TWITTER AND TEAR GAS

ZEYNEP TUFEKCI

Twitter and Tear Gas

THE POWER AND FRAGILITY
OF NETWORKED PROTEST

Yale

UNIVERSITY PRESS

NEW HAVEN & LONDON

Yale University Press books may be purchased in quantity for educational, business, or promotional use. For information, please e-mail sales.press@yale.edu (U.S. office) or sales@yaleup.co.uk (U.K. office).

Set in Scala type by Westchester Publishing Services.
Printed in the United States of America.

Library of Congress Control Number: 2016963570
ISBN 978-0-300-21512-0 (hardcover : alk. paper)

A catalogue record for this book is available from the British Library.

This paper meets the requirements of ANSI/NISO Z39.48-1992 (Permanence of Paper).

10 9 8 7 6 5 4 3 2 1

To my grandmother,
whose love and devotion made everything else possible.

CONTENTS

Preface   ix

Introduction   xxi

PART ONE: MAKING A MOVEMENT

1 A Networked Public   3

2 Censorship and Attention   28

3 Leading the Leaderless   49

4 Movement Cultures   83

PART TWO: A PROTESTER'S TOOLS

5 Technology and People   115

6 Platforms and Algorithms   132

7 Names and Connections   164

PART THREE: AFTER THE PROTESTS

8 Signaling Power and Signaling to Power   189

9 Governments Strike Back   223

Epilogue: The Uncertain Climb   261

Notes   279
Acknowledgments   309
Index   313

PREFACE

IN 2011, AS THE NASCENT UPRISINGS OF the Arab Spring shook the world, I marveled at the new abilities the internet seemed to provide dissidents. Perhaps I appreciated the wonders of digital connectivity more because I had come of age in Turkey after the 1980 military coup. I had witnessed how effective censorship could be when all mass communication was centralized and subject to government control: radio, television, and newspapers. In the early 1990s, working at IBM as a programmer, I had glimpsed the future through IBM's internal global "intranet" network, which allowed me to talk with colleagues around the world. In the mid-1990s, when the internet was finally introduced in Turkey, I eagerly enrolled as one of its earliest users.

I hoped that digital connectivity would help change the state of affairs in which the powerful could jet-set and freely connect with one another while also controlling how the rest of us could communicate. With my newfound power to connect through a shaky, sputtering modem, and full of curiosity, I participated in the earliest global social movement of the internet era. In 1997, through contacts made online, I arranged to attend an "Encuentro"—an encounter, a physical meeting of activists from around the globe—called by the Zapatistas, an indigenous rebel group in the southern Mexican highlands. They had begun their rebellion on the very day the North American Free Trade Agreement (NAFTA) among the United States, Mexico, and Canada was enacted. Passage of NAFTA had required the cancellation of a clause in the Mexican constitution that protected communal tribal lands from privatization. The indigenous farmers feared that powerful transnational corporations would swoop down and steal their lands. Because of the timing of the rebellion and the nature of their demands—asking that the new global world order prioritize human development and values, not corporate profits—they had become a focal point of resistance to a form of globalization that further empowered those who were already powerful.

I met people from all over the world through this movement; I am still in touch with some of them almost twenty years later, both in person and now sometimes through Facebook, Twitter, and WhatsApp. I watched the internet evolve and connectivity explode. In 1999, my e-mail networks informed me of the upcoming World Trade Organization demonstrations in Seattle. These demonstrations would manage to shut down the meetings, to the profound surprise of many powerful people and pundits. The Seattle protests and the massive direct action that disrupted the meeting were among the earliest manifestations of an emerging, networked global movement— "networked" here refers to the reconfiguration of publics and movements through assimilation of digital technologies into their fabric. This movement was empowered by emerging technologies and driven by people all over the world who were hungry for accountability from the transnational institutions and corporations that held so much sway and authority, but were so opaque and unresponsive. Now, the people, too, could talk among each other easily and relatively cheaply. In the first decade of the twenty-first century, I saw social media rise, and phones capable of much more than my bulky early computers make their way into almost every pocket.

It was hard not to be hopeful.

Finally, 2011 seemed to herald the true beginning of a new era, with a transformed communication landscape. The 2011 uprisings across the Middle East and North Africa had taken the scholarly community—and the activists themselves—mostly by surprise. Ebullient crowds celebrated, waving their phones and flags and taking selfies. As regime after regime fell, the world watched transfixed, glued to the social media feeds of thousands of young people from the region who had taken to tweeting, streaming, and reporting from the ground. At the time, the process, of disenfranchised peoples rising up and shaking off aging autocracies, modes of rule on which history had already seemingly rendered its verdict long before, seemed unstoppable, even irreversible.

As my own experience in Turkey had taught me, however, progress rarely proceeds in a linear fashion. Just two years later, in 2013, I stood in the midst of tear-gas clouds circulating in and out of Gezi Park in Istanbul, Turkey, a few blocks from the hospital of my birth. As I stood among yet another ebullient crowd of protesters who had used the internet to great effect to stage a massive protest, my sense of both the strengths and the weaknesses of these digital technologies had shifted dramatically. I had become much less optimistic and significantly more cognizant of the tensions between these protesters' digitally fueled methods of organizing and the long-term odds of their having the type of political impact, proportional to their energy, that they sought. Over the years, both the latent weaknesses of these movements and the inherent strengths of their opponents had substantially emerged.

I had come to understand the historical transition I was witnessing as part of a broad shift in how social movements operate and how they are opposed by those in power. This is a story not only about technology but also about long-standing trends in culture, politics, and civics in many protest movements that converged with more recent technological *affordances*— the actions a given technology facilitates or makes possible. (For example, the ability to talk to people far away is an affordance of telephones—one could shout or use smoke signals or send messages with pigeons before, but it was much harder and limited in scope). This is a story of intertwined fragility and empowerment, of mass participation and rebellion, playing out in a political era characterized by mistrust, failures of elites, and weakened institutions of electoral democracy. I had begun to think of social movements' abilities in terms of "capacities"—like the muscles one develops while exercising but could be used for other purposes like carrying groceries or walking long distances—and their repertoire of protest, like marches, rallies, and occupations as "signals" of those capacities. These *signals* of underlying *capacities* often derived their power from being threats or promises of what else their participants could do—if you could hold a large march, you could also change the narrative, threaten disruption, or bring about electoral or institutional change. And now, digital technologies were profoundly altering the relationship between movement capacities and their signals. In 2013, neither social movement participants nor those in power had yet fully adjusted.

I conceptualize the relationship of the internet to networked protests of the 21st century as similar to the relationship of Nepalese Sherpas to climbers attempting to scale Mount Everest. Not merely guides, the Sherpas give a boost to people who might not otherwise be fully equipped to face the challenges that routinely occur above eight thousand meters. As climbing Mount Everest became a staple on the bucket lists of relatively privileged adventurers, a whole industry sprang up, employing the mountaineering people of Nepal—the Sherpas—to assist inexperienced people in making the climb. The hardy Sherpas carry extra oxygen for the climbers, lay out ladders and ropes, set up tents, cook their food, and even carry their backpacks along the way. In an ironic twist, the very last part of the climb before reaching the summit, the Hillary-Tenzing steps, has permanent ropes on it—and thus shares a feature with climbing walls in indoor gyms. Benefiting from this aid, so many people without much mountaineering experience attempted the climb that Everest started experiencing traffic congestion! Too many people were crowding narrow passages on shaky glacial icefalls or on ladders that connect the deep crevasses.

The assistance may have helped many under-experienced mountaineers to reach the summit, but Everest remains Everest: supremely dangerous and difficult, especially if anything goes even slightly wrong. Mountaineering above eight thousand meters is a serious endeavor and poses extraordinary challenges that can have fatal consequences. The perils of thin air at high altitudes can be overcome with the oxygen tanks carried by the Sherpas, but only if nothing else goes wrong—a sudden storm, a crowded queue causing delays that increase the risk of frostbite, a malfunctioning oxygen tank, an avalanche. On Everest, people without the requisite skills found themselves facing obstacles that required capabilities they did not possess, exactly when the stakes were highest.

The internet similarly allows networked movements to grow dramatically and rapidly, but without prior building of formal or informal organizational and other collective capacities that could prepare them for the inevitable challenges they will face and give them the ability to respond to what comes next. By deploying digital technologies so effectively to mobilize, movements can avoid many of the dreary aspects of political organizing. There is real power here. Clay Shirky's influential book on collective action in the digital age, *Here Comes Everybody,* had an important subtitle: *The Power of Organizing without Organizations.* The ability to organize without organizations, indeed, speeds things up and allows for great scale in rapid time frames. There is no need to spend six months putting together a single rally when a hashtag could be used to summon protesters into the streets; no need to deal with the complexities of logistics when crowdfunding and online spreadsheets can do just as well. However, the tedious work performed during the pre-internet era served other purposes as well; perhaps most importantly, it acclimatized people to the processes of collective decision making and helped create the resilience all movements need to survive and thrive in the long term—just as acquiring mountaineering skills through earlier climbs helps climbers develop their capacity to survive the crucial moments when something, almost inevitably, goes wrong.

What was particularly striking about the post-2011 movements was their struggle with tactical maneuvering after the initial phase of large protests or occupations was over. As sociologist Doug McAdam and others have explored, tactical innovation is crucial for movements over the long term. For example, between 1955 to 1964, the civil rights movement went through multiple major tactical innovations, from bus boycott to sit-ins to freedom-rides to community-wide protest campaigns and more—all are very distinct in what they target and how. In contrast, these networked movements would often devise initial innovative tactics and pull off a spectacular action, but they were unable to change tactics along the way. They also found themselves unable to sustain and organize in the long term in a manner proportional to the energy they had been able to attract initially and the legitimacy they enjoyed in their demands. Having arisen so suddenly and grown so quickly, they hit their first curve requiring agile tactical shifts at great speeds, with little or no prior experience in collective decision making and little resilience. Thus, they often faced greatest peril in their infancy when they were both powerful and large, but also underprepared and fragile.

The year after I started using the analogy of the Sherpas and the internet in my talks and writing, a series of tragedies hit Everest climbs, some of which were indeed the result of too many inexperienced climbers facing circumstances for which they were ill-prepared. As the death toll rose, some Nepalese guide companies started discussing banning extra oxygen and other aids to dissuade inexperienced climbers from attempting to reach the summit. I wondered whether I should stop using the analogy, given the grim news from Everest that kept piling up. But grim news also kept piling up from the movements I had studied. Friends and acquaintances I had met were in jail or had been forced into exile; cities I had visited lay in ruins. My Facebook feed became a chronicle of sorrow, suffering and disappointment.

Despite this ongoing tragedy, it is not correct to label any of these movements as failures. Their trajectories do not match those of past movements, and neither should our benchmarks or timelines for success or impact. In the networked era, a large, organized march or protest should not be seen as the chief outcome of previous capacity building by a movement; rather, it should be looked at as the initial moment of the movement's bursting onto the scene, but only the first stage in a potentially long journey. The civil rights movement may have reached a peak in the March on Washington in 1963, but the Occupy movement arguably *began* with the occupation of Zuccotti Park in 2011. The future trajectory or potential impacts of networked movements cannot be fully understood by using only the conceptual models, indicators and benchmarks that we have gathered from the histories of earlier movements. Similar-looking moments and activities—large marches, big protests, occupations—do not represent the same points in the trajectories of the networked movements as they did in movements organized along traditional models and without digital tools.

In Istanbul in 2013, I was struck by how the protesters' language about technology, protests, and politics resembled those of protesters elsewhere in the world, even though such spontaneous protests had no true Turkish historical counterpart. Egyptian youth and New York youth, different in many ways, also sounded similar themes in discussions: antiauthoritarianism, distrust of authority, and desire for participation. These grievances powering the rebellions were wrapped up in the possibilities of connection and voice afforded by phones they carried everywhere.

Globalization from below had arrived.

The Gezi Park protests, like many other protests around the world, favored self-organization and rejected formal politics and organizations. Volunteers ran everything, including communal kitchens, libraries, and clinics that cared both for protesters with minor ailments and those with life-threatening injuries. The park had a sharing economy where nothing was purchased and nothing was sold. People exchanged whatever they had and received whatever they needed. Many protesters told me that these money-free exchanges were among the most pleasurable, fulfilling aspects of their Gezi experience. It may seem counterintuitive but many protesters also treasured what happened *after* they were teargassed, pepper-sprayed, water-cannoned, and otherwise attacked by police: strangers helped and protected them. There is nothing pleasurable about being teargassed, but the experience of solidarity and altruism within communities engaged in collective rebellion was profoundly moving for people whose lives were otherwise dominated by the mundane struggles for survival and the quest for money.

A come-seemingly-from-nowhere protest of this scale was very novel for Turkey, which had no substantial previous political culture of large, leaderless movements. In Gezi, I was seeing the product of a global cultural convergence of protester aspirations and practices. If I squinted and ignored that the language was Turkish, I felt that it could have been almost any twenty-first-century protest square: organized through Twitter, filled with tear gas, leaderless, networked, euphoric, and fragile.

I come to my analyses after a long journey experiencing and studying protests and the technologies on which they rely—observing and pondering as a social scientist, a technologist, and a participant. I lived through, observed, or studied the impacts of digital technologies on movements ranging from the Zapatista uprising in Chiapas in 1994 to the anti–World Trade Organization (WTO) protests that rocked Seattle and surprised the world in 1999 and the tumultuous global-summit protests in various cities during the early years of the twenty-first century, where the meetings of opaque global institutions like the International Monetary Fund (IMF), the World Bank, and the WTO—transnational organizations that seemed beyond the reach of influence by ordinary people around the world—were met by throngs of protesters. I witnessed and studied the wave of protests and uprisings against authoritarianism and inequality that began in 2011 and that have swept the world from Egypt to Hong Kong to Turkey to the United States. Through a stroke of bad timing for me, I was even present during an attempted coup in Turkey in 2016 that was defeated with the help of digital technologies.

This book is mostly based on an examination of movements that are antiauthoritarian and on the left. However, the conceptual analyses of the mechanisms that are developed here often apply to other movements elsewhere on the political spectrum—though obviously within the context of their own political culture and structural factors.

For example, I talk about what I call "tactical freeze," the inability of these movements to adjust tactics, negotiate demands, and push for tangible policy changes, something that grows out of the leaderless nature of these movements ("horizontalism") and the way digital technologies strengthen their ability to form without much early planning, dealing with issues only as they come up, and by people who show up ("adhocracy"). This is often quite specific to antiauthoritarian movements, as it aligns with their political culture. However, this is also a partial corollary of other, deeper underlying dynamics that I have also analyzed, like the collapse of gatekeepers and gatekeeping organization—dynamics which apply quite broadly to all types of social movement. Similarly, my overall "capacities and signals" approach for thinking about the causal role of technological change in social change, and my emphasis on the role of algorithms and social media platform policies, among other things, are intended to apply much more broadly than just to my core examples. I have also brought in analyses of other movements—like the Tea Party movement in the United States—as a means of comparative investigation, especially to illustrate conceptual points. This book also explores how governments have since responded to the networked public sphere, with a discussion ranging from more open democracies to the methods more authoritarian regimes like Russia and China use to suppress or trammel dissent.

The empirical research and the conceptual and theoretical frameworks that I present in this book represent years of observation, participation, and analysis as well as a great deal of systematic, multi-method empirical research. My own primary research included in this book includes hundreds of formal and systematic interviews with and participant observation of Istanbul's Gezi Park protesters in 2013; peer-reviewed quantitative analyses of a survey of more than a thousand participants in Cairo's Tahrir Square protests of early 2011; visits in 2011 and beyond to many countries involved in the Arab uprisings in the Middle East and North Africa, including Egypt, Tunisia, Lebanon (many Syrian activists fled to Beirut), and Qatar (including a visit to Al Jazeera Headquarters) for interviews and observations. I have also observed or participated in many other social movements over the decades, with a keen interest in how digital technologies interacted with movement dynamics. Among these are anti–corporate globalization protests in between 1997 and 2002, antiwar movements in the United States around 2002 and 2003, and the Occupy movement in 2011 and 2012.

All eras have continuities with the past and antecedents, and many dynamics that predate them, but the start of this book's analysis with the Zapatista solidarity networks is not just an accident of my personal history. The Zapatista solidarity networks marked the beginning of a new phase, the emergence of networked movements as the internet and digital tools began to spread to activists, and general populations. Having lived in Turkey, Europe, and the United States for most of my life, both informs and limits my analyses, of course; I acknowledge my multi-cultural, multi-continent immigrant life-trajectory both as a strength and as a limit of my own experience.

I have also had access to multiple "big data" sets that record aspects of the online activities in the movements that I study. Some of these sets were publicly available; others were privately collected and shared with me. These collections ranged a great deal; some involved data from millions of movement participants, selected by geography, hashtag, or other classifications. My background as a computer programmer—in addition to my training as a social science as a scholar—allowed me to explore these databases as another dimension of observation. I have also published peer-reviewed articles on the strengths and limitations of big data research based on this work, and this work has guided me as I incorporated what I considered were sound and enriching conclusions on social movements using big-data methods.

Over the years, I have also conducted online ethnographic observations of many movements: for example, between September 2015 and the U.S. presidential election of November 2016, I followed a purposive sample of Donald Trump supporters. My observations included daily examinations of these supporters' online behavior and personally attending or watching Trump rallies. Such observations are only one part of systematic research, but they do allow me to ground my conceptual analyses. The *New York Times* and other outlets have published my work in this area, and I was able to make the case early on, even as most pundits thought his candidacy was a joke, that Donald Trump was viable both as a nominee of the Republican Party, and as a strong contender for the presidency.

My own experience allows me to present stories and examples to explain the concepts and analysis I develop in this book. I picked these examples when I considered them to be representative of broader conceptual points. Such examples are necessarily incomplete; they should be read as vignettes. My goal in this book was above all to develop theories and to present a conceptual analysis of what digital technologies mean for how social movements, power and society interact, rather than provide a complete empirical descriptive account of any one movement.

Later in this book, you will notice that I often use the U.S. civil rights movement as a point of comparison. I do this for several reasons, not least that it is one of the most studied movements in history. It is also a movement that many of my students are familiar with, thus providing me with a comparative tool, though I tried to make sure to push beyond the typical summary—"Rosa Parks got tired; Martin Luther King, Jr gave a speech"— to show how complex, dynamic, and multilayered this movement was. This choice, of course, is also a limitation. The civil rights movement is far from the only important movement in history, and I do not mean to position this one movement as a benchmark for success or failure. In fact, I try to avoid imposing any sort of teleology in my approach. My goal is not to judge success or failure, much less to provide recipes for either. I aim primarily to examine networked movement trajectories and dynamics in the light of protesters' capacities and signals.

In presenting a "big-picture" look at any substantial field of human endeavor, no author can rely only on her own data or scholarship. Thus, I also
did not limit the analyses in this book to my own primary research. I have
also drawn heavily on much excellent research, published and unpub-
lished, of both academics and journalists.

I tried to make the text readable and my arguments understandable to a
general audience—ranging from an interested student in college or high
school, to activists involved in these movements, to people who care about
how digital technologies and social change impact the world. In trying to
reach this broad base, I have inevitably fallen short of presenting the depth
of academic scholarship on these topics, even though my own research
and analyses obviously benefited greatly from this rich legacy. To keep
things manageable, and the book at a reasonable length, and with consul-
tation with my publisher, Yale University Press, I have published a more
extensive bibliography on the website for this book, http://www.twitterand
teargas.com.

Collective actions, social movements, and revolutions are woven into the
fabric of human history. They have been studied at great length and for
good reason: they change history. Whether their actions lead to social revolution, as historically they did in France, China, and Russia, to regime
change, as in Tunisia in 2011 or Ukraine in 2013, or simply to reform and
new legislation, like the U.S. civil rights movement, people gathering to
demand attention, action, and change have helped shape the world for centuries. They will no doubt continue to do so, but they now operate in a
newly altered terrain. Digital connectivity reshapes how movements connect,
organize, and evolve during their lifespan.

As of 2016, many protest movements, from Egypt to Turkey, appear to
be in retreat or dispersal. And not all movements using these digitally
fueled strategies are seeking positive social change: terrorist groups such
as ISIS and white-supremacist groups in North America and Europe also
use digital technologies to gather, organize, and to amplify their narrative.
Meanwhile, new movements are popping up, from Brazil to Ukraine to
Hong Kong, as hopeful communities flood the streets in protests and
occupations. Some protests have even transformed, at least partially, into

electoral forces, like Podemos in Spain, Syriza in Greece, and the surprisingly strong effort to elect Bernie Sanders as the Democratic Party nominee for president in the United States, supported by many members of the Occupy Wall Street movement.

Like all human stories, the evolution of modern protest has deep historical and cultural roots. But studying it also requires new ways of understanding the fragility of the power of these new movements. I observe it all not with a scholar's eye, but as a participant-observer in these movements, I also try to feel the moment. Often I have a distinct sense of a cyclic process, of déjà vu, like living in a film I have already seen, but one that I still do not know the ending of. I spend my days listening to protesters, often experiencing the same ups and downs as they do. As people chat with me and learn that I have studied movements elsewhere, one question keeps coming up: "How do you think this will end?" I say that I do not know. In the mountains of Chiapas, I learned a Zapatista saying: "Preguntando caminamos." It means "we walk while asking questions." It is in that spirit that I present this book.

INTRODUCTION

ON FEBRUARY 2, 2011, A HORDE OF MEN, armed with long sticks and whips and riding camels and horses, attacked the hundreds of thousands of protesters who packed Tahrir Square in Cairo, Egypt, parting the crowd as if it were the Red Sea and scattering protesters as they went. The horses' saddles were a brilliant red, traditional and ornate, but the day was anything but cheerful. A dozen people died. Many believe that the attackers were undercover agents of President Hosni Mubarak's regime, although trials afterward were unable to verify this. Egyptians call the event the "Battle of the Camels," a sly reference to a seventh-century internecine struggle among Muslims.

A prominent Egyptian dissident later told me the story from his perspective, starting with his shock at hearing the trampling hooves on the asphalt, seeing the heads of the animals above the crowd, and watching confusion and anger spread in waves through the packed square. "I laughed very hard," he said, "because, for the first time since it all began, I was sure we had won. Surely, I thought, we had won."

I wondered whether he had lost his mind. That would have been understandable after ten days of violence, tear gas, tension, and no sleep.

But he was right. It had been a turning point.

As he explained to me, letting loose thugs on camelback showed just how desperate and out-of-touch Mubarak's regime had become. While camels flooded the square, Tahrir activists were busy giving live interviews to the BBC and other international media outlets via smuggled satellite phones, and tweeting over contraband internet connections. Although Mubarak had shut down the internet—except a single ISP; the Noor network—and all cell phones just before the "Battle of the Camels," protesters had pierced the internet blockade within hours, and remained in charge of their message, which was heard around the world, as was news of the internet shutdown. Mubarak's acts were both futile, because the protests were already under way, and counterproductive, because worried families, unable to call their younger relatives, rushed to Tahrir Square. The sheer, unrestrained brutality of the camel attack and the clumsiness of shutting down all communication networks underscored the inability of Mubarak's crumbling autocracy to understand the spirit of the time, the energy of the youthful protesters, and the transformed information environment. Camels and sticks versus satellite phones and Twitter. Seventeenth century, meet twenty-first century. Indeed, the internet in Egypt soon came back online, and Mubarak, unable to contain or permanently repress the huge crowds, was forced to resign shortly thereafter.

As uprisings spread throughout the region, many felt optimistic. The revolutions had not yet turned into military coups, as would happen in Egypt, or bloody civil wars, as would happen in Libya and Syria. Activists were flying high. Digital technologies had clearly transformed the landscape, seemingly to the benefit of political challengers. Rising in opposition to crumbling, stifling regimes that tried to control the public discourse, activists were able to overcome censorship, coordinate protests, organize logistics, and spread humor and dissent with an ease that would have seemed miraculous to earlier generations. A popular Facebook page, created to decry the beating death of a young man by the Egyptian police, had been the forum for organizing the initial Tahrir uprising and had mustered hundreds of thousands of supporters.[1] An Egyptian friend of mine would later joke that this must have been the first time in history when a person could actually join a revolution by clicking on "I'm Attending" in response to a Facebook e-vite. But such social media sites were important to audiences beyond the protesters; the world also followed the uprising through the Facebook and Twitter posts of young, digitally savvy and determined protesters.

Networked protests of the twenty-first century differ in important ways from movements of the past and often operate with a different logic. (I use "networked" as a shorthand for digitally networked, to refer to the reconfiguration of movements and publics through the incorporation of digital technologies and connectivity.) Many of these developments have cultural and political roots that predate the internet but have found a fuller expression in conjunction with the capabilities provided by technology. Networked protests have strengths and weaknesses that combine in novel ways and do not neatly conform to our understandings of the trajectory of protest movements before the advent of digital technologies.

For example, the ability to use digital tools to rapidly amass large numbers of protesters with a common goal empowers movements. Once this large group is formed, however, it struggles because it has sidestepped some of the traditional tasks of organizing. Besides taking care of tasks, the drudgery of traditional organizing helps create collective decision-making capabilities, sometimes through formal and informal leadership structures, and builds a collective capacities among movement participants through shared experience and tribulation. The expressive, often humorous style of networked protests attracts many participants and thrives both online and offline,[2] but movements falter in the long term unless they create the capacity to navigate the inevitable challenges.

These movements rely heavily on online platforms and digital tools for organizing and publicity, and proclaim that they are leaderless although their practice is almost always muddier. The open participation afforded by social media does not always mean equal participation, and it certainly does not mean a smooth process. Although online media are indeed more open and participatory, over time a few people consistently emerge as informal but persistent spokespersons—with large followings on social media. These people often have great influence, though they lack the formal legitimacy that an open and recognized process of selecting leaders would generate. The result is often a conflict-ridden, drawn-out struggle between those who find themselves running things (or being treated as de facto leaders) and other people in the movement who can now all also express themselves online. These others may challenge the de facto spokespersons, but the movements have few means to resolve their issues or make decisions. In some ways, digital technologies deepen the ever-existing tension between collective will and individual expression within movements, and between expressive moments of rebellion and the longer-term strategies requiring instrumental and tactical shifts.

The internet's affordances—what a given technology facilitates or makes possible—have changed greatly during the past two decades.[3] When I showed up at a Zapatista-organized "Encuentro" in the 1990s, for example, many people greeted me with surprise that I was not "Mr. Zeynep." Our main communication tool was e-mail on slow dial-up modem connections that did not allow much visual information, such as pictures. Most users were assumed to be male, and they often were. We had no smartphones, so we had no connections when we were not at a fixed physical "place."

But the major affordance—the ability to cheaply and easily connect on a global scale—was already emerging and was transforming social movements.[4] The internet may have been slow and available only in offices and homes (since phones did not have internet then), but the protest and movement culture that flourished in the 1990s already displayed many cultural elements that would persist. These movements shared an intense focus on participation and horizontalism—functioning without formal hierarchies or leaders and using a digitally supported, ad hoc approach to organizing infrastructure and tasks. The Zapatista Encuentro lasted a week, during which friendships formed around the self-organized functioning of the camp where it took place. Plurality, diversity, and tolerance were celebrated and were nicely expressed in the Zapatista slogan "Many yeses, one no." There was a general reluctance to engage in traditional, institutional politics, which were believed to be ineffective and, worse, irredeemably corrupt. Digital technology was used to support organization in the absence of formal structures. An alternative social space was created, and it felt like, and was celebrated as a new form of politics.

These elements would reappear in protester camps and prolonged occupations of public spaces worldwide in the next decades, and would become thoroughly intertwined with digital technologies. These technologies were not merely basic tools; their new capabilities allowed protesters to reimagine and alter the practice of protests and movement building on the path that they had already been traveling but could finally realize.

I visited Tahrir Square after the most tumultuous days of 2011 were over in Cairo, but protests were still ongoing. The Egyptian military had not yet organized the coup that would come two years later. The square seemed vast while I was standing in the middle of it during a protest, but from my high-rise hotel next to it, it seemed small and insignificant, lost in the sprawling expanse of Cairo, home to more than twenty million people in its metro area. It was a choke point for Cairo traffic, but traffic seemed to be in a perpetual jam.

Yet in 2011, Tahrir became a choke point for global *attention*. Digital networks allowing the protesters to broadcast to the world raised the costs of repression through attention from a sympathetic global public. Digital connectivity had warped time and space, transforming that square I looked at from above, so small yet so vast, into a crossroads of attention and visibility, both interpersonal and interactive, not just something filtered through mass media. Throughout the eighteen days of the initial Tahrir uprising, I turned on the television only once, wanting to see how networks were covering the historic moment of Mubarak's resignation. CNN was broadcasting an aerial shot of the square. The camera shot from far above the square was jarring because I had been following it all on Twitter, person by person, each view necessarily incomplete but also intimate. On television, all I could see was an undifferentiated mass of people, an indistinct crowd. It felt cold and alienating. The television pictures did not convey how today's networked protests operate or feel.

Scholars have often focused on the coordination and communication challenges that people engaged in collective action face.[5] If authorities control the public sphere, how will activists coordinate? How will they frame their message in the face of corporate or state media gatekeeping and censorship?[6] How will they keep free riders, who want the benefits that protests might win but do not want to pay the costs of protest, from skipping out and waiting for others to fight and take risks?[7] How will they counter repression by security forces that have superior means and can inflict suffering, torture, and death?[8]

None of those dilemmas have gone away, but some of them have been dramatically transformed. Digital technologies are so integral to today's social movements that many protests are referred to by their hashtags—the Twitter convention for marking a topic: #jan25 for the Tahrir uprising in January 25, 2011, #VemPraRua ("Come to the streets") in Brazil, #direngezi for Gezi Park protests in Istanbul, Turkey, and #occupywallstreet.[9] Activists can act as their own media, conduct publicity campaigns, circumvent censorship, and coordinate nimbly.

Sometimes, networked online political action is derided as "slacktivism" or "clicktivism," terms that suggest easy action requiring little effort or commitment. At other times, people assume that movements fueled by social media are organized by people with "weak ties"—people we do not know well—unlike protests of the past.[10] However, these perspectives assume that people who connect online are doing things only online, and that the online world is somehow less real than, and disconnected from, the offline one. In contrast, people nowadays also join protests with people with whom they have "strong ties"—family and close friends—and people connect online with other people with whom they have both weak and strong ties. Symbolic action online is not necessarily without power either—rather, the effect depends on the context. When Facebook friends change their avatar to protest discrimination against gay people, they also send a cultural signal to their social networks, and over time, such signals are part of what makes social change possible by changing culture. Many protesters I talked with cite their online political interactions as the beginning of their process of becoming politicized. It is not even clear that all online acts are really as easy as "just clicking." In a repressive country, tweeting may be a very brave act, while marching on the streets may present few difficulties in a more advanced democracy.

In 2011, I observed how four young people, only two of whom were in Cairo, coordinated supplies and logistics for ten large field hospitals at the height of some of the worst clashes in Egypt. They accomplished this feat through creativity and youthful determination, but it would have been nearly impossible without Twitter, Google spreadsheets, SMS (text messaging or "short messaging services"), and cell phones. In the same time frame, I watched another four college students in Turkey establish a countrywide citizen journalism network, reporting news, busting censorship, and otherwise countering deep polarization. They did this in their spare time, with no funding, fueled only by grit, creativity, and caffeine (preferably from coffee shops with free Wi-Fi). I saw countries with authoritarian-leaning governments lose control over the public sphere, while in democratic countries, issues that had been sidelined from the national agenda, from economic inequality to racial injustice to trade to police misconduct, were brought to the forefront through the force of social media engagement and persistence by citizens.

But I have also seen movement after movement falter because of a lack of organizational depth and experience, of tools or culture for collective decision making, and strategic, long-term action. Somewhat paradoxically the capabilities that fueled their organizing prowess sometimes also set the stage for what later tripped them up, especially when they were unable to engage in the tactical and decision-making maneuvers all movements must master to survive. It turns out that the answer to "What happens when movements can evade traditional censorship and publicize and coordinate more easily?" is not simple.

If the politics of protest do not look like those of the past, neither do some of the obstacles the protesters face. In the United States, the same week the Gezi protests erupted, Edward Snowden revealed details of the existence of a massive U.S. government surveillance program, and we thus glimpsed a scope of what state surveillance capabilities may exist. The United States is almost certainly not the only government to surveil at large scale. In fact, as I stood in Gezi Park, tweeting from a phone tied by law to my unique citizenship ID number in Turkey, I knew that the government surely had a list of every protester who showed up at the park with a phone. Despite this fact, once protests broke out on a large scale, the threat of surveillance deterred few people, partly because they felt protected by the scale of the massive protest.

Many movements face severe repression, much as they did in the preinternet era. In Egypt, a few years after the initial uprising, things were not going well for the revolutionaries. Many of my friends there were now

in jail or in exile. Although Mubarak was ousted, the military was not. The
Muslim Brotherhood had won the election but had not managed to unseat
the old guard from the state apparatus, nor manage to win over the whole
population—many people were alarmed at their acts in government, too.
In the polarized atmosphere, supporters of the military also began to flood
online social networks with their message. People opposing the Muslim
Brotherhood, some of them open supporters of the military but others just
concerned about the state of the country, held a large rally in Tahrir Square
in July 2013. Soon afterward, the Egyptian military took over the country
in a brutal coup, citing the protests as legitimizing its actions. The new
military government mowed down more than six hundred protesters in
Rabaa Square in Cairo. Sufficiently brutal governments seem not to bother
too much with scientific network analysis and the minutiae of secretly sur-
veilled online imprints. Instead, they are often guided by the philosophy
"Shoot at them all, and let terror sort them out."

Other governments, less willing or able to engage in such indiscriminate
mass violence, have learned to control the networked public sphere—the
reconfigured public sphere that now incorporates digital technologies as
well—through a set of policies more suited to the new era. Surveillance and
repression, do not operate primarily in the way that our pre-digital worries
might have forecast. This is not necessarily Orwell's 1984. Rather than a
complete totalitarianism based on fear and blocking of information the
newer methods include demonizing online mediums, and mobilizing
armies of supporters or paid employees who muddy the online waters with
misinformation, information glut, doubt, confusion, harrasment, and distraction, making it hard for ordinary people to navigate the networked public sphere, and sort facts from fiction, truth from hoaxes. Many governments
target dissidents by hacking and releasing their personal and private information to try to embarrass or harass them, rather than acting directly on
their political communication. If anything, Aldous Huxley's *Brave New
World* appears on point in capturing the spirit of the age compared with Orwell's *1984*, which imagined totalitarianism with centralized control of
information—more applicable to the Soviet Union than to today's networked
public sphere.

Whereas a social movement has to persuade people to act, a government or a powerful group defending the status quo only has to create enough confusion to paralyze people into inaction. The internet's relatively chaotic nature, with too much information and weak gatekeepers, can asymmetrically empower governments by allowing them to develop new forms of censorship based not on blocking information, but on making available information unusable.

The networked public sphere carries along many other challenges. Many activists face harassment and abuse organized by governments or their opponents on social media. Ad-financed platforms use algorithms—complex software—to control visibility, sometimes drowning out activist messages in favor of more advertiser-friendly content. Their filtering can entrench "echo chambers" where like-minded people get together (including social movement activists) but then go on to undertake vicious battles online, increasing polarization and thus turning off many people from politics.[11] But movements can also use these very platforms to further their goals, as these technologies allow people to find one another, to craft and amplify their own narrative, to reach out to broader publics, and to organize and resist. Movements are making their own history, but in circumstances, and with tools, not entirely of their own choosing.

This book examines the transformations brought about by digital technologies in the trajectories of social movements and the public sphere, and it situates this analysis within the context of specific affordances of digital technologies and specific features of giant software platforms like Facebook, Twitter, and Google that have become central to social movement organizing around the world. The main goal of this book is to provide empirically grounded, rich conceptual analyses of mechanisms that operate in the networked public sphere and that impact the trajectories and dynamics of networked social movements.

The book is organized into three sections. The first, "Making a Movement," looks broadly at digital technologies and social movement mechanisms. In chapter 1, I examine the networked public sphere, and consider how it affects the ways social movements can form, how rebellions take off (sometimes seemingly out-of-nowhere), and why platforms like Facebook—which combine the personal and political—have become so politically potent. In chapter 2, I conceptualize attention as a distinct, crucial, limited, and limiting resource for social movements—one that is no longer the monopoly of mass media—and censorship broadly as the denial of attention through multiple means. I do this partly through tracing the ever-evolving stories of citizen journalism and examining the new intermediaries of the networked public sphere. Chapter 3 dives into how networked movements operate organizationally, how they take care of tasks, and shows why the *how* of organizing is so crucial to understanding movement trajectories. Finally, chapter 4 examines how the protest culture in networked antiauthoritarian movements interacts with affordances of digital technologies, and how leaderless, adhocratic, and participatory movements actually function, with all the strength and challenges that come from this style.

The second section, called "A Protestor's Tools," focuses more on the technology itself, with analyses of affordances, policies, and algorithms that shape digital tools and their multi-faceted, complex, and even sometimes contradictory impact of social movements. The opening chapter of this section, chapter 5, titled "Technology and People," is a deeper dive into the philosophical and methodological questions that underlie the theoretical approach to technology used in this book, and discusses why we should approach causality in technology and sociology interactions as a multi-layered and multi-pronged dynamic that intermixes social dynamics with technological materiality. As such, it is perhaps the most abstract chapter. Chapter 6 is an in-depth look into how and why a few platforms—Facebook, Twitter, Google, and YouTube—have emerged so dominant in the networked public sphere, and what their user policies, business models, and algorithms mean for social movements—including a case in which Facebook's real-name policies almost tripped up the most influential page of the (yet to come) Egyptian revolution, and its algorithms might have smothered emergent social movements, like the Black Lives Matter movement, while promoting feel-good (and worthy) charity drives. Chapter 7 examines the affordances involving identity and reputation—from anonymity to pseudonymity to real-name policies—in online spaces. This chapter includes examples ranging from the striking and disturbing case of child pornographers who find community online to mothers who realize that they can discuss most difficult questions freely in anonymous digital boards, to hoaxes, fabrications, and harassment campaigns online.

The last section, titled "After the Protests," develops theories to understand both movement trajectories over the longer term and how power also strikes back, reconfiguring networked spaces for its purposes. Chapter 8 develops the *capacities* and *signals* theory of social movements that guides all the analyses in this book, and uses comparative cases from Occupy Wall Street to the civil rights movement to understand what this might mean for narrative, electoral, and disruptive capacities movements can develop. Chapter 9 examines the networked public sphere and movements through the lens of power, governments, and their countermeasures—all which have evolved greatly in the past few years, as networked movements have shaken the world. Authoritarian governments like those of Russia and China have evolved just as social movements have. Finally, the epilogue situates historically the processes discussed so far. The scale, scope, and speed of this transformation in the access of ordinary people to digital connectivity and its affordances, and to active participation in the production and consumption of global information flows, merit comparison with the rise of movable-type printing. The contradictory and sometimes counterintuitive dynamics unleashed by the emergence of the printing press indicate all too clearly that there is little that is straightforward about understanding the strengths, weaknesses, challenges, opportunities, and future of networked movements—and we have likely just begun to see what it may all mean.

PART ONE

MAKING A MOVEMENT

A Networked Public

WHEN MY GRANDMOTHER WAS ABOUT THIRTEEN YEARS old and living in a small Turkish town near the Mediterranean coast, she won a scholarship to the most prestigious boarding school in Istanbul. Just two years earlier, after she had completed the fifth grade, her family told her that her formal education was over. As far as her family was concerned, that was more than enough education for a girl. It was time for marriage, not geometry or history.

My grandmother didn't know her exact birth date. Her mother had said that she was born just as the grapes were being harvested and pressed into molasses in preparation for the upcoming winter, and just as word of the proclamation of the new Republic of Turkey reached her town. That would put her birthday in the fall of 1923, when a new world was struggling to emerge from the ruins of World War I. It was a time of transition and change for Turkey, for her family, and for her. The new central government, born from the ashes of the crumbling Ottoman Empire, was intent on modernizing the country and emulating European systems. It pushed to build schools and standardize education. Teachers were appointed to schools around the country, even in remote provinces. One of those teachers remembered a bright female pupil who had been yanked from school, and, without telling her family, entered her in a nationwide scholarship exam to find and educate gifted girls. "And then, my name appeared in a newspaper," my grandmother said. She told me the story often, tearing up each time.

It was a small miracle and a testament to the unsettled nature of the era that my grandmother's teacher prevailed over her family. My grandmother boarded a train to the faraway city of Istanbul to attend an elite school. She was joined by dozens of bright girls from around the country who had made similar journeys. They spent their first year somewhat dazed, soaking in new experiences. They all excelled in their classes, except one. Almost all of them flunked Turkish, their native language.

The cause was not lack of smarts or hard work. Rather, it was something we now take for granted. A national public sphere with a uniform national language did not exist in Turkey at the time. Without mass media and a strong national education system, languages exist as dialects that differ in pronunciation, vocabulary, and even grammar, sometimes from town to town.[1] These studious girls did not speak the standardized "Istanbul Turkish" that would emerge through the mass media and the national education system in the coming decades.

Like the other students, my grandmother had grown up without any real exposure to mass media because there were none where she lived.[2] Fledgling radio broadcasts were limited to a few hours a day in a few big cities. Standardized mass education was just starting. Newspapers existed, but their readership was limited, and my grandmother rarely encountered one. Without such technologies, her world and her language had been confined to her small town and to the people who saw one another every day.

These days it seems unlikely that citizens of the same country might have difficulty understanding one another. But it is historically fairly new that so many of us understand one another and have common topics to discuss, even on a global scale. Even European languages like the French language became standardized into the Parisian version—derived from a hodgepodge of dialects—only after the emergence of the French Republic and the rise of mass media (newspapers). Political scientist Benedict Anderson called this phenomenon of unification "imagined communities." People who would never expect to meet in person or to know each other's name come to think of themselves as part of a group through the shared consumption of mass media like newspapers and via common national institutions and agendas.[3]

The shift from face-to-face communities to communities identified with cities, nation-states, and now a globalized world order is a profound transition in human history. Because we have been born into this imagined community, it can be hard to realize how much our experiences, our culture, and our institutions have been shaped by a variety of technologies, especially those that affect the way we experience time and space.[4] Technologies alter our ability to preserve and circulate ideas and stories, the ways in which we connect and converse, the people with whom we can interact, the things that we can see, and the structures of power that oversee the means of contact.

In the nineteenth and twentieth centuries, changes to the architecture of our societies mostly happened through the newspapers, railroads and telegraph, followed later by telephone, radio and television. In the early twenty-first century, digital technologies and networks—computers, the internet, and the smartphone—are rapidly altering some of the basic features of societies, especially the public sphere, which social theorist Jürgen Habermas defined as a people "gathered together as a public, articulating the needs of society with the state."[5] Gerard Hauser explains this same concept as "a discursive space in which individuals and groups associate to discuss matters of mutual interest and, where possible, to reach a common judgment about them."[6] It should be understood that there is no single, uniform public sphere. Instead, different groups of people come together under different conditions and with varying extent and power, sometimes in "counterpublics"—groups coming together to oppose the more hegemonic public sphere and ideologies.[7]

Habermas focused on the emergence of a public sphere in Europe in the eighteenth and nineteenth centuries through interaction and idealized reasoned dialogue among people in settings other than the privacy of homes, especially in cities.[8] Cities can also alter how we interact by gathering people in large numbers and creating places for interaction outside of private spaces. Thus, the public sphere was facilitated by the rise of spaces like coffeehouses and salons, where people who were not immediate family members mingled and discussed current affairs and issues that concerned everyone.

The dynamics of public spheres are intertwined with power relations, social structures, institutions, and technologies that change over time. My grandmother, for example, would never have been allowed inside the Turkish version of coffeehouses where people discussed politics among their community since they were (and still are) male-only places. French salons were accessed mostly by the wealthy. Newspapers require literacy, which was not always widespread. Before the internet, broadcast mass media meant that millions could hear the same message all at once, but if you wanted your message heard, it helped if you owned or had access to a radio or television station or a newspaper. And so on.

As technologies change, and as they alter the societal architectures of visibility, access, and community, they also affect the contours of the public sphere, which in turn affects social norms and political structures. The twenty-first-century public sphere is digitally networked and includes mass media and public spaces, such as the squares and parks where many protests are held, as well as new digital media.[9] I use the term "digitally networked public sphere" or "networked public sphere" as a shorthand for this complex interaction of publics, online and offline, all intertwined, multiple, connected, and complex, but also transnational and global. "Networked public sphere," like the terms "digitally networked movements" or "networked movements," does not mean "online-only" or even "online-primarily." Rather, it's a recognition that the whole public sphere, as well as the whole way movements operate, has been reconfigured by digital technologies, and that this reconfiguration holds true whether one is analyzing an online, offline, or combined instantiation of the public sphere or social movement action.

Thanks to digital technologies, ordinary people have new means of broadcasting—the potential to reach millions of people at once. We also have methods of interpersonal communication that can easily connect many people who are not in the same physical space, or even people who do not know each other at all. Ubiquitous cell-phone cameras have greatly increased the ability of citizens to document wrongdoings and potentially move the conversation beyond "authorities said, activists claimed."[10] The authorities, too, have changed and altered their tactics to control and shape the public sphere even though their aims have remained similar. Producing information glut, inducing confusion and distraction, and mobilizing counter-movements, rather than imposing outright censorship, are becoming parts of the playbook of governments that confront social movements.

Although the recent changes have been rapid, digital technologies are not the first technologies that have affected how we interact over space and time and have shaped our sense of community, identity, and the public sphere. Looking at some past transitions is helpful in understanding the scope and scale of newer ones. Writing, for example, is among the earliest technologies that changed the relationship between our words and the passage of time.[11] We are so used to writing that it is difficult to imagine societies without it and to realize that writing is a technology that shapes our society. Before the invention of writing (a long process rather than a single breakthrough), people relied on memory in passing on knowledge or stories. This affected the type of content that could be effectively transmitted over time and space; for example, a novel or an encyclopedia can exist only in a society with writing. An oral culture—a culture without any form of writing—is more suited for poetry with repetitions and proverbs, which are easier to remember without writing down, that are committed to memory and passed on. Writing is not important only as a convenience; rather, it affects power in all its forms throughout society. For example, in a society that is solely oral or not very literate, older people (who have more knowledge since knowledge is acquired over time and is kept in one's mind) have more power relative to young people who cannot simply acquire new learning by reading. In a print society, novels, pamphlets, and encyclopedias can be circulated and made widely available. This availability affects the kinds of discussions that can be had, the kinds of people who can have them, and the evidentiary standards of those discussions.

The power of technologies to help shape communities is not restricted to information technologies. Transportation technologies not only carry us, but even in the digital era they still carry letters, newspapers and other media of communication. They also alter our sense of space, as does the architecture of cities and suburbs. Indeed, the wave of protests and revolution that shook Europe in 1848—and were dubbed the People's Spring, the inspiration for referring to the 2011 Arab uprisings as the "Arab Spring"— were linked not just to the emergence of newspaper and telegraphs, but also to the railways that increasingly crisscrossed the continent, carrying not just people who spread ideas, but also newspapers, pamphlets, and manifestos.[12]

In her lifetime, my grandmother journeyed from a world confined to her immediate physical community to one where she now carries out video conversations over the internet with her grandchildren on the other side of the world, cheaply enough that we do not think about their cost at all. She found her first train trip to Istanbul as a teenager—something her peers would have done rarely—to be a bewildering experience, but in her later years she flew around the world. Both the public sphere and our imagined communities operate differently now than they did even a few decades ago, let alone a century.

All this is of great importance to social movements because movements, among other things, are attempts to intervene in the public sphere through collective, coordinated action. A social movement is both a type of (counter) public itself and a claim made to a public that a wrong should be righted or a change should be made.[13] Regardless of whether movements are attempting to change people's minds, a set of policies, or even a government, they strive to reach and intervene in public life, which is centered on the public sphere of their time. Governments and powerful people also expend great efforts to control the public sphere in their own favor because doing so is a key method through which they rule and exercise power.

The dizzying speed of advances in digital networks and technologies, their rapid spread, and the fact that there is no single, uniform public sphere complicate this discussion. But to understand dissident social movements and their protests, it is crucial to understand the current dynamics of the public sphere. Digital technologies play a critical role in all stages of protest, but they are especially important during the initial formation of social movements.

In 2011, a few days after yet another major protest in Tahrir Square, Cairo, Egypt, Sana (not her real name) and I sat in a coffee shop close to the square where so much had happened in a few months. In the immediate aftermath of Hosni Mubarak's resignation, the protesters' spirit and optimism seemed to shine on everything. Even corporate advertisers were using the theme of revolution to sell soft drinks and other products. Ads for sunglasses highlighted revolutionary slogans and colors.

Sana came from a well-off Egyptian family that, like many, had maintained a fiercely apolitical stance before the revolution. Politics was never discussed at home. She was a talented young woman who went to one of Egypt's best universities, spoke English very well, and, like many of her peers, had a view of the world beyond that of the older generation that still ruled Egypt and the timid elders who feared Mubarak's repressive regime. She told me about feeling trapped and about frustration with her family and social circle, all of whom rebuffed her attempts at even mild discussions of Egyptian politics. She could not find a way to cross this boundary in the offline world, so she went on Twitter.

In an earlier era, Sana might have kept her frustrations to herself and remained isolated, feeling lonely and misunderstood. But now, digital technologies provide multiple avenues for people to find like-minded others and to signal their beliefs to one another. Social media led Sana to other politically oriented young people. Over a strong brew in a trendy Egyptian coffee shop, she explained that she had gone online to look for political conversations that were more open and more inclusive than any she had experienced in her offline personal life, and that this had led to her participation in the massive Tahrir protests.

There is much more to be said about the aftermath of the movements in which Sana participated, but the initial stages of these movements illuminate how digital connectivity alters key social mechanisms. Many people tend to seek people who are like themselves or who agree with them: this social science finding long predates the internet. Social scientists call this "homophily," a concept similar to the notion "Birds of a feather stick together."[14] Dissidents and other minorities especially draw strength and comfort from interactions with like-minded people because they face opposition from most of society or, at the very least, the authorities. Digital connectivity makes it easier for like-minded people to find one another without physical impediments of earlier eras, when one had to live in the right neighborhood or move to a city and find the correct café. Now, people may just need to find the right hashtag.

Sana was different from those in her immediate environment. She had been unable to find people who shared her interests in politics and were motivated enough to brave the regime's repression. When she turned to

Twitter, though, she could easily find and befriend a group of political activists, and she later met those people offline as well. They eventually became her social circle. She said that she finally felt at home and alive from being around young people who were engaged and concerned about the country's future. When the uprising in Tahrir broke out in January 2011, she joined them at the square as they fought, bled, and hoped for a better Egypt. Had it not been for social media leading her to others with similar beliefs before the major uprising, she might never have found and become part of the core group that sparked the movement.

Of course likeminded people gathered before the internet era, but now it can be done with much less friction, and by more people. For most of human history, one's social circle was mostly confined to family and neighborhood because they were available, easily accessible, and considered appropriate social connections. Modernization and urbanization have eroded many of these former barriers.[15] People are now increasingly seen as individuals instead of being characterized solely by the station in life into which they were born. And they increasingly seek connections as individuals, and not just in the physical location where they were born. Rather than connecting with people who are like them only in ascribed characteristics— things we mostly acquire from birth, like family, race, and social class (though this one can change throughout one's life)—many people have the opportunity to seek connections with others who share similar interests and motivations. Of course, place, race, family, gender, and social class continue to play a very important role in structuring human relationships—but the scope and the scale of their power and their role as a social mechanism have shifted and changed as modernity advanced.

Opportunities to find and make such connections with people based on common interests and viewpoints are thoroughly intertwined with the online architectures of interaction and visibility and the design of online platforms. These factors—the affordances of digital spaces—shape who can find and see whom, and under what conditions; not all platforms create identical environments and opportunities for connection. Rather, online platforms have architectures just as our cities, roads, and buildings do, and those architectures affect how we navigate them. (Explored in depth in later chapters.) If you cannot find people, you cannot form a community with them.

Cities, which bring together large numbers of people in concentrated areas, and the discursive spaces, like coffeehouses and salons, that spring up in them are important to the public sphere exactly because they alter architectures of interaction and visibility. Online connectivity functions in a very similar manner but is an even more profound alteration because people do not have to be in the same physical space at the same time to initiate a conversation and connect with one another. The French salons and coffeehouses of the nineteenth century were mostly limited to middle- or upper-class men, as were digital technologies in their early days, but as digital technology has rapidly become less expensive, it has just as rapidly spread rapidly to poorer groups. It is the new town square, the water cooler, the village well, and the urban coffeehouse, but also much more. This isn't because people leave behind race, gender, and social class online, and this isn't because the online sphere is one only of reason and ideas, with no impact from the physical world. Quite the opposite, such dimensions of the human experience are reproduced and play a significant role in the networked public sphere as well. The difference is the reconfigured logic of how and where we can interact; with whom; and at what scale and visibility.

Almost all the social mechanisms discussed in this book operate both online and offline, and digital connectivity alters the specifics of how the mechanisms operate overall rather than creating or destroying social dynamics or mechanisms wholesale. Twitter became a way for Sana to find like-minded others. This is analogous to the role offline street protests play as a way in which people with dissenting ideas can find one another and form the initial (or sustaining) groups that make movements possible.

For example, on April 15, 2009—the day on which tax returns were due in the United States—protests were held all over the country called by the Tea Party Patriots, a right-wing movement with strong views on taxes and their use. Some protest locales were sunny, but others were rainy. An ingenious long-term study later looked at how the weather on that day had affected the trajectory of the Tea Party movement born of those protests.[16] Researchers compared areas where protests could be held to those where protests were not held because of being rained out—a naturally occurring experiment since the weather can be considered a random factor. Compared with rainy locations, places where the sun shone on tax day, and thus could hold a protest, had a higher turnout in favor of the Republican Party in subsequent elections, a greater likelihood of a Democratic representative retiring rather than choosing to rerun, and more changes to policy making in line with Tea Partiers' demands. Sunny protest locations spawned stronger movements with "more grassroots organizing," "larger subsequent protests and monetary contributions," and "stronger conservative belief" among protest participants.[17]

The rain on that initial day of protest had significant long-term effects on the fortunes of the Tea Party movement. The main driver was simple, but not surprising: people met one another at the protests that could be held and then continued to organize together.

Finding other like-minded people, a prerequisite for the formation of a new movement, now often occurs online as well. The internet allowed networks of activists in the Middle East and North Africa to connect before protests broke out in the region in late 2010 and early 2011. Drawing strength from one another, often scattered across cities and countries, they were able to overcome what was otherwise a discouraging environment and to remain political activists even amidst the repressive environment partly because they could find friends.

It is sometimes assumed that activists in the initial wave of a networked movement do not know one another well, or may be online-only friends. There were certainly some people in the Middle East and North Africa who fit that mold, but many of the committed activists had overlapping and strong friendship networks that interacted online and offline. Some of those networks stretched across many countries thanks to easier travel and international organizations that connected activists across the region at conferences and other shared events. However, some had indeed first met online but then had used digital connectivity to find one another offline as well, just like Sana. Even those who used pseudonyms online often knew each other offline.

Such tight networks allow people to sustain one another during quieter times, but that is not all they do. These networks also play a crucial role when protests erupt.

* * *

Activists can become catalysts for broader publics who can be mobilized, but to make a significant impact, large social movements require the participation of large numbers of people, many of whom may not have much prior political experience. These people usually do not seek out political and dissent outlets and thus are less likely to encounter dissident views. This is why people in power are greatly concerned with controlling the broader public sphere, especially mass media.

For decades, authoritarian states in Egypt, Tunisia, and other countries in the Arab world built up extensive control and censorship of the mass media, the most powerful society-wide means of information dissemination. The public sphere was closed, controlled, characterized by censorship, and ruled by fear. Egyptian media did not report news that reflected badly on the government, especially news about protests. People feared talking about politics except with their close family and friends—and sometimes even with them. In this climate, many people in the Middle East did not know whether their neighbors also hated the autocrats who had ruled with an iron fist for decades.

Digital technologies, along with the satellite TV channel Al Jazeera, changed this situation.[18] In 2009, Facebook was made available in Arabic, greatly expanding its reach into the growing digital population in the Arab world. Facebook wasn't the first site to which activists were drawn, but it was the first site that reached large masses. Activists generally are among the earliest adopters of digital technologies. When they are asked about their technology use, many activists recite a long history, describing how they seized on the first tools available. For example, Bahraini activists told me about discovering Internet Relay Chat (IRC)—essentially the chat channel of the early internet—long before such sites were well known. My first encounter with smartphones, including early BlackBerries, goes back to anti-corporate globalization activists in 1999 who embraced the technology almost as soon as it came out, ironically when its use was otherwise mostly limited to high-level businesspeople.

However, Facebook is different from earlier digital technologies. It came out as computers and smartphones were already spreading, and many ordinary people quickly adopted the platform because it allowed easy connectivity with friends and family. This gave it strength. Since it was so widely used, it couldn't be shut down as easily as an activist-only site.

About one year after Facebook rolled out its Arabic version, toward the end of 2010, things started heating up more openly in the Arab world, first in Tunisia, which had been ruled for decades by the autocrat Zine El Abidine Ben Ali. To understand the impact of Facebook, ponder an earlier protest, just as the site—and digital connectivity—was getting started in the region.

In 2008, Ben Ali had endured organized, persistent protests in the mining town of Gafsa in central Tunisia. The Gafsa protests erupted after the residents objected to a corrupt employment scheme that ensured that mostly relatives of those already in power and people closely connected to the regime were being hired. The police were unable to quash the unrest, so the military was called in, and many leading trade unionists were jailed. Their relatives started a hunger strike to draw attention to their protest. Ben Ali responded by suppressing the story, and effectively silencing news of the city.[19] Town residents were united and persisted in struggling for months, but their actions were like a tree falling in a forest where there were few people besides themselves who could hear it. Despite stalwart efforts, they were unable to get most of the news of their protests out to a wider world.[20] A few months later, mostly unheard, exhausted, and broken, they folded. Ben Ali continued to rule Tunisia with an iron fist. The residents' lack of success in drawing attention and widespread support to their struggle is a scenario that has been repeated the world over for decades in countries led by dictators: rebellions are drowned out through silencing and censorship.

Less than two years later, another round of protests broke out in Tunisia. This time they occurred in Sidi Bouzid, a small town near the coast, after the self-immolation of a street vendor, Mohammad Bouazzizi—an individual act of desperation after he was humiliatingly treated by the police and his fruit cart was confiscated. As Tunisians took to the streets in Sidi Bouzid, Ben Ali tried the same strategy he had used against the people of Gafsa. In 2009, at the time of the Gafsa protests, there were only 28,000 people on Facebook in Tunisia.[21] But by the end of 2010, the number of

Tunisians on Facebook had exploded to 2 million. The burgeoning blog community in Tunisia had also forged strong ties during campaigns to oppose censorship. Remarkably, food, parenting, and tourism blogs were in dialogue with the political blogs in the fight to stay online in the face of a repressive regime.

The protests took most of the world by surprise, but now Tunisian groups like Nawaat, a small Tunisian anticensorship and internet-freedom organization that had been working together for many years, were there to help people in finding, vetting, and spreading information. The Nawaat activists were tightly plugged into groups like Global Voices, a grassroots citizen journalism network that spans the globe. Global Voices holds conferences every other year so that people from different countries in the network can meet one another face-to-face. Neither Nawaat nor the Tunisian section of Global Voices was very large, but they became crucial bridges for local information to journalists abroad, as well as a significant resource for Tunisians, making the suppression of news about the protests more difficult. Global Voices was able to use its preexisting relationships with Tunisian bloggers and its accumulated digital know-how and social capital to get the word out quickly and widely.

To be ready to play key roles in movements that emerge quickly, activists must maintain themselves as activists over the years even when there is little protest activity or overt dissent. Following the revolution in Tunisia, I interviewed many members of Nawaat and Tunisian Global Voices contributors, some of whom I had already known for many years. I asked them what had sustained their political work before the revolution, and the widespread global attention. Many cited the Global Voices organization. "It kept me going," one of them said to me, "because they were the people who were listening to me when nobody was, and cheering me on when nobody was. I might have given up had it not been for them."

With a community of digitally savvy activists and a nation that had higher rates of use of social media tools and more people equipped with smartphones than before, the 2010–11 protests took a different path from those in 2009. Unlike the Gafsa protests, pictures of Sidi Bouzid protesters defying the police quickly spread in Tunisia and abroad. The region-wide satellite TV station Al Jazeera also played a key role by broadcasting video taken from social media on its channel that was accessible to many people inside the country. Despite killing dozens of people, after weeks of protests, the police and the army were unable to contain the movement. As the unrest spread, Ben Ali fled to exile in Saudi Arabia.

Until that time, most of the world had not noticed the events in Tunisia. Remarkably, the very first mention of Tunisian protests in the *New York Times* appeared on January 4, 2011, only one day before Ben Ali fled. Just like the autocratic rulers, many in the West thought that the internet would not make much of a difference in the way politics operated, and they did not anticipate the vulnerability of Ben Ali. He was forced out as the widespread and already existing discontent in the country erupted online and offline—discontent that in earlier eras had fewer modes of collective expression or synchronization available to it.

Tunisia was not an aberration; it was the beginning. After Ben Ali's fall in neighboring Tunisia, the political mood in Egypt also started to shift. The ignition of a social movement arises from multiple important interactions—among activists attempting to find one another, between activists and the public sphere, and among ordinary people finding new access to political content matching their privately held beliefs.

In 2011, why didn't Mubarak's regime crack down harder on online media? Partly because back then, many governments, including Mubarak's, were naïve about the power of the internet and dismissed "online" acts as frivolous and powerless. Indeed, authorities in many countries had derided the internet and digital technology as "virtual" and therefore unimportant. They were not alone. Many Western observers were also scornful of the use of the internet for activism. Online political activity was ridiculed as "slacktivism," an attitude popularized especially by Evgeny Morozov.

In his influential book *The Net Delusion* and in earlier essays, Morozov argued that "slacktivism" was distracting people from productive activism, and that people who were clicking on political topics online were turning away from other forms of activism for the same cause.[22] Empirical research on social movements or discussions with actual activists would have quickly dissuaded an observer from such a theory. Most people who become activists start by being exposed to dissident ideas, and people's social networks—

which include online and offline interactions—are among the most effective places from which people are recruited into activism.[23] However, because of the appetite in the Western news media for anything that scorned (or hyped!) the power of the internet, contrarian writers like Morozov quickly rose up to fill that space. Ironically, these provocatively written articles were often used in the competition for clicks online, and often paired with equally unfounded analyses hyping the internet in simplistic and overblown ways.[24] Morozov especially specialized in scathing, polemical commentary full of colorful insults that often mischaracterized the views of his opponents ("targets" might be a better word).[25] This style helped create an unfortunate dynamic where nuanced and complex conversation on the role of digital connectivity in dissent was drowned out by vitriol and over-simplification, as the "sides" proceeded to set up and knock down strawman, helped by a heaping of personalized insults, which made for entertaining reading that could go viral online, but muddied the analytic waters. In that environment, an underdeveloped concept of slacktivism   a catchphrase that insulted activists and non-activists using digital tools without adding to understanding the complexity of digital reconfiguration of the public sphere—took hold.

This broadly erroneous understanding of the relationship of people to the internet, along with an oversimplification of how it affects social movements, stems from a fallacy that has long been recognized scholars, and one that has been dubbed "digital dualism"—the idea that the internet is a less "real" world. Even the terms "cyberspace" and "virtual" betray this thinking, as if the internet constituted a separate space, like the digital reality in the movie *Matrix* that real people could plug into.[26]

All these misanalyses were also fueled by the ignorance of people in positions of power who had not grown up with digital communication technologies, and were thus prone to simplistic analyses. Government leaders around the world remain remarkably incognizant of how the internet works at even a basic level. As of this writing, one still encounters reports of top elected officials (and Supreme Court justices) who never use computers. Their aides print their e-mails. This degree of technical ineptitude among the people who run many governments poses problems for Western countries, but it proved to be crippling for dictators in countries whose rule depended on controlling the public sphere.

If the internet is virtual, what harm could a few bloggers typing in an unreal space do? Besides, while the internet was often characterized as politically impotent, it was also seen as a place for economic activity and development, and for consumers too. Some activists told me that they had taken to setting up "technology" companies to disguise their political activism from the doltish authorities. For years, because of the obliviousness of officials, political activists in many countries, including Egypt, were allowed to write online relatively freely. There were pockets of censorship and repression, but they were hit-and-miss rather than broad and effective attempts to suppress online conversation. (However, since the Arab Spring, regime after regime has been forced to recognize that a freewheeling, digitally networked public sphere poses a threat to entrenched control. See chapter 9 for an in-depth exploration.)

Another line of reasoning has been that internet is a minority of the population. This is true; even as late as 2009, the internet was limited to a small minority of households in the Middle East. However, the role of digital connectivity cannot be reduced to the percentage of a nation's population that is online. Digital connectivity alters the architecture of connectivity across an entire society even when much of it is not yet connected. People on Facebook (more than four million Egyptians around the time of the January 25, 2011, uprising) communicate with those who are not on the site by sharing what they saw online with friends and family through other means: face-to-face conversation, texting, or telephone.[27] Only a segment of the population needs to be connected digitally to affect the entire environment. In Egypt in 2011, only 25 percent of the population of the country was online, with a smaller portion of those on Facebook, but these people still managed to change the wholesale public discussion, including conversations among people who had never been on the site.

The internet's earliest adopters tended to be wealthier, more technically oriented, and better educated. This also has consequences for politics, but it is not the whole story. Two key constituencies for social movements are also early adopters: activists and journalists. During my research, I found that activists in many countries were among the first to take up this new tool to organize, to publicize, and in some places to circumvent censorship.

In my home country, Turkey, I was also among the earliest users of the internet, mostly because I wanted to freely access information, including political information that was censored in Turkey's mass media.

In 2011, a few months after the Tunisian protests, I visited Al Jazeera headquarters in Qatar and interviewed some of the young journalists who had spread the news of the then-emerging Arab Spring protests. Al Jazeera employs journalists from dozens of nations. How did they navigate the Tunisian blogosphere and social media where so overwhelmingly many videos and images were being posted? Many explained that they had been drawn to the internet as a political space from early on, and they had long-time friendships with the leading activists of the region who also understood the power of connectivity. While many Westerners were surprised by the use of social media during Middle East protests, these young journalists were habituated to it since, like their activist counterparts, they lived in repressive countries with tightly controlled public spheres.

The political internet in the first decade of the twenty-first century in the Middle East featured blogs that not only published political essays but also exposed government wrongdoing, from small outrages to large-scale atrocities, aided by their improved ability to document events with cheap cameras and cell phones that recorded and transmitted pictures and video. One well-known Egyptian blogger published videos on subjects ranging from images of women being harassed in the street to police torturing detained people. Before internet activism emerged in Egypt, these topics had rarely been discussed openly.[28]

The region's autocratic rulers might have been somewhat perturbed by these flares of public attention on formerly taboo subjects, but they probably comforted themselves with the thought that internet users in their country were and would remain a peripheral subset of the population consisting of the technically oriented and a few political activists.

But then, Facebook arrived.

Facebook changed the picture significantly by opening to the masses the networked public sphere that had previously been available only to a marginal, self-selected group of people who were already politically active.[29] Facebook has been adopted rapidly in almost every country where it has been introduced because it fulfills a basic human desire: to connect with family and friends. Once a computer was in the house, the site offered connections much more cheaply than alternatives like the telephone, especially as the price of computers dropped over time. In countries like Egypt and Tunisia with large families as the norm and with long working hours, horrible street traffic, and large expatriate communities, it was especially popular. Just one year after Facebook was made available in Arabic in 2009, it had quickly acquired millions of users.

Facebook also has specific features: such as a design that leans toward being open and non-privacy respecting. This was often a privacy nightmare, but it was also a boon to activists—it meant that things spread easily. Ben Ali briefly tried to ban Facebook, but the attempt backfired because so many Tunisians used Facebook to connect with far-flung family, friends, and acquaintances. Facebook had become too useful for too many in the general population to be easily outlawed, but also too politically potent to ignore. In that way, the platform created a bind for the authoritarian governments that had tended to ignore it in its earlier stages.

Ethan Zuckerman calls this the "cute cat theory" of activism and the public sphere. Platforms that have nonpolitical functions can become more politically powerful because it is harder to censor their large numbers of users who are eager to connect with one another or to share their latest "cute cat" pictures.[30] Attempts to censor Facebook often backfire for this reason. This is one reason some nations, like China, have never allowed Facebook to become established, and likely will not do so unless Facebook succumbs to draconian measures of control, censorship, and turning over of user information to the government.[31] Additionally, these internet platforms harness the power of network effects—the more people who use them, the more useful they are to more people. With so many people already on Facebook, there are huge incentives for new people to get on Facebook even if they dislike some of its policies or features. Network effects also create a twist for activists who find themselves compelled to use whatever the dominant platform may be, even if they are uncomfortable with it. A perfect social media platform without users is worthless for activism. One that is taking off on a society-wide scale is hard to stop, block, or ban.

The arrival of Facebook introduced another aspect of the power of networked dissent. Ordinarily, people have social ties of varying strength. Some people are closer to one another and serve as one another's primary or strong ties. Other people are more distant friends, acquaintances, or workplace colleagues or have other weak ties. Traditionally, most people have strong ties to only a few people, but the number of people to whom they have weak ties may vary widely. Strong ties are very important to people's well-being and are often formed between people who tend to live or work close to each other—though immigration and moving internally for education or jobs has helped weaken that connection. People tend to try to keep up with those to whom they have strong ties no matter what technology is available. That is not necessarily true for weak ties. Without Facebook, there is little chance that I would still have contact with my middle-school friends from a place where I lived for only a few years. Through social media, people can announce significant events like births, marriages, and deaths to a wide range of people, including many with whom they have weak ties, and can maintain relationships that were never strong to begin with and relationships that without digital assistance might have withered away or involved much less contact. For people seeking political change, though, the networking that takes place among people with weak ties is especially important.

People with strong ties likely already share similar views, so such views are less likely to surprise when they are expressed on social media. However, weaker ties may be far flung and composed of people with varying political and social ties. Also, weak ties may create bridges to other clusters of people in a way strong ties do not. For example, your siblings already know one another, and news travels among them in many ways. However, a workplace acquaintance—someone with whom you have a weak tie— who sees a piece of political news from you on Facebook may share it with her social network, her relatives and friends, a group of people you would ordinarily have no access to, save for the bridging role played by the weak tie between you and your work colleague. Social scientists call the person connecting these two otherwise separate clusters a "bridge tie." Research shows that weak ties are more likely to be bridges between disparate groups.[32] This finding has important implications for politics in the era of digital connectivity because Facebook makes it much easier for people to stay connected with others through weak ties. Thus Facebook creates more connections over which political news can travel and reach other communities to which one lacks direct access.[33]

For perhaps the first time, dissidents in the Mideast were able to quasi-broadcast their views, at least to their Facebook friends (and the friends of their Facebook friends, who could easily number in the tens of thousands). If a few people who were not overtly political "liked" or positively commented on their posts, not only were they sharing their thoughts with others, but also everyone else seeing the interaction knew that others had been exposed to this information. Through these symbolic interactions, activists created a new baseline for common knowledge of the political situation in Egypt—not just what you knew, but also what others knew you knew, and so on—that shifted the acceptable boundaries of discourse.[34]

In 2010, a young man named Khaled Said was brutally murdered by the Egyptian police. The details are murky, but the precipitating incident was probably a petty crime. Some say that he smoked pot. There were rumors that he might have documented police misconduct. He was tortured and killed, and the police acted with impunity, as they often did. A distraught relative took a picture of his mangled face in the morgue. The photograph spread online in Egypt along with a "before" picture of him: a young, healthy man smiling, full of potential and hope, juxtaposed to a photograph symbolizing everything wrong with the country.

Wael Ghonim, an Egyptian who worked for Google and resided in the United Arab Emirates, was outraged, like many other Egyptians. He set up a Facebook page called "We Are All Khaled Said" to express his outrage. He kept his identity hidden. Nobody at Google knew what he was doing, nor did anyone else. The page quickly grew and became a focal point of dissident political discussion in Egypt. In 2015, I met with Ghonim in New York. Like many other activists I have known, he told me that he had realized the political potential of the internet early on. He was an early adopter of all things digital, going back to the initial days of the internet's introduction in the Middle East. When Facebook came along, he quickly realized that it was not just a place for baby pictures or Eid holiday greetings.[35]

After Ben Ali's fall in neighboring Tunisia, the Egyptian "We Are All Khaled Said" Facebook page became even more animated as thousands of Egyptians debated whether they, too, could overthrow their autocrat and replace the repressive regime with a democracy. Egyptians had followed the protests in Tunisia with great interest, and every day many people posted suggestions, arguments, desires, and political goals at the page. Finally, after much heated conversation and a poll of the page's users, Wael Ghonim posted a "Facebook event" inviting people to Tahrir Square on January 25, 2011. He could not know that it would eventually lead to the ouster of Mubarak.

Less than a year after those protests, I talked with "Ali," one of the leading activists of the movement, who had been in Tahrir the very first day, and also for the eighteen days of protest that led to Mubarak's fall. We were all in Tunisia at the Arab Bloggers Conference, where Egyptians, Tunisians, Bahrainis, and others who had played prominent roles in political social media had gathered. We sat in a seaside cafe, surrounded by activists from many Arab countries after a long day of workshops. The movements were still young, and the full force of the counter-reaction had not yet been felt. The beautiful Mediterranean stretched before us, and some people danced inside the café to rap music making fun of their fallen dictators while others sipped their drinks.

As Ali explained it to me, for him, January 25, 2011, was in many ways an ordinary January 25—officially a "police celebration day," but traditionally a day of protest. Although he was young, he was a veteran activist. He and a small group of fellow activists gathered each year in Tahrir on January 25 to protest police brutality. January 25, 2011, was not their first January 25 protest, and many of them expected something of a repeat of their earlier protests—perhaps a bit larger this year.

I had seen a picture of those early protests, so I could imagine the scene he described: a few hundred young people, surrounded by rows and rows of riot police and sometimes tanks, isolated, alone, and seemingly without impact on the larger society. During some years they were allowed to shout slogans; in other years they were beaten up and arrested. Yet they went on, year after year, on principle and out of bravery and loyalty to their friends. Then 2011 happened. Ali didn't know what to expect but confessed that he had not expected much—certainly not toppling the regime. But as soon as he arrived at the square, he knew. "It was different," he said. That year's protest was larger, he said, but that was not the only difference. "People who showed up in Tahrir weren't just your friends."

Ali paused, searching for a way to describe the people who had shown up that year. "They were your Facebook friends."

He meant that rather than the small core group of about a hundred activists, thousands of people—friends and acquaintances who were not very political, who were not hard-core activists—also showed up on January 25, 2011. His weak-tie networks had been politically activated. Although the crowd was not huge yet, it was large enough to pose a problem for the government, especially since many were armed with digital cameras and internet connections. My research of that showed that people with a presence on social media, especially Facebook and Twitter, were much more likely to have shown up on the crucial first day that kicked off the avalanche of protest that was to come.[36]

Now the annual crowd of a few hundred in the square had grown to thousands. There were too many people to beat up or arrest without repercussions, especially because the presence of digital cameras and smartphones meant that those few thousands could easily and quickly spread the word to tens and hundreds of thousands in their networks of strong and weak ties. More people joined them. These people in Tahrir Square were more powerful not only because there were more of them, but also because they were making visible to Egypt, and to the whole world, where they stood, in coordination and in synchrony with one another.

Humans are group animals—aside from rare and aberrant exceptions, we exist and live in groups. We thrive and exist via social signaling to one another about our beliefs, and we adjust according to what we think others around us think. This is absolutely normal for humans. Most of the time we are also a fairly docile species—and when we are not, it is often in organized ways, such as wars. You could not, for example, squeeze more than a hundred chimpanzees into a thin metal tube, sitting knee-to-knee and shoulder-to-shoulder in cramped quarters, close the door, hurl the tube across the sky at great speed, and always expect those disembarking at the other end to have all their body parts intact. But we can travel in airplanes because our social norms and nature are to comply, cooperate, accommodate, and sometimes even be kind to one another.

Some social scientists (mostly economists) who imagine humans as selfish and utility-maximizing individuals theorize that people would descend into self-absorbed chaos as soon as external controls on them were lifted. But things are far from that simple. For example, it has been repeatedly found that in most emergencies, disasters, and protests, ordinary people are often helpful and altruistic.[37] This is not a uniform effect though; pre-existing polarization can worsen, for example, under such stress. It is true that humans can be rational, calculating, and selfish, but it is also true that humans want to belong and fit in, and that they care deeply about what their fellow humans think of a situation. From preschool to adolescence to adulthood, most of us are highly attuned to what our peers and people with high status or those in authority think. It is as if we are always playing chess, poker, and truth-or-dare simultaneously.

However, that desire to belong, reflecting what a person perceives to be the views of the majority, is also used by those in power to control large numbers of people, especially if it is paired with heavy punishments for the visible troublemakers who might set a different example to follow. In fact, for many repressive governments, fostering a sense of loneliness among dissidents while making an example of them to scare off everyone else has long been a trusted method of ruling.[38] Social scientists refer to the feeling of imagining oneself to be a lonely minority when in fact there are many people who agree with you, maybe even a majority, as "pluralistic ignorance."[39] Pluralistic ignorance is thinking that one is the only person bored at a class lecture and not knowing that the sentiment is shared, or that dissent and discontent are rare feelings in a country when in fact they are common but remain unspoken.

To understand how fear and outward conformity operate hand in hand, think of sitting in a cramped middle row at an awful concert or lecture. You may wish to leave, but who wants to stand out and perhaps feel stupid and rude by leaving when everyone else appears to be listening attentively? Pretending to pay attention, and even to enjoy the event, is the safest bet. That is what people do, and that is what those in authority often rely on to keep people in line. Now imagine that the performer controls not only the microphone but also a police force that will arrest anyone who shows signs of being bored or uninterested. The first person to yawn will be carted away screaming, and you know or imagine that bad things will happen to anyone who signals displeasure or boredom. Imagine that the theater is dark—a controlled public sphere, censored media—so you can hardly see what fellow members of the audience are doing or thinking, although you are occasionally able to whisper about the awful performance to the few friends you are seated with. But you whisper lest the police hear you, and only to those closest to you. Imagine that there are rumors that the police have installed microphones in some of the seats. Most of the time you sit still and remain quiet. It feels dangerous even to give your friends an occasional knowing, disgusted nudge during the worst parts of the performance. Welcome to the authoritarian state.

Now imagine that there is a tool that allows you to signal your boredom and disgust to your neighbors and even to the whole room all at once. Imagine people being able to nod or "like" your grumblings about the quality of the event and to realize that many people in the room feel the same way. That cramped seat in the middle row no longer feels as alone and isolated. You may find yourself joined by new waves of people declaring their boredom.

This is what the digitally networked public sphere can do in many instances: help people reveal their (otherwise private) preferences to one another and discover common ground. Street protests play a similar role in showing people that they are not alone in their dissent. But digital media make this happen in a way that blurs the boundaries of private and public, home and street, and individual and collective action.

Given the role of pluralistic ignorance in keeping people who live under repressive regimes scared and compliant, technologies of connectivity create a major threat to those regimes. Even in the absence of repression, pluralistic ignorance plays a role simply because we like to belong; however, the effect is weaker since people are less likely to be quiet about their beliefs. The threat that pluralistic ignorance might be undermined is one of the reasons that the government of China, for example, hands out multi-decade sentences to bloggers and spends huge sums of money employing hundreds of thousands of people to extensively censor the online world. A single blogger does not pose much of a threat. But if one person is allowed to blog freely, soon there might be hundreds of thousands, and they might discover that they are not alone.[40] That is a crucial aspect of what happened in Egypt, leading to the uprising in 2011.

Thanks to a Facebook page, perhaps for the first time in history, an internet user could click yes on an electronic invitation to a revolution. Hundreds of thousands did so, in full view of their online networks of strong and weak ties, all at once. The rest is history—a complex and still-unfinished one, with many ups and downs. But for Egypt, and for the rest of the world, things would never be the same again.

2

Censorship and Attention

CURIOUS ABOUT THE CLAIM THAT THE ZAPATISTAS, an uprising of indigenous peasants in southern Mexico, were using the internet in new and impressive ways, I traveled in 1997 to the mountainous regions of Chiapas, Mexico, to visit an insurgent Mayan village nestled high up in the border region between Mexico and Guatemala. I found a place without electricity, let alone the internet, ruled by a brutal struggle for survival.[1] Children succumbed to diseases from polluted water, and the villagers spent much of their time doing things that we seldom have to worry about. The children spent a big chunk of their days searching for wood to burn for heat and cooking in the perpetually cold and damp highlands, and women arduously ground corn by hand to make tortillas. Without electricity, it took the women half their day, every day, just to do this task.

Toward the middle of my visit, a young woman approached me, clutching her children, a boy and a girl, both of whom looked under age five, and asked me to take pictures of them. I was used to the opposite: local people asking me not to take their pictures, a sentiment especially common among the indigenous people in the Mayan region, who were understandably suspicious of strangers after five hundred years of colonization. I agreed to take the picture, of course, but asked her reason.

It was simple: she had no pictures of her children. There were no cameras in her village, and there had never been any. Her children were growing up without a single record of them for her to cherish over time. I arranged to leave my camera at the village, although I was unsure whether they would be able to find a way to print any pictures. I still have a copy of that picture of those children, who would be around college age today. It wasn't that long ago.

If I returned to the same Chiapas village now, I am fairly sure that it would be awash in cell phones with digital cameras even though the villagers might still be living in mud-floor huts, as they did then. They might even have internet access, although they still might not have electricity. The mobile revolution has been swift and widespread. In 2012, I traveled to Kenya and visited rural regions without electricity. Even when I was traveling over roads that barely existed, I almost never lost internet connectivity. I couldn't help but notice how the roads were dotted with stalls for charging cell phones and buying minutes. In one village, I met an old lady, about the same age as my grandmother, who wore her phone like a necklace around her neck, just as my grandmother in Turkey does. And just like my grandmother, she didn't use the phone very often, but she always felt connected to her children and grandchildren, many of whom had left in search for a better life.

I once asked YouTube's news director (who leads arguably one of the biggest and most important news-aggregation sites in the world) how long it took for footage of significant events to be uploaded to the platform. Usually under an hour, she said. Because it is almost mundane to us now, we forget how striking it is that within an hour of anything major happening almost anywhere in the world, YouTube expects to see footage uploaded, and we expect to see it soon. In about one generation, we have gone from a world in which cameras were a rarity in many places to one in which billions are connected, almost instantly.

We no longer live in a mass-media world with a few centralized choke points with just a few editors in charge, operated by commercial entities and governments. There is a new, radically different mode of information and attention flow: the chaotic world of the digitally networked public sphere (or spheres) where ordinary citizens or activists can generate ideas, document and spread news of events, and respond to mass media. This new sphere, too, has choke points and centralization, but different ones than the past. The networked public sphere has emerged so forcefully and so rapidly that it is easy to forget how new it is. Facebook was started in 2004 and Twitter in 2006. The first iPhone, ushering in the era of the smart, networked phone, was introduced in 2007. The wide extent of digital connectivity might blind us to the power of this transformation. It should not. These dynamics are significant social mechanisms, especially for social movements, since they change the operation of a key resource: *attention.*

Attention is rarely analyzed on its own; a significant oversight given its importance. Attention is oxygen for movements. Without it, they cannot catch fire. Powerful actors try to smother movements by denying them attention. Censorship is usually thought of as a dichotomous concept: something is either censored or not, often by a centralized gatekeeper, such as governments or mass media. For example, governments may censor an unfavorable story by banning it outright or pressuring mass media not to cover it. It is difficult to understand today's social movement trajectories using this traditional notion of censorship.

In the twenty-first century and in the networked public sphere, it is more useful to think of attention as a resource allocated and acquired on local, national, and transnational scales, and censorship as a broad term for denial of attention through multiple means, including, but not limited to, the traditional definition of censorship as an effort to actively block information from getting out.[2] Chapter 9 examines attention and censorship more from the point-of-view of governments; this chapter focuses more on the relationship between movements and the shifting landscape of attention.

Movements also experience other kinds of obstacles from mass media in their quest for favorable attention. A movement may not get favorable media coverage because of ideological or corporate reasons, rather than government censorship. Traditional journalists may trivialize, marginalize, or ignore a social movement because they disagree with it or dislike it, or a corporate parent may decide that a social movement doesn't fit well with its financial interests—for example, that the movement is unsuitable for the corporation's advertiser-dependent business model.[3]

In the past, mass media operated like it held a monopoly on public attention, and movements needed mass media to publicize their cause and

their events to tell their story. This dependency involved many considerations and trade-offs for social movements. News media were more responsive to formal nongovernmental organizations (NGOs), so movements
would try to get the resources to create one. This meant that movements of
poorer people were greatly disadvantaged. A movement shut out of mass
media could try being disruptive or provocative as a strategy to get attention, but this strategy ran the risk of provoking negative coverage: discussion only within a framework of disruption.[4] Movements often faced having
their causes trivialized or distorted by mass media, with no chance to talk
back. Mass media's near monopoly on attention often meant that the two
were conflated, and an analysis of attention would often be confined to
analyses of media. Now that mass media no longer hold a monopoly on
attention, neither censorship nor the competition for attention operates in
the same way.

The evolution of the public sphere in Turkey in the past few years exem-
plifies many of these dynamics. In my lifetime, my home country went
from a nation under severe military censorship to one in which over half
the population is online. The changes have been dramatic.

After enduring a coup and a military regime in the 1980s and a still
heavily censored public sphere in the 1990s, Turkey's media environment
began to change in the twenty-first century. First, the internet was introduced and was quickly and widely adopted by the people, especially so they
could use social media platforms like Facebook and Twitter that allowed
them to connect with family and friends. Second, despite a proliferation of
mass-media channels, a new censorship regime emerged based on ownership of mass media by corporations that depended on government favor
for profit. Owners of these pliant mass-media outlets voluntarily censored
and adjusted their coverage to please the ruling party. Media outlets that
did not toe the line faced significant pressure. In effect, Turkey went from
one censorship and control regime to another in mass media, although
with a difference: the latter regime existed alongside a burgeoning digitally
networked public sphere.

In this complex new regime in the 2010s, I watched a single tweet inspire
a few college students to form a citizen media network that challenged the

established mass-media giants. What followed was a movement that, using mostly social media to organize and publicize itself, would become the country's biggest protest in decades, the Gezi Park protests of 2013.

To understand the evolution of the networked public sphere in Turkey, and its relationship to the Gezi Park protests of 2013, it is important to start a little earlier, and understand some of the events that helped shape it going into 2013—especially an earlier incident in a Kurdish village in southern Turkey.

The Kurds are a minority group who live mostly in the southeast part of Turkey. For a long time they had been deprived of official recognition and linguistic rights. The "Kurdish question" in Turkey has always been sensitive, wrapped up in a history of conflict and tragedy. During the military regime of the 1980s, the Kurds were referred to in the mass media as "Mountain Turks"—Turks who were just a little misguided about their ethnicity and language—rather than an actual minority. This was, of course, ridiculous (Turkish and Kurdish don't even belong to the same language family), but in the censored military regime, such outlandish claims could be made with a straight face, and children like me had no way to know better—unless they had a direct personal connection to people who were Kurdish and willing to talk about their origins. There were many allegations of widespread human rights abuses of Kurds, including extrajudicial killings and torture, but, in other parts of Turkey, we didn't hear much about any of this. While people outside the region were kept in the dark, an insurgency spread in the region.

In the 1990s, the Kurdish conflict spread and tragically claimed forty thousand lives. This time, the news wasn't made to disappear, as it had been in the 1980s, but was presented in a single version: the government was fighting terrorists, and all those who died were terrorists. It was a time of heavy-handed control of news, with little in the way of independent journalism on mass media.

In 2002, a new political party came to power. More Islamist and less beholden to the military and the Turkish nationalism of previous eras, the new government held talks with the insurgent Kurdish group. A truce was declared, and the guns went mostly quiet. More of the reality of the three-decade insurgency and the counterinsurgency trickled into mainstream consciousness. Meanwhile, political progress was made. Openly Kurdish deputies were elected to Parliament, and the Kurds' existence as a minority became acknowledged. Still, the truce remained fragile and incomplete.

Under the new government, Turkey also moved into a new control regime in the mass media, one that operated through the agency of large corporations that purchased mass-media outlets mostly to curry favor with the new government. Media watchdogs reported that in return for obsequious coverage, media outlets were awarded lucrative contracts, while companies and journalists who did not acquiesce were penalized. News outlets that remained even slightly defiant faced significant pressure.[5] After publishing a piece about corruption involving a large charity that was close to the government, a media group that had not been overly friendly to the government was fined 2.5 billions of dollars in newly discovered "tax fines"—an amount pretty close to the total worth of the conglomerate.[6] After it stopped publishing such investigative news, the fine was quietly but drastically reduced in a "tax amnesty" deal.[7]

One working journalist described the pressure she was under this way: "I first censor myself, as I know I'll be in trouble if I write something critical of the government. And then my editor censors me, if I haven't been mild enough. And then owners of the newspaper also check, to make sure nothing too critical gets through. And if something is published anyway, especially if in defiance, someone from the government calls our boss. And then the tax inspectors are sent in, to find something to fine the newspaper with." Such pressure on the media from government officials and corporate owners is common around the world.

A vague, uneasy truce held in the Kurdish region with many years of relative peace, without large-scale killings on either side, and a complex control regime in the mass media that relied on voluntary shaping of news by corporate owners. Then, in late 2011, Turkish military jets bombed and killed thirty-four Kurdish smugglers making a run over the Iraqi border. The smugglers lived in a nearby village, Roboski, and almost all were from a few large families.

About a year later, a young man, "Cengiz," from one of the families that had lost so many to the bombing, recounted to me what had started as a regular day and had transformed into the worst day of his life. He had been a student in a nearby town when his phone rang a very long time too early in the morning. He became alarmed. His father was on the line, screaming and crying. Cengiz learned that a military plane had bombed and killed many members of his family during a smuggling run. All other details were unclear.

Cengiz caught the first bus to his hometown and noticed that it was equipped with a television, a relatively common sight in inter-city buses in Turkey. He watched a report that mentioned terrorists being caught and killed at the border. Then the anchor moved on, as if there was nothing else worth mentioning. He told me that he sobbed when he realized that his family had been reduced on the news to terrorists in a bombing of supposedly little significance. He had hoped for an acknowledgment that the "terrorists" were poor, young smugglers and that many had even been employed in the government's counterinsurgency program as "village guards"—far from a terrorist group. Their crime was carrying some petrol and cigarettes over the border, making a tiny profit by avoiding taxes—a routine activity in a region where members of the same family sometimes lived on both sides of the border. Later, in interviews, the villagers would mention that they would wave at police and soldiers on their way to their smuggling runs. Their activity was not a secret. The brief mention also didn't acknowledge that twenty-one of the thirty-four dead were teenagers, like Cengiz's brother and many cousins. Cengiz told me that he wanted to crush that television, as if to take out all his sorrow on a physical object. "I thought it might help me deal with my anger without hurting anyone," he said, growing silent at the memory of helplessness, sorrow, and anger.

On that day, while Cengiz struggled to understand the horrible news, TV-station owners and top-level editors were struggling to figure out what they should report, and how they should report it. The incident left them in a bind. The situation was ambiguous. Smuggling in that part of the country was routine, and the village, Roboski (Uludere in Turkish), was thought to be friendly to the government. In the 1980s, the deaths might have been completely censored; in the 1990s, the incident might have been merely blamed on terrorists. This time, too, "terrorism" was offered as a knee-jerk explanation, but the coverage wavered. Now, grievances of a minority population were acknowledged, but whether this was an incident to be censored or reported was unclear. Something had gone wrong in Roboski, but what? And what should they say about it on the news? Lacking clarity, mass-media managers decided to simply wait for instructions from the government and to sit on the news. In newsrooms, the tension rose as journalists were instructed to remain quiet. However, in the era of the internet, this was not enough.

In 1996, I had accompanied a group of journalists to the Kurdish regions of Turkey to assist them with production tasks as they went over the border to film a crisis in northern Iraq. There was a shortage of video from the crisis, so news organizations spent hundreds of thousands of dollars to ship a lot of heavy equipment along with camera people, producers, assistants, sound engineers, and correspondents. We were a large team, and our equipment was worth millions of dollars. We may have had the only high-end video camera in the area, and the footage had to be taken to the one station with a satellite uplink in the region. If we did not film an event, there would probably be no video record of it. But if we filmed it, and if it aired on network news, it would be broadcast to an audience that might number in the tens of millions. The team, and the television station, held make-or-break power.

By 2011, everything had turned upside down. The potential number of cameras filming each event was enormous. In many events of public importance, what is striking is not just that there is video of it, but that the video of the event shows many other people with their phones out, filming the same event. On that morning of December 29, 2011, it was as if TV-station owners in Turkey were yearning for an alternate universe with censorship tools of the past. They would have their way for only a few hours.

Serdar Akinan was a journalist in one of those newsrooms where the corporate bosses had shut things down during a tense wait for government orders. Akinan couldn't sit still. He bought a ticket with his own money, jumped on a plane, took a cab, and went to the village where the bombing had occurred.

Sometime after the event, I met him in Istanbul. We sat at a seaside table in a restaurant near the beautiful Sea of Marmara, and he explained to me how awful he had felt, and how he was unable to contain his journalistic instincts.

Almost upon arrival at the village, he encountered a snaking line of coffins coming down a small hill as families wailed all around. He told me that he was overwhelmed by the grief and the number of coffins, in the dozens. Ten or even five years earlier, that might have been all he could have done: look at the scene, stunned. But it was 2011. He took out his iPhone, snapped a picture, and posted it on Instagram, a service then barely two years old, and on Twitter, about five years old.

Just like that, the story of the Kurdish deaths in Roboski could be censored no more. The agonizing images went viral online especially on Twitter, and denial became impossible. Shortly afterward, television news stations were forced to report it, admitting that those who had been killed had been ordinary villagers, and that the smuggling run had been routine. In a country of increasingly controlled mass media, it was the biggest crisis the government had faced in a long time, and all it took was one reporter with a phone and a digitally networked public sphere of sufficient depth—about half the country was online by that time.

As Akinan continued to tell me the pressures he faced after he broke censorship so blatantly, a seagull landed near our table, eyeing my food, a delicious plate of fish I did not intend to share with anyone, bird or human. I praised Akinan for his choice of restaurant, clearly approved by those who know their fish the best, seagulls. He laughed as I snapped a picture of the overly eager bird and tweeted it out—a typical occurrence in my day, an act that creates an "ambient awareness" with my friends through social media. We chatted a little more about the food, and it became clear that Akinan's interest in food and restaurants wasn't just personal.

Powerful people could not block the news from traveling on the internet, but they could make sure that people like Akinan could not work as journalists. He was devoted to the job; he had started his journalism career at the age of seventeen, by showing up at a newspaper, begging to be hired (it would take many years before he was formally hired). He had hung on for one more year before being fired, unable to find any other job in journalism, and turning to the restaurant business. Indeed, job changes or unemployment would be in store for many independent journalists in Turkey who refused to comply with the new regime. Many, like Akinan, would be forced to find new avenues to make a living—avenues that would take up all their time and prevent them from carrying out their roles as reporters, smartphone or not.

When Akinan tweeted out that picture of the line of coffins, a few young people received the shock of their lives. Their story, and what they did next, is a crucial piece of the puzzle of understanding the emergent structures of the digitally networked public sphere.

During the same week in which a village mourned its dead, a son cursed at the television that censored the news, and a journalist attempted to report news despite his employers, a few young people in Istanbul, barely in their twenties, were undergoing an epistemological shift. They were young, technologically savvy, and somewhat interested in politics. They were college students and friends, and later, sitting in a breezy Istanbul rooftop café, they told me their stories. They explained how they had founded "140journos," a citizen journalism collective that became arguably the most reliable source of news during the Gezi protests. They told me that the first time they had set up their Twitter accounts, they had gotten bored and shut them down. "I wasn't that interested in sharing pictures of my food, frankly," one of them told me. But they had lingered on, somewhat uninterestedly, in many of these platforms, occasionally logging on but not much else, until the Roboski killings revealed both the scale of the tragedy and the extent of the censorship of Turkish mass media. They had seen Akinan's tweets and his pictures of the snaking line of coffins.

"I kept refreshing all the news channels," one of them said. "From CNN Turkey, to NTV to Haber Turk back to NTV to CNN Turkey. Refresh, refresh, change channel. Nothing. Nothing. Nothing." This story was familiar to me from activists around the world who turned on their television to find news of something important that they knew had happened, but encountered cooking shows, entertainment programs, or talking heads chattering about some other topic—anything but the real news. It was a rude, depressing awakening. Here, in one fell swoop, they had learned that the "news" channels were censoring profoundly important news, and that censorship could be broken through social media. They responded at first by getting depressed and going out to a bar together.

In Turkey, like much of the Mediterranean, there is a tradition of slow, conversational drinking that is the opposite of a loud, hurried bar scene. Such conversational drinking often leads to discussions of politics. The stereotype of these all-night drinking locales in Turkey is that everyone has a plan to "save the nation" after the first glass of raki, a strong aniseed-based drink that is considered the national liquor (it is nearly identical to ouzo, the Greek national drink).

In a previous era, an all-night drinking and talking session on the sorry state of news and the extent of censorship might have ended merely in a hangover the next day. Even if it might have gone further—for example, the people might have decided to try to start a journal or a newspaper—a lot of work, resources, and luck would have been required. However, unlike citizens in a previous era for whom frustration with mass-media bias had engendered little more than sour feelings the next day or an uncertain, lengthy, journey, these young men—only four of them—immediately conceived 140journos, a crowdsourced, citizen journalism network on Twitter.

"So you thought about it one day and started the next morning?" I asked, somewhat bewildered. They had. It resembled stories I had heard elsewhere: Tahrir Supplies of Egypt, which I will discuss further in chapter 3, had gone from an idea to a website and a Twitter page in one day and an effective field medical-supply coordinator in just a few more. A decision to expand the Occupy protests in the United States to the world and to call for global protests in dozens of countries had also happened with just few weeks of preparation beforehand.

These young people had indeed thought about the project one day and started it the next. The details of what they wanted to do were vague: turn social media into a platform for journalism, break the censorship they knew dominated mass media, and become intermediaries for the public. They did not know what the result would be, or that it would turn out to play a crucial role. With all the digital technologies at their disposal, they could start building, and ask questions later.

The example of a tweet breaking censorship in Turkey might seem to suggest that nothing more is necessary for an informed public. That conclusion would be misleading. Rather, the openness of this new part of the public sphere should be seen as the first salvo of its evolution, and as with many technologies before it, the initial stages do not tell us the whole story.

Cell phones in almost every hand certainly have had important consequences for the public sphere, but they do not, by themselves, mean that the correct information will always or easily reach broad audiences. There are many layers in the problem of gathering attention and the tactics for denial of attention by those in power. Another crucial dynamic in the new public sphere is the role of verification and trust, as many more people acquire the ability to become broadcasters, and as information diffuses in networks rather than through a few gatekeepers. Often there is simply too much information, and too much of it is unverified.

Just like the mass-media world, the networked public sphere includes formal and informal institutions, gatekeepers, hierarchies, and curators who shape and influence attention flows. These emerging networked structures have evolved rapidly in the past decade, and this evolution makes them fluid and hard to pin down. The digitally networked public sphere does not replace the old media environment wholesale; it integrates with and interacts with it in complex ways. The result is a new public sphere that is more open than the past, but one that is not flat in the sense of all information and nodes having equal reach, attention, and credibility.

Old-style gatekeepers may have denied attention to a variety of subjects that movements cared about, but that was not all that they did. Traditional journalism was supposed to check its facts, at least normatively, and when direct censorship was severe, it was an explicit failing and a divergence from journalism's stated norms.[8] On the internet, in contrast, the problem is not too little information or even direct censorship (since it is often very hard to block all sources of information). Rather, the challenge is that there is too much information, some of it false, and there is often little guidance for sorting through it. Even when important and correct information is available, making sure that this correct information spreads from the corner where it originates to the rest of the network is not easy or automatic.

This is not to claim that the previous era's gatekeepers were great or never erred through mistakes, ideological biases, or government manipulation or pressure. On the contrary, journalists in many countries certainly censored news and even fabricated stories. Even in nations with more press freedoms, like the United States, there have been spectacular failures of the press. The United States was taken to war after almost all major news publications, including the most elite and distinguished ones, repeated false government lines about Iraqi weapons of mass destruction without sufficient probing or investigation.

Still, as a profession, journalists have an ethos of verification, investigation, and accuracy, even if real-life practice falls short to varying degrees. And there are always some outlets striving for accuracy and in-depth reporting, even during times of governmental pressure. Traditional mass media may have fallen short of the ideal of a complete, accurate reflection of important events delivered by saintly journalists with only the public interest in mind, but it provided boundaries of discourse and often delivered on at least some of their normative functions of investigative journalism, fact-checking, and gatekeeping.

The complex and often chaotic world of the digitally networked public sphere lacks such trusted intermediaries. There is too much content competing for attention, and it is hard to tell what is verified from what is false, whether through honest error or deliberate misinformation. People often tune in to ideologically resonant sources of information and become suspicious of everything else they see, both because of well-known human tendencies to seek information we agree with and to defend against information glut. Traditional journalism failures had also fostered an environment of mistrust in all gatekeepers and intermediaries. Although traditional journalism continues to exert influence in the networked public sphere, the increasing number of people acting as both providers and distributors of news, the resulting torrent of information, and the already existing environment of mistrust has meant that the problem facing ordinary people is wading through it all and determining what is true and worth paying attention to. This is not easy.

It was exactly this problem that the four young people of 140journos wanted to tackle. They realized that news and information could no longer be easily blocked, but it was unclear that it could always find its way around. They set out to try to figure out how to make that happen.

* * *

The role that 140journos sought did not come with a script. In fact, much of what its founders knew about news and journalism wasn't helpful at all. Their first impulse was to become volunteer journalists. They started going to events, including significant political court cases, that they thought were newsworthy but were not being reported on, and they would tweet from them. They would often be the only reporters remaining in the room after the judge would throw out all the traditional journalists. What could a few youngsters be doing on their phones? They also started going to observe protests and other events across the political spectrum just so they could report on them.

When I first met these young people, early in their journey, I told them that I noticed that they were acting like journalists who happened to be citizens rather than capitalizing on the special capabilities of the tool. Often, they traveled to various venues—important court cases, demonstrations, and other events—and reported from the scene. This clearly limited what they could do because they could report only from where they were.

They soon decided to shift course. Replicating old-style journalism and merely using social media were not going to harness the potential of having so many connected phones in so many ordinary hands. As a tentative experiment, they started seeking social media reports from citizens to verify and put on their own feeds.

As I watched the young people of 140journos work, I was reminded of other scrappy outlets that acted as intermediaries in the new public sphere. In the initial Arab uprisings of 2011, when Tunisia was in revolt, and media outside the region were roiled in confusion, the long-established Tunisian anticensorship activist group Nawaat curated key videos that were picked up by mass media around the world. In Tunisia, after the revolt died down and elections were about to be held, I asked the founders of Nawaat how they knew where to look for citizen videos documenting the protests, and how to vet them. "We had long-term relationships in many places of the country," they told me, and they had also been developing methods of verification suited to the networked public sphere.

Nawaat activists did much of their curating and monitoring from abroad, a practice that seems antithetical to understanding the dynamics of a movement. However, when social media curating is done correctly, it can be far more conducive to a comprehensive reporting effort than being in one place on the ground, amid the confusion, as traditional journalists tend to be. A traditional journalist can see what is in front of her nose and hear what she is told; a social media journalism curator can see hundreds of feeds that show an event from many points of view. Traditional journalism tries to solve a problem of scarcity: lack of cameras at an event. Social media curatorial journalism tries to solve a problem of abundance: telling false or fake reports from real ones and composing a narrative from a seemingly chaotic splash-drip-splash supply of news.

I had seen the power of such reporting elsewhere. A blogger and journalism student (later hired as the Saudi correspondent for the *Wall Street Journal*) named Ahmed Omran had spent months as an intern for NPR, monitoring the citizen reporting coming from Homs, Syria, during the early days of the Syrian civil war. I could not make sense of the steady stream of horrible videos and pictures, but he could, even from afar, because he had developed this into a "beat." He was so familiar with the scenery that when he was asked whether a video showing injured people coming to the hospital was recent, he might reply by noting that the doctor shown was not on duty that night. He could identify hospital staff by name and note what they wore, and when. It was a combination of investigative journalism and reporting on a regular beat; but performed through digital tools.

I watched 140journos work in Turkey. Its members were mobile and lightweight; they could operate anyplace where the internet was fast enough. I saw them work in internet cafés and in offices, huddled around their laptops, one eye on their phones.

The members of 140journos developed novel techniques for verification of citizen reporting. Once, for example, they started hearing reports that a civic organization devoted to defending secularism in Rize, a fairly conservative town, was being surrounded by threatening mobs. For Turkey, this is a sensitive topic. In 1993, a mob of extremist religious men had surrounded a group of artists, writers, and poets—a group that was known also as a staunch defender of secularism—in a hotel in the town of Sivas and had then set fire to their building, killing thirty-five. Given this history, rumors that a building housing a secular organization was surrounded by mobs understandably set off many alarms, especially since this was during a tumultuous period, the Gezi Park protests. They agonized whether to tweet the rumor out, potentially creating conditions to help people who were surrounded but also risking their reputation if the report turned out to be false. Their reputation was important, too, since trying to report uncensored news in Turkey meant facing many challenges, and a misstep would be costly when credibility was hard to gain but easy to lose. They also did not want to alarm people if this was one of the many false rumors that circulated at the time.

So they set to work. They looked for metadata in the sources: a time stamp, a geolocation, an author. Checking such metadata was something they had taken to doing regularly to verify geographic and temporal information through digital triangulation. They pulled up a Google map of the area, seeking potential witnesses. They tried to call the institution that was alleged to be surrounded, and people inside told them that this was the case. They heard glass breaking in the background. To their later regret, they did not record the phone conversation. This became a moment that led to learning: from then on, they started recording all such calls so they had evidence. They noticed that there was a small local radio station nearby in Rize and called it, asking the people there to go out on the balcony and take a picture or record a short video. Just then, they found a Vine—a short Twitter video—made by someone nearby. With that confirmation, they tweeted out the news, once again breaking the story in the national public sphere.

This was a moment that would be repeated many times over the next few years as the young team of 140journos honed and developed a multilayered strategy for taking in the chaotic, complex, and unfiltered input from the open world of social media and separating fact from fiction, news from deliberate fraud, and noteworthy information from the glut.

The group 140journos was not the only intermediary organization in the emerging networked public sphere in Turkey. There were other groups of young people who had started to take up such roles, building the formal and informal institutions of the new public sphere. In the spring of 2012, with a few friends, I helped organize a panel titled "Digital Troublemakers" at a university in Istanbul.

Very few people in authority in Turkey at the time thought that there was anything troublemaking about digital connectivity. The mistaken perception of the digital world as virtual and the faulty analysis of online political acts as slacktivism had influenced how many people in Turkey, too, thought about social media. The panel of five speakers attracted only a few dozen listeners. However, listening to the panelists, I became increasingly convinced that something was bubbling beneath the surface. The sites they talked about were attracting very large numbers of participants and developing forms of discourse that were rare or nonexistent in Turkey. It was clear that they were impacting the public sphere, and that millions of people were participating in this transformation.

One of the panelists was Sedat Kapanoğlu, the founder of Ekşi Sözlük, which can be translated as "Sour Dictionary." The site had been inspired by Douglas Adams's *Hitchhiker's Guide to the Galaxy*, which envisioned such a universal dictionary, and the name was inspired by the song "Sour Times" by the musical group Portishead.[9] Ekşi Sözlük was founded in 1999, long before Twitter or Facebook. The site was neither a dictionary nor a social media site, though it had elements of all of that and more. On the platform, internet users were invited to collaboratively "define" various concepts, which meant that users ranging from a few to thousands of people would be collectively commenting on and "defining" the entries— in effect, in conversation with one another. This was a radical notion for Turkey because the site emerged as a hub of participatory free speech. Ekşi Sözlük became one of the country's top digital destinations, a freewheeling site where ideas about what things meant or referred to played out in front of its growing audience, tens of millions of visitors each month.[10] It has grown to half a million registered users, some of whom add every day to collective knowledge of the country in a fashion that is hard to explain using metaphors from old media. Site users enter discussions, add basic facts, dispute with one another, and discuss and highlight important stories that never make their way to traditional mass media (although they often circulate on social media). To this day, and despite its necessarily somewhat chaotic nature, the site acts both as a social gathering point and as a crucial reference and collective memory. Rarely a day goes by for me, for example, in which I do not consult or refer to one of its entries.

Another panelist had founded a popular humor site that generated a range of "memes"—humorous images or videos that people share online. The outlet was like a cross between the *Onion* and *BuzzFeed*. Parody and humor have a long history in Turkey as genres for dissident politics. I remember people gingerly purchasing humor magazines as the only outlets in which political criticism—indirect and somewhat veiled but always funny—survived during the early years after the military coup of 1980. But in 2012, political criticism, youth culture, and humor sites had merged and had become part of the networked public sphere, which meant the ability to generate information cascades and go viral through funny and biting political satire. This humor-laced but sharply political meme culture echoed hundreds of years of tradition in Turkey when poets and jesters would use sarcasm to criticize what was seemingly untouchable—even the Ottoman caliphs. But now, this centuries-old method was reborn and reimagined online, often in ways that seemed obscure to those outside of the youth culture that fueled it. Thus, many had missed its scale. It was like slowly bubbling lava, rising higher and higher through the mantle of a volcano, but invisible to people who saw only a calm, majestic mountain. The last panelist we invited was Serdar Akinan, whose tweet of a line of coffins from the Kurdish village had in a way ushered in a new era as large numbers of people had been alerted to the potential of the internet to break censorship.

Reshaping of publics and the flow of attention often occurs without being noticed by those who are used to looking only at old structures. Its consequences can suddenly burst into life. We did not know then that just a year later, all those platforms, the connectivity they afforded, and the flourishing and spreading dissident culture would play a major role in one of the biggest spontaneous protest movements in Turkey's history at the end of May 2013, shaking the country from top to bottom.[11]

It wasn't supposed to be much of a protest—a few environmentalists, concerned locals, and a few people who had been watching the "urban reconstruction" in Istanbul with dismay. The government was razing and developing many traditional areas, destroying the historic fabric of the city. Istanbul's existing buildings and parks created a special challenge to the government, which specialized in new construction as an economic model of development and awarded many large bids to favored companies. In Istanbul there is a mosque called "the New Mosque" because it is only four hundred years old. Some parts of the city are much older. As in other such historic cities, space in Istanbul was at a premium, and it was practically impossible to find central locations on which to build anything without knocking down old buildings and tearing up roads and parks. The city was also growing; taking in large amount of migration, and housing was an important need as well as a vibrant market.

Now, the bulldozers were coming for Gezi Park. Although most of the neighborhoods near Taksim Square were quite expensive and upscale, the hills on the north side had been populated by the poor and by minority populations like the Roma that had traditionally been discriminated against. A building company, headed by the powerful prime minister's son-in-law, slated their narrow cobblestone streets and crowded, dilapidated buildings to be razed and replaced with expensive new housing. That made Gezi Park, the last remaining open space near Taksim Square, even more valuable. Prime Minister Erdoğan, who was also the former mayor of Istanbul, was personally involved in the project and was deeply invested in restructuring the city he had once ruled as mayor, and where he had gotten his start in politics. His government had been elected for the third time and was at the height of its power.

It appeared that Gezi Park could not be saved, but a few dozen people showed up anyway. Many were locals who lived nearby. They had filed lawsuits, but the courts had mostly stonewalled them. They had tried attracting media attention, but Turkey's mass media were not about to cross the powerful prime minister. So they hugged the trees as the bulldozers approached. A legislator from the opposition showed up, and his parliamentary immunity meant that he could not be arrested. That gave the otherwise small protest some power. On May 29, 2013, the legislator stepped in front of a bulldozer and stopped the razing for the day. The workers went home, and the few dozen activists set up some tents around the park, hoping to gain a few more days, but without a clear plan or hope.

On May 30, 2013, just before dawn, municipal police raided the protesters' tents before burning them down. The few activists who remained were pepper-sprayed again, as they had been the day before. One image stood out: a woman in a red dress, her head turned in pain, pepper-sprayed in the middle of the park as burly police in masks and shields moved aggressively toward her.[12] These pictures of ordinary people under attack and bulldozers moving into the park went viral on Twitter, Facebook, Instagram, Viber, WhatsApp, and other digital networks; they seemed to be everywhere on social media almost instantly. Because the protest area was so central, some in Istanbul simply went there, and crowds started growing to a few hundred and more. People called one another, took more pictures and posted them on Twitter, sent text messages, and shook their heads. People then turned on their televisions to check the news. It wasn't there.

Of course, at this point, such mass-media censorship wasn't surprising. The experience of the news blackout of the bombing of the Kurdish village of Roboski had exposed many people to the fact that the mass media could block out major news stories.

But the public sphere had been transformed. It was now a digitally networked public sphere. People had learned to pull out their phones, not just to see what was up, but also to document and share.

The team members at 140journos told me that they had struggled in their first year to find citizen journalists reporting from events, and they would sometimes have to call and try to persuade people to take a picture and tweet it. People used to ask them, why bother? Who is going to see this, and why will it matter? But in the year leading up to Gezi, social media became the place where real news circulated, and many people learned the importance of documentation by ordinary citizens. As soon as they noticed something, many people pulled out their phones and took pictures, and they expected groups like 140journos to curate and share. Ekşi Sözlük and similar sites exploded with information about the protests. People tweeted, blogged, added entries to Ekşi, posted on Facebook, and sent messages to one another. More people showed up, and more news and pictures circulated. Unlike a remote Kurdish village, Taksim Square was easy to get to in a city of more than ten million people. It was simple to compare what was on the phone with what was on the television screen by showing up at the site. That is just what many people decided to do.

As all this was happening, I was in Philadelphia at a conference on the role of data in elections. I sat in the back and kept an uneasy eye on Twitter. By the next day, I could not believe what I was seeing. Huge numbers of people around Taksim were apparently clashing with the increasingly overwhelmed and certainly outnumbered police. Like millions of Turks, I was learning about the events from social media, not Turkish mass media.

At one point, the clashes around Taksim were so intense that CNN International started broadcasting live. At that very moment, CNN Turkey, owned by a Turkish corporate conglomerate eager to please the government, was showing a documentary on penguins. Enraged, a viewer put his two television screens side by side, one tuned to Gezi protests on CNN International and the other to the plight of penguins on CNN Turkey, and snapped a picture of both. The picture documenting the stark media blackout went viral. Later on, a penguin would come to symbolize censored media.

As more and more people came to Gezi Park, the overwhelmed police withdrew. Tens of thousands of people poured in. They set up living spaces with tents, blankets, and whatever they could find and occupied the park. A large spontaneous protest was now gearing to set up a prolonged protest occupation. Both were an anomaly in Turkish politics and in Turkish protests. Still in disbelief, I booked a plane ticket to Istanbul.

3

Leading the Leaderless

WHEN I LANDED IN ISTANBUL IN JUNE 2013, I had little idea what to expect. The movement that had not existed a few days earlier had mobilized millions of people in large-scale protests around the country. Ground zero of this movement was Istanbul's Gezi Park, now hosting thousands of protesters. Would it be a tightly organized, well-run place? Would it be chaotic and confusing? How were issues like supplies, medical care, and publicity being organized?

An old proverb warns that a kingdom can be lost "for want of a nail." It traces a chain of dependencies—from lost horseshoe nail to lost horse, lost rider, lost message, lost battle, and lost kingdom.[1] A modern military strategist will also tell you that logistics can make or break a battle. Weapons need lots of ammunition and spare parts. Vehicles, which need fuel that must also be transported, have to carry all the weapons, parts, and people who know how to use and maintain the weapons. Personnel, including soldiers, must be fed, and that requires a huge kitchen that can work on the road. The kitchen needs equipment, staff, and provisions. The soldiers who fight on the front lines are only a small part of the military undertaking, and a strategy that ignores logistics is likely to fail.

Much of modern life is similarly dependent on complex infrastructures held together by people who often toil in obscurity. When we go shopping and buy ready-made food and clothing, we are participating in a complex global chain of interdependencies. The same is true for modern protests, especially the occupations and prolonged protests that have become common. There are many mundane details; much more is involved than merely showing up: How will the protest be organized? Who will get the word out? Once people show up, what will they eat? Where will they sleep or use the toilet? Who will take care of any ill or wounded? How are donations organized? Who makes the signs?

In the past decade, digital tools have made this work much easier to undertake, and to organize in a more horizontal and egalitarian manner. A lot of such work now operates more as a network or in peer-to-peer fashion rather than under a strict hierarchy. This is more than a mere shift in tools, as it comes wrapped up in cultural expectations and consequences of antiauthoritarian movement culture—many of which predate social media platforms (and which are covered in greater depth in chapter 4).

Another crucial aspect of organizing protests is communication among people before and during events. Historically, police have had helicopters and radios to talk to one another, and a bird's-eye view has given them an advantage in the ability to respond more quickly. In general, pre-digital-era protesters often faced adversaries who were able to communicate in real time and who were more organized, numerous, experienced, better equipped and wealthier. However, the rebels are now at much less of a disadvantage. Protesters, too, have ample tools to communicate in real time. They have bird's-eye capacity because almost every protester has a phone that can relay and collect location information. Many tasks that once required months or years and large numbers of people to organize can now be accomplished with fewer resources and in a more dispersed manner. Using social media and digital tools, protesters can organize at a large scale on the fly, while relying on a small number of people to carry out work that previously required much infrastructure and many people.

When I walked into the Gezi Park protests in June 2013, I saw an agile, competently organized place: three hot meals a day, clothes and blankets, an operating clinic with basic capabilities, a street library stocked with books, workshops on a variety of topics, and a steady stream of donations, volunteers, and organizers who, of course, talked face-to-face in the park but also coordinated broadly through digital technology. There were also communication systems relying on social media and smartphones to warn of potential police movements to evict the protesters from the park, various groups organizing to print leaflets and billboards, people keeping spreadsheets of supplies to ensure that protesters who slept overnight had tents, and much more. And despite being largely shut out of mainstream media, especially at first, the protesters managed to circumvent censorship and organize by using social media to disseminate their message.

All this had not happened under easy conditions. The Gezi Park protests faced significant police responses, including multiday clashes involving tear gas and water cannons before the protesters occupied the park. Gezi Park and Taksim Square are located in a vast central area of Istanbul, with many main and small streets that can be used to enter and exit the space. Taksim Square is on top of a hill, with steep and winding roads on many sides. The clashes covered the whole area. People who knew one another created groups in chat applications and sometimes just added one another on the spot. Some local businesses in the trendy arts district opened their Wi-Fi to protesters (the cellular internet—the internet that is transmitted by phone networks like T-Mobile or Verizon in the United States—as far as I knew or could tell, was not censored but was overwhelmed). Some people who were far from the scene monitored social media platforms like Twitter, chat applications, and Facebook groups to provide updates to their friends on the ground.

Almost all this was done on the fly. Extensive interviews with participants made it clear that preexisting organizations whether formal or informal played little role in the coordination. Most tasks were taken care of by horizontal organizations that evolved during the protests, or by unaffiliated individuals who had simply shown up, alone or in groups of friends.

There was a "solidarity" platform associated with the protest, composed nominally of more than 120 nongovernmental organizations (NGOs), but formal meetings of this group were sparsely attended. One of the meetings I attended had only about thirteen people, three of them from the same organization. It was clear that this umbrella organization had little reach and authority in the protests, though it was composed of real—and some of them substantial—NGOs. Although many members of these NGOs were active in the protests, very little seemed to be accomplished by using the NGOs' traditional hierarchical organization. Many of the hundreds of people I formally interviewed or informally talked with inside Gezi Park during the occupation told me that they did not consider themselves represented by those organizations or bound by their decisions. Instead, to take care of tasks, people hailed down volunteers in the park or called for them via hashtags on Twitter or WhatsApp messages to their own social networks.

Meanwhile, the occupation at the park was a bustle of activity. Hot food was served three times a day in a community kitchen where volunteers both coordinated with one another and called for supplies using their phones. In one corner of the park, volunteers dropped off food and other supplies that would quickly be brought to the kitchen using chains of people who passed boxes or watermelons or water bottles from hand to hand in a human conveyor belt. A hashtag on Twitter called for a library on the site, and it quickly became a reality as books poured in. Because of tear gas and police incursions, the library had to be moved from its initial location in the perimeter of the park, but in its new location toward the middle of the park, people busily exchanged books, an activity overseen by a "librarian" in a rainbow-colored wig. The festive atmosphere continued to be interrupted by tear gas and clashes with the police. A makeshift clinic staffed with doctors and nurses treated the wounded in a quiet corner that was closed off by some drapes that appeared to be bedsheets someone had brought and had simply hung between the trees. Minor injuries were treated on-site, and serious cases were transferred to hospitals. Overall, this digitally enhanced capacity allowed a movement that came to being with zero preparation beforehand and with little or no institutional leadership, to pull off perhaps the largest spontaneous demonstration and occupation in the history of modern Turkey—a country with little history of such movements—and to sustain it for weeks.

The desire of modern protesters to operate without formal organizations, leaders, and extensive infrastructure can be traced at least back to the movements that flourished in the 1960s. New digital technology did not create this but allows protesters to better fulfill pre-existing political desires. Without a tool similar to Twitter with its hashtags, and without all this digital connectivity, it would be quite difficult to call up or sustain spontaneous protests of this size.

This model of networked protest can be thought of as an "adhocracy"—tasks can be accomplished in an ad hoc manner by whoever shows up and is interested. This has has become the central mode of operating for many networked movements, especially those on the left, and with antiauthoritarian leanings.[2] Replacing printed fliers with tweets, large donations with crowdfunding, and in-person organization with online spreadsheets, might seem unremarkable or trivial technicalities. But the consequences of this shift to digital connections as a form of organization can be surprisingly complex because the *how* or organizing is more than an afterthought. How protests operate—even to take care of trivial and mundane tasks—reverberates through many layers of movement dynamics.[3]

To understand how adhocracy in networked protests operates, consider Tahrir Supplies—four young people who organized logistics for field clinics that cared for thousands of people. Their result was an impressive feat by itself, even if you did not know that it took the founder all of five minutes from conception to action.

It began when Ahmed woke up and looked at his Twitter feed. What he saw, he told me, broke his heart. It was another turbulent November morning in 2011, less than a year after Cairo's original Tahrir protests that brought down Egyptian president Hosni Mubarak. Thousands of protesters were in intense clashes with security forces on Mohamed Mahmoud Street, which snaked south from Tahrir Square and led to the Interior Ministry. Security forces loyal to the military council that had ruled Egypt since Mubarak's fall had forcefully dispersed a group taking part in a sit-in to demand a transition to civilian rule. Families who had lost loved ones during the original eighteen days in Tahrir were among those arrested and beaten. As pictures of bruised, battered, and heartbroken family members of such "Tahrir martyrs," as they were often called, flooded social media, activists who had been watching in frustration as the military consolidated its power flocked to Tahrir Square once again.

The security forces were there, ready to confront them. When the dust settled a few weeks later, more than fifty people were dead, and thousands were injured.[4] And, as had occurred during the initial uprising in Tahrir earlier in the year, volunteer medical personnel treated most of the injuries at ten field hospitals set up around the perimeter of the sprawling square and its environs. These field hospitals were all ad hoc—they were just areas set up, sometimes even outdoors, with doctors, nurses, makeshift beds, medical supplies, some curtains, all thrown together, but they were not small. Many treated hundreds of people, including grave injuries leading to fatalities.

Ahmed, a twenty-two-year-old pharmacy student, did not simply watch his Twitter feed. He noticed a hashtag that was prominent that day: #Tahrirneeds. People in the area were posting desperate calls for medical equipment and supplies. Others would respond to these people's pleas and retweet them to their own followers. Ahmed saw that there was confusion about which requests had been fulfilled. Old messages were mixed with those still needing urgent attention. People would retweet the previous day's calls for medical equipment without knowing the situation on the ground. Many people offered help, but there was no way to determine what requests had already been taken care of. As a result, some field hospitals were over-equipped, while others lacked essential supplies.[5]

As a pharmacy student, Ahmed had a general knowledge of medical supplies, although most of the Tahrir requests were oriented toward first aid and triage. But he had no military or first-responder training. He was not a military buff, an ex-paramedic, a battle-hardened protester, or an organizer of logistics in any other capacity.

He was not even in Cairo.

Over a thousand miles away, Ahmed sat in his apartment in a Gulf state, stared at his screen, and decided to do something. Digital connectivity has altered our experience of space and time. He later told me that it took him five minutes from deciding that he should get involved to starting to do things. He set up a new Twitter handle, @TahrirSupplies, on November 21, 2011. "Test," he typed as the first tweet. It went out, but nobody saw it because the account had no followers.

Ahmed quickly recruited help, posting a call on his personal Twitter account for people to help with "a humanitarian project." Three women, all in their early twenties, and only two of whom were in Cairo, quickly answered the call. One of them was about to be engaged. She told me that turned the engagement preparations over to her mother and returned to her Twitter feed, where she had been spending most of her time anyway, glued to the political news. Another young woman had just finished pre-doctoral studies in London, so she had some time on her hands. Remarkably, it is possible, even routine, for an ordinary Londoner to be able to connect with someone in Cairo through someone in the United Arab Emirates instantly, not just to exchange information, but to start *organizing* to take care of crucial tasks.

None of the four were Twitter "stars" with a large presence online. They were ordinary people and were not even prominent activists. Their own followers numbered merely in the hundreds—friends and acquaintances. None had any experience or previous interest in logistics. They had never worked together before, let alone on a project like this. They would not even meet in person until long after the event was over.

The next message from @TahrirSupplies was breathtaking in its boldness: "We have created this account to deliver the needs of the #Tahrir field hospital to the world." What was unusual was not that a young person would make such an ambitious claim, but that he and his friends could fulfill this mission with the help of digital technology.

The small group started by tweeting their message to prominent Egyptian Twitter users with high follower counts, as well as to people abroad who they thought could help publicize their effort by "mentioning" them in their messages—a common way to talk to people on Twitter, even those who do not follow you, by adding their user name to your message. They tried to reassure these people that they were going to take care of the whole problem of coordinating supplies for the field hospitals into which the injured and bleeding people were pouring.

Digital tools are not uniform. Rather, they have a range of design affordances that facilitate different paths—a topic that I will explore in depth in the next section of the book—especially chapters 5 and 6. For the moment, I focus on Twitter, Tahrir Supplies' tool of choice. A common misconception about Twitter is that one must already have a high follower count to gain attention. In fact, two key features of Twitter enable anyone with compelling content to generate a whirlwind of attention. One was just described: Twitter provides a "mentions" column that shows any user of your Twitter handle in a post by another user, providing a record of how people are interacting with you. Since anyone may "@mention" or "tag" you, this feature provides an opening for people to reach you even if you do not know or follow them. You can, of course, ignore your mentions, but most people look at them since that is how people talk to them. @TahrirSupplies used @mentions to access high-follower users and, through them, to quickly reach thousands or even millions of people. In contrast, Facebook is designed more for communication by mutual consent—you mostly talk to people who have agreed to be your Facebook friends, especially if your privacy is set at a high level. This makes Facebook more suitable for conversations among presumed equals, where both parties agree to the conversation in advance. As a result, Facebook has different affordances for political organizing than Twitter's ability to ping anyone.

The specifics of different digital tools' advantages and weaknesses arise from their design, as explored in later chapters. But the fact that specific affordances are offered to social movements via architecture is not unique to online platforms. For example, in 1853, after a history of major uprisings in Paris, during which narrow roads made it easier for rebels to put up barricades, Georges-Eugène Haussmann, under Emperor Napoleon III's direction, redesigned large, grand boulevards—partly to make it harder to barricade them.

I was among those who noticed @TahrirSupplies' first call for help with publicity. It may be that group members first "mentioned" me, using Twitter's mention function, but I may have simply noticed them through someone else's feed. "Let people know we are taking this on," their messages implored. I started following their handle, and watched it closely. The first thing they needed was attention, a crucial resource for activists. They called out to the doctors and other medical accounts that they knew were at the field hospitals surrounding the square—the one in front of the Makram Field, the one in the church on Fahmy Street, the one in the mosque on Mahmoud Street, and the "KFC clinic" in front of a now-boarded-up Kentucky Fried Chicken restaurant right at Tahrir Square. The harried medical workers at these sites, all volunteers, often turned to Twitter to call for help but had no time to engage in the resulting discussions or organize logistics.

The doctors, nurses, and volunteers may have been skeptical when they read @TahrirSupplies' first tweets, but they were quickly convinced. I watched as a few conversations unfolded publicly and then were taken to a private "backchannel"—direct messages on Twitter, text messaging, or apps like Viber. Much of the building of trust happened in this backchannel, out of public view, as the @TahrirSupplies four privately messaged or chatted on the phone with those on the ground—the doctors, the nurses, and the volunteers on their motorcycles ferrying supplies and the injured.

A list of needs flowed into @TahrirSupplies, and the word was getting out about the service they were offering. I had started interacting with them early—I was the twelfth person they followed, but that was just the beginning for them. In one night, @TahrirSupplies acquired more than ten thousand followers—far more than I had at the time. Within a day, these four young people were coordinating almost all supplies for ten field hospitals. To keep in touch with doctors on the ground, they also used Skype and other messaging apps. To keep track of supplies, they used publicly viewable Google documents and spreadsheets embedded on the website they had hastily put up. They used the spreadsheets, updated in real time, to list supplies and needs by hospital and to organize the volunteers who were transporting supplies. The public nature of the spreadsheets lent transparency and accountability to the effort, as well as aiding coordination.

Having organizers in different time zones, two in Cairo, one in London, and one in the Gulf, served them well. They slept in shifts, albeit short ones, over the next few weeks full of frenzy, duty, and caffeine.

Although I was following @TahrirSupplies closely, I did not interact much with them, not wanting to distract them from their mission. I could see, however, that the organizers were about to hit a roadblock that they had not anticipated. I reached out to tell them that their account would soon be frozen by Twitter for tweeting too often—a precaution Twitter takes to limit spammers from taking over the network. That they were unaware of this limit before they became activists was a testament to how normal and relatively infrequent their previous Twitter use had been. I suggested that they set up an alternate account and authenticate it as theirs before their original account was frozen. Sure enough, they were soon "Twitter jailed" for tweeting too often. At that point, I checked in with a friend, Andy Carvin, NPR's social media chief at the time. He was also glued to his devices as he undertook an extensive reporting effort about the uprisings that were sweeping through there region from social media, and had been following the travails of @TahrirSupplies. Through contacts at Twitter, Carvin was able to facilitate "unjailing" the account so the group could continue tweeting.

Onward they went, four Egyptians, fueled by youthful energy, sleeping in shifts, guided by little more than ordinary experience with social media and digital technologies. Soon the repetitive and confusing calls for medical supplies disappeared from my timeline. People who tweeted about urgent needs often tweeted them only to @TahrirSupplies. People who wanted to volunteer or had medical supplies to deliver or collect at drop-off points around the city also asked them to coordinate. Within a few days, an orderly and transparent system had solved a messy logistical problem through the efforts of four people.

This ad hoc centralization of coordination also facilitated a significant increase in the scale of resources that the protesters could obtain. The donated supplies they collected were not limited to small items like bandages but included other large medical equipment, even general anesthesia devices.[6] Increases in eye injuries—often caused by police shooting tear-gas canisters at protesters' faces and eyes—prompted a need for special surgical equipment that cost tens of thousands of dollars. @TahrirSupplies made an appeal and collected over $40,000 to pay for two machines in under five hours.[7]

This kind of technologically mediated interaction via screens located far from the physical scenes of the clashes does not imply psychological distance. Many who do this type of work report suffering genuine trauma, because the online world is not unreal or virtual. The picture, the voice, or the tweet belongs to a real person. Our capacity for empathy is not necessarily limited by physical proximity. In fact, an informal support network sprang up during the Arab uprisings among people who interacted heavily online with those had been subjected to violence. The experience of trauma was later recognized as a distinct phenomenon occurring among reporters and NGO workers who collected or interacted with social media from violence-plagued situations.[8]

Some of the @TahrirSupplies tweets were heartbreaking, for example, when they asked for more coffins for a morgue near Tahrir. The first tweet said (sic), "NEEDED URGENTLY IN ZENHOM MOURGE: coffins and money."

Just one minute later, as if struck by their own words, the group continued: "Zenhom Mourge out of COFFINS. This is a sad day. Moment of silence for all the dead."[9]

They experienced many profoundly sad moments. When a person for whom they had been desperately trying to locate some plasma died, the organizers kept the heartbreak to themselves. Years later, when they finally talked about such incidents publicly, it was clear that they blamed themselves, although almost certainly more supplies could not have kept every severely injured person alive. They wondered about their decision to stay home while other people went into the streets. One of them recounted her ambivalence: "People were telling me I did something important, but I was hiding behind my computer screen. In the meantime, I could hear the fear in the doctors' voices, and people were dying."[10]

In reality, they had taken on a big responsibility, and they almost certainly had helped save lives as volunteer doctors and nurses desperately performed triage, stitched, bandaged, stabilized, applied tourniquets, gave oxygen to those choking from tear gas, and administered atropine shots and anesthetics, with supplies and equipment provided through @TahrirSupplies. Their work helped to heal injuries ranging from tear-gas suffocation to bullet wounds.[11] And their work was appreciated by the activists: "I nearly died today but my life was saved, thanks to God & @TahrirSupplies," said one injured protester.[12]

A few weeks later, when things had temporarily calmed down in Egypt, I chatted with Ahmed, the founder. I asked him whether there had been another example of social media being used so spectacularly to coordinate such a complex scenario that had inspired him but that I did not know about. I also asked him about the history behind such a quick but impressive effort that came seemingly from nowhere, and whether his studies or experience had included an interest or training in military logistics.

What was the source of his confidence?

What was his inspiration?

"Cupcakes," he said.

Cupcakes.

He had been impressed by a cupcake store in Cairo that had used social media to successfully advertise and sell its products or, in internet lingo, make its cupcakes "go viral." He was not aware of historical precedents for what he and his three comrades had done. With very little planning, they had altered one part of the balance of power between protesters and organized government forces. Formerly, only one side could coordinate on the ground and in real time, because only one side had radios, training, and organized medical interventions. No more. Now, protesters could organize and coordinate in ways that would make Napoleon envious and would likely impress even a modern army general with how little effort was needed. They were just four youngsters with cell phones, computers, and reliable internet connections who had acted on the spur of the moment.

Of course, they had an advantage over the past. In traditional military logistics, the principle of organization is that there are too few necessary things, and hence errant messages or overconcentration of resources in one area and underconcentration in another will be wasteful or even disastrous. This is often different for modern movements. If people around the world who sympathize with a movement can perform crucial tasks or contribute money or resources (for example, through crowdfunding), the ratio of resources available to the need is much greater than for a large army which faces ultimate limits of physical scarcity. Here, the protesters in Egypt were indeed tapping into resources on a very large scale—a metaphorical army of people around the world who wanted to help them. These people who were not physically present could not perform every job and solve every problem, but they could certainly take care of many backchannel or behind-the-scenes duties—tasks requiring only connectivity rather than physical proximity, or perhaps donating a little bit of money. It added up quickly when the reach was so big.

The @TahrirSupplies story is an example of the arrival of the "smart mobs" heralded by technology writer Howard Rheingold in 2003: groups of people congregating quickly to undertake a single action.[13] However, it would be a mistake to see this tale as just one of a technical solution to organizational challenges.

In much popular writing about social movements, the *how* of organizing is mentioned only as an afterthought. Logistics and practical details are generally undramatic and do not lend themselves to journalists' narratives, which tend to be focused on the deeds of a few leaders. Great speeches and successful boycott campaigns are remembered; the organizers who oversaw the transportation of hundreds of thousands of people, under tense conditions and sometimes significant repression, are largely forgotten.

However, lack of attention to infrastructure and logistics by popular and mass media—in movies, schools, books and journalistic accounts—is a problem but not only because it fails to give appropriate credit to the hard-working activists who organize things. Not looking at the "how" can blind us to significant differences, both in their nature and in the political capacities they signal to power, between the types of protests that require onerous labor and deep organizational and logistical capacity to make things happen, and those that use digital technology to take off as soon as they tap into a vein of grievance in the zeitgeist and that scale up quickly using digital affordances. In contrast to the past, when movements first built up capacity over a long time and only then could stage large protests, today's movements that are initially organized mostly online generally start the hard work necessary to build a long-term movement after their first big moment in the public spotlight.[14]

One may be tempted to compare marches from the past with marches of today by using the same metrics for both, such as the number of participants or the number of cities in which the marches were held. Especially for younger activists today, it may be hard to imagine how movements were organized in the past, without social media, phones, laptops and spreadsheets. But the visible result, the march, seems familiar and understandable. That conflation of past and contemporary protest events is misleading. They are different phenomena that arise in different ways, and, most important, they signal different future paths.

Logistics can alter the trajectory of a movement in ways not captured by historical accounts that focus on the small number of people whose names dominated news coverage. The civil rights movement in the United States succeeded because of the courage, persistence, and dignity of millions of participants. One of the great achievements of this movement was the yearlong boycott of the segregated bus system by the African American population of Montgomery, Alabama, which kicked off a decade of protests.

Another was the remarkable March on Washington for Jobs and Freedom in 1963, one of the largest up to that date in U.S. history, which ended with the momentous "I Have a Dream" speech by Dr. Martin Luther King Jr. The popular history of the civil rights movement tends to focus on the acts of a few men and women who played crucial roles: Rosa Parks, whose steadfastness and bravery catalyzed the Montgomery bus boycott, or King, whose strong vision and brilliant oratory moved millions and continues to do so today.

What gets lost in popular accounts of the civil rights movement is the meticulous and lengthy organizing work sustained over a long period that was essential for every protest action. The movement's success required myriad tactical shifts to survive repression and take advantage of opportunities created as the political landscape changed during the decade.[15] Consider what it took to organize the Montgomery bus boycott of 1955 and the March on Washington almost a decade later, the first of which catapulted King onto the national scene and the second of which cemented his status as a great figure in American history.

The 1955–56 Montgomery bus boycott to protest racial segregation and mistreatment in the bus system faced major logistical challenges at every juncture. Although Montgomery's African American population had suffered great hardships, on the surface, the town had been relatively quiet for years. Underneath, a flurry of organizing had been taking place that would become visible to the rest of the world only with the historic boycott.

Although many people know the name of Rosa Parks, she was not the first to be arrested for protesting racial segregation on a bus in Montgomery. Earlier that year, in March 1955, a fifteen-year-old girl, Claudette Colvin, was arrested under circumstances almost identical to Rosa Parks's December arrest: refusing to give up her seat and move to the back of the bus. There were others as well.

The head of the Montgomery NAACP chapter, Edgar Nixon, had been looking for a case to legally challenge and protest the segregated bus system in which African American riders were often treated cruelly; some had been shot at for challenging mistreatment. Each time after an arrest on the bus system, organizations in Montgomery discussed whether this was the case around which to launch a campaign. They decided to keep waiting until the right moment with the right person. Finally, Rosa Parks was arrested for her defiance. Unlike young Claudette Colvin, Parks was an NAACP secretary and volunteer, a committed and experienced activist. Nixon had been organizing in Montgomery for decades, and he thought that Parks would be a good candidate who would be able to withstand the intense pressure and danger that would come her way.[16]

After Parks accepted the challenge, the Montgomery organizers decided to launch a one-day bus boycott. Another longtime activist and local educator, Jo Ann Robinson, stepped up to lead and organize the many tasks that would need to be performed, the first of which was getting the word out for a boycott.

From our twenty-first-century vantage point, where we are used to sharing a tweet through a few clicks with a potential audience of hundreds of millions, the challenge may not appear to be the huge obstacle it actually was. Montgomery had more than one hundred thousand residents. African Americans constituted more than half the population and represented 75 percent of the bus ridership. Rosa Parks was arrested on Thursday, December 1. The decision to boycott was made later that day, and the boycott was set to start on the following Monday. Between Friday and Monday morning, organizers had to get the word out to tens of thousands of people.

Jo Ann Robinson, an English professor at Alabama State College, asked a colleague in her university for access to the mimeograph, a duplicating machine. Mimeographs do not create brilliant or glossy reproductions, but they work well enough, especially for typewritten material. Robinson typed up an announcement of the boycott. She kept the description short, only a few paragraphs long, which meant that three copies fit on a single page that could be cut up, minimizing the number of pages that needed to be printed. She then spent the night in the duplicating room and, with the help of two students who were enrolled in her 8 a.m. class, mimeographed fifty-two thousand leaflets.

Printing the copies was only the first step. Without the digital tools we take for granted today, without even universal home telephones, distributing the leaflets required using a substantial number of previously existing organizations. In all, there were sixty-eight African American organizations in Montgomery, such as church groups, women's groups, and labor unions.

Within one day, practically every African American home had a copy of the leaflet.[17]

The boycott was originally planned to last a single day, the Monday after Rosa Parks's arrest. At the end of the first day, the organizers and the community, assembled in a mass meeting, decided to continue, although they were unsure of their goal. At the time, the phrase "integrated buses" was not even mentioned publicly because it seemed too radical a goal. Before any ideas for long-term plans could be debated, there were many immediate practical challenges. The boycotters were not wealthy and needed transportation to and from their jobs. Activists coordinated a massive carpool. About 325 private cars transported passengers from "43 dispatch stations and 42 pickup stations" from five in the morning to ten at night. Some were group rides, while others were organized to pick up just one person. Tens of thousands of people walked, often long distances, through all kinds of weather. In the end, the boycott required an enormous number of meetings and gatherings just to take care of organizational tasks, ranging from the carpools to raising money for fuel, managing the legal challenges that were proceeding, and responding to maneuvers of the city council. This required a high level of sheer dedication of the community.

With the advent of digital tools, it seems no loss to avoid having to stay up all night with a mimeograph machine or to meet many times a week to organize carpools. However, the work that went into traditional organizing models generated much more than rides and fliers. The presence of movement organizations before and during the boycott in the African American community of Montgomery allowed the creation of both formal institutions and informal ties that were crucial for the boycotters to weather the severe repression and threats they received, as well as the legal and extralegal pressure and economic challenges they suffered.

During the boycott year, King's house was bombed while his wife and infant daughter were inside, and many other boycott leaders were threatened. Riders and walkers were harassed. Multiple legal challenges were launched, including a temporary but significant ban on carpools as loitering that forced many to walk for hours each day. City officials shifted their tactics for dealing with the boycott many times, sometimes offering mild concessions and at other times making grave threats. Participating in the boycott meant putting one's life and livelihood on the line. The boycott movement also had to respond to the changing tactics of its adversaries in the police, the courts and others, and to maintain discipline and resilience within its ranks in an environment in which the acts of a few could have dire consequences for many.

The capacity developed in organizing various structures of the boycott movement was crucial to its success. After both long-term organizing and working together during the boycott to take care of a myriad of tasks, the movement possessed a decision-making capability that saw it through challenges as they came up, and one that was strong enough to survive outside pressure and internal strife. The formal organizations constituting the movement were bolstered by the informal ties—the community and friendships—among participants that carried the boycott through its challenges, and were no doubt strengthened along the way as people met, gathered, and undertook the lengthy and tedious logistical work. There was certainly internal strife, but it did not play out publicly on social media, with a persistent record that could be brought up again and again. Despite enormous obstacles, the Montgomery bus boycott persevered for the year-long battle—and triumphed, winning much more than its original demand for a bit more decency in the segregated bus system.

When the authorities saw a group of people who were able to organize and finance far-flung carpools and stick together through tribulation for more than a year despite everything that was thrown at them, they must have understood that what was at stake was more than lost revenues from the bus system. They saw a community that seemed ready to take up the next set of challenges as well. The opportunities created by the mass media's new willingness to cover its struggles, as well as the Cold War environment with its attendant concerns about international perceptions of the United States as a racist nation, which increased pressure on federal authorities to eliminate racism's most glaring manifestations, were also factors that would enhance the movement's future ability to achieve major milestones in the struggle to attain civil rights. But the community— the protesters—were ready and able to navigate the treacherous path lying ahead. The Montgomery bus boycott was far more than a boycott; it was a signal of the movement's capacity to undertake the most arduous journeys.

Through the lens of history, the 1963 March on Washington, which took place eight years after the Montgomery bus boycott, might seem like an inevitable success, but a cool-headed evaluation at the time would have deemed it likely to fail. There had never been such a huge demonstration in the nation's capital before, and it took place at a time of significant tensions. The civil rights movement was in full swing, along with a surge of repression and backlash. Before the march, the mass media repeatedly speculated about the rioting that would occur if "100,000 militant negroes" were brought to the capital. The *New York Herald Tribune* warned that "the ugly part of this particular mass protest is its implication of uncontained violence if Congress doesn't deliver" and cautioned organizers not to persist with their plans.[18] The military readied thousands of troops in the suburbs of Washington, D.C., ready to intervene. Expecting mass arrests, the authorities emptied jails. Even the organizers were uncertain until the morning of the march whether it would succeed.

We know now it was a day for the history books. Hundreds of thousands of people, a quarter of them white, traveled from around the country, marched without incident, and made it back home safely the same day. The march ended with a speech almost every schoolchild in the United States and many around the world have heard of: the "I Have a Dream" speech made by King at the Lincoln Memorial. It is one of the most stirring speeches in history, and it was beamed live to millions of American homes, deeply affecting many. The march was significant, however, not just for what happened on that day, but for the means through which it came to be—a manifestation of the vast organizing capacity that the civil rights movement had built over many years.

The chief organizer of logistics for the March on Washington was Bayard Rustin, a name less well-known than Martin Luther King or Rosa Parks, but that of a man who had spent his lifetime mobilizing people for political causes. He may seem to have been an unusual choice for the role: a black man arrested for being gay in a time when his sexuality was a crime, a former Communist (who would later turn staunchly anti-Communist), and a devoted pacifist who had spent World War II in prison as a conscientious objector. Rustin played a role in encouraging and deepening King's convictions about the use of nonviolence as a political strategy during the early days of the Montgomery bus boycott. Even within the civil rights movement, Rustin was often viewed with suspicion and treated as a liability. However, his decades of experience in the trenches of organizing marches, events, meetings, fund-raisers, and boycotts, meant that he was the ideal person for the job.

It might come as a surprise to learn that the March on Washington was not the first large-scale civil rights march that year. It was not even the first time King recited the "I Have a Dream" speech, just like Rosa Parks was not the first person to be arrested for resisting segregation; in fact, the 1955 arrest was not even Parks's first arrest. The civil rights movement was not a quiet, obedient group led by an infallible Martin Luther King any more than Rosa Parks was merely a tired seamstress who wanted to sit down one day. Instead, the movement was a lively band of rebels, united under the umbrella of a cause but also with many differing ideas about how and why they should proceed. However, they had spent years working together and had a shared culture of mutual respect—even if it was quite tense at times.

Rustin knew that without a focused way to communicate with the massive crowd and to keep things orderly, much could go wrong, so he insisted on renting the best sound system money could buy. His idea was resisted by others within the movement because the expense was so great. Rustin insisted on a $16,000, state-of-the-art system instead of the $1,000 or $2,000 systems that usually were leased for marches. An example of the esteem in which his logistical acumen was held was that he persuaded large unions, many of whom he had worked with for a long time, to provide the funds for the rental.

Then disaster struck: the night before the march, the top-of-the-line sound system was sabotaged. Leading march organizer Walter Fauntroy made a direct appeal to Attorney General Robert Kennedy and Burke Marshall at the Justice Department, who arranged for technicians from the Army Signal Corps to dismantle and rebuild the sound system on the platform of the Lincoln Memorial overnight. The sound system worked without a hitch during the day of the march, playing just the role Rustin had imagined: all the participants could hear exactly what was going on, hear instructions needed to keep things orderly, and feel connected to the whole march.

The organizers had to bring in hundreds of thousands of people to Washington, D.C., for the day and then get them back home. It was not possible for that number of people to stay in the city overnight, not only because of logistical difficulties but also because of political infeasibility given the hostility toward black people and the lack of accommodations in the largely segregated city before the Civil Rights Act of 1964. The details of transportation were many. Everything had to be done without modern computers; most of the clerical tasks were performed with paper forms and 3″ × 5″ index cards. The building in Harlem, New York, that served as the organizational headquarters of the march was filled with desks, telephones, mimeograph machines, and assistants borrowed from participating organizations. The young organizer charged with overseeing transportation worked so hard during the eight weeks before the event that she fell asleep from utter exhaustion on the day of the march. She missed the whole march, even King's speech, but the transportation worked perfectly. The buses had drop-off locations that were convenient for demonstrators disembarking to join the march, and preassigned parking places to enable marchers to find them at the end of the day. "Internal security marshals from the ranks of black police officers" guarded against troublemakers who might attack the crowd or who might try to discredit the march through acts of vandalism and violence.[19]

Before the event, tens of thousands of signs were constructed with carefully crafted messages of racial equality and pleas for the upcoming and uncertain civil rights bill. The organizers made sure that there were enough portable toilets for the crowd and arranged for twenty-two first-aid stations with doctors and nurses at each. Marchers were given food and water in lunch boxes. The organizers even made sure that the sandwiches did not contain mayonnaise that could spoil in the August heat and cause food poisoning. More than a thousand media members were credentialed and provided with answers and space to work. Getting reporters to cover the march and persuading TV networks to carry it live required considerable effort.

Hundreds of people worked directly on organizing for two months, although overall preparation took six months. The entire organizing staff met at the end of the day, almost every day, for those months. But the organizational capacity and know-how that went into the march benefited from networks of people that went well beyond its Harlem headquarters. Dozens of large formal organizations, ranging from unions to the NAACP, and many informal networks of people who had participated in the civil rights movement for years worked together to make the day happen.[20] The atmosphere in which the organizing work took place was not always harmonious; internal strife broke out constantly. March organizers constantly had to adapt to political reality and negotiate with the groups forming the march, as well as with the authorities. There was even a tense negotiation right before the march about the contents of the speech of the chairman of the Student Nonviolent Coordinating Committee, John Lewis, which some considered too radical and off-putting. After much back-and-forth, including personal appeals by A. Philip Randolph and Martin Luther King Jr., Lewis agreed to alter his speech, although the rewritten version shrewdly conveyed many of the same ideas. Lewis did not, however, call the White House's civil rights bill "too little and too late," as he had originally planned. Negotiation softened the speech's political edges but also allowed the march to proceed without internal divisions becoming more public.[21]

Without such mobilized organizing capacity and the history of the principal players working together that established bonds of trust and influence, King's "I Have a Dream" speech might never have happened in the way we historically think of it, even if he had gotten on a podium and recited the speech's exact words. The day could have been overshadowed by violence, or a sound system that did not work, or internal divisions and recriminations that eclipsed the message of progress. It might have been ignored or distorted. After all, King had given the speech before to much less effect. The magical power of the day was not only in the content of his message or the power of his oratory. Again, like the bus boycott, the March on Washington attested to the capacity to hold a large protest under very challenging circumstances—and to do much more in the future. For history books, the march may have been over at the end of King's speech. For those in power, his speech may have been only a beginning, a moment when they realized the power of the organized participants. The following year, the U.S. Congress passed the historic Civil Rights Act of 1964, and many of the march's key organizers and participants went on to play other significant roles in U.S. history.

If one looks at the form that today's protests take, they may seem indistinguishable from earlier styles of demonstrations: people gather at a designated place at a designated time or walk together on a predetermined route, shouting slogans and holding signs. There may be speakers and festivities. Most marches end on the same day, and protesters go home after having made their statement. But a comparison of the logistics and organization of pre-digital protests like those of the civil rights movement with post-digital ones like the Tahrir or Occupy protests of 2011, the Gezi protests of 2013, or the Hong Kong protests of 2015 makes the differences clear. Older movements had to build their organizing capacity first, working over long periods and expending much effort. The infrastructure for logistics they created, using the less developed technology that was available to them at the time, also helped develop their capacity for the inevitable next steps that movements face after their initial events (be it a march, a protest, or an occupation) is over.

Modern networked movements can scale up quickly and take care of all sorts of logistical tasks without building any substantial organizational capacity before the first protest or march. Consider what a Gezi protester told me about how he came to be involved in the protests (his statement has been slightly edited for brevity):

I didn't know anyone who was in the initial small protests; the ones whose tents were burned down early in the morning, around 5am. I had a Twitter account, but it was mostly dormant until then. I used it to check news. The day the tents were burned down, I started logging on to Twitter, to try to see what was happening. A relative from another city called and asked me if I knew what was going on. I turned on the television, but there was no real news. There were some small reports on television, but the whole thing was driven by Twitter. I kept working, with an eye on Twitter. I could see a lot was going on, but hard to really verify all of it. After work ended, at 7 p.m., I decided to go to Taksim Square. . . . It was so startling. I saw many thousands had gathered. Even after we gathered during the clashes, everyone checked Twitter to try to make sense of it all.

This account is similar to ones I heard from hundreds of people I interviewed formally, and from many others with whom I discussed the triggers for their initial participation in the protest. Many people, like the one just quoted, had gone from merely hearing about the news on social media—most for the first time on that day—to becoming full-fledged participants in the country's largest-ever spontaneous protest movement, eventually involving hundreds of thousands to millions of people around the country with no lead-up. No formal or even informal organization was leading, preparing, publicizing, or doing any of the many things a protest of this size would traditionally have required. Another formal survey (conducted by KONDA; a polling firm in Turkey) found similar results: Only about 21 percent of the protesters had an affiliation with a political party or an NGO, and 93 percent of participants said they were joining the protest as ordinary citizens, rather than as associates of organizations. And of the protesters in the park, a whopping 69 percent said they first heard of the protests through social media, not TV, which they named as their first source of news.[22]

This Gezi Park moment, going from almost zero to a massive movement within days, clearly demonstrates the power of digital tools. However, with this speed comes weakness, some of it unexpected. First, these new movements find it difficult to make tactical shifts because they lack both the culture and the infrastructure for making collective decisions. Often unable to change course after the initial, speedy expansion phase, they exhibit a "tactical freeze." Second, although their ability (as well as their desire) to operate without defined leadership protects them from co-optation or "decapitation," it also makes them unable to negotiate with adversaries or even inside the movement itself. Third, the ease with which current social movements form often fails to signal an organizing capacity powerful enough to threaten those in authority.

* * *

In Gezi Park, toward the end of the protest, when the Turkish government invited a delegation to negotiate, it was unclear who would attend. The protest had no recognized leadership. Although there were two organizations that became prominent during the protests, one of which encompassed more than a hundred NGOs, these were not necessarily accepted, formally or even informally, as leaders of the movement. Protester after protester in the park told me that these platforms did not necessarily represent them—they had not elected them and often were not open to electing or delegating power, especially decision-making power, to anyone. At first, the government invited a group of people who were not connected to the movement, including television actors, as if they were representative of people gathered in Gezi. This move by the government met with howls of derision from the park. Choosing TV stars who were not part of the movement to represent it was a charade too obvious and absurd to be accepted. The government tried again, next inviting activists and leaders of the NGOs who had been involved in the park and the protest. The second invited group displayed a more representative and legitimate appearance, at least according to many protesters I talked to at the time. Nonetheless, in effect, by not choosing its own leaders and representatives, the Gezi movement yielded power to the government, allowing it to usurp the choice of negotiators.

The second group met with government representatives in Ankara, including the prime minister and cabinet members. The protesters in the park knew that the meeting was taking place and settled in to await the outcome, mostly gathering around the center of the park, where a stage with a television had been set up. The evening passed pleasantly in the lovely June weather as people ate dinner and chatted, occasionally checking their phones to see whether the negotiators' meeting had ended. Around 3 a.m., word spread in the park that it was over. Awaiting the outcome of the meeting, many people stayed awake during the night, making the park almost as crowded as during the day. People milled around the fountain and the stage, which had become the quasi-center of organizational activity. A large television was set up to display a video feed from Ankara. (I would later listen to details of the meeting firsthand from participants as well.)

As a voice started booming through the speakers, I watched along with a crowd that grew silent. I saw on the screen one of the most visible persons in the movement, a member of Turkey's Chamber of Architects and Engineers, an organization that had taken a prominent early role in opposing the government's plans for Gezi Park, as well as gentrification projects generally. He outlined the offer—to make the status of the park subject to a national plebiscite. What began as a local issue had become symbolically important nationally, and the government's offer appeared to concede this. In the park, people voiced mistrust of the government, and many were unsure how to react. Some thought that this would be a good opportunity to declare victory. Some booed; others clapped. Some cheered; others jeered. The crowd was split. Unlike previous times when government plans had clearly been seen as illegitimate by majorities within the park, this proposition produced a division in the movement.

The next day, the protesters at the park initiated a "small-forum" process, inviting people to break into small groups to discuss the government's proposal. This was the first attempt to initiate a formalized discussion among everyone during the protest. It was not clear who could participate, or how decisions would be made. Nonetheless, there was much enthusiasm for discussion because many felt that this was a potential turning point. People divided into a few groups, clustered around trees and tents and sitting on the lawn—there was no way for the whole assemblage to meet at once. However, even the smaller groups were quite large, in the hundreds. The discussion lasted about nine hours. Meanwhile, adding to the tensions, the governing party announced a rally, as a show of force, in another part of Istanbul.

The next day, the atmosphere remained just as confused. The forums had met for a long time, but without established mechanisms for making binding decisions, the meetings had no clear outcome. Without a binding decision as a group, or even a means of making one, people had started to make decisions individually. Some organizations advocated declaring victory and going home, leaving a single tent on the site as a symbol of intent to watch over the rest of the process. Others wanted to continue the occupation, although their goals were unclear. Some believed that the government had given up its plans to raze the park. Others thought that it was all a trick and that as soon as they were gone, the park would be demolished. Amid the

confusion, some protesters started dismantling the structures of the occupation, like the tents and some shared areas, while others stayed put.

Later, I heard accounts from the government side that its inability to find
a negotiating counterpart had been both a source of frustration and an opportunity to shape the moment to the government's liking—and also to
shore up their own base. Some government officials had wanted a negotiated end to the occupation. Others had thought that no concessions should
be given, so as not to encourage further protests.

At the ruling party's rally that day, the prime minister announced that
the government had made its offer, and that was that, and the protesters
should clear the park. A few hours later, during ongoing confusion among
the protesters about how to respond, the police swooped into Gezi Park
with a massive force and dispersed them. With that incursion, amid tear
gas and riot police, the occupation was expelled from Gezi Park.

After that tumultuous day, there were many attempts to organize neighborhood forums in other parks, some of which started one day after the loss
of Gezi. At first, these drew large numbers of those who were still upset and
looking for further discussion. I attended neighborhood forums in many locations. The forums tried to replicate the Gezi Park experience, which people
had taken calling the "spirit of Gezi." People gathered and took turns speaking, but no formal decision-making or organizational mechanisms emerged,
and there were no existing networks of civil society that were widely accepted
and able to mediate conflicts that arose in these spaces.[23] Over time, energy
waned, and the forums were attended increasingly by younger people with
time to spare, or by ideologically less representative but more committed
people from fringe political groups. Ordinary people started appearing less
and less in what was a chaotic, time-consuming, and lengthy process that
seemed to produce no decisions, no forward momentum, no tactical shifts.

On the government side, despite more tumult, its organizational efforts
were geared toward the upcoming elections—organizing voter contacts, setting up candidates, and preparing the resources. In interviews, ruling-party
members were clear that they had stepped up their organizational and mobilization efforts in response to the protests, which they hoped to exploit to
rally their base. Less than a year after the Gezi protests that shook the country and changed the national conversation, the ruling party still won two

major elections by comfortable margins. Although the goal that sparked the initial protest, saving Gezi Park, was at least temporarily realized, many protesters later told me that they felt that their broader objectives—more representative democracy and less media censorship—remained unaccomplished.

The experience of the Gezi protesters was not due only to peculiarities of Turkish dissident movements. Of course, the country had been suffering from censored media and a restrictive constitution, legacies of the military coup of 1980 that had stifled democracy in the country. However, the protests were fairly large and relatively popular—even though the country was also polarized. If anything, the Gezi occupation was unprecedented in Turkey in that a movement without clear organizational infrastructure and leadership made so many waves.

However, the use of digital technology to quickly convene prodigious numbers of people brings these movements to a full-blown moment of attention to their protest when they have little or no shared history of facing challenges together. The minor organizing tasks that necessitated months of tedious work for earlier generations of protesters also helped them learn to resolve the thorny issues of decision making, tactical shifts and delegation.

Undertaking the tasks that are required for organization, logistics, and coordination together over time has benefits I call "network internalities." Network internalities are the benefits and collective capabilities attained during the process of forming durable networks which occur regardless of what the task is, or how trivial it may seem, as long as it poses challenges that must be overcome collectively and require decision making, building of trust, and delegation among a semidurable network of people who interact over time.[24] I contrast these with "network externalities," an established phrase that is often defined as an increase in benefit from a good or service when the number of people using that good or service goes up. For example, a fax machine is much more useful if there are many people using fax machines. In contrast, network internalities refer to the internal gains achieved by acting in networks over time.

Network internalities are not always easily visible, because most of the time, analysis of the gains attained from the work itself focuses on the task: Was the rally organized and held? Did the word get out? In the long term, however, the process of organizing may be as important as the immediate outcomes. This is why it matters whether the word gets out via fliers (a more laborious task) or hashtags (which lend themselves to decentralized organization), and whether meetings were held every day to organize a carpool, or whether a Google spreadsheet maintained by a few people was used.

Network internalities do not derive merely from the existence of a network—something digital media easily affords—but from the constant work of negotiation and interaction required to maintain the networks as functioning and durable social and political structures. Building such effective networks is costly; they are not "cheap-talk networks" in the sense that people are merely connected to one another. Instead, people have invested time and energy and gained trust and understanding about the ways of working and decision making together. Sometimes, doing seemingly pointless or unimportant work gives groups the capacity to do more meaningful things under other circumstances, like negotiating with adversaries and shifting movement tactics. Building network internalities can be viewed as similar to building muscles. There is no loss in terms of getting there if you drive a car instead of biking to the place, and you can climb a mountain by carrying your own gear or by having a Sherpa carry the gear. However, if the next steps require muscles or mountaineering experience, the capacity gained by biking or carrying one's own gear is a benefit in itself and may be crucial to the person's ability to respond to the next challenge. (This conceptualization of movement capacity will be explored in greater depth in chapter 8.)

Technology can help movements coordinate and organize, but if corresponding network internalities are neglected, technology can lead to movements that scale up while missing essential pillars of support. In the past, organizing big protests required getting many people and organizations to plan together beforehand, which meant that decision-making structures had to exist in advance of the event, building the network internalities along the way. Now, big protests can take place first, organized by movements with modest decision-making structures that are often horizontal and participatory but usually lack a means to resolve disagreements quickly. This frailty, in turn, means that many twenty-first-century movements find themselves hitting dangerous curves while traveling at top speed, without the ability to adjust course. Although participatory leaderlessness and horizontalism are a source of strength in some ways, it is also a treacherous path over the long haul.

The lack of decision-making structures, mechanisms for collective action, and norms within the antiauthoritarian, mostly left-wing networked movements examined in this book often results in a *tactical freeze* in which these new movements are unable to develop and agree on new paths to take. First, by design, by choice, and by the evolution of these movements, they lack mechanisms for making decisions in the face of inevitable disagreements among participants. In addition, their mistrust of electoral and institutional options and the rise of the protest or the occupation itself as a cultural goal—a life-affirming space (a topic examined in chapter 4)—combine to mean that the initial tactic that brought people together is used again and again as a means of seeking the same life affirmation and returning to their only moment of true consensus: the initial moment when a slogan or demand or tactic brought them all out in the first place.

In Egypt, during the initial uprising, "Tahrir Square" (protest participants often referred to themselves as "Tahrir Square" or "the Square" in conversations) was unable to deviate tactically from the demand that had brought people together to begin with: that Mubarak resign. When, eighteen rocky days after the protests began, the military stepped in and announced that Mubarak had resigned (or more likely, had been forced to), and that its own council was taking over, there was great trepidation among many of the more experienced activists that this would mean a return to full military rule rather than a transition to democracy. "The Square," however, did not have a structure to negotiate with the newly announced military council or even to deliberate among itself. Decisions, it seemed, would be made via the original method by which people had assembled: they could choose to stay or to leave. But even if some left, it was difficult for those who stayed to claim the same legitimacy because an explicit decision was not taken. In the end, most people left in a few days, starting the multiyear process that would indeed culminate in a full return to a military rule as brutal as Mubarak's, or even more so.

Part of the experience of a tactical freeze stems from the fact that many of these networked movements appear leaderless—there is no designated spokesperson, no elected or institutional leadership. This is a technological and cultural phenomenon. Many movement participants view the idea of leadership with deep and profound suspicion and find the lack of it to be empowering. They have strong historical reasons for this: leaderless movements are less prone to decapitation by co-optation or, as is unfortunately very common, killing of the leaders. It is fairly clear that being leaderless is not a pure disadvantage or irrational in every aspect, either politically or operationally. Yet even if it enhances resilience in other ways, as it did in Tahrir Square, leaderlessness greatly limits movements' capacity to negotiate when the opportunity arises.

Somewhat late in the initial Tahrir uprising of January–February 2011, Mubarak's regime realized something about a young man named Wael Ghonim, who was discussed earlier as the founder of the Facebook page that became an organizing hub for protesters: it had held him in custody for a while without knowing his identity or his role. Ghonim was released while the protests were still going on, shaken but alive, and he was received joyously by the protesters.

Seeing him as a potential negotiator, the government attempted a tactic that it had likely tried many times before. Ghonim and a few other prominent members of the youth opposition were invited to the presidential palace probably to find out what it would take to buy them off, or maybe to intimidate them. However, Ghonim was in no position to concede anything. He was not an elected leader or even an informal one. He had recognition and appreciation among the crowd, but he had no special power over "The Square." He did not intend to betray the protest, but even if he had wanted to, he could not have. He could not have negotiated or sold out or have been intimidated, even if the government had tried hard. At that moment, leaderlessness may well have been an advantage, allowing the movement to survive potential infidelity by any leader, or worse, direct targeting or even murder.

Over the longer term, though, this strength means that there is nobody with the ability to nudge the movement toward new tactics. Like many other dynamics explored in this book, weaknesses and strengths are inseparably entangled.

There is another weakness in the lack of formally or informally institutionalized leadership or decision-making processes that protesters will recognize as legitimate. Ostensible leaderlessness does not stop de facto leadership from springing up, and the de facto leadership is often composed of those with the most time, tenacity, energy, extroversion, preexisting social status, and even plain aggressiveness. This is not a new dynamic, of course—participatory movements have long dealt with these issues.[25]

However, social media add new twists to problems of the lack of formal organization and leadership, especially because of novel dynamics of the online "attention economy"—the struggle to get the most likes, views, or other endorsements on social media—that create de facto spokespersons.[26] These de facto leaders find themselves in a difficult position: they attract much attention that is desirable for movements, but they lack formal recognition of their role as de facto spokespersons. These leaders are also unable to exert influence without facing significant attacks from within the movements—attacks that often happen publicly, visible to all and recorded for the future, rather than in an argument in a union hall or a living room that might soon be forgotten, or at least not relived again and again through retweets and screenshots of old arguments. This internecine fighting inevitably deepens tensions and polarization within movements, all the while simultaneously exposing the most visible people to attacks from outside the movement.

Battles among those who vie for attention and influence and those who criticize them now play out openly, publicly, and around the clock on social media and leave participants and targets without the means to resolve tensions. Wael Ghonim, for example, chose to disappear from social media for two years, mostly because of the stress of being constantly attacked from within the movement for which he was seen as a spokesperson. He told me that he found dealing with the internal movement criticism, which often turned into or merged with vicious personal attacks, much harder than standing up to the military because the critiques were voiced by his friends and by people whose views he cared about. "I once sarcastically said that I feel like it is much harder to actually stand up against the mainstream on Twitter than stand up against a dictator." Although Ghonim said this as a quip, it was clear that the hurt was real.[27]

The two tumultuous years after the January 25, 2011 uprising witnessed efforts by the liberal, secular-leaning movement in Egypt to occupy Tahrir Square again. The activist core tried to repeat the difficult, gut-wrenching, life-threatening, but also exhilarating and transformative eighteen days in Tahrir Square that forever altered their country and their lives. These efforts were unsuccessful; the crowds were never as massive, and many times, the attempts ended with repression and discouraging results.

The flawed but real elections that took place in Egypt after Tahrir were, for the most part, not popular with many of the young people who had played a major role in the protest.

Many of these young activists boycotted the first elections held in the country. "Elections will never change anything," some of them told me, with the same distrust of electoral politics as their seasoned counterparts in the West even though they had not experienced a single election or a duly elected government in their lifetime. "How do you know?" I would ask them, somewhat bewildered that they were so firm in making up their mind about elections in a country without elections. They would confidently repeat that they knew that elections never changed anything. Their values were already aligned with the mistrust of representation that was widespread in global movements elsewhere, and also stemming from their own local experience with an autocracy.

It was globalization from below: the protest culture wrapped up with the shortcomings of electoral politics in more advanced countries was affecting how activists in Egypt responded to conditions in their own country. "What's the way forward, then?" I would ask. The answer almost inevitably came back to Tahrir. It was a freeze: tactically, politically and emotionally. Tahrir or bust.

There was no organizational structure or leadership in place that was strong enough to overcome this freeze. Suggestions that came up had no way of gaining legitimacy unless activists voted with their feet and flocked all at once to something new. But the unstructured, freewheeling internet environment made this difficult because there was no way to stop the free flow of recriminations and accusations of selling out that seemed to occur daily online.[28]

The experience of tactical freezing is not limited to a few countries. Occupy, the movement that started in New York as a protest against income inequality and that occupied Zuccotti Park near Wall Street for many months, resisted even the limited spokescouncil model of organization, in which working groups on certain topics reported back to the full assembly. Even that most horizontal form of organization was seen as too hierarchical by many protest participants. Like protesters in Gezi, Occupy protesters were also unable to advance a next-phase agenda after the Zuccotti Park protest was forcibly expelled. The movement largely dispersed until an external event—the 2016 presidential election—mobilized many of them in support of Vermont senator Bernie Sanders's candidacy. Sanders's campaign ultimately fell short, but, as a testament to the power of movements once they do get moving, what started as a quixotic effort by a senator from a small U.S. state turned into a campaign that mounted a significant threat to an otherwise institutionally strong candidate, Hillary Clinton.

After their expulsion, Gezi Park protesters tried, like Tahrir protesters, to formulate a response that focused on the spirit of Gezi Park, with an intense emphasis on the park. But they were unable to turn their energy into a sustained political movement with the strength to counter the government's response. Iranian protesters told me that they faced similar moments, when most of the movement, lacking the ability to make a new decision, seemed stuck at wanting to repeat the last tactical move.

Exceptions to this rule of the tactical freeze do sometimes occur, for example, in Greece and Spain, where groups broke from the movement and started political parties, Syriza and Podemos. In both instances, the small group initially faced much internal resistance but jumped in anyway. This, of course, is another side of the same coin: lack of institutionalized leadership opens up space for taking such initiatives, although the process is often taxing and psychically difficult. Sometimes it succeeds; in other cases it results in destructive public conflicts within movements, with no means to settle them.

In contrast, the civil rights movement was able to shift tactically, moving from boycotts and lunch-counter sit-ins to pickets, freedom rides, and marches by people working together as a movement and able and willing to follow decisions by a leadership. The sociologist Doug McAdam found that their constant tactical innovation was key to maintenance of a high level of activity over time.[29] Obviously, this was a difficult, complex, and messy process that involved much internal strife and tension (which happened more privately in an age before social media), but they were able to proceed and strike a balance between leadership and participation that allowed the movement to endure and produce major change.

The rapid growth fueled by digital technology, along with the power and the fragility that come from bursting onto the scene on a large scale without corresponding network internalities, are among the most significant defining features of antiauthoritarian networked movements in the twenty-first century. It is important to remember that the lack of institutionalization and the lack of leadership are not just happenstances or mere by-products of technology. They are deeply rooted political choices that grow out of a culture of horizontalism within these movements—a topic explored in chapter 4—and that are enabled by current information technology.

4

Movement Cultures

A PIOUS EGYPTIAN WOMAN ARRIVED IN NEW YORK at the height of the Occupy protests of 2011. She was quickly drawn to Zuccotti Park, where the original Occupy Wall Street protest was encamped. A hijab-wearing religious woman from the Middle East and the dreadlock-sporting anarchists of Zuccotti Park were not what I thought of as a natural constituency. The Egyptian woman felt differently. She enthusiastically announced herself to the crowd in the park: "I'm from Tahrir, and I support you guys!" She was not wrong in her expectation of the protesters' response. Not only was she welcomed, she was even recognized, as she had been a prominent Twitter voice from Tahrir Square during the Egyptian initial uprising. There was mutual rejoicing. A few months later, she was tweeting pictures of the view from her hotel room overlooking the Ka'ba in Mecca, Islam's holiest site, while on hajj pilgrimage.

The global antiauthoritarian protest culture—with its emphasis on participation, horizontalism, institutional distrust, ad hoc organizations eschewing formal ones, and strong expressive bent—that is shared by many of the movements discussed in this book, cuts across political ideology in nontraditional ways.[1] This shared culture allowed common sentiment and connections to develop between a deeply religious Muslim woman and the defiant occupiers in Zuccotti Park despite starkly different beliefs about religion, family, modesty, and other issues.[2] These networked protests have taken on collective identities outside traditional political and social divisions.

Rebellious Egyptian youth referred to the "Republic of Tahrir," while Turkey's protesters talked about those who carried the "spirit of Gezi"—using the place of their rebellion as a form of identity. Anyone could be a part of the community if they shared that spirit.

This culture of protest and its intersection with digital tools as it is created, practiced, and shared are of great significance in understanding how these protests happen. Each country has specific influences, and each movement has many specific features and grievances. Yet there are commonalities across different movements that occur partly because of global cultural shifts in present era and due to other identifiable factors as well. Nowadays, thanks to digital media, protesters in different locations can interact directly. Increased global travel also allows the establishment of more direct interpersonal connections. Networks of global activists are much tighter and more interpersonally connected than many outside observers may assume, although the ways they interact—and the divisions that exist between them—do not always fit traditional political categories.

In Tunisia, I watched as an American anticensorship activist hacker arrived with one of his girlfriends—he was polyamorous—to teach computer security to a crew of Arab bloggers, who themselves reflected great diversity, some deeply religious and others downright anarchist. The gathering was not without cultural differences: almost all the Arab activists smoked and ate stewed lamb dishes whenever they could, while the Western hacker and activist was a tattoo-sporting, vegan teetotaler. The Arab activists were polite enough not to smoke in the room, but they did congregate just outside the training room for smoking breaks, often directly in front of the big "No Smoking." As they puffed away, the smoke slid under the door, slowly filling the room. The Western security educator's voice would get higher as he tried to breathe, and he would start coughing, which would be a warning sign to those outside the room to extinguish their cigarettes, at least briefly. Meals were another space where such cultural conflicts played out as the vegetarians, who tended to be non–Middle Easterners, ended up eating a lot of hummus and bread. (Both were delicious.)

Even among the Arab activists, the lines were not drawn according to traditional politics: people from families belonging to different cultures and sects whose older members would likely never be seen together mingled freely and protested together. I watched, for example, Shia activists from Bahrain initiate a hunger strike that was joined by an atheist founder of the Tunisian Pirate Party. In Qatar, where I attended a multinational meeting of both youth activists and long-term dissidents from perhaps a dozen countries around the region, I watched the lines being drawn not according to sect or even ideology, but according to generation. Religious youth banded with the secular youth and sat in the back of the meeting, phones in their hands, "tweckling"—heckling on Twitter—the more established speakers on the stage across the political spectrum.

These global networks of protest that do not fit into traditional political demarcations are no flash in the pan.[3] Their roots go back decades and their latest iterations are linked to the rise of the internet, which provided, for the first time, a cheap and easy way to be part of a global communication system without being part of the global elite.

This interpersonal network also had a major impact on my own life, and I have observed it throughout my adulthood. I have seen many people keeping in touch for decades. I have seen key events, conferences, and networks bring together people who would later play major roles through the years, including protests. For example, in the Gezi Park protests in 2013, I ran into a friend from Ireland whom I had first met in the Zapatista solidarity networks of the 1990s, when we had both traveled to events in countries other than our own. We had kept in touch over the years, online and offline. He was, coincidentally, in Istanbul as a tourist, and had heard of the protests—naturally coming to the park to check them out. In Gezi Park, I introduced him to some local protesters, and he immediately started chatting away and exchanging information—I am sure they keep in touch now. When I have met with activists from around the world, I have also often found it easy to identify acquaintances we have in common, conferences people attended together, and key junctures in which crucial players met with one another—long before significant political upheavals took place.

These networks persist over time as many activists travel to participate in the ongoing global protest movements. For example, walking in Tahrir Square in 2011, I accidentally bumped into a person, mumbled an apology, and looked up. I soon recognized that I had just bumped into an international crew of prominent hackers and activists who often provided technical support for many dissidents around the world, including those in East Asia and the United States. I already knew them from elsewhere, but here we were, literally walking into each other in yet another country.

The longevity and durability of these networks means that know-how, especially infrastructural know-how, can be shared across time and place. In the Occupy protests of 2011, some seasoned activists who played central roles had also participated in the Seattle 1999 protests against the World Trade Organization, especially handling technology infrastructure, for example. Frequently, when I would mention one activist from a different country or even a different continent to another, I would find that they already knew each other, or at least heard of one another.

Once, while watching a video stream of an Occupy protest march in Oakland, California, I noticed that the marchers had picked up an Arabic chant that was popular in Egypt. Puzzled, I scanned my social media networks and asked around. It turned out that an activist I knew from Egypt but had also seen in other countries was in San Francisco for a conference on the internet and human rights, and he had, naturally, skipped the end of the conference to attend the protest. He was warmly welcomed and probably recognized because he has hundreds of thousands of Twitter followers. That day, he led part of the march and taught Bay Area activists how to chant protest slogans in Arabic.

This shared protest culture and politics of twenty-first-century networked protests has a material basis rooted in friendship and solidarity networks that have been built over decades of travel, digital connectivity, solidarity, friendship, and even strife. By design, there are few formal organizations in this landscape. Their absence obscures the lines through which this culture flows, but they are quietly familiar to those within. To understand many questions posed about these movements—their leaderless nature, their participatory impulse, their sudden rise and fall, their emphasis on expressive politics, and the role of digital connectivity—it is important to understand the specifics of this political culture that can bring together dreadlocked anarchists, devout Muslims, Shia hunger strikers, and Tunisian Pirate Party founders. But first, let us ask a broader question to illuminate how today's political protest culture operates the way it does. Why do people protest in the first place?

* * *

When protesters achieve their goals, the resulting benefits (if any) may be enjoyed even by those who did not participate. At the same time, the act of protesting takes time and energy, and may be dangerous, depending on the country, with risks ranging from arrest to tear-gas exposure—even death in extreme cases. Given these risks, many scholars have asked, why don't more people "free ride"? Why not let others take the risks and shoulder the burdens when the positive results derived from protests cannot be denied to those who stay home?[4] Such gains are called "public goods." For example, a public park is available for everyone to use, even people who do not pay taxes. There are also other questions that are more specific to twenty-first-century networked protests but are intertwined with the puzzle of the free-rider phenomenon. Why is this new style of protester so adamant that the protest must be leaderless? Why do so many of the protests occupy parks and squares, sometimes for weeks at a time? Why is there so much emphasis on methods that emphasize as wide participation as possible, even at times when it makes things slower?

To understand all this, let us start with a simpler question that had long puzzled me: Why do so many protest camps set up libraries?

The Occupy protest in New York's Zuccotti Park erected a library, as did many other Occupy encampments around the world. Hong Kong's democracy protesters set up a library as well. The Plaza del Sol protests in Madrid, the biggest protests of the Indignados movement that swept much of southern Europe, had libraries. Libraries seem to be one of the most typical fixtures of these protests.

Libraries do not seem like a necessity in the middle of protests that may come under police attack, but they are among the first structures constructed by protesters and are subsequently stocked and defended with enthusiasm. Many protest camps also include soup kitchens, free clinics, clothing exchanges, and other hubs that are usually explained by demonstrators as necessities. There are many people in the protest camp who must eat; hence it is important to have a soup kitchen. Although that is true to a degree, a closer examination reveals that even these are not as essential as they have been portrayed. Yes, there are many people in a protest camp, and they do need food and clothes; but my experience is that generally speaking, protest camps gather far too much donated food, and most people attending the protest do not really need any extra clothes. In fact, tellingly, most protest camps struggle to manage the opposite problem—too many volunteers and too many donations coming in too quickly.

Clearly, all these donations, libraries, and exchanges are not merely an outgrowth of obligatory necessities that protesters take care of grudgingly because they are indispensable to the act of protest. Rather, this model of participation reflects something about the spirit that moves people to protest in the first place. The sense of rebellion that is felt at a protest and the work that people perform in protests are inseparable.[5]

This model is not new to the twenty-first century, but it has become both more visible. For example, historically, we consider the taking of the Bastille a turning point in the French Revolution in the eighteenth century. However, it was more a symbolic event. Only seven prisoners—"four forgers and three madmen"—were freed at a cost of one hundred lives lost in storming the prison. Yet it was important because of its symbolic, expressive power in opposition to the monarchy through "cultural creativity" and "ecstatic discovery" via storytelling afterward rather than its instrumental use.

Protests cannot be described as a single entity; they have a multitude of components, some in tension with others. They are an outgrowth of protesters' grievances, as well as demonstrations of a demand. Protesters want the world to change and may be demanding a set of policies or attention to their issues. But protests are also locations of self-expression and communities of belonging and mutual altruism.

Protests have always had a strong expressive side, appealing to people's sense of agency. Finding meaning in rebellion is not a new concept; rather, it goes back to the earliest days of modern protests and occurs even in massive events like revolutions. The English poet William Wordsworth, writing about the French Revolution, said, "Bliss was it in that dawn to be alive," a sentiment that would be at home in twenty-first-century Istanbul, Madrid, Hong Kong, New York, or Cairo during a protest—or in many other occupied squares and parks around the world.[6] For many, taking part in a protest is a joyful activity, and often provides a powerful existential jolt—especially if there is an element of danger and threat to the safety and the well-being of the protesters, as there often is.

The French sociologist Émile Durkheim wrote of "collective efferves-cence," the emergence of a sense of being swept through one's actions by a larger power when one is "within a crowd moved by a common passion." When he wrote this, he was studying "elementary forms" and "rituals" of religious life, but Durkheim showed that rituals also extend to secular ac-tivities.[7] That transcendent feeling of being part of something larger than oneself applies also to protests, however secular their aims may be. This relationship between belonging and individual expression is a key compo-nent of protest participation, and today's protests, like those of the past, indeed have rituals that are recognizable to their participants and that are included in what scholars term their "repertoires of contention."[8]

Throughout history, protests have often had strong instrumental aims—a set of demands or desires they wish to see enacted, or policies they want changed—up to toppling a government for revolutionary movements. The protesters may be trying to save a park, oppose a war, or demand recogni-tion of their (minority or denied) identity or their legal rights. Most pro-tests are identified by these instrumental demands: they are for civil rights for African Americans, or against the war in Iraq, and what they are about is how people know who they are.

The answer to the question about free riding becomes more apparent in this context: Why would people protest to achieve instrumental aims given the costs of protesting, especially since, if enough other people show up to demonstrate, the benefits will go to everyone? Risks are cer-tainly a part of the decision-making process and vary in proportion to the threat a protester faces. If the risks are high enough, they will dissuade people from participating. For example, I have no doubt that the conse-quences that may be incurred by an act of protest in mainland China are dire, making people reluctant to participate. But in some countries, risks have declined, and participation in protests remains quite high despite the potential benefits that may be obtained by free riding. Why? Because the expressive side of protest is a significant part of the reward that pro-testers seek.[9]

Even though the success of many protests is judged on whether they achieved their expressed instrumental aims, protests can be ends as well as means. People wish to belong, especially to communities that make them feel good while offering Durkheim's collective effervescence. This occurs online and offline as people join viral conversations, adding their voice to the collective even though it is just one more voice, and join protests even though they are just one more person. We wish to express ourselves, and protests in today's world often intermingle expressive and instrumental aims.

When people protest because of their great distrust of traditional institutions and electoral politics, as often happens today, their choice of participatory and antiauthoritarian methods of organizing is not simply an afterthought. Instead, the environments that demonstrators are quite deliberately fashioning are a major part of what makes participation in protest worthwhile.

Viewed through this lens, setting up libraries amid the tear gas makes perfect sense. Libraries express a set of values that are aligned with the deeply held values of the protesters.

In Gezi Park, the library was in the middle of the park, staffed by a man in a clown suit and a curly-hair wig in the colors of the rainbow. He waved merrily at passersby and handed out books. Protesters told me that the library had been relocated because the first library, a smaller one located at the front of the park, had been knocked down during a police incursion. The second library was constructed from cinder blocks and was stocked with hundreds of books. People brought more donations of books all the time, and others came to take out a book to read in the pleasant, almost perfect June weather. Like many things in the park, the library was organized in both online and offline spaces. A publishing house was the first to start a hashtag, #gezikütüphanesi—Gezi Library.[10] As soon as the initial online call went out, people responded, bringing in books, and the hashtag took on a life of its own. Other demonstrators in the park noticed the on-site library and toted books to donate the next time they came to the park.

Gezi protesters I interviewed often mentioned the presence of the library as a symbol of how the park was different from everything wrong with "out there." Libraries are core symbols of an ethic of non-commodified knowledge. Anyone, regardless of how much money she or he has, can check out a book, and a book is passed from person to person in a chain of knowledge sharing. Perhaps more than anything, libraries represent a public good and a public space that is non-monetized and shared. In setting up the library, protesters also express a desire for people over profits or money, a slogan that comes up in many such protests. And unlike other items that one can buy, like food or clothes or cigarettes, but that are often distributed for free in protest camps, books symbolize knowledge and occasionally rebellion, and embody intellectual values.

Occupy Wall Street had a library containing more than five thousand volumes, including books, magazines, and newspapers. The police destroyed the library during the eviction of the group's occupation, and the city was later ordered to pay hundreds of thousands of dollars in restitution.[11] From Toronto to Oakland to Hong Kong to Tahrir, libraries were among the first spaces protesters provisioned in occupied protest encampments, exactly because they encapsulated the spirit of the protest: that people can and should interact with one another and exchange ideas in a relationship not mediated by money.

Karl Marx—known for his political theory of communism but also considered a founder of the field of sociology because of his analysis of capitalism—pondered the phenomenon of "commodity fetishism," the tendency of market exchanges to blur and hide the economic relations that are embedded in the social relations that underpin them.[12] In modern terms, a cell phone, for example, may be manufactured in China in a factory with few labor protections, transported via containers in transpacific ships to rich nations in accordance with complex and often opaque and convoluted trade accords, have software written in San Francisco by companies with offshore headquarters, and be marketed with an ad campaign that includes undisclosed product placement in mass media. At each step in the chain of supply, distribution, and marketing, there are laws, history, trade agreements, and treatment of humans within a variety of social contracts required for that transaction. Even the basic existence of money that undergirds this transaction rests on social relations and political structures. There is nothing ordinary about handing over a piece of paper and receiving valuable material goods in return. Yet that transaction—handing over money or sending credit—hides this complex social relationship and makes it appear to be a simple exchange. Marx called this act of hiding social relations in monetary exchanges "fetishism" because using money in return for the commodity—the item being purchased—blinds the buyer and the seller to the deeper social nature of the exchange that makes the whole transaction possible.

Many people are drawn to protest camps because of the alienation they feel in their ordinary lives as consumers. Exchanging products without money is like reverse commodity fetishism: for many, the point is not the product being exchanged but the relationship that is created, one that is an expression of their belief that money is not necessary to care for one another. Unlike commodity fetishism under capitalism, where the exchange of money obscures the social relationships that are involved, in protest camps, the conspicuous lack of money is less about resources than about taking a stance regarding the worth of human beings outside monetary considerations. Under ordinary capitalism, people also exchange gifts and valuable items to signify their feelings, but they do so within discrete, small circles (family, friends, lovers) embedded in reciprocal relationships. In protest camps, the pursuit of unencumbered, often anonymous giving to one another and to the community is an exchange that is explicitly not reciprocal. Hence in most protest camps I visited or people told me about, there was always a surplus of donated food, clothes, blankets, and raincoats because people *wanted* to give.

In Gezi, a woman told me how she had fallen asleep, tired from the activity and the occasional tear gas, her phone next to her, completely unsecured. She woke up, she said, in a slight panic and then noticed her phone next to her, untouched. But something had changed while she was asleep: someone had placed a blanket over her so she would not get cold. She shook her head as she recounted the story. She was in disbelief that this was a common, expected occurrence, as it truly was. Similarly, I was offered food or cigarettes (I do not smoke, but many protesters do) at every turn. People donated clothes and were eager to volunteer. All day, every day, there was "gifting"—someone would come up with a tray of borek, a Turkish pastry, and pass it around.

Gezi Park was also repeatedly cleaned. I started joking that I was going to take my shoes off before entering the park. People attributed this cleanliness to Turkish customs: many Turks do clean their houses obsessively

and remove their shoes at the door. But the collective cleaning of the occupation area was not limited to Gezi Park protests. Tahrir protesters repeatedly cleaned the square, even setting up recycling stations—and
neither street cleaning nor formal recycling is common in Egypt. Wisconsin
protesters who occupied the state capitol in 2011—before the Occupy Wall
Street movement began in the United States, but after the Tahrir Square
protests in Egypt—to protest an anti-union bill also frequently cleaned the
place. Hong Kong protesters cleaned the Admiralty area they occupied
repeatedly as well, garnering press coverage about their cleanliness. So did
the #electricyerevan protesters in Yerevan, Armenia, in 2015, and Ferguson protesters in St. Louis, Missouri, in 2014. Occupy protesters, too, undertook massive cleaning efforts.

In fact, if anything, Gezi Park was cleaned almost too often—I kept seeing people with brooms, sweeping. Any call for volunteers to clean elicited
an overwhelming response. There is a practical side to the popularity of
cleaning in protest camps: authorities often claim that such protest camps
are filthy and need to be closed because of unsanitary conditions. But beyond practical considerations, this incessant cleaning is a statement about
the sense of sacredness of the space, and the prodigious amount of cleaning performed by activists in these places stems from that desire to protect
their "home" and their space of rebellion.

"People are good" was a sentiment voiced many times to me in Gezi
Park. "I'd have never imagined people could be so good," I was repeatedly
told. In Hong Kong, a protester described the intimacy of the protest camp
by saying, "It was like my home."[13] A demonstrator who had been at Plaza
del Sol at the beginning of the Indignados protests in Spain told me how
her faith in humanity had been revived after the Indignados occupied
Madrid's central square. You can find similar quotes from the people at
almost any occupation enactment or major protest camp. Many people I
talked with recounted their time at protest camps as among the "best days
of their lives"—even those whose lives had been in danger.

During the Gezi Park protests, I would occasionally describe the assemblage as a cross between the music festival at Woodstock and the Paris
Commune—an uprising in Paris in 1871 that formed a temporary, insurgent government. Other times, people would joke that it was like the Smurf

village, where blue cartoon characters live happily under mushrooms and fear only occasional attacks by the evil wizard Gargamel—or, in the case of Gezi, tear gas or rubber bullets. This mélange of community, rebellion, and altruism creates a special moment, a sense of sacredness, among the protesters.

The French Revolution's slogan was "Liberté, égalité, fraternité"—the revolutionaries' protest was not solely about freedom, but also about equality and brotherhood.—of course, we would now talk of sisters too. Dr. Martin Luther King Jr. called the civil rights movement "the beloved community," referring to the bonds formed within the movement. This intense sense of, and desire for, belonging in protest is not an aberration; it is an integral part of the reasons that people protest and rebel.

Once while visiting insurgent Zapatista villages in the Chiapas mountains during the 1990s, I attended a service in a village that had been occupied by indigenous people after the Zapatista rebellion. On Sundays, they met in their churches—huts with mud floors and wooden benches. The lay priest, a Mayan villager, opened the Bible and read a single sentence: "Greater love hath no man than to lay his life down for his friend." He shut the book, and that was it for traditional religion that day. The rest of the day in "church" was spent discussing the problems with the chicken cooperative (too few chickens were surviving). In that one sentence, the Mayan lay priest had captured the core of what creates that "beloved community": the brotherhood and sisterhood of people who sacrifice for one another without expecting money or favors in return.

This affirmation of belonging outside money relationships and of the intimacy of caring for people is the core of what motivates many to participate in protests. It explains the presence of libraries, the sites' cleanliness, and people's deeply felt desire and motivation to stand with one another in rebellion. That longing also explains many other aspects of networked antiauthoritarian protest movements, even as it also sheds light on other kinds of movements and past movements.

The intense horizontalism and participatory practices ingrained in these protests—because they are what the protesters feel are missing in their lives—have complex effects on how movements proceed and how they organize, especially when they lack formal structures and use digital technologies to organize and take care of tasks. The mechanics of these participatory democracy processes can seem nonsensical or baffling at times because they are time consuming, tedious, and difficult. One nuanced academic book that explain the power of participatory methods carries the ironic title *Freedom Is an Endless Meeting*, which makes the method sound undesirable.[14] However, as Francesca Poletta explains in the book, participation correlates with strong buy-in and a sense of belonging. It builds relationships and has strategic value. The most serious weakness of these methods, especially those that prioritize—or even fetishize—consensus above all, is that they are often unable to resolve even minor disagreements, even when most agree on a course of action.

Consider what happened in Atlanta, Georgia, on October 6, 2011, less than two weeks after the Occupy movement started in Zuccotti Park, New York. Hundreds began to gather in Woodrow Park in Atlanta and launched the Occupy movement in their hometown. It was a pleasant day, with a high temperature of eighty-one and little humidity. Like Zuccotti Park and elsewhere, the protesters chose to meet in an "assembly" in a park.

Assemblies and "human microphones" (or "mic checks") have become the dominant methods of meeting in Occupy protests. Assemblies are gatherings that use horizontalist meeting techniques and consensus to conduct business. People sit down together, often on the lawn or in a park, and as they speak one by one, everyone else repeats the phrases of the speaker. This is called "human microphone," a method adopted by Zuccotti protesters after they were denied legal permits for the use of sound amplifiers like bullhorns and loudspeakers. Assemblies conduct their business by reaching consensus and allow individual people to block decision making by signaling their dissent. This means that the discussion continues till everyone agrees on the course of action.

Assemblies are led by facilitators who manage the "stack": the list of people who can speak. The sound is amplified by the crowd collectively yelling each phrase after each speaker. An assembly often starts with "mic check," called out by someone or the facilitator, and then everyone repeats "mic check" to confirm his or her participation. The crowd repeats whatever the last speaker has said; speakers have to speak in short phrases since long phrases are hard to repeat. "Mic checks" have become more than a means of amplification and have evolved into the signature meeting format of Occupy protesters around the country, even when they have been allowed amplification. In Atlanta, there was a facilitator with a bullhorn, and the human microphone served no practical need. It was used anyway.

When the facilitator, a middle-aged white man with glasses and a beard wearing a red shirt with a victory hand sign on his chest, announced through the bullhorn, "We have someone here," the crowd did not miss a beat. "We have someone here," they chanted in unison. "Who would like to speak," the facilitator said, and the crowd repeated, "Who would like to speak." "That person," "That person," "is Congressman," "is Congressman," a pause, "John Lewis."

Upon hearing the name of prominent civil rights movement activist, hero, and icon John Lewis, now a congressman from Atlanta, the crowd broke into cheers and applause. Many did the "up twinkle fingers"— raising their hands and wiggling their fingers to signify agreement. These "occupy hand signals" had become common in these assemblies, a method for people to indicate support or dissent without clapping. There were hand signs to indicate dissent, agreement, a request for clarification, and other sentiments.

"How do we feel about Congressman John Lewis addressing the assembly at this time?" the facilitator asked, phrase by phrase, as the human microphone laboriously repeated each phrase after him. More cheers went up. Someone who had been on the ground later said that "there were 400 for and 2 against" Lewis speaking.

It seemed like a good moment to expand the movement's reach: a man who had marched with Martin Luther King Jr., and had risked his life to bring about change that had happened, addressing a movement that was picking up the baton. In fact, it later turned out that he had been invited by some protesters who wanted to expand Occupy Atlanta's range by inviting a civil rights hero from Atlanta. This was especially important since Occupy in general had been criticized for being primarily a white movement, even in Atlanta, an overwhelmingly black city. Indeed, the crowd that night looked overwhelmingly white.

The facilitator paused. "Are there any blocks?" he asked, still through the bullhorn. His question was repeated through the human microphone.

Occupy's consensus-based model included giving people the right to block—to hold up a decision if even one person objected. There was one objection. A white man, also in a red shirt like the facilitator's, and with black-rimmed glasses and a beard, got up. "Mic check," he yelled. The crowd repeated after him, "Mic check."

He started by acknowledging Lewis's long history of activism. The crowd cheered again. They might have been thinking of how Lewis had risked his life to oppose an unjust and racist system and had joined a dangerous and long-term struggle before becoming a congressman from Georgia, a seat he held for decades while taking many positions when they were not popular, including opposing welfare reform during the Clinton presidency and extensive government surveillance after 9/11.

The blocker, who later gave an interview and revealed that he was a graduate student in philosophy at Emory University in Atlanta, said that he did not want Lewis to speak because he thought that "no particular human being is inherently more valuable than any other human beings." After his statement, the facilitator asked for a "temperature check," emphasizing that this was not a vote. Some people did "twinkle hands" in agreement with the block, but many turned thumbs down. The facilitator looked around and continued, "It seems we are close to consensus in agreeing with the block," at which point people started shouting, "No, no. Let him speak."

From the video, the crowd looks quite divided, nowhere near a consensus in favor of the block, but the facilitator was holding the bullhorn. The facilitator asked whether anyone would like to address the block. A white young woman got up and supported Lewis' request to speak. She said, "Letting John Lewis speak does not make him a better human being. It just says that we respect the work he's done and that we respect the position he holds in the government we want to change. People like John Lewis have just as much right to be part of the change as to be part of the problem. I hope we hear what he has to say."

As the crowd shifted uneasily, the facilitator asked for revised proposals, and another white woman who already knew the blocking person— she addressed him by name, Joseph—proposed that Lewis should speak after the assembly was over. The facilitator called for a "straw poll," asking how many people would like to hear John Lewis right then. Hands shot up. Visually, it seemed like an overwhelming majority. Nonetheless, the facilitator continued and asked how many people would like to have him address the assembly later. Some hands went up for that too. The facilitator then decided that the group was divided, and that there was no consensus. Therefore, he said, "I propose we continue with the agenda," denying John Lewis the right to address the assembly.

It was an exercise of implicit power by the few that I had seen again and again in these protests. Because they lack formal means of resolving disagreements, often the most aggressive person, or simply the one holding the bullhorn, can push his or her own preference to a de facto decision. Rather than participation, the result is exclusion.

There were boos, and people started chanting, "Let him speak." But the facilitator was still holding the bullhorn, and he repeatedly yelled "mic check," which the crowd repeated, drowning out the boos and challenges. The only two objectors had been young white protesters who clearly knew each other—hardly representative of the city, the protest, or even that crowd. None of the black people—some of whom were sitting toward the back and had started waving their hands vigorously—had gotten to speak.

The facilitator continued to say, "The assembly did not have a consensus," and that was that. The method of decision and the implicit power of the facilitator meant that the assembly could not make a decision to move forward; it could only be stopped from making one. People could only murmur as the facilitator continued. The debate over letting Lewis speak had consumed over ten minutes because of the cumbersome "mic check" procedure, probably more time than Lewis would have spoken. Despite all the talk of participation and leaderlessness, the facilitator wielded an enormous amount of power; he was the only person speaking at least half the time and he made significant decisions while acting like the community had made them.

John Lewis walked away. He later said that he understood the process—that when he had been the head of the Student Non-violent Coordinating Committee, its members, too, had held long meetings and had tried to work by consensus. The next day his office released a statement supporting the activists and the Occupy movement. But the moment was lost, and a critical potential alliance was spurned.

If assemblies are so burdensome and sometimes tactically disastrous for movements, why do so many movements adopt these methods of decision making? In Tahrir, there was no single leader, nor was there one in Gezi, or among the Indignados, or in the antiausterity protests in Europe. The Hong Kong protest had a few student leaders, but it was clear that they did not hold formal authority. Almost all the protests held assemblies. To understand this, we need to go back to the reasons people take part in these protests and to recognize that this form of movement building has real strengths despite its obvious problems.

Many protesters turn up to take part precisely because they desire to have a voice, have lost faith in delegating responsibility to others to act for them, and believe that all leaders will inevitably be corrupted or co-opted. Most networked protests include many political novices, especially since movements of this style emerge so quickly and use social media to organize rapidly. There was a widespread belief among protesters that the lack of leaders empowered to make decisions for the group was a positive feature. A woman in Gezi Park told me that "it was a breath of fresh air" to know that there was no authority who would be making decisions for her; she was at Gezi to protest this very thing, the excessive authority she thought was wielded by the prime minister.

Using the "human microphone" even when electronic amplification is available is cumbersome, but it also serves the paradoxical function of unifying a movement whose style places so much importance on individual voices. It is obviously hard to deny the problems the method poses for movements, which are apparent in the preceding example, but it is more than a mere hang-up. Although many protesters come with groups of close friends and family, as in the past, there is no institutional framework, previous collective experience, or previously agreed-on conceptual umbrella to hold the whole movement together. Besides, many people have a social media account through which they continue to have an individual voice about the movement. The "mic check" creates a counterbalance to this heightened individual participation by providing a moment where everyone collectively repeats someone else's point of view in unison. Psychically, it makes the assembly, a place where strangers gather, into a unified voice—at least for a moment.

This mode of organizing, which depends so heavily on those present and outspoken, clearly includes many other biases. It is favored by the people who end up holding the bullhorns; and have a vested interest in these methods—ideologically participatory on the surface, yet allowing the few seasoned activists to remain in control without accountability. There are also structural biases. People without jobs (and thus with time on their hands) tend to be overrepresented in assemblies. Over time, this imbalance leads to students becoming dominant blocs of influence, which can limit the scope of the movement. It's not that these voices are unimportant. Students have long been a staple of protests, but the assembly format excludes most people with jobs, children, responsibilities, illnesses, and travel challenges, since showing up every night for many hours is a prerequisite for participation.

Voluntary public speaking as a mode of decision making is another impediment to participation because people willing to speak up, especially in a challenging way in public, tend to be from privileged backgrounds, people who already like to wield authority and power, and, in my observations around the world, mostly men. Extraverted, assertive, and even aggressive people have an advantage, as do those who are used to being in decision-making positions. In the end, the loudest voices in assemblies are not homogeneous, but neither are they representative of the movement in any straightforward way.

The participatory impulse should not be seen as exclusively negative, despite its challenges and problems examined above, nor entirely as a phenomenon of post-internet protests. Participation is deeply empowering, and it arose specifically as a challenge to the failures of the "representative democracy plus techno-bureaucratic administration" model in the twentieth century.[15] The student, youth, and antiwar movement that shook the world in 1968 was a major precursor of today's protest culture and was shaped by that participatory impulse that grew from the feeling of being left out of important decisions in one's life, of a loss of autonomy. Much of the Port Huron Statement that helped define that generation's movement—

crafted in 1962 by fifty students from Students for a Democratic Society—
would resonate among today's protesters:

> Loneliness, estrangement, isolation describe the vast distance between
> man and man today. These dominant tendencies cannot be overcome by
> better personnel management, nor by improved gadgets, but only when a
> love of man overcomes the idolatrous worship of things by man.
>
> As a social system we seek the establishment of a democracy of individ-
> ual participation, governed by two central aims: that the individual share
> in those social decisions determining the quality and direction of his life;
> that society be organized to encourage independence in men and provide
> the media for their common participation.
>
> In a participatory democracy, the political life would be based in several
> root principles:
>
>> that decision-making of basic social consequence be carried on by pub-
>> lic groupings;
>>
>> that politics be seen positively, as the art of collectively creating an
>> acceptable pattern of social relations;
>>
>> that politics has the function of bringing people out of isolation and into
>> community, thus being a necessary, though not sufficient, means of
>> finding meaning in personal life;
>>
>> that the political order should serve to clarify problems in a way instru-
>> mental to their solution; it should provide outlets for the expression of
>> personal grievance and aspiration; opposing views should be orga-
>> nized so as to illuminate choices and facilities [sic] the attainment of
>> goals; channels should be commonly available to related men to knowl-
>> edge and to power so that private problems—from bad recreation
>> facilities to personal alienation—are formulated as general issues.[16]

This statement above from 1962 would be at home in Zuccotti Park,
Tahrir Square, Gezi Park, or Plaza del Sol, though today's protesters would
surely replace the word "man" with "human." The culture and politics of
protest in these left, anti-authoritarian movements over the decades might
be (very) broadly summarized as follows:

1. Monetary transactions should not have more value than human
   interactions.
2. Representative democracy has failed, captured by corporate powers
   and elites.[17] Protesters therefore distrust delegates and leaders and

instead desire direct participation. Many protesters seek agency in protest as they see a world in which their voice does not matter and their creative capacity is devalued.

3. Modernity and the rise of the individual come with a sense of loss of community, and protests take on communitarian tones.

4. Many protesters feel that the world encourages conformity or polarization, and they instead value diversity and pluralism in ways that don't fit into traditional political categories.

Although these sentiments are not new, digital technologies make the expression of this protest culture connect in ways that may not have been possible before.

The challenges are not new either. The participatory strain in movements goes back decades, and movements going back to the 1960s experienced the same challenges. The famous 1972 essay "The Tyranny of Structurelessness" by feminist Jo Freeman outlined how movements that eschew typical hierarchies become dominated by unaccountable leaders and informal and exclusionary friendship networks, often much like today's horizontalist movements.[18] Occasionally, I give this 45 year old text to younger activists. "This could be describing us!" they often exclaim, somewhat in shock to learn that their experiences are part of a larger historical pattern.

Protest experience can be individually transformative, especially through its community dynamics.[19] In 2011, as I walked around Tahrir Square, then adorned by many speaking podiums for yet another protest in the early days of Egypt's tumultuous revolution, I noticed that many groups of people who came in from different parts of the square would shriek in delight, and people would run to hug each other. I asked them where they had met; many said that it had been during the first days of the uprising. The community that had sprung up in "the Square" had continued to be part of their community. Others had come with family and social networks, as has always happened in most protests, but had found their bonds strengthened.

In Gezi Park, I saw the same dynamics. Friends sat around in tents, chatting, eating sunflower seeds as piles of husks grew, smoking, checking their phones, and showing one another pictures and news. Some met for the first time in the park, but their friendships did not end when the protests dispersed. Years later, I keep encountering groups of friends that formed after first meeting in the park in June 2013. Gezi Park was among the chattiest places I had ever seen in Turkey—and Turkey is a nation where people talk, even with strangers. Stories from other protests, from Occupy encampments to Hong Kong, paint a similar picture.[20]

A protest, if nothing else, is a community.[21] The evolution of community occupies a great deal of space in twentieth-century sociology. The political scientist Robert Putnam's book *Bowling Alone* about the decline of community in the United States—supposedly exemplified by the decline of neighborhood bowling leagues—is among the most influential scholarly books in sociology, although some have criticized it for painting an incomplete picture and overemphasizing old forms of community.[22]

Challenges to traditional communities come from many converging factors: extended families have shrunk to nuclear ones living in suburbs, and parents work long hours; the rise of TV as entertainment at home has isolated people; and local institutions like union halls that provided space for interactions between people who are neither immediate family nor work colleagues have declined. However, people have also started creating "networked communities"—communities based on affinity of interests rather than happenstances of geography.[23] Some kinds of community may be in decline, but the search for community and belonging is, if anything, on the rise.

It is thus unsurprising, though striking, that community building may be among the most important functions that a protest march or a persistent occupation serves. This occurs both in the expression of shared grievances and in the creation of a network of people who can become the anchors of longer-term movement activities. These protest communities form quickly but are quite intensely active because of the existentially rousing conditions under which they emerge.

During the Gezi Park protests, more than one protester compared the "spirit of Gezi" to the community that formed after the 1999 earthquake in Izmit, Turkey, my childhood town. I knew what they meant because I had traveled to the quake-devastated region in 1999 and had spent a few weeks helping with rescue efforts amid the rubble. It was, of course, a horrible, tragic time—seventeen thousand lay dead around us. Against a background of death and sorrow, though, the solidarity and the altruism displayed by the survivors and the rescue teams were unlike anything I had experienced. It was indeed an existentially rousing moment. Witnessing the way people lent a hand to both strangers and friends without a thought, shared everything they had left, and came together in an impressive effort to rescue people trapped under the wreckage was a life-changing event for many who experienced it.

As protest occupations sprang up around the world, I kept hearing people talk about them in the same way I had heard people talk about post-disaster communities. If you examine a protest camp, it becomes apparent that in many ways, it resembles the formulation "paradise in hell" that Rebecca Solnit has proposed for the communities that spring up in post-disaster situations and defy the norms of ordinary life.[24] Indeed, furthering the analogy to a protest situation, Solnit recounts how the authorities sometimes respond to disaster scenarios with paranoia and repression, while ordinary people act with altruism and solidarity. Contrary to misleading media reports that disasters descend into chaos or a Hobbesian war-of-all-against-all, sociologists have often found that under the right conditions, altruism, collective help, and effective self-organization dominate such scenarios. Such altruism does not always occur, of course, especially if there are previous cleavages and deep polarizations within the society, but neither is it an uncommon response. In the United States, the September 11 terrorist attack was met by New Yorkers coming together immediately to help the survivors. When Hurricane Katrina hit New Orleans, contrary to media reports at the time which were grossly incorrect, the mostly African American survivors trapped in the Superdome without power, water, or functioning toilets nevertheless assembled an impressive self-organization that saved many lives.[25]

Of course, post-disaster situations often involve significant trauma and death, but protests have risks too. In both cases, the risk and the trauma contribute to the existential jolt. Gezi Park was frequently tear gassed, and I witnessed significant injuries to some protesters, including life-threatening head traumas. Many people lost their sight to tear gas canisters that were shot directly at them rather than angled into the sky, as police are supposed to do in order to avoid such injuries. Overall, seven protesters died in the protests around the country from various causes: three were hit by tear gas canisters; one was shot under murky circumstances; one died after being beaten by the police; one died from a heart attack after tear gas overload; and one was run over. The scale of the violence had been much worse in Egypt. Just during the initial uprising in Tahrir Square, in January and February 2011, nearly a thousand people lost their lives.[26] But even there, many described the protest as the best days of their lives—not as a means to dismiss the deaths, but as a description of the meaning they found in collective rebellion. Similarly, the "Gezi spirit" is talked about with nostalgia and longing.

Obviously, protesters are not pining for death or threats, but rather for the interruption of ordinary life they experience under conditions of mutual altruism. Many protesters I talk with especially hold dear the moments when a total stranger helped them through tear gas, pressurized water, live bullets, camel attacks, or whatever came their way. For many, the protest is the pinnacle of an existential moment of solidarity when strangers become family, united in rebellion. For many, that feeling of solidarity is a core part of why they protest; rebellion is a place for extraordinary communities, however brief or lengthy they may be. And the participatory impulse is not an afterthought, but another dimension of those extraordinary communities, however long they last.

Another feature of these extraordinary protest communities is that they can bring together groups that ordinarily do not interact. This is especially significant because pluralism and diversity are among the chief normative aims of many of the protests covered in this book. Consider an encounter that I might not have believed if it had not happened right in front of me.

In Gezi Park, I spotted "Meral," one of the most prominent transgender activists in Istanbul, recognizable from a distance by her tall stature, as well as the combination of a rainbow flag and a traditional yemeni—a delicately embroidered, thin colorful head scarf used by women in villages— that kept her hair swept back in the June sun. Gezi Park had a reputation as a meeting place for Turkey's LGBTQ community, an unsurprising fact given its location next to Turkey's arts and clubs district, bordering its hippest neighborhood, which boasted a community of openly LGBTQ individuals.

LGBTQ community members had been among the first to show up for the protests to save the park and had been on the ground since the first day. The queer community of Istanbul was also well accustomed to police brutality because it frequently suffered from raids, and worse, at the hands of the police. Meral had gained notoriety after lying down in front of a TOMA— one of the armored antiprotest vehicles of Turkey that spray tear gas, pepper spray, or pressurized water and that were ubiquitous at Gezi Park protests— to stop it from moving toward the park in the early days of the protest.

The LGBTQ movement was an organic part of the protest and among the few groups allowed to bring their flags into the park; the anti-formal-institution protest culture in the park meant that organizations were not allowed to bring their own banners and flags into the park unless they were one of the three or four groups that had started the Gezi protest. I had seen Meral around the park and had intended to interview her to get some insight into the earlier days when there had been far fewer protesters. When I approached her, Meral was busy chatting with a middle-aged woman, "Leyla." Leyla spoke with a distinct Zaza accent (Zaza is a dialect of Kurdish). Her hair was dyed with henna, a common choice among many women from more traditional backgrounds. She was from one of the most embattled Kurdish regions of Turkey, the site of many deaths and much trauma in history. She looked to be in her fifties, so she had experienced the insurgency and the conflict that had begun in the 1970s most of her adult life. Like many Kurds from the region, she was dressed conservatively, although her hair was uncovered. My experience with the heavy censorship of the Kurdish conflict in the 1990s was one of the key reasons I had become interested in the role of the internet in social movements. When I was growing up, at a time when offline protest was mostly banned or repressed, and online encounters did not exist, and the mass media worked to isolate, not connect, I could not even have imagined the encounter I was about to witness.

These two women, Leyla and Meral, from as different segments of Turkey as I could imagine—the secular, hip LGBTQ neighborhood of Istanbul and war-weary, conservative, rural, and traditional Kurdish areas of Southeast Anatolia—were hugging and crying. A few people were huddled around them, nodding and dabbing their eyes as the women told each other their stories of oppression—and, crucially, resistance. "Why have we never talked to each other before? We have so much in common," exclaimed Leyla. Meral wiped a tear with her yemeni.

"I know, mother, I know," she said, using a form of address a traditional Turkish woman might use with her mother-in-law or actual mother. "They always keep us apart, and that is how they oppress us both." They continued to cry and hug and spent most of the afternoon talking.

This was far from the only encounter in Gezi Park in which protests brought together people from very different walks of life, people who rarely had an opportunity to talk to one another. Besides the LGBTQ community of Istanbul, there was another group that was truly battle tested in encounters with the riot police: young male soccer fans. As in many countries, Turkey's soccer fans are rowdy, boisterous young men, and the fan culture is infused with machismo and bravado. Rivalries between teams are deep and are taken very seriously. Around the time of the Gezi protests, fans of one club had stabbed a fan of another one, killing him. Many times, after matches, fans who were unhappy with the result or were overjoyed at the outcome would clash with the police. The police had recently started an electronic surveillance system in the stadiums, which also threatened the ability of fans to swap tickets, and this had caused even more conflicts between fans and the police.

In Tunisia, in Egypt, and to a degree in Greece, these soccer fans, often called the "Ultras," played a key role in anti-austerity or anti-dictatorship protests. Likewise, in Turkey, soccer fans were among the first to show up to defend the park against the police and were also the best equipped: many already had masks to protect them from tear gas. Nonetheless, even those without masks were hardy and used to the gas. In many videos, you can see and hear them chanting loudly through tear gas so thick that you can barely make out their faces. How they can breathe in that cloud of gas, let alone chant loudly, I have never figured out.

Their chants, though, were at odds with the political makeup of Gezi Park's more secular, educated and much less macho crowd. The soccer fans were used to chanting sexist and homophobic insults against the referees and other teams in soccer matches; in the context of the protest, they adopted the same style for their chants about Prime Minister Recep Tayyip Erdoğan and other prominent politicians. The macho nature of the fan clubs was also reflected in insults directed at women. The word "whore" came up often in their chants, and they used that term to refer to politicians, male and female, again as a means of insult. The culture clash was inevitable, but it provided perhaps one of the most interesting twists to Gezi's many intersecting groups, including the LGBTQ community.

The protest's well-respected participants from the LGBTQ community approached the soccer fans, explaining to them that gay people, rather than persons to be insulted, were fighting alongside everyone—actually, often in front of everyone—to save the park. They used terms like "faggot" that had been hurled at them as insults and turned their meaning around. "Real faggots oppose oppression, you see," they explained to the bewildered macho fans, who had never encountered this community so directly or heard its members speak so openly. The LGBTQ community asked the soccer fans to stop using personal, sexist insults to make political points.

One sign in the park said, "I'm a whore, and [that politician] is most certainly not my son—signed sex workers," and some sex workers even marched with that sign to object to the use of "son of a whore" as a political insult. The soccer fans, most of them young men in their teens and early twenties, were taken aback and willing to concede that they had indeed seen these LGBTQ individuals defend the park with all their might and face the police with as much bravery as anyone. But they were less willing to let go of their beloved slogans without an alternative.

"What should we call politicians, then?" they asked. The new chant "Sexist Erdoğan" proposed by LGBTQ communities and the park's feminists did not scan as well because it had too many syllables in Turkish. Still, as I went around the occupied park, the soccer fans I interviewed were almost startled by their new understanding that "faggot" or "queer"—one of the terms most frequently hurled as an insult—was a term of honor among some of the hardiest protest fighters against police, besides themselves, whom they had met.

In the park, there were many similar diverse intersections of class, ethnicity, religion, and other traits. I watched men draped in a particularly nationalist version of the Turkish flag watch intently as a group of Kurdish youngsters held a boisterous line dance under banners and colors associated with the Kurdish movement—a sight that would have been almost impossible to imagine a few months earlier. The men were clearly curious but not hostile. Some started tapping their foot with the rhythm. During the day, there would be heated but civil arguments. Considering a recent history of insurgency, counterinsurgency, and forty thousand dead people in Turkey, such scenes felt surreal.

This coexistence is another reflection of the movement culture that values voice and community and came into being without strong and formal organization that might impose an ideological framework and homogeneity. But there is something more: plurality and diversity are explicitly sought and celebrated, and understanding "the other" through an empathic moment of rebellion is a core value.

Almost two decades ago, the Zapatistas, indigenous rebels in Chiapas, Mexico, whose global visibility, outreach, and organizing efforts arguably mark the beginning of the current wave of post-internet networked protests, crystallized this outlook explicitly. Their leader, the enigmatic and mask-wearing Subcomandante Marcos, had issued this statement in response to questions about his identity:

> Yes, Marcos is gay. Marcos is gay in San Francisco, black in South Africa, an Asian in Europe, a Chicano in San Ysidro, an anarchist in Spain, a Palestinian in Israel, a Mayan Indian in the streets of San Cristobal, a Jew in Germany, a Gypsy in Poland, a Mohawk in Quebec, a pacifist in Bosnia, a single woman on the Metro at 10pm, a peasant without land, a gang member in the slums, an unemployed worker, an unhappy student and, of course, a Zapatista in the mountains.
>
> Marcos is all the exploited, marginalized, oppressed minorities resisting and saying "Enough." He is every minority who is now beginning to speak and every majority that must shut up and listen. He is every untolerated group searching for a way to speak. Everything that makes power and the good consciences of those in power uncomfortable—this is Marcos.[27]

In the spirit of Marcos's statement, the Zapatistas organized an "En-cuentro" against "neoliberalism" and for "humanity" and invited activists from all over the world. I heard about it on the internet, which had just come to Turkey. I saw the Zapatistas' call and, intrigued, traveled to such an "Encuentro," where, as I mentioned earlier, I heard another Zapatista slogan that I would recognize over the next decade in many other move-ments: "Many yeses, one no," emphasizing this new type of movement's insistence on bringing together diverse voices against something they all felt strongly about. That was the dynamic that later paved the way for the type of movements that had brought Leyla and Meral together and in so doing had created a community that the protesters both yearned for and drew strength from.

Digital technologies are integral to this type of community. "Do you ever go home?" I asked some of the Gezi protesters who lived nearby but were now occupying the park. Most tried not to because they felt that it was important to keep up the numbers in the park in case of a police incursion. But some had responsibilities, either work or family, that took them away from the park at times. Many told me that they kept connected online: "I try to check in online as much as I can, and see what's needed. I also sit down and write longer posts to share with family and friends who are not part of the protest. I sometimes curate and find the best stuff, to help spread the cause."

This use of digital technologies was not simply instrumental; protesters felt a strong sense of loyalty to the cause and to their new and old friends who faced danger, and they wanted to retain a sense of connection. "I couldn't [sleep in bed elsewhere] unless I checked and made sure people were safe." The online flow of information, appeals, news, and humor also facilitated the formation of community in the park by ensuring rapid shar-ing of cultural products, and by creating a frankly hilarious, lighthearted, and joyful expression of protest.

A common media trope imagines connectivity devices functioning as mere "alienating screens."[28] In fact, especially in protests, they act as "inte-grating screens" because many people use their devices to connect with other people, not hide from them. Social uses are among the most widespread functions of digital technology across the globe. The reasons for the media trope "alienating screens" are complex, and it is not wholly without merit in other contexts, especially the collapse of the divide between work and the rest of life in the face of constant pressure for connectivity from bosses. However, in the context of rebellion and protest, digital technologies play a fundamentally communitarian role. Digital media also allow individual expressiveness. Through this expressiveness and community building, digital affordances and core goals of most protesters are interlaced.

Digital media enhance the visibility of a cause and can assist the breakdown of pluralistic ignorance, but what is less noticed is how connectivity also supports a sense of camaraderie and community—even a hashtag storm can create a sense of belonging. Digital connectivity can help create, set, and maintain a mood in a protest, even if it is completely decentralized otherwise. Digital tools also allow the protest to feel bigger than the location or the boundaries of an occupation camp. Especially in real-time situations, it is as if social media create an umbrella that envelops the protest and at the same time reaches out to people, potentially millions, who feel that they are part of the movement. In fact, sometimes it is unclear whether online or offline protest is riskier. Tweeting a protest hashtag connects a person to the protest in a way that is more easily traceable by the authorities; while offline protest risks tear gas, online protests risks surveillance. For most protest movements, a large group that identifies with the protest helps empower the cause of the protesters, and hashtags can certainly contribute to building and spreading that collective identity.

Digital connectivity also helps set a collective mood during a protest. In Gezi Park, even during the worst times, people turned especially to Twitter for the latest joke or meme. I watched people go to the front lines of the park during clashes (where the barricades kept the police away), get tear gassed, return to the back of the park to catch their breath, take out their phones to catch up, and then start laughing at the latest meme making fun of the authorities—although the laughing usually included a hacking cough closer to a seal's bark because of the lingering effects of the tear gas. Energized, they would then return to the front lines. The role of ritual in creating community has been explored by many social scientists. In the twenty-first century, meaning making and ritual creation during protests also occur online.[29]

Whatever their context, be it saving a park in Istanbul or protesting inequality in New York or overthrowing a dictator in Egypt, these protests are characterized by a desire for nonmarket human connections, participation, voice, agency, community, and diversity. It is not that today's protesters do not care about the moment beyond the protest, or that they do not take policy goals seriously. Rather, many of these protests spring from a deep lack of faith that they will be able to achieve these goals through institutional or electoral means. These types of protests cannot just increase their instrumental side, focusing more on elections, for example, and remain what they are. Their profound alienation from ordinary politics is inseparable from their commitment to protest, and this affects all levels, from the top to the bottom. Their desire for participation creates challenges, especially to tactical decision making and shifts, but it is also part of the bedrock of the movement they want to participate in precisely because they are seeking a voice and a community.

For protesters, digital tools and street protests are parts of the same reality. Social media allow protesters to share information, of course, but also to create a counter-narrative and culture that go beyond immediate physical boundaries. Through physical protest, offline connections, and online connectivity, protesters exposed wrongdoings as they perceived them, but perhaps more important, they created a shared protest culture that spread widely, and one in which millions of people can participate. That is how in Turkey the term "spirit of Gezi" or the "Republic of Tahrir" in Egypt or just the word "Occupy" in the United States has come to mean a celebration of rebellion, community, and diversity far beyond the emotions of people located in one park or square.

PART TWO

A PROTESTER'S TOOLS

5

Technology and People

ON A BREEZY OCTOBER DAY IN 2011 IN TUNISIA, I was attending a meeting of Arab bloggers, the first international gathering of some of the most prominent bloggers after the wave of uprisings had swept through the region. It felt distinctly different from the first two meetings of the group, which had attracted little attention beyond the few dozen in attendance. Now, the region was in turmoil. Journalists crowded at the perimeter of the closed event; one of the attendees was said to be nominated for the Nobel Peace Prize, which was about to be announced. Many of the Arab bloggers had last seen one another offline while in exile and had grown accustomed to connecting through social media and blogs. They had supported one another in jail, cheered one another through historic protests, and worried about one another's safety through thick and thin. During the upheavals, they had taken to tweeting "low battery" or "offline" before turning off their phones so friends would not wonder whether they been arrested, kidnapped, or killed.

Now, following the regional political turbulence in which they had played major roles, dozens of leading Middle Eastern and North African bloggers were physically in the same place. Joy, disbelief, and easy laughter filled the meetings. There were workshops on effective data visualization and usable cryptography, debates about electoral politics and constitutions, late-night dancing to music mocking fallen dictators, and celebrations of imminent births of babies.

It was almost time to leave Tunisia, and a few of us chatted in the hotel lobby about catching a taxi to the airport the next day. If only, I joked, there was a way to coordinate cab rides. The group of experienced organizers immediately understood the joke. In jest, they came up with solutions that did not involve digital technologies. A bulletin board, one suggested, where we could list everyone's name and departure time? I countered that it was now evening, and who would see that board? Another suggested that we each write our departure time on identical pieces of paper and slip one under every person's door. Those who woke up early enough to share a ride would see the papers. But the paper was a one-way communication, so the original person would not know whether she had anyone joining her, and everyone interested in sharing a ride would have to follow the same routine—slipping dozens of paper slips under dozens of doors. Maybe, we reasoned in jest, we could tell people to give their departure times (in thirty-minute windows) to the person at the hotel reception desk, and everyone could check there. But this approach had the same problem as the bulletin-board suggestion. The non-digital scenarios for coordinating proliferated, each one getting more complicated and then being shot down by the activists, who knew all too well the weaknesses of schemes for organizing and coordinating large groups of people without digital technologies. After the laughter subsided, I did the obvious. I took out my phone and sent out a single tweet with the conference hashtag and my time of departure, asking whether anyone else was going then. And that was that. My morning ride was organized. A Bahraini blogger and I rode to the airport together, while others also used tweets with the conference hashtag to organize their rides.

Twitter allowed me to easily communicate a one-to-many message to a broad group and to solve a coordination problem that would otherwise have been thorny.[1] This may seem a trivial convenience, but in historical terms, it is a powerful development.[2] Technology is helping create new ways of organizing and communicating and is altering how we experience time and space.[3]

Political dissidents have long recognized that the specifics of the way we communicate dictate the range of actions available to political movements. As early as 1949, George Orwell wrote a piercing essay questioning whether

Gandhi's methods would work in the Soviet Union, for example, where there was virtually no free expression.

> Is there a Gandhi in Russia at this moment? And if there is, what is he accomplishing? The Russian masses could only practice civil disobedience if the same idea happened to occur to all of them simultaneously, and even then, to judge by the history of the Ukraine famine, it would make no difference.[4]

Of course, now we have many tools that allow people to do just that: coordinate so that ideas can be expressed "simultaneously." Communication technologies, however, do not come in only one flavor. Rather, the tools have a wide range in what they allow us to do, and what they do not, and the ways they organize and shape communication. Each of these aspects makes a difference in what can be accomplished with them, as can be seen in the example of the bulletin board versus Twitter to organize ride sharing. This chapter goes in depth about the ways of thinking about technology and society and its complex interactions. It is not necessarily a chapter about social movements, but a means to clarify the conceptual approach that underlies the analysis of technology, networked movements and society in the rest of the book. This is the most abstract chapter; but the approaches developed here guide analyses of not just social movements but how technology and society interact.

To understand the role technology plays in human affairs, we must examine its effects at many levels. The first level of effects requires understanding how the entire societal ecology changes in correspondence with the technological infrastructure. An internet society differs in significant ways from a pre-internet society, and this affects all members of that society, whether a person uses the internet or not. A print society functions through a different ecology of social mechanisms than does a society with an internet public sphere.[5] Who is visible? Who can connect with whom? How does knowledge or falsehood travel? Who are the gatekeepers? The answers to each of these questions will vary depending on the technologies available.

After that first level—the ecological effects—we must analyze what an individual technology does at a particular moment or in an interaction given the existing ecology. For that, we must understand a specific technology's particular affordances—what its features allow or encourage you to do.[6] A pane of glass, for example, has an affordance of transparency, so you can see through it and use it as a window; a brick wall does not have that affordance.

The internet played a major role in how the 2011 uprisings in Egypt unfolded—an ecology-level effect. That Twitter allows many-to-many coordination via hashtags is a specific affordance of a technology that contributed to Twitter's role as a bridge, for example, in connecting activists in Egypt with journalists and observers abroad.

Digital technologies are especially complex because they have a huge range of potential affordances and serve many functions since they operate not just through hardware but also through software, which affects what can be achieved with the hardware. A smartphone combines numerous functions. It is a television, a phone, a notebook, and performs other actions for which we have no historical analogs. The programs that run on it make an additional range of connections possible. Facebook pages allow people to post messages, refer back to them in time, and share them across a wide network, unlike Snapchat, for example, which, in its current iteration, makes messages unavailable after the intended recipient has seen them.

In 2011, the first year of the Arab uprisings that are sometimes called the Arab Spring, there were many articles in the Western press about the upheaval. But, as a group, reporters overwhelmingly focused on the technology. Journalists asked whether social media themselves caused these movements, sometimes referring to "Twitter revolutions" or "Facebook uprisings."

I fielded many questions from reporters at that time about the technology, but their framing was not useful. Of course, new technologies played a major role, but the media coverage did not always evaluate that role in the context of protesters' goals or the political culture in which the technology was operating. The excessive (and often ill-considered) questions focusing solely on technology as a driver of revolutions became so irritating to some activists that they told me that they would roll their eyes and terminate interviews as soon as the topic came up. They objected to the intense focus on technology's role in social movements from an ethical viewpoint, arguing instead that the conversation should be about people fighting bravely to overthrow dictators against enormous odds.

Activists also wondered whether Westerners focused on technology in large part because many of the technology companies were headquartered in the West. They felt that the media was not giving Middle Eastern activists credit for the genuinely innovative and novel uses they had developed for these tools. In private, however, they continued to talk at length about the use of digital media because these tools and their specific features continued to be crucial to their efforts as they strove for freedom, democracy, and human rights—the topics they wanted to discuss with journalists.

A common middle ground in these discussions is that people accomplished the revolution, not technology. However, this is not always a satisfying compromise because this statement is true for almost everything people do—people make things happen. Would people do just the same thing under a different technological regime? Would the outcomes have been the same no matter the technology involved?

In academic circles, there is often concern about not falling into the trap of "technodeterminism"—the simplistic and reductive notion that after Twitter and Facebook were created, their mere existence somehow caused revolutions to happen.[7] Causation in this case is not a question that can be easily answered by selecting one of two binary opposites, either the humans or the technology.[8] Activists used these technologies in sundry notable ways: organizing, breaking censorship, publicizing, and coordinating. Older technologies would not have afforded them the same options and would likely have caused their movements to have different trajectories. Technology influences and structures possible outcomes of human action, but it does so in complex ways and never as a single, omnipotent actor—neither is it weak, nor totally subject to human desires.

It is natural to want to fit events around us into stories of cause and effect. That is how we make sense of life. There are tens of thousands of articles linking technology to solutions or ailments (attention-deficit/hyperactivity disorder [ADHD], addiction, stress, depression).[9] Many of us can name things we do differently now than we did even a few years ago because of technological developments. It is clear that historic change is under way, and that it is rapid.

Technology certainly causes things, but not as straightforwardly as we might think. Take automobiles, a complex technology with multifaceted affordances that generate new capabilities and have powerful effects on society, somewhat like information technology. Studies find a link between increasing car ownership and increasing rates of obesity in many places.[10] Research also shows that as poor countries have more cars, people walk less and become less healthy in general. However, the relationship is not simple cause and effect—more cars cause poorer health. Wealth also allows access to, for example, the Western diet of more processed and cheaper food that is high in sugar and fat. As countries become richer, more cars and new diets arrive too, both of which may contribute to rising levels of obesity. On some level, however, there is generally a correlation between wealth and better health care, meaning that infant mortality may fall even as adult health deteriorates. Therefore, it is hard to say that wealth is uniformly bad for health. In individual cases, cars may contribute to good health. For example, if you live in an isolated suburb where you cannot walk anywhere, car ownership might mean that you will drive to a place to exercise or to shop for better, healthier food.[11] For other people, not owning a car may lead to a more sedentary lifestyle since they cannot easily travel to locations where they engage in exercise—the opposite of the general societal trend. Cars certainly promote certain behaviors and nudge people's activities in new directions, but they do not do this in a simple, uniform manner.

Disentangling different kinds of causal dynamics can help us understand how this works for complex processes. Greek philosopher Aristotle, in his theory of causation, breaks down causes into four types: material, formal, efficient, and final.[12] Material causes refer to the substrate of things. Do metals cause cars? Does bronze cause statues? Metals do not make cars to come into being, just as bronze or marble does not turn into a statue by itself. However, a statue cannot come into being without suitable material, and it is hard to imagine cars—as we understand them—spreading in a society that has not figured out how to work with metals. In that way, metals are a causal input into the existence of cars.

Formal causes refer to the design or arrangement of things. A car is not just a heap of metal and plastic; it is a very particular arrangement of those materials that emerges from a very specific design. There is a logic to how metals become a car. To make the design work requires other inputs and knowledge; there must be sufficient understanding of force, acceleration, combustion, and other factors in order to be able to design a car that works. Manufacturing an automobile requires a certain level of understanding of engineering concepts. The knowledge that goes into design is not static over time, but at any given moment in history, there is a range of what is possible based on what is known. Manufacturers have been able to cram more and more processing power into silicon chips because of advances in design technology, but these capabilities did not just happen overnight. Formal causes bridge the symbolic and the material because they involve both the plans and knowledge in the minds of creators and the objective arrangement of things.

For information technology, the idea of "formal cause" acquires a new layer of meaning because software is not an arrangement of physical components. Instead, like language, it is a symbolic arrangement: it is the way we tell computers to make computations. An iPhone would not be an iPhone without the software, and with different software it is another type of tool—but the hardware in the iPhone also shapes what software can reasonably run on it. A set of instructions for the tasks that a computer is told to perform is often referred to as an algorithm, and new algorithms change what we can do even if the hardware does not change at all. Although the physical materiality of the computer—the amount and type of computational power and memory available, for example—affects the type of algorithms that it makes sense to pursue, that relationship is not absolute or rigid. Different programs running on the same networks and computers can do distinct things. Accounting, social media, video, and games on computers are made possible by separate programs that provide disparate affordances even though they run on the same piece of hardware.

Efficient cause in Aristotle's schema is the act that brings about the change. This is often closest to the everyday meaning of the word "cause," and closest to philosopher David Hume's sense of the word as it is used in modern times. Efficient cause is all about the doing and who is performing the actions. We can talk about movement participants' actions as the "efficient cause": people who took to the streets, posted about democracy on Facebook, tweeted as citizen journalists breaking censorship, occupied a park in protest, or braved repression are the efficient cause of a movement. Efficient cause focuses on agency. If a car hits a tree and knocks it down, the efficient cause is just that: the car hitting the tree. Because it is closest to everyday usage, this layer of causality needs the least explanation.

The final cause, sometimes called the "root cause," is the purpose that catalyzes events leading toward an outcome. The final cause is the reason that activists join or work in social movements or the dissatisfactions and grievances that motivate them to undertake all the work and brave the risks. In the case of the Arab uprisings, many activists I interviewed spoke about their desire to have a say in their future and to be free to express themselves. That is the final cause of these movements. For events occurring in the natural world and other situations where there is not necessarily a "mind" planning a sequence of actions, the final cause can be interpreted as the eventual end.

In a twist of interpretation, digital technology can also be seen as an aspect of the formal causes of events. Digital technologies of connectivity affect how we experience space and time; they alter the architecture of the world—connecting people who are not physically near, preserving words and pictures that would otherwise have been ephemeral and lost to time. Digital technologies are the most recent historical versions of communication and information technologies that create these important changes in the architecture of the world. Importantly, current digital technologies allow many more of us to do this in ways that were once difficult or confined to the elites. You no longer need to own a television station or be the publisher of a newspaper to make a video or an article available to hundreds of thousands or even millions of people.

In talking about cause, most public discourse refers to the category of efficient cause (what or who led to what) and occasionally final cause (the purpose of something). However, technology is also an important part of the other two layers of causality. We can think of technology as part of both the formal and the material causes that change the environment in which people (efficient causes) strive toward their goals (the final causes). A war fought with nuclear weapons, for example, is certainly going to have different effects on the planet than a war fought with sticks and stones even if the parties are equally "bad," or if the nuclear war is seen as "justified." The materiality of the event, no matter the final or efficient causes, has effects. "People kill people" is true, but what they kill with is of great consequence—especially if the tool is a weapon of mass destruction.

Causes also do not appear singularly. Most historically noteworthy events have many causes at all the layers. Social media and the internet certainly changed the communications environment in the Middle East, but so did new satellite television channels.[13] Easier and cheaper travel and decades of globalization were factors, too, as more young people traveled internationally and interacted with other young people and activists around the world. Activist networks formed during the Iraq War protests, which were the first publicly permitted political rallies in a long time in many countries in the region, allowed activists to meet one another. Increasing corruption in government and rising food prices also contributed to that moment in early 2011 when the region shook. Hence "Did this one factor cause this complex event?" is rarely an apt question. The answer might be yes, but always with qualifications to account for multiple factors.

It is also important to distinguish between necessary and sufficient causes. Many elements contribute to an event, but that does not mean that the presence of those elements in other situations will always have the same consequences. It may be that the introduction of social media enabling freer communication between individuals greatly facilitated the chain of events that led to the Arab uprisings, but that does not mean that the introduction of social media in other locations or at other times will necessarily have the same consequences. Think of fire: to start one, there must be combustible material, oxygen, and a spark. All three are causative factors, and all three are necessary, but two out of three are not sufficient to start a fire. You can sit all day and stare at the driest kindling in the open air, but it is not going to catch fire without matches, a lighter, a lightning strike, or concentrated heat from the sun's rays.

Realizing that causes occur at multiple levels and can be necessary without being sufficient, and that complex events have many causes, helps avoid false dilemmas. "Was it the people or the technology that caused the Arab

Spring uprisings?" Posed in this way, the question is incoherent. We do not have to declare technology unimportant in order to credit and honor people.[14]

"Technology is just a tool" is a prosaic saying that is often followed by pointing out that as a tool, it can be used for good or bad ends. There is obviously truth to this: technologies are tools, and tools have a variety of consequences and potential uses. However, the notion is too imprecise to be helpful in understanding the role of a particular technology. Are all technologies equally useful for good or bad? Would "good" or "bad" be equally achieved with any technology, no matter what it was? One could murder someone with a chair. But while it would be quite difficult to commit genocide using only chairs, a nuclear weapon in the wrong hands could easily be used to this end. A world in which some major countries have nuclear weapons is altogether dissimilar from one in which there are none. The distribution of these hypothetical nuclear states also significantly influences possible outcomes. (Do all countries have these devices? Or only the large powers? Warring nations? Ones that are able to protect the weapons from accidental launches? Who makes the decision to launch? Are the nuclear weapons on hair-trigger alert?)[15]

Technologies can also have different *efficiencies* and *potencies* which coexist with their affordances on multiple spectra. A baseball bat may be a potent weapon for murdering one person at a time, but it is not a very *efficient* tool for mass murder. A machine gun or a bomb, however, is.

One can appreciate the impulse to ask that humans shoulder responsibility for their choices, but history shows that technology is not just a neutral tool that equally empowers every potential use, outcome, or person. The historian Melvin Kranzberg perhaps stated this best with his first law of technology: "Technology is neither good nor bad; *nor is it neutral*" (my italics).[16] Technology alters the landscape in which human social interaction takes place, shifts the power and the leverage between actors, and has many other ancillary effects. It is certainly not the only factor in any one situation, but ignoring it as a factor or assuming that a technology could be used to equally facilitate all outcomes obscures our understanding.

Another problem with the "technology is just a tool" approach is that the phrase is often used to dismiss the real structuring that technology may bring to a situation. It is correct that technology is a human-made tool with a multitude of impacts, and that we should carefully consider the relationship among design, implementation, ecology, and social consequences. However, the phrase should not be used to mean that as humans, our intent in using a technology is all that counts in determining consequences. The relationship between technology and society goes two ways. Technology, too, has structuring power within its constraints that are dependent on its materiality,[17] its formal cause, and its design.

Let us look again at the example of a car. A car's affordance is taking us from one place to another speedily over roads designed for cars. In moments of desperation, or while traveling, people may live out of their cars. A car can also be used as a decoration in a yard, for example, or as an art piece in a museum, but transportation is a car's raison d'être. Cars differ depending on their design and their intended uses: some are better suited to speeding (more powerful engine), others to carrying goods (bigger trunk), and others to transporting families with children (stain-resistant seats).

With information technology, the question of affordances becomes even more important because the hardware provides only the base on which the digitally shaped affordances are built. Hardware has its own affordances: a mobile phone is always connected and easy to carry around and thus creates differently structured opportunities for activists than desktop computers, which must be located in physical buildings. A phone with the right hardware and software can take pictures, communicate with social networks, manipulate sounds and music, take notes, or make calculations— or, minus the software, none of the above. A social networking site can be designed to maximize visibility or privacy; it can be made more open to people or have higher barriers of use; it can make it easy for political news to go viral, or it can obstruct the news. Depending on its design, a social networking site may make it easier or tougher for activists to expand their reach. Even seemingly simple user interface choices such as the ubiquitous presence of the "Like" button on Facebook have significant consequences for political movements, like tilting the platform toward cheery topics.

Overall, it is important to keep in mind that understanding digital technology's role in social movements requires multilevel analyses that take into account the way digital technology changes society in general, that the particular design and affordances of each technology have complex consequences, and that people make active choices in how they create, influence, and use technologies.

Another common idea about technology is that it is socially constructed. This is certainly true in the sense that our social arrangements and power relationships affect everything we do. However, technologies are not constructed only socially, and "socially constructed" does not mean that they are unreal or without structuring power.[18]

To understand the concept of social construction, let us first take an example from outside technology: the social construction of race. Throughout history, there have been varying definitions of race in the United States.[19] At one time, Irish Catholics were not considered "white" in the same way white Anglo-Saxon Protestants were. Similarly, people of Italian, Greek, Polish, Turkish, or Russian origin are still sometimes called "white ethnics," a term intended to denote a difference between them and higher-status white people—Anglo-Saxon Protestants. For most of the history of the United States into the twentieth century, a person with any amount of African heritage was classified as black—the so-called one-drop rule. During the time of slavery, this meant that children born of any slave parent were also considered slaves, even if one of their parents or grandparents were white.[20] Over the past century, these definitions shifted as people's understanding of the concept of race and its role in determining legal and social status changed. Today in the United States, people of Italian and Irish extraction are considered white, and little distinguishes them from other ethnicities in terms of race.[21] As someone of Turkish origin, I am always treated as white in the United States, although not necessarily in Europe—a fact that highlights the culturally based nature of the distinction. Of course, today in the United States, people with some African heritage may identify as white, biracial, or black depending on their self-conception.

That said, the influence of social and cultural factors on how we define race, a fluid category, does not mean that race as a category has no effects or is somehow unreal. Regardless of one's self-conception, people who fit a certain look that, in the United States, is defined as black will often be subject to treatment based on the perception of them as "black," sometimes even if the person is of high status. Consider how Harvard professor Henry Louis Gates Jr., an African American, was arrested for attempting to enter his home in Cambridge, Massachusetts, through the back door after the front door jammed. The police appeared and, according to Gates, refused to believe that he lived there. In contrast, white people living in the neighborhood told journalists stories of Cambridge police helping them break into their own homes by entering through unlocked doors or windows on the second floor without even asking for identification or proof of ownership of the house. Although this tale is only one anecdote, it fits the findings of many studies that demonstrate that black people face negative effects from racial discrimination in hiring, interactions with police, housing, finance, and other areas. That the boundaries of race are socially constructed does not make their effects any less real or patternless. Additionally, that people choose to identify themselves as members of particular racial categories does not negate the fact that people with certain physical features will be viewed in the United States as black and sometimes treated differently because of that perception.

"Socially constructed" also does not mean "unreal." Race is what sociologist Émile Durkheim defined as a "social fact," a social reality that is capable of exerting external constraint over an individual.[22] Such social facts have power regardless of our opinion of them, although, since they are socially constructed, they can change over time as society changes. One can think of them as static at any given moment but dynamic over longer periods. Race has power and influence, but its meaning and consequences can certainly change over time.

The social construction of *technology* is an academic approach that posits that technology design is "an open process that can produce different outcomes depending on the social circumstances of development," and that technological artifacts are "sufficiently undetermined to allow for multiple possible designs."[23] There is no single output for any design process, and designers may make a range of choices. This is true to some degree for almost all technologies, but the range of possibility is not infinite during the design process or thereafter. Properties of objects are also rooted in laws of nature and mathematical findings and, for software, in the possibilities inherent in algorithms. At a minimum, such properties pull toward certain kinds of affordances rather than others. In the case of technology, "socially constructed" also doesn't mean that material facts about the technology are irrelevant, or completely open to reinterpretation as social facts. Material facts about the world and laws of nature constrain and enable, for example, what electronic products can do, how big they can be, how they can be sur‐veilled, and what affordances can be provided at what price ranges. In addi‐tion, the social and political forces that influence a technology's design and use are social facts—you cannot alter them by merely wishing that they were different, although they can be changed over time.

The social dynamics structuring the design process are not physical limitations like, say, the speed of light, but they exert real power. It is far from a mere coincidence that Facebook originally chose the "Like" button as a key signal to order and rank posts on the site. "Like" is an advertising‐friendly signal, and advertising finances Facebook. A "Dislike" button might help activists, for example, by letting them express displeasure with power‐ful groups, individuals, or brands, but it would upset the marketers who pay for Facebook ads because of the risk that brands would be subjected to withering public criticisms. A "Dislike" button could also be used for bul‐lying, so there are many complex considerations to all such decisions.

Major commercial companies that shape the affordances of digital plat‐forms are necessarily embedded in the socioeconomic realities of their countries and their own financial incentives, and those realities influence the range of choices they can consider and implement on these platforms. This influence should not be read as straightforwardly mechanistic: the mere fact of financing by corporations under capitalism does not mean that every aspect of the design of a platform will favor certain features, since markets require consumers as well as producers, and politics and regulations also play a major role. Founders and programmers of software companies are also not powerless in this complex interaction. Also design‐ers do not have total control over every other factor that determines how a particular technology will interact with other political and social dynam‐ics. As a result, what they think they are designing and the actual conse‐quences of their designs can differ significantly.

Almost all of Twitter's key affordances, for example, were first introduced by users and only later were taken up by the company as regular features. We can even say that one of Twitter's affordances is openness to user experimentation and reappropriation. Users can take tools that were meant to do one thing and find ways to use them in significantly different ways, such as hashtags, a Twitter feature allowing people to congregate around various topics. Hashtags are so heavily used by social movements that many movements are referred to by their hashtag (#blacklivesmatter, #occupy, #Jan25). Hashtags are an innovation developed by users, as was the use of the @ sign to ping a user on the site. These new features were inspired by even earlier user innovations in Internet Relay Chat and other earlier technologies that were later recognized by Twitter and incorporated into the platform.

I have often found myself using digital tools as anticensorship tools—purposes other than the ones the designers intended. Computer programs can run Twitter accounts—called "Twitter bots"—that automatically follow a coded script. For many years, a Twitter bot called "Magic Recs" (short for recommendations) would notify people about the new accounts being followed by people they had just started following—a means of alerting people to the existence of new and rising content. For example, if a movie star who was popular in your social circles opened a Twitter account, and many of your friends followed her, the bot would let you know that your friends were rushing to follow this new account. It was meant to highlight popular content. In the Turkish context, though, the bot became a tool to find new accounts created by people whose old account had been blocked by a court order. When the court ordered the blocking of an account, the censored person would open a new account, "@MyNewUncensoredAccount," for example, and reach out to friends and followers to let them know. As people started following this new account, Magic Recs would alert me to its existence as if it were a popular trend.

How do these concepts apply to digital technologies? Like other communication technologies, digital technologies alter the spatial and temporal architecture of society. Information technology is the latest in a series of consequential communication technologies that include writing, telegraph, print, telephone, photography, television, and even transportation carrying people or media from place to place. However, information connectivity is more layered because it comes with algorithms—software and computation that allow these technologies to do things beyond just connecting people. Thus, the transition to digital technologies is particularly significant because they are so flexible and powerful in the range of functions they offer. A digital phone is much more than a phone, for example. These technologies have very quickly moved from being used by only a few to being mundanely common devices. The rollout is uneven across multiple divides in wealth and connectivity, but billions of people now have access to potentially instantaneous communication.[24]

When technologies are new, many early theories about them assume that they will breed new kinds of people. For example, during the early days of the internet, there were many theories that speculated that the internet would make race and gender less important, that our bodies would become irrelevant, and that "cyberspace" would become a place that would be free of bodies, a place where ideas and rationality ruled. Take this early statement by John Perry Barlow in his "Cyberspace Independence Declaration":

> We are creating a world that all may enter without privilege or prejudice accorded by race, economic power, military force, or station of birth.
>   We are creating a world where anyone, anywhere may express his or her beliefs, no matter how singular, without fear of being coerced into silence or conformity.
>   Your legal concepts of property, expression, identity, movement, and context do not apply to us. They are all based on matter, and there is no matter here.
>   Our identities have no bodies, so, unlike you, we cannot obtain order by physical coercion.[25]

Obviously, this statement is not just utopian and unrealistic; it reflects a profound digital dualism, with the expectation that people typing words would somehow remain isolated on the internet, with no consequences for our corporeal presence. It may be tempting to dismiss this as merely one poetic statement, but this approach of assuming novel social dynamics on the internet (people being judged on the merits of their ideas regardless of status dynamics, for example), isolated from the rest of the world or its materiality, has influenced both scholarship and public commentary on the internet's effects. Although it is now fairly clear that the internet is not isolated from the rest of the world, and that status, race, gender, class, and nationality continue to matter greatly online and offline, our analytic capabilities have not fully caught up.

In discussing social movements, for example, it is still possible to encounter commentary that talks of "the real world" and the need to "take to the streets" without considering the mechanisms by which street protests work, how functions of protests relate to online connectivity, and whether it makes sense anymore even to separate the world into such categories. For one thing, there is no reason to believe street protests necessarily have more power than online acts—such an evaluation depends on the capacities conveyed by the action, something explored in chapter 8, rather than just looking at whether the acts were online or offline. Besides, most street protesters today organize with digital tools, and publicize their efforts on social media.

The problem with Barlow's statement is not just its reliance on digital dualism, but also the assumption that new technologies breed completely novel types of human behavior, common fallacy in technology writing—for example, witness the moral panic about selfies, which actually reflect mundane human behavior over millenia. Technology rarely generates absolutely novel human behavior; rather, it changes the terrain on which such behavior takes place. Think of it as the same players, but on a new game board. Culture certainly evolves, but many core mechanisms that motivate people are fairly stable, and this is true for social movements as well. People in movements still try to find and connect with people like themselves, get attention for their cause, convince people of their ideas, seek legitimacy and strength, and hope to bring about change. Now, this all happens at a different scale and under a different architecture of connectivity.

The internet is not a separate, virtual world, but it is also not a mere replica of the offline one that is just a little faster and bigger. The attributes of a society with digital technologies differ from those without them, regardless of whether a person is connected to the internet at any one point, and a person living through the digital revolution is subject to different forces and dynamics than a person living in a predigital world, even if she or he does not have access to digital technologies.[26] People make technology, but technology also has structuring power. The specifics of technologies, their spectrum of affordances, and the way layers of causality interact and intermix all matter if we want to understand networked protest.

6

Platforms and Algorithms

I TRAVELED TO CAIRO IN THE SPRING OF 2011, a few months after the fall of President Hosni Mubarak. Egypt was unsettled but jubilant. One of the Egyptians I interviewed was a blogging pioneer whom I will call "Hani."[1] In the early years of the twenty-first century, Hani had been among the first to take advantage of the internet's revolutionary potential. Most Egyptian bloggers made it through the Mubarak era unscathed because the government could not keep up with or fully understand the new medium. Unfortunately, the government noticed Hani; he was tried and sentenced to years in prison for the crime of insulting Mubarak. At the time, there was little open dissent in Egypt. The public sphere was dominated by mass-media outlets controlled by the government, and Egyptians were in the early stages of experimenting with the use of the internet for sharing political information.[2] When he was released in November 2010 after six years in prison, Hani was still defiant. Before his prison term, Hani's blog had been a bustling crossroads of discussion, with his voice reaching farther than he had ever thought possible. After his involuntary hiatus, Hani told me that he had resumed blogging with enthusiasm, but he found that his blog, which had formerly been abuzz with spirited conversations, as well as the rest of the Egyptian blogosphere, seemed deserted. "Where is everybody?" Hani asked me before answering himself, "They're on Facebook."

A few years later, I heard a very similar story from Hossein Derakshan, an Iranian blogger, who had become the primary actor in a similarly unfortunate "natural" experiment. Before 2008, he operated a lively blog in Farsi with a large readership in Iran, gaining a reputation as Iran's "blogfather." Tragically, he was put in jail in 2008 for six years, missing the whole shift to Facebook. When he was finally released, in 2014, he started enthusiastically blogging again—to crickets. There was no response or readership. Assuming that he just had to keep blogging via Facebook, he took it up and wholeheartedly put his material there. Hossein told me the story in 2016: how his Facebook posts just disappeared into the site, his weighty subjects unable to garner the cheery "Likes" that are a key currency of the algorithm that runs on the platform. The web is all turning into a form of television, he sighed and pondered if, at this rate, the powers-that-be may not even have to censor it in Iran. Facebook's algorithmic environment would bury them, anyway.[3]

For many of the Egyptian activists I talked with, especially in the early days of the revolution, Facebook's ability to reach so many Egyptians felt empowering. Ordinary people who otherwise might not have taken to the internet were joining the site for social reasons: to keep in touch with family and friends. For many Egyptians, joining Facebook was the entry to becoming connected to the their family and friends, but it also meant joining the networked public sphere. Exposure to the ideas and information circulated by political activists was a side effect of their Facebook membership. A study based on a survey of Tahrir Square protesters—that I coauthored—confirms that social media platforms like Facebook and Twitter drove the crucial early turnout of protesters in Tahrir Square that triggered the avalanche of dissent.[4] More than a quarter of the protesters surveyed had first heard about the protests on Facebook, and Twitter users significantly more likely to were among the initial group that showed up in Tahrir Square on the first day of the protests. Overall, the study found that social media had played a crucial role.

During January and February, many Egyptians were riveted by the power struggle being played out between the Tahrir Square protesters and the country's leadership, who had heretofore seemed invincible. Mubarak's government did not grasp the power that the ability to document, communicate, and coordinate via social media placed in the hands of ordinary people. By the time Mubarak was forced to resign, Facebook had become a major player in the civic sphere, and its use continued to grow after the initial uprising. Even the new military council that replaced Mubarak launched a Facebook page. But what did it mean that Facebook had become so central to the political life of the country? This was unclear at the time.

With the advent of social media platforms around 2005, the burgeoning civic space developing online, mostly through blogs, expanded greatly. In the same time period though, it also underwent a major transformation, shifting from individual blogs and web pages to massive, centralized platforms where visibility was often determined by an algorithm controlled by the corporation, often with the business model seeking to increase page-views.[5] In many places, including the United States, the Middle East, Russia, Turkey, and Europe, the networked public sphere largely shifted to commercial spaces. The platforms were chiefly Facebook, Twitter, and YouTube, along with a few others that facilitated sharing content.[6] Some countries had no prior infrastructure to build upon, or to transition away from. For example, Myanmar, just emerging from a military dictatorship under which there had been no active public sphere in the traditional sense, plunged straight into the networked public sphere.[7]

As these changes occurred, scholars and civic activists worried about how these new "sovereigns of cyberspace," platforms like Facebook and Twitter, would wield their power.[8] Would they censor and restrict freedoms to serve the interests of advertisers or governments? Would they turn over user information to repressive regimes? Internet-freedom advocate Rebecca MacKinnon was prescient in identifying the core problem: the growth of privately owned spaces that functioned as a new kind of public space, as if street corners or cafés where people gathered were owned by a few corporations.[9]

During the 1950s, when U.S. television networks showed images of the brutal acts of police encountered by civil rights protesters, their often belated editorial decisions to bring these issues to the attention of the American public opened possibilities for activists and ultimately helped shape the trajectory of the movement. During the next decade, when civil rights protesters were planning future actions, reaching network news audiences became one of their key strategic goals. Activists knew that television coverage (or the lack of it) could potentially make or break a movement.

Nowadays, the function of gatekeeping for access to the public sphere is enacted through internet platforms' policies, algorithms, and affordances.

In some ways, this has empowered movements by reducing their dependency on traditional mass media and their editors. In other respects, the current digital communications gatekeeping ecosystem has been reduced to a very few but very powerful choke points. Social movements today are largely dependent on a very small number of corporate platforms and search engines (or, more accurately, one search engine, Google).

While billions of people use the internet, a small number of services capture or shape most of their activities. Facebook has 1.5 billion users, 1 billion of whom log in daily to see updates and news from the hundreds of people they have "friended" on the platform.[10] Google processes more than three billion searches every day. The dominance of a few platforms online is not a historical coincidence; rather, it is the product of two important *structural* dynamics: network effects[11] and the dominance of the ad-financing model for online platforms.

The term "network effects" (or "network externalities") is a shorthand for the principle that the more people who use a platform, the more useful that platform is to each user.[12] Such effects are especially strong for online social networking platforms since the main point is to access other users and the content they have posted. Think of a telephone that could talk only to telephones made by the same company: what good is a wonderful telephone if you cannot call anyone with it? You would want to get the one most of your friends used even if you liked another company's model better. When network effects operate, potential alternatives are less useful simply because fewer people use them. Thus a platform that achieves early success can become dominant as more and more people flock to it. Network effects limit competition and thus the ability of the market to impose constraints on a dominant platform. This advantage is operative for Facebook (where most people know that their friends and family will have accounts) and Google (users provide it with data and resources to make its search better, and advertisers pay to advertise on Google knowing that it is where people will search, hence Google has even more money available to improve its products). This is true even for nonsocial platforms like eBay (where buyers know that the largest number of sellers are offering items, and sellers know that the largest number of buyers will see their items).

It is true that network effects did not provide absolute protection early in the race to commercialize the internet: MySpace was beaten out by Facebook, for example, and Yahoo and Altavista by Google—they had gotten started earlier, but had not yet established in as dominant a position. Network effects doesn't protect companies from initial missteps, especially in the early years before they pulled way ahead of everyone else, and such dominance does not occur independent of the quality of the company's product. Google's new method of ranking web pages was clearly superior to the earlier competitors. Network effects may not mean that the very first companies to enter a new and rapidly growing market and achieve sizable growth will necessarily be the ones to emerge as dominant once the market has matured and growth has slowed. But at that point, whichever companies are dominant will be very difficult for competitors to unseat. Network effects are certainly apparent in the dynamics we see currently in the use of, for example, Facebook, Google, and eBay. Beyond network effects, the costs of entry into these markets have also become high because of the data these companies have amassed. A competitor to these behemoths would need to be massively financed and would still be at a huge disadvantage given the enormous amount of data about users' habits these companies have already collected.

Another key dynamic operating in this commercial, quasi-public networked sphere dominated by a few companies is that most platforms that activists use, the places where user-generated content is produced and shared, are financed by advertising.[13] Ads on the internet are not worth as much to advertisers as print ads in traditional media because they are easily ignored in an online environment and because there are so many of them. This means that immense scale is paramount for the financial viability of an online platform. Platforms must be huge, or they will find themselves in financial trouble. Even Twitter, with hundreds of millions of users, is considered too small to be viable by Wall Street. That each internet ad is worth so little encourages corporations to surveil users' habits, actions, and interests. The only way for platforms to increase the price they are paid for ads is to create tailored ads that target particular users who are likely to buy specific products. The vast amounts of data that platforms collect about users are what allow this tailoring to be performed.

These pressures to achieve huge scale and to minutely monitor users promote the centralization and surveillance tendency of platforms like Facebook and Google and their interests in monopolizing both ad dollars and users. The enormous platforms in turn become even better resourced hubs of activity. These structural factors combine in a runaway dynamic that smothers smaller platforms: the huge platforms are the only ones that have enough surveillance data to profile their users so that the ads they display are worth something, which in turn means that they have even more resources and data on users as more and more people join them because that is where most of their friends are.[14]

Because of this spiral of network effects and ad financing, for an increasing number of people, Facebook and Google are the internet, or at least the framework that shapes their experience of it.[15] For social movements, Facebook is the indispensable platform along with a very few others, like Twitter and Tumblr (owned by Yahoo), and Google is the ne plus ultra of search engines. The picture-sharing site Instagram and the messaging service WhatsApp, which are also important, have already been acquired by Facebook. These platforms own the most valuable troves of user data, control the user experience, and wield the power to decide winners and losers for people's attention by making small changes to their policies and algorithms in a variety of categories, including news, products, and books. These platforms also offer users other strengths and real benefits. For example, like Google provides better security against state snooping (except that of the U.S. government), and Facebook's WhatsApp is encrypted end-to-end, making it more secure than all the poorly financed alternatives while still being widely available and easy to use (a major issue plaguing niche platforms that cater to activists).

Communicating primarily in this networked public but privately owned sphere is a bit like moving political gatherings to shopping malls from public squares or sending letters via commercial couriers rather than the U.S. Postal Service; neither shopping malls nor Facebook nor any other private company guarantees freedom of speech or privacy. Now, one person can reach hundreds of thousands or even millions of people with a live feed on a cell phone but only as long as the corporate owners permit it and the algorithms that structure the platform surface it to a broad audience. Neither of these is always assured for political content.

Internet platforms are much more than gatekeepers to the broader publics, like the mass media of an earlier era. Facebook also serves other essential communication and assembly functions. Activists also use it as a coffee shop, which scholar Jürgen Habermas famously idealized as the cornerstone of a critical public sphere. For activists, the platform also takes on a resemblance to the office of an underground newspaper—a place to mingle and have back-channel conversations in ways that are reminiscent of their historical antecedents in the alternative print press.[16] It also serves as a living room where families gather to socialize and, having usurped many of the functions of traditional telephones, as a tool that makes one-to-one conversations possible.[17] Facebook thus combines multiple functions that are indispensable to social movements, from the public to the private, for access to large audiences and to facilitate intimate interpersonal transactions. Now all these functions are thus subject to the policies, terms, and algorithms of a single platform.

Despite what seems to be merely a transfer of the same type of dependency from one type of media to another, social media platforms filter, censor, and promote in ways that differ from those of earlier forms of mass media, so the dependencies are not transferred identically. Platforms' power over users rests largely in their ability to set the rules by which attention to content is acquired rather than by picking the winners directly, the way mass media had done in the past. These companies shape the rules, which give them real power, but they are also driven by user demand, creating a new type of networked gatekeeping.

In this chapter, I focus mostly on Facebook and the interaction between its policies and social movement dynamics because Facebook is crucial to many social movements around the world, and there is no real alternative because of its reach and scope. Its putative competitors, such as Twitter, capture a fraction of most populations or, like Instagram, are owned by Facebook. In country after country, Facebook has almost universal reach among internet users, dwarfing other platforms. Together, Google and Facebook capture the vast majority of the advertising money in the digital world.[18] Even so, many of the issues raised in this chapter apply to other platforms as well, even ones with a much smaller reach.

In the past, much scholarship on social movements studied their interaction with mass media and probed the operations of mass media from many angles, ranging from institutional studies to ethnographies of their employees.[19] In the age of the digital public sphere, digital platforms are a similar topic: their policies, the ideologies of their founders and engineers, the specifics of their legal concerns, their financing models, their terms-of-service and algorithms all interact in important ways with social movement dynamics. I will highlight a few of the most pressing issues, but mine is not an exhaustive list, only a stark demonstration of the power of a few platforms and the reach of their choices.

At the height of Egypt's revolutionary movement in 2010 and early 2011, as I noted in chapter 1, public discontent coalesced around a Facebook page called "We Are All Khaled Said," named after a young man who had been brutally tortured and killed by Egyptian police. Sadly, his death at the hands of the police was not a rare occurrence in Egypt. But Said's story received a significant amount of attention when "before" and "after" photos of him—one showing a smiling young man, the other a mangled, tortured corpse—went viral. The images made the brutality of Egyptian police concrete and symbolized its horror. The Facebook page "We Are All Khaled Said" became the focal point for the agitation of hundreds of thousands of Egyptians. Eventually a call for protests on January 25 posted on that page roused people to action that turned into an uprising. However, that course of events was almost tripped up because of Facebook's "real-name" policy.

One of the most consequential decisions that social media platforms make for their users is whether people can use pseudonyms—and easily create multiple accounts—or whether there is a formal (legal "terms-of-service") requirement that they use their "real" name, however defined. Few platforms require "real names," but Facebook does. Although its policy is something of an exception for internet platforms, it is hugely consequential for social movements because Facebook's dominant size and extent mean that it is used by the ordinary people whom activists want to reach. Facebook acts as a de facto public sphere reaching large sections of the population in countries that heavily censor mass media news, leaving platforms like Facebook and Twitter as the only alternatives outside the direct control of the state.

Facebook's policy on real names is not an accident. Trying to force or nudge people to use their "real names" is part of the articulated ideology of Facebook and is central to its business model. The rule is also part of the expressed ideology of its founder (who still controls the platform), Mark Zuckerberg. In reference to pseudonym use, Zuckerberg once said, "Having two identities for yourself is an example of lack of integrity"—a statement ignoring the obvious function of social roles: people live in multiple contexts and they do not behave the same way in each of them.[20] A student is not the same way at home, in class, or at a party. For a commercial platform making money from advertising, the advantages of requiring real names are obvious because traceable names allow advertisers to target real people, and to match their information across different settings and databases—following them from voter files to shopping records to their travel and locations. Facebook's policy on names and its method of enforcing its rule have entangled many movements and activists in its web.

The Khaled Said episode, centering as it did on graphic and therefore controversial photographs, echoes an earlier incident in U.S. history, the murder of Emmett Till. Till was a black teenager who had been lynched for allegedly talking to a white woman in Mississippi. His devastated mother held an open-casket funeral for him in Chicago, Till's hometown, that drew tens of thousands of mourners. The inhumanity of the people who had lynched him was exposed in the visage of the mutilated, broken body of the murdered youth. A few newspapers and magazines published grim pictures of Till in the casket. Seeing those images was a galvanizing moment for many persons and exposed many white people to the reality of the ongoing lynchings at a time when the civil rights movement was poised to expand nationally. (The Montgomery bus boycott began within four months of Till's murder.)[21]

Khaled Said's case played a similar role in Egypt. A young Egyptian activist told me about Khaled Said's story and the pictures moved him from being a political bystander to being an activist: "He [Said] wasn't even political. Yet the police tortured and killed him. If it could happen to him, it could happen to anyone, even me."

Wael Ghonim, the administrator of the "We Are All Khaled Said" Facebook page, told me that he had focused on Said's case because it was representative and was not tied to a particular political brand or leadership.[22] From the stance of an activist, it was a good case to make a point because it was easy to identify with this unlucky young man who had done little more than fall prey to police. Ghonim chose to remain anonymous as the administrator of the page rather than using his legal name to keep attention on political issues rather than himself, but also, importantly, to protect himself and his family from retaliation by Egypt's repressive government. Soon, hundreds of thousands of people began conversing with one another on the page, yet unaware of either the essential role it and they would play in toppling the thirty-year autocracy of Hosni Mubarak or the challenges they were to face just to keep the page open.

In November 2010, a couple of months before the uprising to come, Facebook abruptly deactivated the "We Are All Khaled Said" page. There was immediate speculation that this might be an act of censorship by the Egyptian government. But how had the censorship been accomplished? How was Facebook pressured by the government? An intense discussion raged as puzzled people—including activists around the world—tried to make sense of why the page was yanked.

A Facebook spokesperson confirmed that Facebook made the decision without pressure from the Egyptian government. Facebook deactivated the page because the account holder, Wael Ghonim, had used a pseudonym.[23] Facebook said that his use of a fictitious name was "a violation of our terms," reason enough to delete the page despite its huge following and political significance. Just like that, through its internally decided naming policy, Facebook had censored one of the most important spots for political gathering in Egypt, at the height of political activity, without even a request by the Egyptian government.

The international human rights community pleaded with Facebook to reverse the takedown. In the end, the page was reactivated after a courageous Egyptian woman living abroad offered to allow her real name to be used in connection with the page. Her offer to publicly associate herself with the Said Facebook page, which she made simply to satisfy Facebook's terms of service, meant that she risked permanent exile from her native country and reprisals against members of her family. If she had not stepped up, the page might never have returned and might never have played the major role it did just a few months later, on January 25, 2011, as one of the top coordination and information sources for Egyptian protesters. Even this reactivation was only possible after employees inside Facebook also stepped up to pressure the company. A page without such visibility might have simply disappeared.

This is far from the only such example. Michael Anti is a Chinese journalist and a former reporter for the Beijing bureau of the *New York Times* who goes by that name in his offline life. He was awarded fellowships at Harvard and Cambridge, and is well known as a democracy activist. Anti specializes in using new media to write about Chinese censorship. In March 2011, he was thrown off Facebook, the place where he stayed in touch with thousands of people. The reason? Even though Michael Anti is what his Chinese friends call him and is his byline in the *New York Times,* the name is a pen name. Anti never uses his legal name, Zhao Jing, which is completely unknown to his circle of friends and colleagues, let alone his readers. Anti angrily decried the contrast between his treatment and that of Facebook cofounder Mark Zuckerberg's puppy, named Beast, which is allowed its own page. Because of Facebook's real-name policy, to this day, Anti does not have a Facebook page.

Even in developed nations where people are not necessarily hiding from the authorities, Facebook's policies cause problems for social movements. LGBTQ people have been some of the sharpest and most vocal critics of Facebook's real-name policies. LGBTQ people may go by names that are different from their legal ones as a preference or as a protection against family members who are angry about their sexual orientation or gender identity and who may act abusively toward them. There have been numerous incidents where LGBTQ people with public visibility—either as activists or as performers—were pushed off Facebook by vengeful people who reported them for not using their real names.[24]

If you use Facebook, you may be surprised by the preceding stories, and also by my claim that activists regularly encounter problems with the real-name policies, because you may have noticed that some Facebook friends do not use their real names. The vast majority of people use their real name on Facebook. Although a significant minority do not, they never encounter problems as long as they are not political activists.

It is true that a sizable portion of Facebook's users avoid using legal names on the site. In my surveys of college students, I often find that about 20 percent use a nonlegal name—often nicknames known only to their friends. A quick search reveals that there are many individuals on Facebook who use names like "Santa Claus" or "Mickey Mouse" and continue to have a perfectly normal Facebook experience. Why, then, did Wael Ghonim run into such trouble?

Facebook's real-name policy, like most policies of almost all social media platforms, is implemented through "community policing"—a method with significantly different impacts depending on the community involved. Community policing means that the company acts only if and when something is reported to it and mostly ignores violations that have not been flagged by members of the community. This model, also called "report and takedown," is encouraged by U.S. laws that declare that these platforms are not legally responsible for content that gets posted unless they fail to take down items that they are told violate the law. Community policing puts social movement activists—indeed, anyone with visibility—at a distinct disadvantage. The more people who see you—especially if you are commenting on or advocating for social movements or on politically sensitive issues, which makes you more of a target—the more opportunities there are for someone to report you.

This model also allows the companies to have a very small staff compared with their user base, significantly lowering their expenses. For example, at its height, General Motors employed hundreds of thousands directly and perhaps millions indirectly through its supply chain. In contrast, Facebook directly employs a little more than 12,600 people despite a user base of 1.5 billion. This combination of legal shelter for "report and takedown" and dramatically lower costs means that the model of a tiny employee base compared with the number of users, and indifference to terms-of-service violations of ordinary users, is common among software companies.

However, activists are not ordinary users of social media. People active in social movements tend to be more public, focus on outreach to people beyond their immediate social networks, and hold views that might be minority perspectives, polarizing stances, or opinions targeted by governments. Activists are more likely to be targeted for reporting by social media "community" members, people who oppose their ideology, or the authorities or people in the pay of the authorities. If your Facebook friends are close friends and acquaintances, you generally mind your own business, and do not comment publicly on potentially controversial matters, no one is likely to report you for calling yourself Mickey Mouse. Activists behave exactly the opposite way on Facebook. Activists ruffle feathers and challenge authorities. Most activists I have interacted with over the years make many of their political posts public (visible to everyone, not just their Facebook friends) to try to attract attention to their ideas. Activists also often try to broaden their social networks as much as they can in order to spread their message. Many activists I know maintain thousands of friends on social media and in many other ways stand out from the crowd.

All this leaves movements vulnerable to being targeted directly through community policing because their opponents seek to report them for infractions, real or imagined. Often, such reporting takes place in an organized manner, which means that companies are more likely to take it seriously as if it were a real infraction since the number of complaints is high. For example, on Turkish Twitter, there are often calls for reporting political opponents as "spam" to the degree that spam has now become a verb: "Can we please spam Myopponent99?" (meaning not "Let's send spam to Myopponent99" but "Let's all falsely report Myopponent99 as a spammer and hope that results in the account getting suspended"). Such mass reporting of opponents as spam or abusive is often successful in getting accounts suspended temporarily or even permanently. And this does not happen only in other countries; even in the United States, false reports of violations of terms of service are routinely attempted and sometimes successful—often targeting feminists, LGBTQ people, or political dissidents.

Activists, especially in repressive countries, use nicknames on Facebook for a variety of reasons. For example, I have seen activists use pseudonyms to keep random vigilantes from finding their home addresses—they are not necessarily hiding who they are, but just making it not too easy for people with low motivation or competence to quickly find them. If opponents report them, their accounts are in jeopardy unless they begin using their legal names, which must be verified by submitting documents like images of a driver's license or passport in what can be a risky and time-consuming process. Just the verification process may endanger their lives, depending on the severity of the repression in the country. I have seen this happen repeatedly but will not list examples—it would put these activists at further risk.

Even activists who use their real names are at risk of having their accounts suspended when political opponents and authorities make false accusations against them. When activists are reported, even if the report is false, they often must go through the verification process anyway, which sometimes disables their profile for weeks, especially in cases when their non-English but accurate, real names appear plausibly fake to Facebook's employees or algorithms.

After a great deal of harsh criticism, Facebook has slightly modified its policy, shifting to "first and last names" people use in everyday life. However, the documents that they accept for account verification are almost overwhelmingly legal documents such as checks, credit cards, medical records, and bank statements. Some of the choices they accept for identity verification, such as a yearbook photo, may work for Western activists, but activists or LGBTQ people in developing countries rarely have these options. Ironically, implementing these slight modifications to the real-name policy may have taken some of the heat off Facebook because LGBTQ communities in Western nations, those in the best position to make noise about their plight, have found ways to work with the company, but non-Western activists and affected communities elsewhere around the world, who have a lot less power vis-à-vis Facebook, continue to suffer.

In one instance, a politically active Facebook friend of mine who lives in a Middle Eastern country racked by violence was caught in a catch-22. Facebook's terms of service mandate "no vulgar names." But vulgar in what language? Her very real and legal non-English name corresponds to a vulgar word in English—which ended up with her account getting suspended. To get around this cultural imbroglio, she tried to use a nickname, but Facebook then asked her to verify that it was her legal name. She could not because it was not. She ended up having to send many copies of her passport over Facebook's system, a process that put her at risk of identity theft. She repeated the process many times, getting suspended on and off, sometimes because of her "vulgar" name other times because her replacement name was a nickname. She was finally able to reinstate her account after much effort, largely because she was connected to people who could alert Facebook to the issue. For others, such an ordeal might mean that they are, in effect, banned from the biggest public square in the world, which is also the biggest private social network. The stakes could hardly be higher.

What determines the kind of content that is allowed on platforms and the kind that is removed, censored, or suppressed? There is no simple answer. Platforms operate under a variety of pressures, ranging from commercial and legal ones to their own business models, as well as their ideological choices. Many platforms have explicit policies about the type of content that is allowed or forbidden. These policies are partly driven by financial concerns but are also influenced by a company's own vision of its platform. Many of these companies are quite young and are run by founders who own large amount of stock. Therefore, the role of individual ideology is greater than it is in an established, traditional company that is fully securitized and subject only to Wall Street considerations. Platforms are also subject to a multitude of different legal regimes because they operate in countries with dissimilar and sometimes conflicting free-speech, hate-speech, libel, and slander laws. Tellingly, intellectual property laws are a prominent exception to the rule "Let the community handle it." Copyright, an aspect of intellectual property law, is generally implemented in a much more proactive and comprehensive manner. Somewhat unsurprisingly, social media platforms, which are corporate entities, are far more concerned about intellectual property rights that corporations care most about, and where they have more legal remedies, than about individual privacy or political agency.[25]

The most important social media platforms for social movements, Facebook and Twitter, and the video-sharing service YouTube, owned by Google, have significantly different terms of service reflecting various editorial policies as well as the norms adopted by users. In the more freewheeling Twitterverse, fairly little is banned by the terms of service, although Twitter has been making some of its rules stricter (or at least applying them more strictly). In particular, Twitter has been pressured to act because of concerns about abuse, especially of female and/or minority people and activists, the use of the platform by groups seeking or inciting violence, racism, hate speech (illegal in much of Europe), and lately the rise of ISIS in the Middle East.

Facebook, on the other hand, has stricter rules and is more trigger-happy in deleting content for terms-of-service violations. Facebook has removed content ranging from breast-feeding pictures to posts considered to denigrate a community, often with little recourse for the people whose posts are removed. In September 2016, Facebook removed a post by a Norwegian journalist because it included a picture of a naked child. The picture was the Pulitzer Prize–winning 1972 photo showing a nine-year-old Vietnamese girl, Phan Thi Kim Phuc, running naked and screaming "Too hot, too hot," having just been badly burned by a napalm attack. The picture had been published on the front page of the *New York Times* and seared into many people's memories as a symbol of the brutality of the war in Vietnam. It had been reprinted countless times as an iconic photo showing the tragedy of war.

Facebook was criticized for censoring the post and was rebuked by the prime minister of Norway, who also had posted the photo to the platform. Facebook then responded by deleting the prime minister's post as well. After global expressions of outrage, including stories in leading traditional newspapers, Facebook finally backed down and reinstated the post. It's worth pondering what might have happened if Facebook had been the dominant channel of distribution in 1972. Except for publicity campaigns to pressure Facebook to reverse its decisions, users have little or no recourse against the actions Facebook takes.

Making these types of decisions is not straightforward, nor are there easy answers—especially ones that scale with the low employment business model of technology giants. Google, too, has struggled, especially because its video platform, YouTube, is a major means of propaganda for both activists and terrorists, ranging to ISIS beheadings in the Middle East and rampaging mass shooters in the United States. An activist in Egypt once recounted to me his battles with Google about taking down content that depicted violence. A policy against depictions of violence might seem to make sense when the video depicts an ISIS beheading or a mass shooting. But what about a video that documents misconduct of the police or the army? Some of the videos were horrifying, but, as the activist told me, "That was the only way we could get the word out." In response to the pressure, Google decided to allow such videos to remain on the site because of their "news value." Only a few years later, other antiviolence activists tried to pressure Google to take down videos showing beheadings carried out by ISIS. This policy too, was applied inconsistently. Videos of Westerners murdered at the hands of ISIS were removed fairly quickly, while similar videos of executions of local Syrians, Iraqis, or Libyans often remained on YouTube. As this example shows, there is no simple, easy-to-implement answer or method that applies uniformly to all cases, which means such decisions can neither be easily automated nor outsourced to lowly-paid, harried employers.

To get a better grasp of the complexities of the policies and practices that govern what content is allowed or disallowed on social media platforms, let us look at the example of activists and political parties in Turkey aligned with a particular perspective on the Kurdish issue in the country. The military coup of 1980 in Turkey unleashed a brutal wave of repression that was especially harsh in Kurdish southeastern Turkey. In the same period, an armed militant group called the Kurdistan Workers' Party (PKK) launched what would become a multidecade insurgency. The conflict claimed forty thousand lives, mostly in the 1980s and 1990s. I lived in Turkey for most of those years but knew few details about the situation—besides the fact that something awful was going on—because coverage was heavily censored both on state television and in privately held newspapers.

Change came in 2002, when a new Islamist-leaning party without the same historical commitment to Turkish ethnic identity, the Justice and Development Party (AKP), came to power. After a few years, the AKP government initiated a peace process with the PKK, resulting in a fragile cease-fire and improved laws that allowed Kurdish identity to be expressed more explicitly. At the same time, a mostly Kurdish political party also flourished in the region, capturing a majority of the votes in many Kurdish cities, often overwhelmingly. But even though there was no longer just one, state-owned, television station in Turkey, the mass media remained indirectly constrained through pressures on the media's corporate owners.[26] At the time, the southeastern Kurdish region was generally calm (a situation that would change around 2013 and significantly worsen after 2015), and censorship of the mass media was not the primary problem, at least for Kurds.

Despite this more open political environment, for years Kurdish politicians were censored on Facebook. The Facebook page of the mayor of the biggest majority Kurdish city in the region was banned even though almost four hundred thousand people had "liked" his page before it was taken down. The list of Kurds who were banned from Facebook ranged from prominent authors to elected deputies (parliamentary officials). The suppression encompassed an assortment of pages such as a site for Kurdish music and other popular, even mundane pages with hundreds of thousands of followers and likes. Yet Facebook did not provide clear explanations of the reasons for prohibiting the pages. Most of the time, it offered a terse statement about "violations of community guidelines." Some Facebook messages claimed that the proscribed sites had hosted pornography (which, given the traditional nature of the community, seemed quite unlikely). Sometimes no explanation was given. Administrators of these sites appealed, but written requests to Facebook for explanations often went unanswered.

People asked whether the censorship was a result of government pressure. This did not make sense because the same Kurdish officials appeared on traditional news media even as their Facebook pages were blocked and banned.

Curious about the censorship mechanism, I started following these pages, and asked many people in Turkey, including free-speech activists and lawyers, as well as officials, whether they were aware of court orders or backchannel pressures from the government on Facebook to ban Kurdish politics. I knew that many suspected that the government was behind these closures, because Kurdish content had often been suppressed in earlier years. However, all the people I spoke with, including sources close to the government, said that they were not lobbying or communicating with Facebook about these pages. I could find neither motive nor evidence of government interference. It was a mystery.

Some light was shed on the matter when I talked to high-level employees from Facebook, including Richard Allan, Facebook's vice president for public policy, who oversees European and Middle Eastern countries. Allan, a friendly, sharp, and knowledgeable Englishman, listened as I voiced my concerns, and he then walked me through the process. He explained that Facebook had adopted the U.S. State Department's list of "terrorist organizations," which included the Kurdish insurgent group, the PKK. He also assured me that Facebook was taking down only content that promoted violence.

His statement would suggest that Facebook was banning only PKK content. But this did not fully solve the mystery since deputies who had been legally elected, established journalists, and even some Kurdish culture pages were also censored, their pages shut down on and off. There was also much banning of items such as journalists' reports of public events, even when the events were written about in Turkish newspapers without issues. After examining the banned Facebook pages, I realized that the trouble seemed to be that Facebook was failing to distinguish PKK propaganda from ordinary content that was merely about Kurds and their culture, or news about the group or the insurgency. It was like banning any Irish page featuring a shamrock or a leprechaun as an Irish Republican Army page, along with BBC reports about "the troubles" in Northern Ireland.

For example, in March 2015, during the Kurdish New Year celebrations, a Turkish journalist posted on Instagram—a site owned by Facebook—a picture she had taken showing, ironically, elderly Kurdish women who had symbolically taped their mouths shut, wearing T-shirts with the PKK's imprisoned leader's visage suggested by a distinctive outline of black hair and mustache overlain on their white shirts. The reporting suggested that they were protesting the fact that the imprisoned leader of the group had not met with his lawyers recently. Instagram quickly censored the picture, taking the whole post down, and Facebook did the same on the journalist's page. The same thing happened to pictures of the same rally from another prominent Turkish journalist.

Both journalists were known to be sympathetic to Kurdish rights, and Turkish nationalists had long targeted them on social media. But all they had done was post a picture from a public, legal rally of some women wearing a t-shirt with a suggestive outline of the jailed leader. The picture was clearly newsworthy; similar photos from the rally had even appeared on pro-government outlets in Turkey. The outraged journalists loudly took to Twitter, where they had a large following, and complained about the censorship of their pictures. Facebook and Instagram later reinstated the pictures, as well as pictures from the same rally posted by other journalists. But Facebook's reversal occurred only after the journalists' public protests achieved a substantial amount of attention, which less prominent people might not have garnered.

A leaked document from Facebook's monitoring team provided a key insight; it showed that Facebook instructed employees to ban "any PKK support or [PKK-related] content with no context" or "content supporting or showing PKK's imprisoned founder."[27] One possible explanation of what was happening was that Turks who held strong nationalist views were using the community-policing mechanism to report Kurdish pages on which pictures from rallies or other political events from Kurdish cities appeared, even when the image was merely a photo taken in public or as part of a news story, and that Facebook employees who oversaw Turkish content monitoring were targeting those pages, either out of ignorance or perhaps because they were also Turkish nationalists opposed to Kurdish rights—a potential problem for platforms such as Facebook in a country with so much domestic polarization. In fact, in almost any country with deep internal conflict, the types of people who are most likely to be employed by Facebook are often from one side of the conflict—the side with more power and privileges.

Facebook's team overseeing the monitoring for Turkey is also located in Dublin, likely disadvantaging anyone who could not relocate to a European country, or does not speak English. Although I do not have statistics, I have, for example, heard from other sources that this puts women at a distinct disadvantage in the Middle East because their families are less likely to locate outside their home country for the benefit of employment at Facebook. The moderation teams—already pretty small—represent thus but a privileged slice of the countries that they oversee.

It is also possible that workers who knew little about the Turkish or Kurdish context and, possibly, who were not even formally employees of Facebook, did much of this monitoring. Journalists who have investigated the content-monitoring industry have often found that these decisions are outsourced to low-paid workers in countries like the Philippines, who must look at a vast amount of content and make rapid-fire decisions under strict time constraints, sometimes barely a few seconds per decision.[28] Could these workers wade through the nuances of an already-difficult decision-making process and adequately judge the items with news value, those protected by freedom of speech, and those that were an incitement to violence—especially about countries where they had never been and where they did not understand the language? Or did they mostly make decisions in response to the volume of complaints received, something that is easy to quantify and organize?

These are complex situations without easy solutions. In July 2015, a few months after that picture of elderly Kurdish women engaged in a symbolic protest was censored, the cease-fire between Kurdish militants and the Turkish government collapsed again, and the insurgency picked up steam, resulting in more deaths. When reporters cover conflicts, the line between news value and propaganda is not always clear, especially when dealing with the huge numbers of user-generated images. In a nationalist, armed insurgency, where is the line between freedom of the press and images that might fuel a war or be propaganda for acts of terrorism that result in many deaths? And who is qualified to make those decisions?

In the United States, where the First Amendment of the Constitution guarantees broader freedom of speech than in almost any other major country, it may seem that the straightforward answer is to allow all types of content. However, even with the First Amendment as a legal framework, a zero-interference policy would run into problems. The U.S government sometimes seeks to ban content that it considers a threat to itself. This includes posts by ISIS, which uses social media to recruit disaffected people or incite them to commit acts of terrorism. The United States also has strong copyright protections, and thus these platforms are under legal constraints to remove copyrighted content. What about other real cases, such as a graphic picture of someone's death posted on the internet for the purpose of harassing that person's loved ones? What about revenge porn, when a jilted ex-boyfriend releases or steals nude pictures of his ex-girlfriend or wife and posts them as a malicious act (many real cases)? There are many other examples.

Governments, too, have increasingly learned to use these mechanisms to silence dissent. They can encourage or even pay crowds to purposefully "report" dissidents to get them banned or at least make them struggle to stay on a platform. In these cases, the authorities count on taking advantage of the thinly staffed, clunky enforcement mechanisms of major platforms. Officials can also directly pressure the companies.

Michael Anti's problems with technology companies did not begin with Facebook's real-name policies. In 2006, Anti had a popular Microsoft blogging platform that drew the ire of the Chinese government. Microsoft, which does much business in China, shut down his blog at the government's behest.[29] In another case, the internet giant Yahoo provided the details of the e-mail account of Chinese journalist and poet Shi Tao. Shi had used a Yahoo account to pseudonymously release a Communist Party document to a pro-democracy website. The authorities had no easy way to track down the whistleblower, so they turned to Yahoo. After Yahoo turned over information identifying Shi, he was sentenced to ten years in prison and forced labor. The case attracted widespread attention after Amnesty International declared Shi a prisoner of conscience and Shi received an International Press Freedom Award from the Committee to Protect Journalists. After the human rights backlash, Yahoo's CEO apologized to Shi's family. Still, the damage was done. Shi spent almost nine years in prison, and his family members were harassed by the authorities.[30] In 2016, it was also revealed that Yahoo secretly scanned user e-mails at the behest of the U.S. intelligence services, raising questions about the Fourth Amendment, which protects against search and seizure without due process.[31]

Activists trying to reach broader publics find themselves waging new battles, beyond those that involve conflict and negotiation with large media organizations. There is a new era for the dynamics of gatekeeping in the new, digital public sphere, and it is far from a simple one. I have discussed the downsides to social movements of these policies; but this doesn't mean that there is a perfect, easy answer to the question, nor a means to do this both ethically and at scale through automation or poorly-paid contractors judging content in countries not their own. Major platforms could do a lot better by investing resources and giving more attention to the issue, but that their business model, their openness to government pressure, and sometimes their own mindset, often works against this.

Social media platforms increasingly use algorithms—complex software—to sift through content and decide what to surface, prioritize, and publicize and what to bury. These platforms create, upload, and share user-generated content from hundreds of millions, if not billions, of people, but most platforms do not and cannot show everything to everyone. Even Twitter, which used to show content chronologically—content posted last is seen first—is increasingly shifting to algorithmic control.

Perhaps the most important such algorithm for social movements is the one Facebook uses which sorts, prioritizes, and filters everyone's "news feed" according to criteria the company decides. Google's success is dependent on its page-ranking algorithm that distills a page of links from the billions of possible responses to a search query.

Algorithmic control of content can mean the difference between widespread visibility and burial of content. For social movements, an algorithm can be a strong tailwind or a substantial obstacle.[32] Algorithms can also shape social movement tactics as a movement's content producers adapt or transform their messages to be more algorithm friendly.

Consider how the Black Lives Matter movement, now nationwide in the United States, encountered significant algorithmic resistance on Facebook in its initial phase. After a police officer killed an African American teenager in Ferguson, Missouri, in August 2014, there were protests in the city that later sparked nationwide demonstrations against racial inequalities and the criminal justice system. However, along the way, this burgeoning movement was almost tripped up by Facebook's algorithm.

The protests had started out small and local. The body of Michael Brown, the black teenager shot and killed by Ferguson police officer Darren Wilson on August 9, had been left in the street for hours. The city was already rife with tensions over race and policing methods. Residents were upset and grieving. There were rumors that Brown's hands had been up in the air when he was shot.

When the local police in Ferguson showed up at the first vigils with an aggressive stance, accompanied by dogs, the outrage felt by residents spread more broadly and brought in people who might not have been following the issue on the first day. The Ferguson situation began to attract some media attention. There had been tornadoes in Missouri around that time that had drawn some national journalists to the state. As reports of the use of tear gas during nightly protests started pouring in, journalists went to Ferguson. Ferguson residents started live-streaming video as well, although at this point, the protests were mostly still a local news story.

On the evening of August 13, the police appeared on the streets of Ferguson in armored vehicles and wearing military gear, with snipers poised in position and pointing guns at the protesters. That is when I first noticed the news of Ferguson on Twitter—and was startled at such a massive overuse of police force in a suburban area in the United States. The pictures, essentially showing a military-grade force deployed in a small American town, were striking. The scene looked more like Bahrain or Egypt, and as the Ferguson tweets spread, my friends from those countries started joking that their police force might have been exported to the American Midwest.

Later that evening, as the streets of Ferguson grew tenser, and the police presence escalated even further, two journalists from prominent national outlets, the *Washington Post* and the *Huffington Post,* were arrested while they were sitting at a McDonald's and charging their phones. The situation was familiar to activists and journalists around the world because McDonald's and Starbucks are where people go to charge their batteries and access Wi-Fi. The arrest of the reporters roused more indignation and focused the attention of many other journalists on Ferguson.

On Twitter, among about a thousand people around the world that I follow, and which was still sorted chronologically at the time, the topic became dominant. Many people were wondering what was going on in Ferguson—even people from other countries were commenting. On Facebook's algorithmically controlled news feed, however, it was as if nothing had happened.[33] I wondered whether it was me: were my Facebook friends just not talking about it? I tried to override Facebook's de-

fault options to get a straight chronological feed. Some of my friends
were indeed talking about Ferguson protests, but the algorithm was not
showing the story to me. It was difficult to assess fully, as Facebook keeps
switching people back to an algorithmic feed, even if they choose a
chronological one.

As I inquired more broadly, it appeared that Facebook's algorithm—the
opaque, proprietary formula that changes every week, and that can cause
huge shifts in news traffic, making or breaking the success and promulga-
tion of individual stories or even affecting whole media outlets—may have
decided that the Ferguson stories were lower priority to show to many
users than other, more algorithm-friendly ones. Instead of news of the Ferguson protests, my own Facebook's news feed was dominated by the "ice-
bucket challenge," a worthy cause in which people poured buckets of cold
water over their heads and, in some cases, donated to an amyotrophic lateral
sclerosis (ALS) charity. Many other people were reporting a similar phenomenon.

There is no publicly available detailed and exact explanation about how
the news feed determines which stories are shown high up on a user's
main Facebook page, and which ones are buried. If one searches for an
explanation, the help pages do not provide any specifics beyond saying that
the selection is "influenced" by a user's connections and activity on Facebook, as well as the "number of comments and likes a post receives and
what kind of a story it is." What is left unsaid is that the decision maker is
an algorithm, a computational model designed to optimize measurable results that Facebook chooses, like keeping people engaged with the site
and, since Facebook is financed by ads, presumably keeping the site adver-
tiser friendly.

Facebook's decisions in the design of its algorithm have great power,
especially because there is a tendency for users to stay within Facebook
when they are reading the news, and they are often unaware that an algorithm is determining what they see. In one study, 62.5 percent of users
had no idea that the algorithm controlling their feed existed, let alone how
it worked.[34] This study used a small sample in the United States, and the
subjects were likely more educated about the internet than many other

populations globally, so this probably underestimates the degree to which people worldwide are unaware of the algorithm and its influence. I asked a class of 20 bright and inquisitive students at the University of North Carolina, Chapel Hill, a flagship university where I teach, how they thought Facebook decided what to show them on top of their feed. Only two knew it was an algorithm. When their friends didn't react to a post they made, they assumed that their friends were ignoring them, since Facebook does not let them know who did or didn't see the post. When I travel around the world or converse with journalists or ethnographers who work on social media, we swap stories of how rare it is to find someone who understands that the order of posts on her or his Facebook feed has been chosen by Facebook. The news feed is a world with its own laws, and the out-of-sight deities who rule it are Facebook programmers and the company's business model. Yet the effects are so complex and multilayered that it often cannot be said that the outcomes correspond exactly to what the software engineers intended.

Our knowledge of Facebook's power mostly depends on research that Facebook explicitly allows to take place and on willingly released findings from its own experiments. It is thus only a partial, skewed picture. However, even that partial view attests how much influence the platform wields.

In a Facebook experiment published in *Nature* that was conducted on a whopping 61 million people, some randomly selected portion of this group received a neutral message to "go vote," while others, also randomly selected, saw a slightly more social version of the encouragement: small thumbnail pictures of a few of their friends who reported having voted were shown within the "go vote" pop-up.[35] The researchers measured that this slight tweak—completely within Facebook's control and conducted without the consent or notification of any of the millions of Facebook users—caused about 340,000 additional people to turn out to vote in the 2010 U.S. congressional elections. (The true number may even be higher since the method of matching voter files to Facebook names only works for exact matches.[36]) That significant effect—from a one-time, single tweak—is more than four times the number of votes that determined that Donald

Trump would be the winner of the 2016 election for presidency in the United States.

In another experiment, Facebook randomly selected whether users saw posts with slightly more upbeat words or more downbeat ones; the result was correspondingly slightly more upbeat or downbeat posts by those same users. Dubbed the "emotional contagion" study, this experiment sparked international interest in Facebook's power to shape a user's experience since it showed that even people's moods could be affected by choices that Facebook made about what to show them, from whom, and how.[37] Also, for many, it was a revelation that Facebook made such choices at all, once again revealing how the algorithm operates as a hidden shaper of the networked public sphere.

Facebook's algorithm was not prioritizing posts about the "Ice Bucket Challenge" rather than Ferguson posts because of a nefarious plot by Facebook's programmers or marketing department to bury the nascent social movement. It did not matter whether its programmers or even its managers were sympathetic to the movement. The algorithm they designed and whose priorities they set, combined with the signals they allowed users on the platform to send, created that result.

Facebook's primary signal from its users is the infamous "Like" button. Users can click on "Like" on a story. "Like" clearly indicates a positive stance. The "Like" button is also embedded in millions of web pages globally, and the blue thumbs-up sign that goes with the "Like" button is Facebook's symbol, prominently displayed at the entrance to the company's headquarters at One Hacker Way, Menlo Park, California. But there is no "Dislike" button, and until 2016, there was no way to quickly indicate an emotion other than liking.[38] The prominence of "Like" within Facebook obviously fits with the site's positive and advertiser-friendly disposition.

But "Like" is not a neutral signal. How can one "like" a story about a teenager's death and ongoing, grief-stricken protests? Understandably, many of my friends were not clicking on the "Like" button for stories about the Ferguson protests, which meant that the algorithm was not being told that this was an important story that my social network was quite interested in. But it is easy to give a thumbs-up to a charity drive that involved friends dumping ice water on their heads and screeching because of the shock in the hot August sun.

From press reporting on the topic and from Facebook's own statements, we know that Facebook's algorithm is also positively biased toward videos, mentions of people, and comments. The ALS ice-bucket challenge generated many self-made videos, comments, and urgings to others to take the challenge by tagging them with their Facebook handles. In contrast, Ferguson protest news was less easy to comment on. What is one supposed to say, especially given the initial lack of clarity about the facts of the case and the tense nature of the problem? No doubt many people chose to remain silent, sometimes despite intense interest in the topic.

The platforms' algorithms often contain feedback loops: once a story is buried, even a little, by the algorithm, it becomes increasingly hidden. The fewer people see it in the first place because the algorithm is not showing it to them, the fewer are able to choose to share it further, or even to signal to the algorithm that it is an important story. This can cause the algorithm to bury the story even deeper in an algorithmic spiral of silence.

The power to shape experience (or perhaps elections) is not limited to Facebook. For example, rankings by Google—a near monopoly in searches around the world—are hugely consequential. A politician can be greatly helped or greatly hurt if Google chooses to highlight, say, a link to a corruption scandal on the first page of its results or hide it in later pages where very few people bother to click. A 2015 study suggested that slight changes to search rankings could shift the voting preferences of undecided voters.[39]

Ferguson news managed to break through to national consciousness only because there was an alternative platform without algorithmic filtering and with sufficient reach. On the chronologically organized Twitter, the topic grew to dominate discussion, trending locally, nationally, and globally and catching the attention of journalists and broader publics.[40] After three million tweets, the national news media started covering the story too, although not until well after the tweets had surged.[41] At one point, before mass-media coverage began, a Ferguson live-stream video had about forty thousand viewers, about 10 percent of the nightly average on CNN at that hour.[42] Meanwhile, two seemingly different editorial regimes, one algorithmic (Facebook) and one edited by humans (mass media), had simultaneously been less focused on the Ferguson story. It's worth pondering if without Twitter's reverse chronological stream, which allowed its users to amplify content as they choose, unmediated by an algorithmic gatekeeper, the news of unrest and protests might never have made it onto the national agenda.[43]

The proprietary, opaque, and personalized nature of algorithmic control on the web also makes it difficult even to understand what drives visibility on platforms, what is seen by how many people, and how and why they see it. Broadcast television can be monitored by anyone to see what is being covered and what is not, but the individualized algorithmic feed or search results are visible only to their individual users. This creates a double challenge: if the content a social movement is trying to disseminate is not being shared widely, the creators do not know whether the algorithm is burying it, or whether their message is simply not resonating.

If the nightly television news does not cover a protest, the lack of coverage is evident for all to see and even to contest. In Turkey, during the Gezi Park protests, lack of coverage on broadcast television networks led to protests: people marched to the doors of the television stations and demanded that the news show the then-widespread protests. However, there is no transparency in algorithmic filtering: how is one to know whether Facebook is showing Ferguson news to everyone else but him or her, whether there is just no interest in the topic, or whether it is the algorithmic feedback cycle that is depressing the updates in favor of a more algorithm-friendly topic, like the ALS charity campaign?

Algorithmic filtering can produce complex effects. It can result in more polarization and at the same time deepen the filter bubble.[44] The bias toward "Like" on Facebook promotes the echo-chamber effect, making it more likely that one sees posts one already agrees with. Of course, this builds upon the pre-existing human tendency to gravitate toward topics and positions one already agrees with—confirmation bias—which is well demonstrated in social science research. Facebook's own studies show that the algorithm contributes to this bias by making the feed somewhat more tilted toward one's existing views, reinforcing the echo chamber.[45]

Another type of bias is "comment" bias, which can promote visibility for the occasional quarrels that have garnered many comments. But how widespread are these problems, and what are their effects? It is hard to study any of this directly because the data are owned by Facebook—or, in the case of search, Google. These are giant corporations that control and make money from the user experience, and yet the impact of that experience is not accessible to study by independent researchers.

Social movement activists are greatly attuned to this issue. I often hear of potential tweaks to the algorithm of major platforms from activists who are constantly trying to reverse-engineer them and understand how to get past them. They are among the first people to notice slight changes. Groups like Upworthy have emerged to produce political content designed to be Facebook algorithm friendly and to go viral. However, this is not a neutral game. Just as attracting mass-media attention through stunts came with political costs, playing to the algorithm comes with political costs as well. Upworthy, for example, has ended up producing many feel-good stories, since those are easy to "Like," and thus please Facebook's algorithm. Would the incentives to appease the algorithm make social movements gear towards feel-good content (that gets "Likes") along with quarrelsome, extreme claims (which tend to generate comments?)—and even if some groups held back, would the ones that played better to the algorithm dominate the conversation? Also, this makes movements vulnerable in new ways. When Facebook tweaked its algorithm to punish sites that strove for this particular kind of virality, Upworthy's traffic suddenly fell by half.[46] The game never ends; new models of virality pop up quickly, sometimes rewarded and other times discouraged by the central platform according to its own priorities.

The two years after the Ferguson story saw many updates to Facebook's algorithm, and a few appeared to be direct attempts to counter the biases that had surfaced about Ferguson news. The algorithm started taking into account the amount of time a user spent hovering over a news story—not necessarily clicking on it, but looking at it and perhaps pondering it in an attempt to catch an important story one might not like or comment on— and, as previously noted, programmers implemented a set of somewhat harder-to-reach but potentially available Facebook reactions ranging from "sad" to "angry" to "wow." The "Like" button, however, remains preeminent, and so does its oversized role in determining what spreads or disappears on Facebook.

In May 2016, during a different controversy about potential bias on Facebook, a document first leaked to *The Guardian* and then released by Facebook showed a comparison of "trends" during August 2014. In an indirect confirmation of how the Ferguson story was shadowed by the ALS ice-bucket challenge, the internal Facebook document showed that the ALS ice-bucket challenge had overwhelmed the news feed, and that posts about Ferguson had trailed.[47]

Increasingly, pressured by Wall Street and advertisers, more and more platforms, including Twitter, are moving toward algorithmic filtering and gatekeeping. On Twitter, an algorithmically curated presentation of "the best Tweets first" is now the default, and switching to a straight chronological presentation requires navigating to the settings menu. Algorithmic governance, it appears, is the future and the new overlords that social movements must grapple with.

The networked public sphere is not a flat, open space with no barriers and no structures. Sometimes, the gatekeepers of the networked public sphere are even more centralized and sometimes even more powerful than those of the mass media, although their gatekeeping does not function in the same way. Facebook and Google are perhaps historically unprecedented in their reach and their power, affecting what billions of people see on six continents (perhaps seven; I have had friends contact me on social media from Antarctica). As private companies headquartered in the United States, these platforms are within their legal rights to block content as they see fit. They can unilaterally choose their naming policies, allowing people to use pseudonyms or not. Their computational processes filter and prioritize content, with significant consequences.

This means a world in which social movements can potentially reach hundreds of millions of people after a few clicks without having to garner the resources to challenge or even own mass media, but it also means that their significant and important stories can be silenced by a terms-of-service complaint or by an algorithm. It is a new world for both media and social movements.

7

Names and Connections

MOST OF US DO NOT THINK OF CHILD PORNOGRAPHERS and voyeurs as part of a social movement, let alone one that congregates openly in large numbers in public online spaces and draws strength from the assembled community. Yet this describes a phenomenon that occurred from mid-2007 to 2011 on a subgroup of the popular website Reddit—a gathering that would be quite unlikely to occur anywhere offline at that scale.

Reddit is one of the biggest sites on the internet, with hundreds of millions of views every day. Reddit has a simple, austere design that allows users to post links and images and comment on them. Unlike Facebook, Reddit's naming system is very friendly to pseudonymity: people can easily and quickly pick a nickname and start posting without even entering an e-mail address or phone number. But this is not a reputational vacuum. Reddit allows these nicknames to acquire a traceable history, reputation, and ranking setting up a fascinating, if sometimes disturbing, experiment.

Reddit's design and affordances allow us to explore this question: How does reputation operate when there is little direct connection between a person's online (Reddit) identity and their offline identity? Will people still care about the reputation their online avatars acquire? The answer, it turns out is, yes. Many Reddit communities display characteristics of other communities, complete with norms, customs, and hierarchies of status and power—just like other subcultures. Members of those communities influence one another, and the whole group can shift in behavior over time, in some cases further from the norms of broader society.

Reddit's reputation system is called "karma." Karma is represented through points users can earn as other Redditors upvote the links posted or comments made by the user. Karma can also be lost through downvotes. Reddit users can also earn "Reddit Gold," a gold-star symbol displayed next to their name. Other Redditors purchase this symbol to give to fellow Redditors for posts deemed particularly worthy—a practice called "gilding."

A number or star next to a username, not even linked to one's offline identity, may appear to have little significance. But this symbolic universe does not operate in a vacuum; instead, it is embedded in communities (subreddits) that flourish under Reddit's minimal structure. Just like other subcultures, these subreddits generate their own internal norms. Each is a world; some are very large, while others are tiny. Many are vibrant communities with distinct a subculture and regulars who earn significant amounts of karma just through their interactions within the subreddits. Reddit also has regular features that attract attention from outside the site. For example, many public figures, ranging from entertainment celebrities to the president of the United States, take part in "Ask Me Anything" sessions on Reddit in which community members ask them, well, anything.

Unpaid volunteers monitor almost all Reddit forums, and Reddit's management generally sticks to a hands-off approach. As I discussed in chapter 6, this is in line with the Silicon Valley business model of keeping costs down by employing a small staff, turning over monitoring to community members, and basically taking a live-and-let-live approach until legal or corporate trouble hits the site, mostly responding to takedown requests from outside rather than proactively looking at what might be going on at any corner of the site.

Amid the flourishing Reddit community structure and protected by Reddit's anything-goes pseudonymous culture, some unsavory subreddits grew very large. In one particularly troubling subreddit called "Creepshots," Redditors shared with one another photographs of women taken without their knowledge or consent, such as "upskirt" photos of women walking up stairs. Another, perhaps even more disturbing community called "Jailbait" grew large as well. "Jailbait" is a slang term for females younger than the age of consent for sexual relationships. This Reddit group was dedicated to sharing involuntary, sexually suggestive poses of young girls—at beaches, sports meets, or swimming pools. Participants in the forum often defended themselves with claims that they were only posting pictures that were, for the most part, taken in public places. But despite these twisted arguments, and whatever the pictures' legal status might have been, the intentions of the community were clear. Redditors on the Jailbait forum discussed these girls' bodies, rated their attractiveness, and shared sexual fantasies about these children. Some "joked" about raping them, cheered on by fellow community members. The Jailbait community grew disturbingly active and was among the biggest sources of traffic to Reddit. Meanwhile, Reddit's management mostly ignored this alarming phenomenon.

As discussed earlier, members of these subreddits, too, developed an internal sense of norms in the service of legitimizing their activities—this is what human communities do. The men attempted to justify their acts to one another, denying that they were child pornographers or pedophiles with the claim that they were mostly attracted not to very young children, but rather to teenage and tween girls. Jailbait members used this counterargument frequently, especially if a Redditor expressed discomfort with an image, or if another community on Reddit objected to the content on Jailbait. This happened fairly often because the activities on Jailbait deeply disturbed members especially of feminist subreddits who were actively trying to get Reddit's management to take action.

In regular interactions with one another, nestled within a community under avatars accruing reputation and online histories, Jailbait members created internal norms to justify their behavior. Just like other subcultures, they drew strength from one another. Over time, the community members accumulated karma points and learned one another's nicknames to determine who was a regular, trustworthy member and who was a suspicious newbie.

Thus the Jailbait subreddit emerged as a self-affirming community of adult men sexually interested in young girls, openly congregating by the thousands. That the Jailbait forum was allowed to exist in such a public, visible space may be difficult to believe, but it managed to survive and even thrive online for four years. The managers of Reddit (then owned by publishing giant Condé Naste) defended these online assemblies as "free speech" and refused to shut down such forums, which, perhaps not coincidentally, provided a significant amount of traffic to Reddit.[1] Reddit's managers rationalized their actions by saying that the men were carrying out these acts anyway, and that even without a space on Reddit they would continue to share these pictures illicitly, so letting them gather on Reddit caused no additional harm.

The position articulated by Reddit managers expresses a grave misunderstanding of how social norms and social movements form in human societies. Because of their public participation in a community on one of the most important sites on the internet, these men felt protected from the scorn and delegitimization they would receive from the larger world. It is one thing to share these types of pictures illicitly, knowing that what one is doing must stay in the dark or be subject to public opprobrium. It is another matter to be able to use an identity and avatar to share these types of pictures and then participate in an ask-me-anything forum with the president of the United States, using the same identity and avatar.

These men's activities are repellent, but the dynamics seen here are like those exhibited by other types of social movements. Homophily—seeking people who think like you to draw social support—is a universal phenomenon. The internet allows social movement formation not only by legitimate dissidents in Egypt or the United States but also by groups of people like these men, who might never have had the opportunity to meet in physical spaces in large numbers. The affordances of Reddit combined an easy pseudonymity that felt to users like complete anonymity (although technically, Reddit could trace users to their computers unless they took actions to disguise their internet addresses), yet with a means of accruing reputation according to internal norms. Thus Reddit's structure created the perfect cover for this otherwise marginal group. It is no surprise that over time, and given the space to flout the norms of the wider society, the Jailbait community grew bolder.

In 2011, CNN's Anderson Cooper hosted a segment about Jailbait that set off shock waves outside Reddit's self-contained community. Unsurprisingly, the idea that Condé Nast, the same company that published respectable magazines like *The New Yorker* and *Vanity Fair*, owned and hosted a platform with such a large, open forum for trading sexual pictures of minors, out-raged those accustomed to the norms of larger society.

Most pictures publicly shared on the subreddit were suggestive and disturbing but not fully nude pictures of minors. This is morally wrong enough, but sharing naked pictures of a minor in a sexualized manner is a grave federal offense. The subreddit was finally terminated after a Jail-bait Redditor who identified himself as a high school student posted that he had naked pictures of his underage girlfriend and asked whether anyone would like to see them. Many of the frequent visitors to the site, who voluntarily and proudly called themselves "creeps," publicly asked that the pictures be sent to them. I counted many many requests of this type (the thread was later taken down, making an exact count difficult). After that incident, the FBI was called in, and Reddit finally shut Jailbait down.

This episode tellingly displays the way in which internal norms within a community can shift over time through interaction. What would have been rightly alarming to anyone not steeped in the internal norms of Jailbait subreddit—the outright sharing of child pornography—had been greeted by members of the subreddit with enthusiasm and participation instead of alarm.

The story took another turn when an investigative reporter, Adrian Chen, unmasked the pseudonym of Violantacrez, the moderator of both the Jailbait and Creepshots forums.[2] That person, Michael Brutsch, was a forty-nine-year-old computer programmer in Texas and a prolific Redditor. His exposure made national news and awakened many more people out-side Reddit to the existence of these forums.

Cocooned in his Reddit communities and isolated from mainstream views, Brutsch seemed to think that he had a defensible point of view even after his unmasking, and he took part in interviews that offer fascinating insights into the role of reputation, even in pseudonymous spaces, and into the formation of communities. During an interview on CNN, Brutsch vacillated between defending his actions and apologizing. He still seemed stuck between two sets of norms, those of the community of Redditors to which he had belonged for so long, and the mainstream norms he was now facing. The interviewer told Brutsch that, as a father of girls, he wanted to punch him. Brutsch was clearly startled by this confrontation between the distorted norms his community had built and those of the rest of the world, disgusted with his acts.

When asked about what motivated him to moderate the forums, Brutsch replied that it was the "karma points"—the numbers signaling his acceptance by his Reddit community. He had even brought to the CNN interview a statuette, a gold-plated Reddit "alien bobble head" that the Reddit community had awarded him. Brutch proudly waved the bobble head on camera, offering it as an explanation of why he facilitated communities dedicated to sexualizing children or posting nonconsensual photographs of women. As Brutsch brandished the statuette, the CNN interviewer looked as though his eyes might pop out of his head.

This disturbing case is an example of how preexisting human dynamics interact in online spaces. Social scientists have long emphasized that "deviance" has no absolute definition; we understand it only as a departure from the norms of a community.[3] These men found community, acceptance, and a means of bolstering their reputation: positive "karma," codified in numerical scores next to their user names that were awarded for acts that were considered horrible by the broader world outside Reddit but were celebrated within it. This sordid example shows that rules of community formation in offline spaces also work online, that digital affordances shape the ground rules under which they operate, that reputation has an impact on human behavior online and offline, and that the decisions platforms make about whether to allow pseudonymity, the details of their terms of service and rules of speech, and the ways they construct their business model have significant consequences.

Throughout this book, I have emphasized that although the internet is not a virtual place completely separated from the real world, it also is not a mere replica of the offline world that is simply a little faster and bigger. Digital technologies introduce a range of twists to social mechanisms and dynamics through their affordances. Furthermore, through their algorithms, design choices, and terms-of-service rules, increasingly centralized platforms determine the architecture and the ground rules about how people can represent their identities online, as well as their methods of building reputation. Critical parameters include whether online and offline identities are tightly or loosely coupled, and whether social interactions online create persistent histories and a reputation that are visible to those with whom users interact. Social platforms differ in whether a pseudonym can serve to build a reputation and maintain continuity in the online identity even if it is not directly linked to offline identity. Twitter and Reddit, for example, allow both pseudonyms and the accrual of reputation. In the opening case study of the chapter, we saw how the ability to acquire a reputation can have significant consequences. Online platforms are not governed only by the rules set by the companies that own the spaces; they also have cultures and norms created by the platform's users and evolved through their actions. On Twitter, the linking of online and offline identities isn't mandated and the site's culture allows both versions—people using their recognizable name and people using pseudonyms. It is difficult to ascertain what percentage of users choose which path. Reddit, on the other hand, is mostly populated by people who do not link their user name to their offline name. These different combinations of affordances, rules, and cultures create different dynamics for the communities that use them.

There are also sites that make it very difficult to have a persistent identity over time, ranging from 4Chan, a controversial youth-oriented forum, to the seamy side of YouBeMom, a parenting forum where people discuss children and relationships. On these sites, there is no practical way for a person to indicate to others who he or she is (although the site itself can track identities). Each variation across these dimensions of identity and reputation affects the formation of communities and the building of social movements.

Many digital affordances do not have straightforward offline counterparts, although we can try to think of them by using metaphors. The pseudonymous and reputation-accruing sites are like places where people could gather, sometimes in large numbers and sometimes in intimate groups in spaces like coffeehouses or salons—sites suggested by Habermas

Table 1. Affordances of Identity and Reputation

	Reputation building	No reputation
Anonymous to pseudonymous	Reddit, Twitter	4chan, YouBeMom
Real name or offline identity embedded	Facebook, WhatsApp	Not truly possible

as the cornerstone of the public sphere—without ever having to reveal their names to observers or one another. In these types of spaces, however, people are sometimes able to identify themselves to one another through "special masks" which may be recognized across time, for example, online nicknames or avatars. In anonymous places without reputation accrual, it is as if each person donned a new mask at every step. (See table 1 for a simplified classification.)

Most internet users have gotten used to such types of interaction and tend to overlook that this situation is somewhat bizarre and perplexing, as well as fairly recent in human history. Although the absence of identifiable "real names" does not make social interaction meaningless, it does alter its context and consequences. For almost all human history, social interaction took place under conditions where people's actions would affect how others perceived them. The emergence of large cities changed this to some degree, allowing people to have casual interactions or create spaces where identity elsewhere—for example, at work versus a club—did not automatically stay attached to the person. Even so, whether at a club or on a crowded street, there was always the chance that one would be recognized. Many social dynamics that have long been observed and studied in human groups, such as the tendency of like-minded people to seek and draw strength from one another, which I explored in earlier chapters, also operate online, although they are subject to twists introduced by digital affordances.

These social dynamics are familiar from news stories about examples we see as positive: Egyptian dissidents finding each other and making connections on Twitter, for example. However, digital connectivity also affects all types of groups, as in the example that opened this chapter.

When communities forming in online spaces become more visible and reach very large numbers of participants, their size affects behavior in important ways as well. It is one thing to have homophily operate in a geographically grounded physical community where contacts are limited to those who live nearby; it is another to have a potential globe of like-minded people with the ability to congregate online. The dimensions of identity and scale interact, too. On Twitter, for example, which allows pseudonymous identities, women and minorities face a disproportionate amount of organized harassment from mobs of pseudonymous accounts. In a smaller community, pseudonymity might not have such negative effects; indeed, in the early days of Twitter, even with a user base in the millions, it was largely composed of early adopters whose more uniform cultural preferences dominated practices on the platform. Harassment and abusive behavior that now has many users dispirited was not as dominant a complaint as it is now with a much larger and more diverse user base. Persistence and reputation are often intertwined as well. Behavior on Snapchat, which eschews showing metrics to users and discourages persistence, differs from that on Twitter or Facebook.

Some online communities not only are distant from offline identities but also have little or no persistence or reputational impact. It is as if people are talking to each other while walking by without a promise that they will encounter each other again—and without any way to verify that the person they are talking to is the same person as before. Social scientists call this the "stranger-on-a-train" effect, describing the way people sometimes open up more to anonymous strangers (in places such as trains) than to the people they see around them every day. The fact that this person will no longer be in your life in just a few minutes or hours can free you to discuss issues that might otherwise be embarrassing or have deleterious social consequences.[4] Such encounters can even be more authentic and liberating, as is shown by the examples of Chinese youth and Brooklyn moms, discussed next.

Ethnographer Tricia Wang examined how anonymous communication can alter the fabric of a society—in her case, China. Wang looked at the cultural pressures on youth in China to "restrain themselves from emotional expression" and the way "personal relationships are built through favors" (encouraging keeping track of mutual obligations). Reciprocity is an important element in all cultures, but in the case of China, a few factors combine to make the pressure particularly heavy. China's heavy-handed state control of the public sphere restricts the kind of communities that can flourish— civic associations are often under heavy pressures. China's recently ended one-child policy put pressure on young people who were often not just the only child of their parents but also the only grandchild of their only-child parents in a cultural milieu that places great importance on the obligations of youth toward elders. Thus some grandchildren are subject to the focus, attention, and expectations of two generations. Wang explains that this intense pressure makes it especially hard for many Chinese youths to share aspects of themselves that may disappoint their families.

For her research, Wang interviewed young people in China who felt that they could not talk honestly to their parents or even to their peers who were embedded in the same offline social network:

> [Youth], too, withhold personal information from their peers. Confucian principles of emotional restraint, combined with the Communist legacy of emotional attachment as risk, have created a cultural milieu where youth have limited opportunities to explore identities other than those sanctioned by the three primary institutions that oversee their lives: the family, the school, and the state.[5]

Wang found that young people enter China's vast, sprawling anonymous online networks, not necessarily for political communication, but for the moments of honest conversation they offer. This is, of course, much like what young people around the world do.[6] Unlike youth of a decade ago, Chinese youth today have access to online social networks on which expression other than overt calls for collective action or very sharp political

criticism is not heavily censored.[7] The Chinese authorities allow some political expression online as a pressure valve for the population, and also
because they use it to keep abreast of the mood of the citizenry.

In her research, Wang traces the story of hundreds of young people who
use the internet to have conversations "about things that [they] had never
shared with anyone [they] knew," much of it on pedestrian subjects. As
Wang chronicles their journeys, it becomes clear that this path can also be
a catalyst for activism. Many young people discover a more assertive voice
online. Some become activists, sometimes almost accidentally. They might
begin by becoming comfortable with aspects of themselves that they were
previously ashamed of.

In one case, a divorced woman found an online community where she
could discuss her marital situation extensively with strangers, an important outlet in a society where marriage is a strong norm and divorce is
frowned on. She later became an HIV activist. In another instance, "Lily," a
young person who found comfort and expression online in discussing everyday subjects, learned of a polluting chemical factory in her hometown.
Buoyed by the strength of the connections she made online, she turned up
at a protest. Lily was exhilarated by the feeling of standing shoulder-to-
shoulder with people she had known only online and who had been without
voices or faces until that moment. Wang documents many such people who
moved from feeling shame in their lives to achieving a sense of belonging
and acceptance online and sometimes later becoming activists.

Of course, strong social norms exist everywhere. The United States is significantly more tolerant of public discussion of personal worries, but there
are still areas that are taboo. Consider parenting, especially mothering.
Despite the popularity of "mommy blogging," there are still parenting issues that are rarely discussed in public. A quirky forum called YouBeMom
allows parents to discuss these issues anonymously. YouBeMom is a bare-
bones site without a way to gather reputational points because there are no
accounts, avatars, or ways to trace who said what. The design is simple and
text based. YouBeMom threads flow quickly as people ask questions and
others respond.[8] The site describes itself as "an anonymous forum that lets
you engage in open, honest discussion with other parents."[9]

Browsing on any day shows a wide range of topics, some quite mundane: how to get a toddler to eat more varieties of food, for example. There are the types of personal confessions that we are accustomed to seeing in the United States, like frustrations with spouses ("dh" or "dear husband" on the site). Under the cover of anonymity, parents also discuss things they may not have ever said to anyone else. Browsing the site as a parent herself, New York–based writer Emily Nussbaum encountered touchy discussions such as unwanted pregnancies, affairs (women's own and their husbands), and frustrations with misbehaving children.[10]

But that wasn't all.

Mothers on YouBeMom, discussing anonymously and without any avatars or means of any reputation accrual, delved into taboo topics such as regretting having children or treating their children badly. Some confessed favoring one child over another or not liking their children at all. Such feelings are almost never discussed openly in the public sphere and are rarely discussed with one's family or friends. But on YouBeMom, they ignited vigorous debate, with reactions ranging from sympathy to disgust to frank advice.

The discussions on YouBeMom range from the mundane to the taboo, and the emotional tone of the threads can range from cathartic to judgmental. It is clear, however, that these conversations could not easily occur without the site's affordances, which reject both persistent identities and reputation over time. Although there are no doubt regulars on the site, they are not identifiable, nor can cliques and subgroups form easily. There is one question after another in a steady stream of answers, discussions, and musings.

Anonymous spaces are hard to measure and study, and their long-term impacts on participants are difficult to discern. However, we can listen to social movement participants and activists in societies with strictly controlled public spheres who talk about the impact of anonymous online interactions on their journey.

In the early days of the Arab uprisings, in 2011, I traveled to Qatar to attend a forum organized by Al Jazeera. (This was a different group from the Arab bloggers' meeting I would attend later that year in Tunisia.) Tunisian and Egyptian autocrats had fallen a few months earlier. Neither Syria nor

Libya had yet descended into civil wars. Young activists from the region were drawn to the forum, some from countries where not much was happening yet, others from places in turmoil. I asked them about their early internet experiences and heard a term I had not heard in years from ordinary people. Arab Spring activists surprised me by mentioning IRC, or internet Relay Chat, a largely forgotten internet chatroom system that allows for easy and anonymous conversation. Almost all the activists mentioned active participation in IRC chatrooms, and not only to discuss politics.

For these young activists who lived in regimes in which the public sphere was dominated by the elderly and the powerful, where strong social norms made it difficult to have conversations about intimate subjects, and where repression was common, the experience of talking freely was transformative. Once they were able to get online, some became interested in political conversations almost immediately. Others took pleasure in talking about ordinary topics, like the youth in Wang's tales of anonymous online conversations in China. They could explore a sense of self and belonging and had their perspective of what was acceptable move beyond societal norms. Being willing to transcend social limitations sometimes also led to transcendence in their political imaginations. A decade after these youth first started populating IRC chat rooms, they were thronging the streets of Arab countries demanding change and fighting repression by the old guard.

The very large scale of social networks, especially when combined with pseudonymity, raises other challenges for activists. Take the case of a successful dissident author in Turkey who came to me one day in a panic. Because she was a fairly prominent literary figure in Turkey, she enjoyed a large Twitter following. Twitter considers freedom of speech central to its identity. Twitter UK general manager Tony Wang once called Twitter "the free speech wing of the free speech party." Twitter cofounder Jack Dorsey often says that Twitter is a platform for "speaking truth to power." Twitter allows not only pseudonyms and multiple accounts but also parody accounts. These features attract many activists, but this laissez-faire environment fosters other threats.

For this prominent Turkish literary figure, a large-scale social media network that allowed pseudonymity brought significant problems of the kind I would hear about again and again from prominent dissidents and would even experience myself. She tweeted about reports of human rights violations in Turkey and sometime commented on the news of the day. Her creative ability as a fiction writer showed in her deft tweets, even with only 140 characters. Her account became popular and widely followed; her tweets and writings frequently went viral.

But now she was scared. She was getting a barrage of death threats, mostly from seemingly pseudonymous accounts. She asked me how much she should worry about the "eggheads."

"Egghead" refers to the default Twitter profile of accounts that do not bother to change the picture Twitter provides, a gray oval (the "egg") in a color block square. Such accounts can be "bots"—automatically generated profiles that tweet what is programmed—or they can be real people hiding behind anonymity. Many of the accounts appeared to me to be bots or automated (given the speed at which they appeared), but I could not be sure. And along with the accounts that appeared to be automated, there were many others that seemed clearly to be those of real people hurling insults at her. The messages ranged from calling her stupid to threatening to kill or rape her. "It's like this every day," she told me. "Hundreds of people who just come at me. Over and over and over."

I have heard or read similar sentiments from almost every prominent activist. A Black Lives Matter activist with hundreds of thousands of followers tweeted that he had blocked more than ten thousand people, and that there were many people who "sat in his mentions" all day, meaning that they kept "pinging" him on Twitter by using his handle, showing up on his notification tab (if they weren't blocked). Many of these were real people; many others were accounts that used pseudonyms. Others were bots. I occasionally experience this when I write an article critical of a politician with a large-enough following, or address a topic that attracts organized groups of angry people. Once, I became the subject of a vast amount of online fury simply because I wrote that I disliked the trend toward larger and larger phones because they were becoming hard to use for many women, like me, who have smaller hands. I thought it was a minor, obvious point, but the vitriol it provoked was massive. I later realized that the attackers had also been organizing online, using the same affordances as other activists for positive change—but only to attack female writers who touched upon gender-related topics. They were using Twitter's ease of organization and willingness to let them operate freely to target the freedom of speech and assembly of others. Like many platforms, Twitter had wanted to remain "neutral" but, as is often the case, rights of one group—the group who wanted to silence women or minorities—clashed with rights of women or minorities (especially outspoken ones) to freely use the site to speak and assemble. A stance of "neutrality" meant, in reality, choosing the former over the latter.

Over the years, I have watched journalist after journalist and activist after activist being targeted by organized, angry, and sometimes vicious groups who wanted to silence them with harassment. Bots are the least of their problems, but even bots cause trouble since hundreds and thousands of hostile mentions clog people's notifications, absorb their attention, and unnerve them. It is not humanly possible to stare at such threats and to casually brush them off every time. Many times, the threats are directed at people's children, pets, or relatives, making it harder to just shrug them off even if one has decided to accept personal risk. I've seen people take turns reading each other threats because it can become overwhelming to read threats to one's children, trying to assess how credible they are. I have done it for others, and it is hard to bear even when one is not the target.

Often, people are harassed via "doxing": disclosing personal information online against a person's will, ranging from home address to hacked private e-mails. On the other hand, the moderator of Reddit's ugly "jailbait" subreddit, dedicated to sexual exploitation of minors, was "doxed" too—his identity was disclosed against his will. As with many of the issues I study, it is difficult to have a coherent and unified normative view or a simple rule that would apply in all cases that *all* doxing is good or bad by itself. There are always trade-offs. These judgments have to be made in the context of whose rights are allowed to trample whose, what ethical values will be protected and which ones disregarded. Will we protect children's right to be free of sexual exploitation, or the rights of adult men to anonymously gather and exploit? But will we also protect the right of dissidents around the world to be able to post pseudonymously? There is no single, simple answer that covers all ethical and normative questions that come up for platforms and their policies, without the need to judge many of these cases individually, rather than applying blanket rules.

The people organizing targeted harassment campaigns on Twitter against political opponents can also be regular people leading seemingly normal lives. Some are acting on their political beliefs and see their targets as traitors or enemies of their nation. Some are just bored people who enjoy spending a few hours trying to get a rise out of well-known activists or journalists. Others are in the pay of governments. As I discuss in chapter 9 on government responses to digital tools, there have been numerous reports, notably from China, Russia, and Iran, that governments seeking to repress activists have hired people to create pseudonymous accounts to amplify the governments' point of view.

The enormous scale of this new networked public sphere means that older ways of thinking about it don't necessarily apply. One person telling you that your political views are stupid or even treasonous is almost certainly free speech, at least by U.S. First Amendment standards (and the standards of most developed countries). However, it is another matter when tens of thousands of people attack your political views, interspersed with a random scattering of more serious threats. Such an avalanche creates fear and paralysis, especially since those targeted on social media are sometimes also targeted by governments. Is this a form of digital heckler's veto—when free speech is shut down by organized crowds shouting down speakers they dislike? Scale and anonymity combine to change much of our understanding of the obstacles to exercising freedom of speech.

Such targeted harassment campaigns also demonstrate the continued importance of race and gender in the digitally networked public sphere. In the early days of internet studies, the internet was conceptualized as a "cyberspace" where people would play and experiment with gender and race as they wished.[11] The internet would allow disembodied minds to roam freely to engage in discussion, regardless of borders or offline identities.[12]

There is obviously some truth to this; people can engage in discussions online while hiding their race and gender. However, the reverse side of the coin is more disquieting: people can target and harass others online while hiding their own identity, and they can do this on a large scale. Women, minorities, dissidents, and journalists writing about sensitive topics have been especially targeted.[13] This has led to many publicized incidents of women or minority activists withdrawing from online public spaces after being targeted by incessant harassment campaigns. Threats of rape and murder mix with the occasional "swatting"—the term for hoaxing the police by telling them that an armed and violent event is under way at the victim's address. Swatting can literally put the victim's life at risk as police storm into what they expect to be an extremely dangerous situation, guns drawn, ready to shoot—sometimes even knocking down doors—while the victim has no idea what is going on.

Activists and others who have been harassed in such ways have repeatedly called on social media platforms to put a stop to the abuse. The easiest way would be to ban the malicious bots, something most platforms do as soon as they are detected. Unfortunately, it is also easy to create a new bot network, and not all bots are harmful or malicious.[14] Even if all bots were eliminated, the real issue is scale. There is no simple solution to the problem of thousands of people, whether motivated by politics or by lack of employment, focusing on a political actor to make their experience on the platform unbearable. At least, there is no solution platforms can take without upsetting some people investing significant resources, making normative and ethical judgements, and inevitably upsetting some people.

Many platforms are now considering banning or limiting hate speech and abusive campaigns, and we have even seen news of automated and algorithmic filtering of terrorist content.[15] However, defining what constitutes hate speech is difficult—especially if the implementation will be algorithmic or outsourced to low-paid workers. Is it hate speech to tell a politically dissident woman that she is "ugly" and "doesn't deserve a husband"? In isolation, most people would probably say not—it is just pathetic. If it occurs only once, it may not make much difference in the life of a person, especially because people know that the sender might be just a bored teenager sitting somewhere far away. When one receives hundreds and thousands of such messages in quick succession, though, the experience is different.

Should platforms ban all hostile or abusive messages? Many people would find a blanket ban hard to accept or define. This is especially true among activists because rules banning impolite speech tend to be used against activists first.

There is no easy or straightforward way to automate searches only for threats of rape and harm and also catch all of them. Any automated solution would necessarily have "false positives"—things that are mistakenly flagged as hate speech. Mere insults or political opinions (or a mix of both), or even messages with unrelated content, would end up barred from the platform. Would people talking about an act of terrorism be banned as if they were supporting it? How about those inciting or celebrating it? Could algorithms separate one from the other? It is not that difficult for most people to find ways to imply a threat linguistically without triggering automated controls, and threats that are stated in a low key, "it'd be a shame if something happened," can be among the most credible and chilling. Some threats come in the form of images that automated solutions might struggle with. Conversely, many activists use screenshots to protect their content from reprisal and censorship—since pictures are harder to search for, though artificial intelligence is making large strides in this area—and thus any automated solution to searching images might also put them in a potentially difficult situation.

As I noted in chapter 6, most platforms operate on the "report-and-takedown" legal model encouraged by U.S. and European laws: they are not responsible for user content and can be held legally responsible for taking it down only if it is reported by users.[16] In the United States especially, where most social media companies are based, this legal model protects platforms from being sued for libel or slander for content placed on them by users. It also lowers their costs because they rely on "community policing," that is, their users, who are not paid, to identify material to take down. This model puts the burden on the user, a notion that may make sense for small communities but breaks down when hundreds of millions of people or even more are using a platform.

Imagine someone like the author from Turkey facing hundreds or thousands of insults and many threats for her political speech. Is she supposed to spend her time flagging them one by one and hope that Twitter's interpretation of what constitutes a threat (in a language that is not spoken widely within the company and in a country in which the company has no offices) is the same as hers? Can Twitter distinguish between individual threats and those that are part of a targeted avalanche? Even if we assume that the company always sides with her, the problem is not solved. Twitter's remedy might be to suspend all the accounts, including the egghead ones, that have been hurling abuses at her. The pseudonymous account holders then only need to spend another five minutes setting up new accounts—something they might be motivated to do especially if they are being paid by a government, tasked to harass dissidents.

She could stop checking her mentions—people who are trying to talk to her on the platform—and try to mute (silence) or block (prevent from seeing her tweets) the abusive accounts, an arduous process. Manually blocking hundreds of horrible tweets while wondering which ones may constitute a physical threat is draining and time consuming. She can do what many others do: "post and flee" the platform, using it as an occasional broadcast mechanism without engaging with other material. Indeed, this is what she has chosen to do. She now posts less and less and avoids posting directly political content because each political post triggers a torrent of attention and abuse. In theory, Twitter provides a platform she can speak in that is not controlled by the government. In practice, she has been chased away by an orchestrated campaign.

This conundrum of large-scale harassment or attack on more open, pseudonymous platforms has caused some activist groups either to retreat to Facebook, with its stricter real-name policies (as I have examined, that model comes with its own problems), or to refuse to interact with anyone who appears to be using a pseudonym. It is not that most activists prefer Facebook's policy of forcing people to use the names they were legally born with, or that real-name norms or rules completely prevent people from organized campaigns of harassment or abuse. However, in some contexts, activists have decided it might offer a level of protection. One

Russian activist told me that members of her group would not let anyone not using his or her real name into their public groups, often hosted on Facebook. Other activist groups have resorted to using pseudonyms on platforms, simply to make the bar for harassment slightly higher. However, being public is part of the goal of most activists, which complicates this choice. Activists have told me that they do not assume that the government does not know who they are, and they share their offline identity with one another. Some have told me that even though they use pseudonyms themselves, they see those who refuse to share their identity and meet in person as suspect, and they treat them as hostile people, infiltrators, or government agents until they are proved otherwise.

Earlier, I discussed the downsides of real-name policies for activists. However, as in the above discussion, pseudonymous platforms create other threats. Pseudonymous platforms can also raise questions of credibility for dissidents since political opponents, posers, or salaried government workers can use this affordance to create accounts pretending to be activists or beleaguered dissidents and then make provocative statements or claims. These are then used by governments or opponents of social movements' views to discredit, disrupt or sow discord among the activists.

Even one troubled, unethical individual can also muddy the water for many real dissidents. In one particularly egregious case, an American graduate student, Tom MacMaster, then aged forty, decided to pretend to be a young "gay girl" in Damascus named "Amina." He had created "her" first as an online voice that he had used in many platforms, but when the Arab uprisings spread to Syria, he became more outspoken, specifically about events there—events that he knew little about.[17]

On "her" blog, "Amina" wrote heartwarming and defiant dispatches from Damascus in fluent English and became the poster child for the repression many faced in Syria. It didn't hurt that the picture "Amina" used was one of a photogenic and attractive woman (actually Jelena Lečić, a Croatian who had no idea her picture was stolen). Amina created a whole fictional universe, including a fake Facebook profile that she used to friend other activists. Amina even acquired a long-distance girlfriend (a real person) in Canada.

As the Syrian protests ramped up in the spring of 2011, Amina's blog became increasingly prominent. However, just then, MacMaster wanted to go on a vacation with his actual girlfriend and, in a breathtaking act of callousness, decided to have Amina "abducted" by the Syrian government to give him some time off from writing the blog. It seems that the same callousness and depravity that had led MacMaster to engage in the hoax in the first place also prevented him from realizing that the real people who thought the fictional Amina was a real person would care about her disappearance at the hands of a brutal regime.

Unsurprisingly, Western activists who considered themselves Amina's friends became very worried and mounted a full-scale, and very loud campaign, to find her and to save her life. After much commotion and careful sleuthing by some people, it became clear that Amina was merely a cruel hoax. Worse, the hoax now threatened real activists in Syria because it cast a shadow over all their testimonies. In an environment where the Syrian government's supporters claimed that all allegations of regime brutality were false, that all pictures of brutality were doctored, and that all victim testimonies were fake, Amina seemed proof that you couldn't trust anything.

In Tom MacMaster's case, it was uncaring vanity, and perhaps his sexual interests—pretending to be a lesbian and even acquiring an actual long-distance girlfriend in Canada who did not know "Amina" did not actually exist as she interacted with "Amina" only in writing—that led him to pretend to be a gay girl in Damascus.[18] The journalist who had first interviewed MacMaster immediately after he was outed, Irem Koker, told me that MacMaster didn't seem concerned about the intense damage he had caused actual activists (or LGBTQ people in the Middle East, who face much repression). For him, it was a game, one that was made easier by the internet's facilitation of pseudonymous identities. For supporters of the Syrian regime and governments around the world, it was a case study in how pseudonymous claims and identities could be used to cast in a negative light claims that were made online behind assumed identities or pseudonyms. A few months after MacMaster's cruel hoax captured so much attention, a *real* "gay girl blogger in Damascus," who I personally knew, was arrested by the regime. I joined the campaign to free her, which thankfully succeeded, but the shadow of such hoaxes would fall on many real cases from then on.

There are no easy solutions to problems raised in this chapter. There is no perfect, ideal platform for social movements. There is no neutrality or impartiality—ethics, norms, identities, and compromise permeate all discussions and choices of design, affordances, policies, and algorithms on online platforms. And yet given the role of these platforms in governance and expression, acknowledging and exploring these ramifications and dimensions seems more important than ever.

PART THREE

AFTER THE PROTESTS

8

Signaling Power and Signaling to Power

IN FEBRUARY 2003, I ATTENDED AN ANTIWAR march in New York, part of a massive global wave of movements opposing the looming war in Iraq. The Guinness World Records called it the largest antiwar rally in history, with protests in nearly 600 cities around the world.[1] As someone from the region, I understood the monstrosity of Saddam Hussein's brutal autocracy. But wars can break countries in even worse ways, and I worried that this haphazard rush to unleash massive military power in an already-volatile region was a recipe for further disaster.

In New York City, I walked to the end of the march, as I usually do, and climbed on top of a high point to see the entire procession. It went as far as I could see down First Avenue, spilling over to side streets and even other avenues. I estimated that at least, hundreds of thousands were there. And that day was a global day of protest; marches were held in sixty countries, with millions of participants.

I thought to myself that surely world leaders *could not* ignore such a massive, loud, global outcry and drag us into a calamitous war.

I was wrong.

Just a few days later, U.S. president George W. Bush declared that he was not "going to decide policy based upon a focus group"—in reference to the antiwar movement.[2] Just one month later, he launched the invasion. The war would last many years.

Where does the power of social movements come from? The answer may seem obvious; and people often invoke size and scale of participation: large, energetic movements succeed. History shows us that the answer is rarely that simple.

Many large and vibrant movements fail and wither away without proportional impact. The 2002–2003 antiwar movement was large, energetic, and drew heavy participation. Yet, many movements do have power—on many occasions, they change policy and history.[3]

It is easy to criticize President Bush's attitude, but the question is worth considering: What makes a protest more than a "focus group"? What claim to influence over public policy does a social movement have? Through what mechanisms does a social movement lead to change, and how do those mechanisms look to those in power? What aspects of social movements pose a threat to those in power, and when can they decide to ignore them as only unrepresentative "focus groups"?

It is rarely the case that a social movement possesses either the force or the numbers to overcome a modern state, especially a repressive one that can unleash indiscriminate violence. Very few modern social movements succeed via brute force, and most of them do not seek such direct or violent conflict, which they would not win anyway. The police and armies of modern states, equipped with highly lethal or incapacitating weapons and sophisticated capabilities for surveillance, intelligence, communication and logistics, can bring more force to bear than almost any social movement could gather.

Huge numbers of participants alone are not magic either, especially because there are always large numbers of people who are not participating in a protest as well. In 1972, despite years of massive and widespread protests against the Vietnam War, Richard Nixon was re-elected as the U.S. president in a historic landslide. Earlier, he had called for the support "silent majority" to refer to Americans who did not join the protests. It turned out that he succeeded in convincing many people to vote for him.

In 2011, I witnessed another wave of protests sweeping through many countries: the Arab uprisings. Cairo is a city of seven million people, with twenty million in its metropolitan area. A few hundred thousand people in Cairo did not force the longtime autocrat Hosni Mubarak to resign because of their numbers alone. Nor did they physically overpower the military. Indeed, two years later, the Egyptian military took over the country in a coup.

Even very big movements like those that can bring about revolutions are not large compared with the overall population. Most successful revolutions involve only a small percentage of the population. One of the largest revolutions in modern times in a major country with a substantial population occurred in Iran in 1979. Even so, only about 10 percent of the population may have taken part in protests.[4] And 10 percent is an upper limit, a statistical outlier.

If numbers and energy do not tell the whole story, how do we measure a protest's power? Why do some movements have little impact while others are potent agents for change?

Of course, one major part of the story is repression and violence: movements can be silenced by brutality and other techniques—some of the digital dimensions of this are explored in the next chapter. The role of repression in countering social movements is crucial to all discussions of movement efficacy and impact, and should never be overlooked.[5] In this chapter, however, I will focus on an underlying dynamic that operates (albeit with some differences) in environments with various levels of repression: how social movements build and *signal* capacity to those in power.

Strength of social movements lie in their *capacities*: to set the narrative, to affect electoral or institutional changes, and to disrupt the status quo. This is a complex, mutual and intertwined interaction between movements and the powerful as they strive to interpret and respond to each other's signals, and especially as the powerful try to assess the capabilities that are signaled through movement actions—and these signals, as I explore in this chapter, are more complex than indicators like headcounts or number of protests.[6]

"Capacity" as a concept comes from the field of human development. I adapt the term from Nobel Prize–winning economist Amartya Sen's "capability" approach to theories of development, as well as philosopher and legal scholar Martha Nussbaum's capability theory of justice.[7] Sen wants development scholars to focus less on easily measurable outcomes that do not necessarily reflect the "beings and doings" of humans, by which he means their opportunities to obtain education and live a healthy life, to be productive, to live well, and to do things they care about.[8] In the context of social movements, a capacity approach means evaluating the movement's collective ability to achieve social change, rather than solely measuring available benchmarks. Rather than focusing on outputs or indicators like the number of protests or the number of people who attend a protest, we should look at what a protest represents in terms of the movement's capacities in specific arenas. These capacities are often demonstrated through the protest itself: What did it take to organize the protest? What was the threat organizers faced? Was the protest a one-time gathering or a recurrent meeting of a group of people? Does the ability to hold that march also entail the ability to carry out other acts?[9] Though the protest itself provides visibility and unity, the steps required to organize the protest are a stronger signal of a group's underlying capacities.

The advantage of focusing on capacity rather than outcome is especially apparent in understanding the impact of digital technology on social movement trajectories. This is because seemingly similar outcomes and benchmarks—for example, a protest march attended by a hundred thousand people—do not necessarily signal the same underlying capacity to those in power when they are organized with the aid of digital technology as they do when they are organized without such supporting tools.

I focus on three crucial capabilities of social movements from the point of view of power: narrative capacity, disruptive capacity, and electoral and/or institutional capacity. These categories are not the only capabilities movements develop and they are especially applicable to electoral systems, the key systems of governance in much of the world in various incarnations, but they are pertinent most anywhere a government seeks legitimacy and a claim to representation. Narrative capacity refers to the ability of the movement to frame its story on its own terms, to spread its worldview.[10] We might think of this as "persuasion" as well as "legitimacy"—key ideological pillars of any social movement. Disruptive capacity describes whether a movement can interrupt the regular operations of a system of authority. Finally, electoral or institutional capacity refers to a movement's ability to keep politicians from being elected, reelected, or nominated unless they adopt and pursue policies friendly to the social movement's agenda, or the ability to force changes in institutions through both insider and outsider strategies.[11]

As the saying goes, if a tree falls in a forest and no one is around to hear it, does it make a sound? Social movements not only must get the word out that the tree has fallen, but must also spread their own explanation of why the tree fell, and what must be done about it now. These goals—getting attention and convincing people of the veracity of particular narratives— are among core acts of all movements and infuse every stage of a social movement's life.

Almost all movements—the environmental movement, the women's movement, the African American civil rights movement—must first convince people that their issues are important, and that their stance and demands are legitimate. Persuading people does not mean only targeting those outside an interest group to join the cause. Activists must also persuade people inside the movement to undertake the initial, often painstaking work of early movement formation. In the 1960s, women held "consciousness-raising" groups with other women, for example, to discuss and deepen their understanding of feminism.

Not every member of an aggrieved or affected community will automatically join or even necessarily sympathize with a movement that claims to act on his or her behalf. They may also think that the movement is too risky, or that the chances of success are too low. Before the Montgomery bus boycott in Alabama, many members of the African American community were worried that a boycott would fail and leave them worse off for having tried because, in the aftermath of a failure, they would have to deal with the wrath of the white power structure in the city. Some members of an aggrieved community may even think that a movement is not justified. Indeed, social movement initiators sometimes find that people they hope to mobilize already hold some or most parts of the worldviews of those in power. The power to dominate a society is closely related to the power to dominate what are considered accepted (or mainstream) views, and to induce people who may be suffering to accept the way things are as the correct or natural order.

Even after there is a group large enough to form the foundation from which a social movement may emerge, there is a struggle to gain acceptance within the broader society for the movement's version of the issue. Is the problem, as the feminist movement claimed, that women are not considered and treated as equal members of society? Or is it, as some claimed in reaction to feminism's emergence, that a small number of women are rejecting their proper role in society and attempting to become more like men?

Changing the minds of elites and those in law enforcement is important, too, especially in more repressive societies where movements might face severely violent reprisals. The willingness (or lack of it) of police and the army to side with the government may be decisive at crucial turning points. For example, the uprisings that swept Eastern European countries in 1989 ended peacefully in most cases after the elites simply and quickly gave in and the armed forces and police stood down—choosing not to exercise their overwhelming firepower. Such outcomes often depend on the perception of legitimacy of the protesters (in that particular case, the decisive role was that of then-Soviet Union president Mikhail Gorbachev, who signaled that he was not likely to support military intervention).

Given the importance of changing minds and attracting attention to the power of a social movement, it is unsurprising that many governments have turned to media control and censorship. Even in more democratic capitalist societies, movements that threaten the interests of corporations or advertisers can find themselves left out of news coverage, a subtler form of censorship. Also, "mainstream views" are a way in which a movement can find itself shut out if journalists do not believe that an issue is news or is worth covering, simply because they, too, have adopted the dominant framework. In response, movements often struggle for favorable media coverage, and now, thanks to digital tools, they increasingly turn to making their own media.

Narrative capacity is thus a movement's capacity to get attention and to appeal on its own terms to the broader public for redress of its grievances. Is a movement able to make many people aware of its issues? Or are its views smothered via active censorship? Do the mass media represent the movement as unimportant, trivial, or frivolous? Do ordinary people get a chance to hear the movement's version of the events or its cause? Narrative capacity is a movement's ability to articulate a voice, get its voice heard, and have it responded to as legitimate.

In countries with elections, electoral threats put significant pressure on politicians who often desire almost above all to get elected or reelected. To get votes, politicians must have access to money to finance their campaigns and to obtain favorable media coverage. Therefore, electoral threats are not just threats about the ballot box; they are factors in every stage of the electoral process. The first step to electability for a politician might be currying favor with people with deep pockets who can help finance her run. Elections are further complicated by the fact that those with money and power can also buy advertising or finance politicians' campaigns, pay for costly legal challenges that may help them, or even provide favorable coverage as owners of mass media. This category of capacity also includes the ability to impact how institutions behave; how they are formed; whether and what kind of demands they are responsive to; and how they make decisions that shape both the institution and its behavior in the world. Wielding effective electoral and/or institutional capacity by movements crucially includes—indeed requires—the ability to think strategically collectively and act tactically over sustained periods of time, since elections and institutions require long-term work to affect. This capacity thus pertains most to organizational and decision-making structures that movements do—or fail to—develop.

In many democratic societies, there has been a steady capturing of electoral politics by powerful groups that use money and control of media to elect preferred candidates and, after elections when the attention of ordinary citizens wanes, wield armies of lobbyists to make sure the politicians look after their interests. As a result, the responsiveness of electoral politics to the desires of ordinary citizens has dropped in many countries.[12] Unsurprisingly, there is a trend for people to become wary of representative democracy as a solution to social problems because they have seen it fail repeatedly. As this sentiment grows, some movements actively shun electoral politics as a political statement. This, of course, leaves those with money and power to control politicians with even more influence as many of those most interested in social change, including protesters, give up on trying to influence electoral or policy outcomes.

An example of a response to electoral threats by politicians is the differential funding of social welfare programs. In the United States, programs like Medicare, which provides health care for the elderly, are relatively generously funded while higher education, a benefit for young people, suffers from deep funding cuts. Politicians who say that they prefer funding cuts in general will rarely advocate cutting funds for the elderly. Politicians know that the elderly are very likely to vote and to punish leaders for cutting their benefits, while young people are less likely to act collectively as an interest group via social movements or formal organizations that carry electoral threats.

Social movements can also affect electoral politics by influencing politicians and even changing their minds or their reelection calculations after they are elected. This influence can be seen as part of both narrative and electoral capacity since these capacities are not mutually exclusive, although there are sometimes tensions between them.

Protest movements may also develop electoral capacity as the movement evolves, and some even turn into political parties. In Europe, political parties on both the left and the right have emerged from social movements and have captured large chunks of the vote in many countries. In Greece, a movement-formed party named Syriza became the lead party forming the government in 2015, and in Spain, a movement-born party called Podemos has quickly become one of the biggest political parties in the country. The reason people can shift so quickly to these new parties is also connected to the distrust that makes people turn to movements: an alternative party can gather support more easily when there is little loyalty to existing political parties that are seen as ineffective or captured by the powerful.

Electoral capacity thus refers to a movement's ability to credibly threaten politicians and policy makers with unsuccessful electoral outcomes, whether by preventing them from becoming candidates through primary challenges, causing them to lose elections, making reelection less likely or impossible, or even engaging in recall campaigns. Electoral capacity often implies numbers of voters who are mobilized and ready to act electorally by contributing money or effort to campaigns and by voting. In some cases, movements can threaten politicians by threatening to stay home and withdraw support.

Movements signal electoral capacity to those in power in multiple ways, not just through elections—a protest for example may credibly signal an electoral or institutional threat. A movement can also force or nudge institutions to behave in ways aligned with its goals—convincing leaders or bureaucrats, threatening them with replacement, or even joining them and fighting for change from the inside. Like others, electoral/institutional capacity is measured in more than raw numbers or any simple indicators as factors such as the ability to maneuver strategically and shift tactically greatly influence if, when, and how these movements can enact social change.

Protests may signal disruptive capacity when they interrupt business as usual. This interruption may take the form of a momentary intervention (a Black Lives Matter group briefly shutting down a highway in St. Louis) or a prolonged disruption, such as an occupation (protesters taking over centrally located Tahrir Square in Cairo, Egypt). Sometimes, disruption of business is done through boycotts or refusal to cooperate, like the yearlong civil rights bus boycott in Montgomery, Alabama, in which African Americans refused to ride the buses that were imposing segregation and mistreating black riders.

Disruption, whether by civil disobedience or occupation or some other form of direct action, is a complex strategy for movements. Successful use of the tactic requires a delicate balance among challenging authority, bearing the costs of challenging authority, and making a case for the legitimacy of the protest. Although disruption sounds as though it is generally a flash in the pan, disruptive acts sometimes continue for years, if not decades. In the early twentieth century, the leader of the Indian independence movement, Mahatma Gandhi, led the country in a multiyear strategy of noncooperation with the British Empire. During the Montgomery bus boycott, thousands of people had to find a way to get to work for a whole year without using the bus.

Many forms of disruption are carried out to gather attention taking a stance, and to make a symbolic statement. On June 17, 2015, a young man opened fire on a prayer group in an African American church in South Carolina, killing nine people. The openly racist killer had posed in photographs alongside the Confederate battle flag, a U.S. Civil War banner. In the aftermath of the attack at the church, the display of the Confederate flag became the subject of much public discussion across the United States. Some see it as a symbol of Southern identity and heritage, but to many it represents racism and the history of slavery. At the time, state law mandated the flying of the Confederate flag on the grounds of the South Carolina statehouse. The presence of the flag over the state capitol underwent renewed scrutiny, and many people expressed their desire that it be taken down.

While the debate about changing the law dragged on in the South Carolina state legislature, Bree Newsome, an African American activist and filmmaker, decided to act. Newsome strapped on rock-climbing gear and scaled the flagpole at the statehouse in the early morning hours of June 27. As she brought down the contested flag, two police officers were waiting for her. "I'm prepared to be arrested," she told them. A videographer recorded her climb while another team member, a young white man, stood guard underneath the pole as she climbed. They were both arrested, but powerful images of her snatching the Confederate flag from the pole immediately went viral online and were covered prominently by many national news outlets. The many who viewed Newsome's memorable act of disruption, saw powerful symbolism, and she propelled the issue to the front of the political agenda in the nation. A few days later, the legislature voted to change the law and permanently take down the Confederate flag.

Disruptive tactics, though, do not always receive positive media coverage, and they risk angering people if the disruption is perceived as illegitimate, counterproductive, needlessly burdensome or violent. They also run the risk of overexposure because the tactics themselves attract much media attention which may eclipse substantive issues the movement wants to discuss. In many anti–corporate globalization protests, for example, a lot of mass media coverage focused on the very few (and quite marginal within the protest itself) people who threw rocks at stores or burned trash cans—rather than the substantive complaints of millions of people who participated in marches and rallies. These tactics also draw people who may be more interested in acquiring attention for themselves than in addressing the issues, endangering the goals of the movement or risking conflict with other movement participants.

In short, disruptive capacity is a movement's ability to interrupt business as usual with the aim of getting attention, making a point, or making it untenable for those in power to continue as in the past, and to sustain such disruption over time. Disruptive capacity is powerful but also carries the highest risk of backlash. Disruptive capacity, properly interpreted, also includes the ability to bear the costs of either the backlash or the consequences that are doled out by the authorities—abilities which are also indicative of the underlying capacity.

Those in power try to assess a protest's capacity to change the narrative, to alter electoral outcomes, and to disrupt the usual order of business by trying to assess the honesty, cost, and depth of a movement's capacity. Obviously, taking the word of movement leaders will not work. Instead, what happens is a delicate, communicative dance of signaling and interpretation among movements, their participants, broader publics, politicians, and the authorities.

Signaling theory in biology and the social sciences examines how parties to an interaction try to communicate their potential and their intentions to other parties in order to create a favorable outcome for themselves.[13] Signals, which may be rooted in true capacity or be exaggerated bluffs, are direct or indirect signs that indicate what a person (or a movement) is capable of doing and is likely to do. Signaling theory is applicable to many situations in the social world, especially adversarial situations where the parties do not have perfect information about each other. The relationships between social movements and those in power are analogous to these situations.[14]

Signals can be costly or cheap to broadcast, and they can be honest or misleading. For example, many poisonous animals have bright colors to signal to would-be predators that eating them would be deadly. Predator animals have learned to heed such warnings. However, other types of prey will adopt these same colors in an attempt to mimic the appearance of more dangerous animals; their signals are deceptive. The California mountain king snake sports the same ominous-looking red, white, and black bands as the poisonous coral snake. The former is mostly harmless, while the latter is deadly. The king snake thus benefits from faking a signal of danger. Of course, if a predator adapts and learns to distinguish between the true signal of the coral snake and the false one of the king snake, the king snake is now worse off because its conspicuous colors do not allow it to blend into the environment. Instead of signaling danger, it signals lunch.

Costly signals are often more effective, evolutionarily speaking, since animals may have an interest in producing fake signals, signals that are costly and thus harder to fake are more reliable indicators of threat. Deer antlers are a good example. It takes a healthy buck to generate the energy necessary to build and wield big antlers. A healthy deer will also be a more ferocious fighter, assisted by those antlers. Hence a deer can size up an opponent's antlers and figure out whether the odds are in its favor. If a weaker deer chooses to retreat, that is a win for the stronger deer and also a chance for the weaker deer to avoid injury or death.

Another example of a costly signal is gazelle stotting: sometimes while grazing, the animal, seemingly out of the blue, jumps very high in place, lifting all four feet. This action is puzzling because it makes the gazelle visible to predators. But such jumping is also an impressive display of athletic ability and signals an ability to run fast. Stotting is therefore an honest signal, and a predator like a lion is better off chasing a less fit animal rather than one impressively stotting. If a gazelle has the muscles to jump very high, it can also probably run quite fast. But stotting is also a costly signal: the muscles required to jump take much energy to build. If a smart deer could figure out how to attach springs to its hooves and jump very high without having to be so strong and healthy (or jump on a trampoline!), it would have a great advantage through a cheap and deceptive signal.

Finally, some interactions between adversaries are what social scientists call "cheap talk," "costless, nonbinding, nonverifiable messages" that may nonetheless affect the other party's beliefs.[15] The point of cheap talk is exactly what it appears to be: it is cheap to make the noise, and it is up to the recipient to try to figure out what is behind the noise. You don't need to develop a lot of capacity to be able to just talk about having it. To apply this idea to social movements, consider the difference between a movement declaring "We will make sure nobody who opposes our platform wins an election" and a movement holding large protest rallies in hundreds of districts of vulnerable politicians. The declaration is not necessarily without effect: if it were true, it would cause problems for legislators. Thus targeted politicians must assess the credibility of the threat. The rallies, though, are a direct indicator of capacity because they are targeted, local, and involve people power. They show that voters in the appropriate district are committed enough to show up for a protest. "Cheap talk" can generate interest and worry for the powers that be, but costly signals are more likely to be taken seriously.[16]

Signaling to compete or to coordinate in social interactions is common in human relationships. As individuals, we frequently must judge the potential outcome of an interaction on the basis of our best reading of the situation. Is someone likely to accept an invitation to a party or a date? Is proposing collaboration a good idea? Should we confront a liar? We also try to signal our intentions and our capabilities. Dressing up for an interview signals being eager for the job; education and diplomas, we hope, signal our capabilities to potential employers.[17]

Signals are also not limited to aggressive situations. The sociologist Thorstein Veblen's theory of "conspicuous consumption"—the idea that we buy expensive items just to show them off, not to use them—is a form of signaling theory.[18] In class, I sometimes ask my college students whether, instead of expensive diamond engagement rings, they would be satisfied with chemically identical lab diamonds that possess every quality of diamonds (they are not fake diamonds, just ones created in labs that might have fewer flaws than mined ones), or whether they would consider keeping the money as a couple to use as a down payment for their first house. Many hesitate. The costly signal of buying an otherwise useless diamond is an indicator of dedication: the goal is not the diamond but the signal that spending huge amounts of money "just because" sends–a message that has been culturally reinforced through ads and other mechanisms. Understanding interaction as signaling and status-building is applicable to many situations. For example, Alice Marwick examines how technologists and entrepreneurs signaled status and built brands in the technology industry after the dot-com boom and Judith Donath has long examined how identity, deception and signals work online.[19]

What distinguished a few thousand people gathered in Tahrir Square on January 25, 2011, from the hundreds of people who were almost always present anyway? And was the difference between the 150 people who were protesting the police on January 25, 2010, and the few thousand who showed up on January 25, 2011, just a question of a few thousand—a small number in a city of seven million?

The few thousand who showed up in January 2011 represented a drastically different level of capacity than the few hundred who had shown up one year earlier, even though the initial numbers were not greatly different—an extra few thousand people is not a huge difference in a country the size of Egypt. Unlike past years, however, the protesters in 2011 had organized through a Facebook page that reached millions of Egyptians. Hundreds of thousands of people replied "yes" to this Facebook page's electronic invitation to the revolution, publicly signaling broader discontent. The context was important, too: neighboring Tunisia had just experienced a revolution that had caused all eyes to turn to the region, and this meant new global attention for Egypt, too. This changed the legitimacy and momentum of the protests. The few hundred from the previous year had not had millions of people online openly backing them. The few thousand in 2011 were able to set off a chain of events that those in power were inclined to interpret as signaling real capacity that required an effective response.

These activists were social media pioneers; they had been blogging, tweeting, and organizing via the internet for years and knew how to get a story out. Hence, once the protest caught on even a little bit, they knew that they possessed significant narrative capacity to reach broad audiences globally to tell their story. Once the protest grew, the movement also represented disruptive capacity because its members now held one of the most important squares in Cairo, making it difficult for the government to keep the city operating smoothly. Narrative capacity plus disruptive capacity made a powerful combination.

The mostly secular, liberal youth of Tahrir who captured the imagination of Egypt and the world with their brave stance and their youthful, bright outlook had come together using communication and digital technologies as a form of organization. But the online skills that had greatly enhanced their narrative capacity did not do the same for their electoral capacity. The movement lacked electoral capacity both because of the way it emerged (rapidly, using digital technologies) and because of its political culture, which distrusted elections and representations.

Looking at social movements through the lens of signaling capacities also helps resolve some mistaken comparisons, for example, between street protests and online protests. Many pundits (and sometimes activists themselves) believe that street protests are more real and more effective in bringing about social change than online protests. Aside from the fact that many street protests come with an online component (although some protests are indeed online only and have no presence in the streets), this approach is not a useful way to determine the true threat a protest poses to those in power. Depending on which capacities are signaled, and the cost and honesty of those signals, an online protest may well be potent. For example, in China, a country with widespread access to technology but tightly controlled internet platforms, a street protest may pose little danger to the regime unless news of it spreads widely online. Tweeting (or using Weibo, the Chinese version of Twitter) about a protest is almost certainly a bigger threat to the authorities in China than a street protest of a few hundred or even thousands of people if news about the protest can be suppressed and remain local. Bravery itself is a signal: that people are willing to take so much risk to oppose a regime, but it is not a surefire path to success.

Whether an act is online or offline often has no simple relationship to whether it is a costly or even an honest signal. The defiant tweeting of Chinese dissident Ai Wei Wei was no doubt costlier as a signal, in terms of risk and consequences, than many of the antiwar marches I attended in person in the United States. Although the physical act of typing is much easier than walking, understanding the true costs of the act requires examining the political context rather than looking only at the act itself.

Digital tools have greatly affected movements by strengthening, altering, or even weakening some of their capacities. Digital tools are powerful, but they are not only enhancers of capacity; they also affect movement choices and readiness, and lead to a variety of outcomes, especially when they are coupled with the cultural and political choices of social movements. And some movement outputs that look like increases in capacity mask weaknesses that have been introduced. The impact of digital technology is best understood through case studies found later in this chapter that examine the broader affordances of digital technologies in the context of a specific movement.

If there is a broad claim to be made about digital technologies and social movements, it is that these tools often greatly enhance narrative capacity— but they do not just do that. The ability to get attention and frame issues used to be controlled mostly by the mass media and their gatekeepers. Unsurprisingly, many activists spent a great deal of energy trying to acquire mass-media attention and to influence coverage to become more sympathetic to the movement. Many movements developed formal organizations to better respond to requests from the news media, learned how to write press releases, and hired experts with credentials who were more acceptable than the activists. Others staged spectacular events to attract attention. However, all these strategies involve costs and complications.

The sociologist Todd Gitlin documents how the news media's tendency to choose the most flamboyant members of a movement as spokespersons had deleterious effects on the 1960s antiwar movement.[20] A movement that was about a gravely serious issue, war, was reduced to sound bites from flag burners who were handed the microphone by national media seeking to sensationalize and trivialize their concerns. As the news media flocked to political stunts, a cycle was created in which attention-seeking individuals developed more stunts as a strategy to keep attention on themselves.

The problem is not the stunts per se, but rather a movement's strategic ability to manage them, and to channel them into, and in conjunction with other capacities. ACT UP, an organization dedicated to bringing attention to the AIDS crisis, skillfully used spectacular stunts aimed at generating media attention, such as dumping red paint symbolizing blood on presidential candidates and other prominent officials.[21] Receiving attention was a major step forward for ACT UP since its members' plight had previously been largely ignored, but it was not the last step. It was able to deploy institutional and electoral pressures as well, forcing a reorganization of the way medicine is tested and brought to market in the United States by targeting the Food and Drug Administration and the Centers for Disease Control. ACT UP also helped change U.S. policy on generic drug enforcement through the WTO. Its stunts had been tactical moves to get attention, but it followed the attention with more pressure, including lobbying of politicians and government agency officials—without letting go of the possibility of future disruptions. ACT UP represented a true hybrid of narrative capacity and disruption. However, not all movements can navigate this so successfully.

Often, stunts do help get attention but may interfere with the movement's control of the narrative that results. William Gamson and Gadi Wolfsfeld state this dilemma succinctly: "Those who dress up in costume to be admitted to the media's party will not be allowed to change before being photographed."[22] For example, we can question if the media's tendency to trivialize the antiwar movement and focus on its extremes and stunts, documented by Gitlin, contributed to the defeat of antiwar movement candidates in 1972 elections.

The other strategy, forming NGOs that are more palatable to the news media and the public and playing as nicely as possible by media rules, requires large amounts of resources and cultural capital. This strategy is therefore more open to be used by wealthier movements and more privileged people within a movement, at the expense of poorer movements or segments within a movement. The dynamic that emerges from this strategy often puts a strain on the connection between movement grassroots activists and those whom the mass media see as their spokespeople, which tend to come from a different strata. In their 1971 book *Regulating the Poor,* Frances Fox Piven and Richard A. Cloward argue that such mainstream-style organizations mostly served to submerge the radical nature and dynamism that existed in grassroots movements, and that they ended up with few gains.[23]

Digital media have altered all these dynamics and have introduced their own complications. Movements no longer need institutional presence to get their narrative out broadly. For example, consider the evolution of the #BlackLivesMatter protests in the United States, focusing on police killings of black people, especially in poorer communities. #BlackLivesMatter has emerged primarily through a national network that uses social media both to organize and communicate and as a tool for gathering attention and shaping narratives. The network has been able to overcome challenges and to develop narrative capacity without tools that older movements used, such as formal organizations and recognized spokespersons or leaders.

According to NAACP statistics, the rate of killings by police has not gone up drastically in the past decade (or even when it is compared with earlier years). However, there has been a great shift in the amount of attention paid to these killings, thanks to a movement that was fueled by digital technologies, now often called Black Lives Matter in reference to the hashtag that the movement rallied around.[24] Until Black Lives Matter came on the scene, formal organizations like the NAACP had not been able to make the topic part of the national conversation. Instead, most mainstream politicians endorsed "tough on crime" policies, often involving heavy mandatory sentences applied in the absence of judicial discretion, without any discussion of police accountability (or of the fact that crime rates have been falling for a long time).

The movement was sparked after the killing of Trayvon Martin, a teenager on his way home from a store in his neighborhood after he had purchased some candy in February 2012. Martin was followed and attacked by a self-appointed neighborhood-watch vigilante who shot the unarmed teenager dead in the ensuing scuffle. At first, the killer was not even charged with a crime. This created discontent that grew rapidly online. The news and outrage traveled on social media, and I first learned about it there, weeks before there was any mass-media attention. After weeks of persistent campaigning online, which included haranguing journalists on social media about the case, hashtags about the killing were trending nationally on Twitter, and national news media coverage followed. Faced with growing pressure, the state of Florida finally initiated a trial. Although the killer was acquitted (there was no video of the incident, and the only person alive to tell the story was the killer), the social networks that carried on this conversation continued to keep talking to one another and to grow.

Two years later, in August 2014, another black teenager, Michael Brown, was killed by a police officer under murky circumstances in Ferguson, Missouri (see my examination in chapter 6 of how Facebook's algorithm treated this incident, and other details). Some witnesses claimed that his hands were up in the air when he was shot.[25] There was no video of the incident. His body was left in the middle of the street in the hot August sun for many hours. A Justice Department report later revealed the root causes of the tensions between the city's almost all-white police force and its almost all-black residents: the city governance and budget were based on fining the minority residents for every minor infraction. Fines were compounded when people did not or could not pay the initial charge, and people were arrested and jailed to compel payment. More than 60 percent of Ferguson residents had arrest warrants in their names, many because of unpaid fines that had incurred extra interest. Jail time for failure to pay fines led to job loss and more poverty. This miserable cycle of fines, arrests, and tensions continued in this city where the majority of residents were African American, while the city's council and police force were almost all white.[26]

Immediately after Michael Brown's killing, upset, grieving Ferguson residents gathered near the street where the teenager had been shot. The next day, they held a protest. National reporters arrived on the scene partly because a few were already in the state due to tornadoes expected in the region; there was no big, national media story yet. However, armored vehicles with snipers on top of them, holding rifles aimed at the residents, were also on the scene. Journalists who witnessed the events told me that at that point people were merely peacefully protesting; there were many children among them, and there was no visible reason for massing armored vehicles and rifles in the streets. No items had been thrown, and no buildings had been set on fire; these events would happen later.

Journalists and residents started tweeting images showing the massive police force that had been arrayed against the protesters. The photographs of the scene struck a nerve. People around the country started tweeting, many voicing outrage about overpolicing of the protest. On the streets of Ferguson, the police kept pressuring the residents and even journalists. Two journalists were filmed being arrested for just sitting at a McDonald's. At this point, there were few media reports about Ferguson on national television. Yet the conversation on Twitter became very loud—even my friends in Egypt who were awake were tweeting about Ferguson and the fact that journalists seemed to disappear even in the United States. Later analysis would show about three million tweets related to #Ferguson were sent before TV stations started covering the events.

Ferguson was a turning point for what would later be called the Black Lives Matter movement. The social media conversations over the past two years had drawn the attention of more and more people to the issue, and after Michael Brown's killing, some of them got into cars or buses and went to Ferguson. Like many activists I have known or interviewed over the years, meeting other activists and facing tear gas and rubber bullets for protesting stirred them even further. Offline personal connections and collective protest experience strengthened their resolve, and a movement was fully launched.

The Ferguson events propelled the topic to national attention. Some newspapers started counting the number of people who had been killed by the police nationally each year. In the first six months of 2015, the press uncovered more killings than the federal government's slapdash reporting had claimed took place in all of 2014, and it would later find the total for the year to be above one thousand. That year ordinary people filmed encounters with the police and posted more shocking videos, including one in which a police officer shot a fleeing, unarmed black suspect in the back and then proceeded to plant evidence on him. In many instances, official police reports were found to be lies after video evidence emerged. The unusual amount of publicity these killings received contributed to the generation of even more protests and often to mass-media coverage. An incident in Baltimore in which a black young man, Freddie Gray, was chased by the police, placed hurt but alive in a police van, and later taken out dead after having been denied medical care he requested led to days of unrest in the city and charges for police officers.

Through the emergence of the Black Lives Matter movement, the political scene started changing as well. In a reversal of the several-decade trend of "tough on crime" electoral strategies, politicians felt pressure to discuss reforms of the criminal justice system and the differential manner of policing applied to communities of color. Municipalities started requiring police officers to wear body cameras. The Justice Department opened inquiries into some of these killings. Democratic presidential candidates unveiled packages of criminal justice reforms. And polls, too, began shifting. One poll showed a striking twenty-one-point jump in the number of young people—most of whom were more heavily engaged in social media than their elders—who thought that police were unfair to black people in the year after the death of

Travyon Martin (from 42 percent to 63 percent).[27] A 2015 poll showed that al-most half of all Americans now thought that racism was a problem, com-pared with about 28 percent three years before that.[28] Such big jumps in opinions are rare, and the fact that the shift was mostly confined to young people (under age twenty-nine) as the issue gathered so much attention first on social media strongly suggests at least a partial cause of this change.

Black Lives Matter has exhibited great narrative capacity, and like the Oc-cupy movement's success in highlighting inequality, it has changed the public conversation. The Black Lives Matter movement is young, and how it will develop further capacities remains to be seen. Crucially, social media allowed the movement to take local events, like a police killing in Fergu-son, and make them nationally salient. Salience and attention complement each other, and social media, especially with its capacity to document events and to live-stream protests and other important moments, allows move-ments to make the connections of salience among local, national, and even international events.

Different types of movement capacity need not grow at the same rate or in tandem. Thus, it's not that the widespread argument that digital technol-ogy empowers movements in *many ways* is wrong; it's just that this is not a uniform effect on all movement capabilities.[29] At times, the way the inter-net affects movement capabilities may even be at odds with one another. In June 2011, the Canadian anticonsumerist magazine *Adbusters* sent an e-mail to its ninety thousand subscribers: "America needs its own Tahrir." The two people behind this initiative, Kalle Lasn and Micah White, had known each other for a while but had not seen each other in person for more than four years.[30] It took just a few months from that initial e-mail for a global movement to be founded. However, the political culture that characterized the movement had been in the making for decades. Both the speed of that movement, as it went from zero to global in almost a heartbeat, and the steady and slow accumulation of its political influences, which had ante-cedents in movements from the twentieth century, would shape the ca-pacities that Occupy would and would not develop.

The Occupy movement had both strengths and weaknesses that were sur-prising. The movement quickly influenced the conversation (narrative ca-pacity) in ways that were unusual for such a young movement, but it had little or no direct electoral or disruptive capacity (outside of a few minor incidents) in the immediate aftermath. To understand this decoupling of capacities or their time frames, we need to look at Occupy's political culture, as well as the technology used by Occupy activists, and understand how these are intertwined.

Occupy as a movement was inspired, both spiritually and methodologically, by the uprisings in the Middle East, especially in Egypt, where activists occupied Tahrir Square in Cairo for weeks and forced their aging autocrat to resign. Tahrir's young rebels captured the world's attention with their deft use of social media. But perhaps no group was more transfixed by the ground-level view of a revolution in the making than their fellow activists. There were other antecedent movements in Western nations as well: the 2011 occupation of the Wisconsin capitol by students and union workers who objected to collective bargaining being made illegal, and southern Europe's "indignados" who had staged many occupations in multiple countries and had rocked Spain, Italy, and Greece. There are great differences in the material realities of a nation like the United States and one like Egypt, but there was a common thread among activists: a sense of challenging the powers that be whose rule had become increasingly unchecked by balancing forces. In Egypt, this meant the undemocratic regime. In the United States, it made sense to confront another kind of power: that of the super-rich. Activists wanted to see whether inequality and skewed accumulation of wealth could be challenged at their global headquarters, Wall Street.

The call to gather in New York led to a movement that would sweep the world, resulting in protests in eighty countries and almost a thousand cities and involving millions of people. But first, the movement had to be heard and not be ridiculed. This was not easy and might never have happened without the power of social media to balance the ridicule or silence of traditional gatekeepers, especially in the mass media.

The initial encampment took place in Zuccotti Park, New York, a small park near Wall Street. The location was partially coincidence: police had blocked One Chase Manhattan Plaza, the protesters' first choice and a more logical target right across from Chase Bank headquarters. But Zuccotti Park made sense from a legal standpoint because although it was technically open to the public, it was privately owned, which meant that the police were more limited in the rules they could enforce there. About a thousand

people showed up for Occupy Wall Street's first assembly, a gathering emphasizing consensus, meaning that anyone could speak, and one person could
block an idea or an action of the entire group. That night, September 17,
2011, perhaps hundreds of people settled into tents in the park.

Over the next few weeks, the number of people grew, and support poured
in from ordinary people, trade unions, well-known artists, and even pundits. On September 27, over seven hundred pilots from Continental and
United, members of the Airline Pilots Association (union), marched to
Wall Street, wearing their pilot uniforms. Postal workers joined one of the
marches held by the Occupiers. The filmmaker Michael Moore appeared
and addressed the occupation. Almost every day brought new messages of
support and solidarity and news of other occupations popping up around
the country.

Here was a popular protest, an emergent movement that addressed one
of the most important fault lines developing in Western nations, the one
between the super-rich and the rest of the population. It had a catchy slogan, "We are the 99 percent," explicitly pitting the protesters against the
richest 1 percent. The occupation was located at the heart of a media-rich
environment. It should have been major news. But it was not.

If it had not been for social media, where the occupation flourished as a
topic through hastily set-up Facebook pages and Twitter accounts that
shared news, pictures, videos from the protests, and even live-streaming of
its general assemblies, the movement might have hit a wall because of lack
of attention. Obscurity is among the biggest obstacles to movement success. It has smothered many others that were similarly promising but
withered away because of participants' frustration about the impossibility
of getting attention.

The *New York Times* did not cover these protests for the first eight days.
When Occupy finally made it into the paper, the movement was framed by
a headline as confused. The first article, titled "Gunning for Wall Street,
with Faulty Aim," appeared only in the metro pages and described protesters
as clueless—the title said it all. The piece ended with a quote from a stock-
broker ridiculing the protesters for using Apple computers to organize.

A search in Lexis, a news database, for the phrase "Occupy Wall Street"
during the first weeks brings up more international articles about the
movement than articles from the U.S. news. Mass-media outlets from

Australia to Pakistan found the movement more newsworthy than American ones. The *New York Times'* other major story about the protest was titled "Wall Street Occupiers, Protesting till Whenever," also a mocking title that was uncharacteristic of the tone of most *Times* headlines. The article this time gave more voice to the protesters, but there was still little coverage of the issue they were protesting: inequality.

Many movements face this dilemma: the mass media provide them with attention only when there is a confrontation or violence, or when conflict with the police is involved. Occupy was no exception; traditional press coverage spiked only after a pepper-spraying of kettled protesters caught on video ("kettling" is the practice of surrounding and cornering protesters with barricades or tape so they cannot move), followed by mass arrests on the Brooklyn Bridge. Such conflict-driven narratives, however visually striking, tend to drown out coverage of substantive issues. A database search for major newspaper coverage of Occupy Wall Street's first two weeks returns about twice as many mentions of "pepper spray" as of "inequality." The word "police" shows up almost three times more often than "inequality."

Some of the protesters in Occupy were veterans of protests in the previous decade and had lived through this cycle before. The most seasoned protesters (some of whom I knew, and some of whom I met later) had been involved in the antiglobalization protests, although most protesters would use the term "anti–corporate globalization." Many were avid travelers, immigrants, or migrants, not opposed to the knitting together of a global society, but pitted against corporations that were taking advantage of globalization to create a race to the bottom among workers around the world. Workers were mostly not allowed to travel freely while capital hopped from jurisdiction to jurisdiction at will. That was corporate globalization.

This movement came to broader attention through a large-scale disruption in 1999 of the World Trade Organization meeting in Seattle. That year, tens of thousands of people organized to demand accountability from global institutions that were used to meeting behind closed doors. Back then, the internet was beginning to emerge as a tool for movements, and it was already playing a major role for coordination among the activists who were early adopters of these technologies.

The disruption of the WTO meeting in Seattle in 1999 stimulated important conversations about globalization, inequality, and governance of global institutions. More protests followed at the global summits of similarly opaque institutions, such as the International Monetary Fund.

However, the members of a small group among the protesters who called themselves the "Black bloc" used these protests to carry out acts that were both destructive and politically futile, like breaking windows of local businesses after protest marches, including businesses of minorities, immigrants, and whomever they happen to run into in random, and wanton acts of violence. These people, who were accountable to nobody but themselves, who hid their faces behind black balaclavas, and set fires in trash cans, were catnip for the press—a few dozen could generate more press coverage than hundreds of thousands who had marched peacefully, if forcefully. Such violence also threatened the other people in the movement, especially people from vulnerable groups, who would suddenly find themselves between these young (almost all) men setting fire to random objects and provoking the police as hard as they can, and the police who reacted with force. Some activists suspected that this group might have been infiltrated by deliberate provocateurs who wanted the movement to fail—the negative coverage a few anonymous people breaking random windows could generate would scare many more ordinary people who, understandably, did not want to associate with such a group. There was no definite proof, but the broader movement did not develop an effective strategy to deal with (and somehow stop them from carrying out these acts, which were deeply unpopular in and out of the movement) this small group that managed to hijack much attention and make it very negative.

As the twenty-first century progressed, I watched—and many scholars systematically documented—how media coverage shifted to focusing on these tiny groups within the larger protests and further smothered substantive discussions of the topics.[31] The terrorist attacks on September 11, 2001, changed the topic and the mood of the nation even more. The movement trailed off, with few protests or other visible organized activity, until the Occupy Wall Street protests in the next decade.

The smarmy tone of early news coverage of Occupy—"protesting with faulty aim," "till whenever"—signaled the possibility of a similar trajectory, in which the mass media would frame the movement as frivolous, or fringe events would drown out substantial and grave issues. However, this time, there was a significant difference: social media were on the scene, and their use went far beyond the circles of early adopters. Occupy flourished in online space. In the first month of the movement, researchers identified almost four hundred public Facebook pages dedicated to it, and hundreds of thousands of people participated in those pages.[32]

Countering the dismissive depictions in the traditional media and rejecting both disruption and freak frames to tell their story, movement participants created spaces to discuss their issues, featuring inequality and the accumulation of wealth by the super-rich as substantive topics. As people in more and more cities joined the movement by creating their own encampments, the audience for the conversation grew despite the initial reluctance by mass-media gatekeepers to portray the movement's issues as serious. The activists were able to craft their own narrative and to resist being trivialized. Eventually, their framing was picked up by sympathetic journalists; for example, Nicholas Kristof of the *New York Times* wrote a column urging people not to dismiss them, highlighting their framing of inequality.[33] The protesters had struck a chord: growing inequality and stagnant wages, on the one hand, and the growing, almost unbridled wealth of a few, on the other hand. They had a pithy slogan: the 99 percent against the 1 percent. They had a cause and a megaphone: themselves. The movement exhibited prowess in gathering publicity and attention to its cause.[34]

However, despite its impressive ability to change the conversation, Occupy had little or no direct electoral impact in the immediate aftermath. There were no primary challengers to congressional leaders who had opposed (or had not facilitated) policies that might dampen inequality. Almost no seats were lost because of protester demands. None of the conversation that the movement sparked on how to tax the rich—a tax on financial transactions, restoring tax rates to pre-Reagan-era levels, closing corporate tax loopholes, going after offshore tax havens—led to substantive policy changes in the next four years. As of 2016, inequality had only gotten worse (in the United States, at least), and even basic provisions like food stamps were being cut.[35]

Occupy's impressive narrative capacity was not matched by electoral or institutional capacity partly because of emergent conditions of the movement and partly because of the cumulative choices of its participants. Occupy had scaled up quickly, leveraging the affordances of digital technologies to overcome mass-media indifference, local government hostility, and police pressure. Thanks to twenty-first-century technologies, such rapid scaling up can happen without organizational infrastructure, whether formal or informal. With little organizational structure, though, the movement could not easily undertake large-scale efforts beyond the occupation, its original step. It had no effective means to make decisions to do anything else, or any strategic capacity for shifting tactics.[36] It did not signal an electoral, institutional, or disruptive threat to power.

Occupy members were often under strong pressure from the police, and after the occupation of the park was forcibly dispersed, it was unable to undertake a tactical shift and try something else because it had no decision-making mechanism to help it face this inevitable turn. Social movements regularly face police pressure and even severer types of repression, and their ability to shift their protest tactics is often a key determinant of whether they can survive in the long term. Although the amount of repression that Occupy participants experienced was substantial, it was still far less than what many other movements, for example, the civil rights movement, underwent for many decades. Occupy had come into being very quickly and had grown large very rapidly without any experience in weathering such pressure. Additionally, many of its more outspoken and dominant voices were politically against the idea of creating such mechanisms. Although many Occupy participants who were seasoned activists tried to develop decision-making structures and continue the movement after the occupation of the park was dispersed, they were unable to carry the day. It is much easier for a few loud voices to paralyze digitally scaled-up movements that emphasize horizontalism and prize "consensus" than it is to move them forward through tactical shifts.

About a year later, Occupy partially resurrected itself as an aid group during the aftermath of Hurricane Sandy, which devastated parts of New York. The work Occupy Sandy chose to undertake fit the sensibilities of the movement: mutual aid, solidarity and direct participation rather than representation, and a refusal to engage with bigger power structures except through distrust. There were a few other attempts that grew out of Occupy, like a debt collective that undertook creative acts to bring together student or medical debtors to "strike" against unjust debt. These, however, remained relatively small compared to Occupy's original reach.[37]

Occupy's most direct engagement with the electoral sphere would come many years later, in 2016, after Bernie Sanders, an independent Senator from Vermont, would launch a seemingly-quixotic challenge for the presidential nomination of the Democratic Party. His bid was not successful, but it re-mobilized many people who had been part of the Occupy movement earlier, showing the fact that the underlying energy and the legitimacy of the demands had been there, though not matched by proportional electoral or institutional capacity in the 2011 incarnation.

It is unclear what would have happened if Occupy had tried to engage earlier and more directly in forcing changes in policy making. If Occupy had tried to engage in electoral or institutional politics in the period after 2011, it might have looked at representatives of another movement with effective political representation: the Tea Party.[38]

The Tea Party movement has been less studied and less visually spectacular than Occupy, but it has arguably had greater impact on policy in the United States. There are, of course, major differences between the two movements politically: not least that one comes from the right, the other from the left. However, much like other right-wing movements elsewhere (notably in Europe), the Tea Party movement in the United States focused on developing electoral capacity almost above everything else and used both online tools and street protests to gather capacity for that end. Its evolution offers interesting lessons about how participant sensibility intertwines with technological affordances to create different trajectories in turning digital technologies into political capacities.

Like many other movements in the twenty-first century, the Tea Party movement owes its beginning to a viral event, albeit one that began on cable television rather than via e-mail, like Occupy. On February 19, 2009, Rick Santelli, a commentator on CNBC, a cable channel devoted to business and stock news, went on a rant from the floor of the Chicago stock exchange about the "moral hazard" of providing government assistance to people who were behind in their mortgages. Santelli said that he wanted to organize a "Chicago Tea Party"—a reference to early protests against British taxation of colonists before the American Revolution. His lamentations went viral, and a protest was organized, mostly online, for April 15, 2009, also known as "tax day" in the United States, the day by which citizens are required to file their annual income tax forms.

More than half a million people nationwide—perhaps as many as eight hundred thousand individuals in more than five hundred rallies—attended these protests. As discussed earlier, protests serve many functions, and one of them is to demonstrate to others that a belief is widely held and to break "pluralistic ignorance"—the notion that a private belief is held in isolation rather than shared by many others. However, protests are also crucial spaces for protesters to meet one another and to create community. This is especially significant in the age of online tools since holding large protest events no longer requires a tedious and painstaking organizational effort. Like its counterparts across the political spectrum, the 2009 tax protests had little organizational infrastructure: they came mere months after the initial inspiration. However, like most protests, once they were held, they had impacts as participants met one another and gained the collective experience of building a community of protest.

The Tea Party movement differs significantly from the left-leaning movements that are studied in this book: its members are wealthier, and the percentage of whites is larger than average. We can call such right-wing movements "status quo" movements: reactions to changing times and the loss of privilege, especially ethnic privilege.[39] In fact, unease about race after the election of Barack Obama to the presidency was a major factor driving Tea Party protesters in polls, as well as the feeling that the government was taking their money and giving it to undeserving people through taxes and redistribution.[40] Nevertheless, the Tea Party engaged in collective behavior and used tactics similar to those of many other protests. Its focus on electoral capacity, however, shows the importance of political culture in shaping the impact of technological affordances.

Occupy and the Tea Party were both organized without formal structures, and neither had official leadership. Occupy, however, was composed of people who were thoroughly disillusioned with the electoral process and opposed to the idea of representation. "Tea Party Patriots" wanted the policy makers to represent them, and they intervened heavily in the electoral process, using online organizing tools and grassroots efforts, along with support from wealthy donors. Although the presence of wealthy donors is a distinguishing characteristic of status quo movements, donors cannot by themselves make people vote, especially in the earlier stages—like primaries, which are crucial to challenging the existing political order in a two-party system. Interviews and polling data show that indeed, a large number of people identified with the cause, however vaguely it was defined.[41]

Analysis of Tea Party Facebook groups showed this electoral focus: a desire to block the "current Congress" and to replace it with a "new Congress" dominated early discussions. The election of Tea Party congresspersons then led to the Tea Party Caucus (founded by Michelle Bachmann of Minnesota), with numbers ranging up to sixty representatives in the House. The online activity of Tea Party supporters also focused heavily on making sure that this freshman class of members adhered to policy stances favored by the groups.[42]

Researchers also found that Tea Partiers were often full of misconceptions about the provisions of policy proposals, for example, the existence of "death panels" in Obamacare. However, the activists had encyclopedic knowledge of the political process by which policy gets made and implemented: veto points, committee agendas, which person needs to be called when. In fact the Tea Party activists appeared to exhibit such a deep "mastery of the legislative process and arcane party rules" that researchers thought they would do as well as political scientists who specialize in these narrow and obscure topics—topics crucial to anyone who cared about passing legislation.[43] They focused intensely on process—and how to block or shift it to their liking.

Over the next few years, the average conservatism score of Republican representatives shifted significantly to the right as more Republican incumbents adopted Tea Party stances to avoid a primary challenge and as more Tea Party candidates were newly elected, and as elected members of congress got lobbied by this movement. In 2016, a candidate who matched the Tea Party base's sensibilities, Donald Trump, won the Republican nomination for president despite strong opposition from the party's donor class and establishment figures, and went on to win the general election.

Finally, I examine a movement that is almost entirely online, acting to counter the influence of money on legislation, as an example of how digital tools can throw off the cost of signals, but how the powerful eventually learn to read them better. In 2012, a bill known as the Stop Online Piracy Act and Protect Intellectual Property Act (SOPA/PIPA) was introduced in Congress that would have required major platforms and internet service providers to block copyrighted material. This legislation was more than a mere anti-copyright-infringement provision; it threatened to restrict online free speech. Written with the aid of lobbyists from the entertainment industry, "Big Hollywood," the bill would have changed the internet's infrastructure and would have forced internet platforms to block websites or web traffic that potentially enabled or facilitated copyright infringement—a broad, ill-defined mandate that might well have made it impossible to have an open internet. The bill's opponents thought that it was written too broadly, that its technical requirements were absurd, and that it would make it next to impossible to operate any website hosting user-generated content. It would also be a drastic departure from current law that treats internet companies more like telephone companies, which are not liable for what is said over their lines, than television stations or newspapers, where editorial decisions determine what gets included.

An online campaign opposing the bill gained momentum quickly, with many bloggers, including me, joining a single-day blackout as a symbolic gesture. But the battle to stop the bill intensified when the big internet companies—Google, Tumblr, Wikipedia—joined the fight to oppose it. On the day of the SOPA/PIPA protest, anyone who landed on Google or Tumblr's initial page was given the option to dial his or her congressional representative's office directly, without charge. Thousands of calls flooded members of Congress. They "freaked out," a staffer told me. In the perception of Congress, the "internet was angry." Minds were changed quickly, and almost everyone who had previously supported the bill now opposed it. The bill died a quick death.[11]

SOPA/PIPA seems to be a Cinderella story of online activism leading to change, but there are complications to the happy ending. Protests are powerful to the degree that they operate as signals of capacity to threaten or disrupt the machinery of power or to bring about outcomes the powerful would rather avoid. Phone calls from thousands of constituents scare politicians because they perceive the deluge as a signal of power that could bring something more: a primary challenge, a lost election. However, phoning campaigns organized using digital tools, especially those wielded by centralized platforms, may not carry the same capacity, even though the act (calling a representative) is similar. In fact, these protests are a very good example of why looking at outputs (calls, protest size, tweets, or number of signatures on a petition) without looking at the underlying capacity producing those outputs (internet giants facilitating such calls and tweets) can be misleading.

When those phone calls are brokered via Google and Tumblr, they do not necessarily signal a broader movement capacity (although this does not seem to have been apparent to members of Congress during the SOPA/PIPA vote). Rather, coming from "Big Internet," it signals elite disunity and the willingness of large Silicon Valley companies to visibly flex their political muscle. Elite unity or disunity is a major factor in whether protests successfully change policies or have other impacts, and this may well have been a case of elite disunity having a greater impact than a grassroots movement.[45] However, this makes the few giant companies the bigger actors and the parties that need to be negotiated with. In the long run, the interests of these large companies can diverge from those of the grassroots movement whose members made the calls. The movement is there, but it lacks the organizational capacity that both letter-writing campaigns and calls, and even street protests, signified in the pre-digital era.

Undertaking complex logistics and deploying bodies into action without the aid of digital tools required large numbers of committed people who worked for a cause over many years. The magic was not necessarily just being in the street or making phone calls; it was what the act signaled in terms of capacity that affected the calculations of those in power. It is quite likely that a SOPA/PIPA-type protest, where phone calls are generated in a process led by tech giants, may not be as scary to congressional staffers the next time around. They may interpret the capacity represented by this kind of action as that of particular tech giants, and will be less likely to see the protest as signaling the rise from below of a potent, uncontrolled political force.

Interpreting signals generated partially through digital infrastructure has flummoxed many regimes in recent history. Over time, governments have created an array of responses. In Turkey, for example, the government occasionally chose to temporarily ban social media sites. The practical effect of this was to force people who wanted to defy this order to use so-called virtual private networks (VPNs)—a technical means available via many apps and programs that can change where one's device appears to be located. VPNS allow users to bypass government blocks, and at the same time avoid surveillance since information transferred through VPNs is much less traceable. The Turkish state's policy was effectively to forgo some opportunities for surveillance in order to dampen people's use of social media. It appears that an unfettered conversation is considered to be a bigger risk than lack of surveillance capacity.

Signaling and movement capacity as a framework allows us to answer many questions in a conceptually deep manner. All social movements bear a mix of capacities based on their interests, goals, culture, and resources. Digital technology allows new configurations to arise that intermingle the technical, political, and social dynamics of movements. Looking at digital technologies through the lens of capacity formation and signaling allows us to better understand the ongoing unbundling and recoupling of capacities in social movements, and digital technology's interaction with all of this.

Using signaling and capacity theory to anchor our analyses of social movements, we can finally circle back to the initial question that opened this chapter, and understand why the New York antiwar protests of 2003 could be less threatening to those in power than protests of similar size in the past. In 2003, the movement could easily hold a large march—digital tools were already widely used then. However, that march, and the manner in which it was organized, did not reflect significant capacity, and those in power could dismiss it without paying an electoral (or really any other) cost. They had correctly read the capacity that was signaled.

Evaluating movement capacity as multidimensional helps explain why a movement like Occupy can be both so large and successful in some dimensions and so fragile in others. Understanding protest actions as signals, rather than looking at just their labels, brings clarity to the consequences of movement actions. This perspective also affords a better way of comparing past and current movements—by looking at underlying capacities, not just intermediate indicators like protest size. Using signaling and multiple-capacities theory, we can also examine the difference between an orderly act of civil disobedience that may cause a brief disruption but then is followed by normalcy—a narrative act—and a persistent disruption, such as occupying a key central square, which functions as both a narrative and a disruptive act. Despite surface similarities, these acts signal different kinds of capacities.

Throughout this chapter I have noted how the trajectory and the impact of a movement depend on the complex, mutual, and multilayered interactions and signals of capacity between those in power and those who seek to challenge them. The next chapter examines the other piece of this puzzle: the responses and capacities those in power are developing to the threat of networked movements and in order to control the networked public sphere.

9

Governments Strike Back

IN JULY 2016, AT AN AIRPORT IN SOUTHERN TURKEY, I stared in disbelief at the television near the boarding gate. I could make out a tank in the image, oddly juxtaposed with the very familiar background of Istanbul's Bosphorus bridge—a bridge I had been on countless times, and whose outline had been etched in my memory since childhood. Now, with tanks perched at its entrance, it looked surreal and unrecognizable.

I had been on vacation in Antalya, a city on Turkey's southern coast, a brief breather before coming back to the United States to do the final edits of this book. It was a chance to see friends, family, and the beautiful Mediterranean, and to have a quiet, sunny week before I resumed work. I was just about to fly back to Istanbul, ticket in hand, luggage checked, ready to board.

I squinted at the two screens near the boarding gate, each showing a different channel. They were still stuck in that surreal place that I was not sure existed. An anchorwoman repeated that both bridges over the Bosphorus straits had been closed by soldiers, but she gave no other information.

Earlier that month, the country had reeled from an ISIS attack at Istanbul's main airport—the one I was about to fly into. Now, in Antalya, travelers sitting in the café area near the gate started debating loudly, some asking whether this was just a precaution against another terrorist attack.

Sometimes, silence speaks loudly. Where was the prime minister? The president? Neither appeared on the TV channels we were watching. I immediately pulled out my phone to check Twitter and WhatsApp, two of the key sites where political communication occurs in Turkey. There was no news besides what was on television, but much speculation about a potential terrorist act.

"It's a coup," I said out loud, startling the people around me. I tweeted cautiously, only about the bridges being closed, not wanting to make assertions without knowing more facts. Internally, I felt more certain by the minute. It did not seem plausible that this news would be on television screens without any high-ranking member of the government on a television station if this was indeed a mere precaution against a potential act of terrorism. The terrorists would obviously know that the bridges were closed by now. There was absolutely no reason for the government to remain quiet.

I walked to the gate agents and told them that I was not getting on the plane, and that they should not let anyone else fly into Istanbul Airport. It was not a good idea to try to land at the country's busiest airport—one of the most important, obvious targets in any conflict—during a military coup. The gate agents, two young women, shook their heads and assured me that we were just delayed and should be taking off soon. I asked them how I could cancel my ticket—refund or not—and whether I could get my checked luggage back.

Another traveler, a woman, came up next to me and said, "Me, too." She also wanted to cancel her trip. We locked eyes. "My second," she said. "Mine, too," I said. The young gate agents, both of whom looked like they had been born after the last major coup in 1980, looked at us with puzzlement. We had both been through coups before and had an immediate, shared understanding of the gravity of the situation.[1]

I was a child when the Turkish military took over the country in 1980, establishing a multiyear junta that eventually gave way to a restricted democracy. The country had been in turmoil, and Turkey already had a tradition of military intervention. Taking over the precious, single television station had been one of the first acts of the military. It had then forced an anchorperson to read its manifesto to a stunned nation, announcing the military takeover, a complete curfew, the closing of all borders, and dissolution of the Parliament. Tanks had rolled in the streets of many cities.

In an even earlier coup in Turkey, in 1960, the military had faced a dilemma. It had, of course, taken over the country's radio station (there was
no television then). However, a highly anticipated soccer match was scheduled to take place just a few days after the coup. What if the announcer,
describing the game in real time over the radio, said something against the
military? The coup plotters' solution was to point five guns at the announcer
while he described the match. Such was the power, in their minds, of the
public attention that the announcer would command for the ninety minutes
of the soccer game, via mass media.

Growing up after the 1980 coup, I had come of age in an era of censored
media, censored books, censored theater, censored newspapers, and censored textbooks. Independent news was not easy to find. In the time of my
childhood, there was one television channel and one FM radio station. I
learned many basic facts about the history of my country only after the internet came to Turkey in the mid-1990s. That experience had spurred my interest in the internet's impact on society. Indeed, the sentences this book opens
with, about how my appreciation of digital connectivity stemmed from having come of age in Turkey in that era of strict censorship, were among the
first I wrote as I mulled this book. I had always wondered what might have
happened had there been an internet during those censored years, or right
during the coup. I had even given talks, speculating about this question.
Now, to my utter disbelief, I would get to experience what *would* happen during a coup in the era of the internet. I would watch as a government known
for imposing restrictions on the internet itself used the internet and digital
connectivity to thwart an illegitimate attempt to topple it.

Digital tools have changed the ecology of the public sphere and have
profoundly reshaped the architecture of connectivity. Social movements
were quick to adopt these tools and to use them to challenge power. There
is no reason, however, to believe that affordances of digital technology are
like Thor's hammer, which only the pure of heart can pick up, and only for
a single purpose.[2] Since these tools' inception, many governments have
come a long way in understanding and learning how to control the new
public sphere and its digital ecology. Governments have learned how to
respond to digitally equipped challengers and social movements—and
have even adopted portions of their repertoire. Governments sometimes

organize protests to oppose social movements. Nowadays, governments or powerful groups also make rhetorical attacks on bona fide experts by positioning these movements as authorities to be resisted, portraying the media as a tool of elites (often distant or foreign). In Turkey, the events of July 2016 would also show that governments can even use these tools to defend themselves against illegitimate challenges, like an attempted coup.

In Egypt in 2011, Mubarak's clumsy response to the role of the internet in the uprising against him had been an attempt to severely censor it, which had earned global condemnation. Since then, governments have made great advances in devising more sophisticated methods to neutralize those who would use the internet digital tools against them, and even to use it to mobilize populations for their own interests. This chapters examines these new dynamics, ranging from new modalities of censorship to using online information as a means to maintain control to how surveillance operates in practice.

Censorship during the internet era does not operate under the same logic it did during the heyday of print or even broadcast television. When Mubarak cut off internet and cell-phone communication in Egypt in January 2011, just as throngs packed Tahrir Square, his move backfired at all levels. His actions were based on a complete misunderstanding of how communication and censorship work in the age of the internet.

Egypt's huge protest was located in a well-known, central place: Tahrir Square. Cutting off communication between the people at home and the people at Tahrir Square was an ineffective form of censorship because there was little to keep secret about the protest's existence or its location. But the drastic act of censorship sent a strong signal to the country and alerted people who might not have been aware of the scope of the threat the protest posed to the government.

Cutting off connectivity also made it harder for Egyptians to wait out the events at home, since they were suddenly plunged into information darkness. Many protesters told me that the cutting of cell-phone communication was what finally got their extended family to join them at Tahrir Square. They could either sit at home and worry about their children, relatives, kin, and friends or show up at the place where they knew that everything was going on. Unsurprisingly, many did just that.

The protesters were also able to circumvent the internet blockade quickly; all they needed was a line to the outside, and the rest of the world would amplify their message. When Egypt's government cut off the country's internet, it left a single internet service provider (ISP) operating that mainly serviced government offices and large corporations.[3] Fortunately for the protesters, one of them who lived close to Tahrir Square was enrolled in that ISP. The protesters had already set up a media tent within the square, where they collected recordings that people had made during the day. They told me how they would go through the clips they collected, identify the most striking ones, and then walk over one of the bridges between Tahrir and nearby neighborhoods to the house that was connected to the still-functioning ISP. Just like that, they had access to the outside world. The young revolutionaries had also acquired satellite phones that could connect to the internet more directly. The internet and mobile shutdown may have made it difficult for the protesters to communicate within Egypt, which was actually a move that wasn't even helpful for the government, but they were scarcely impeded in the very important struggle to get their message out to the world.

Shutting down the internet also backfired because this draconian move increased both global and domestic attention to the protests. Keep in mind that attention, not information per se, is the most crucial resource for a social movement. Suddenly the protesters had even more of it.

Domestically, losing cell-phone access was jolting in a country where many people owned them, but the effect was even more pronounced internationally. To many people around the world, especially in Western countries, Egypt may seem a distant land, and its politics may not be easy for a casual foreign observer to grasp, but losing access to phones, the internet, Twitter, and Facebook was something people could easily relate to. The global journalism community had gotten used to following individuals on Twitter for the latest updates, but its members were now suddenly cut off from easy interaction with people whom they felt they had gotten to know and whose lives were in danger. The reporters wrote a passel of international stories about the drastic censorship. For the government, the communications blackout did not achieve any of the key goals of censorship in the digital era: impeding attention, discouraging people from participation, and trying to deny protesters control over the narrative.

In the digital age, attempts at censorship can backfire and bring much more attention to the information that was supposed to be suppressed. This even has a name, the Streisand Effect from an incident in 2003, when Barbra Streisand attempted to keep images of her Malibu villa from appearing in a series of photographs of the California coastline—a project documenting coastal erosion—through legal measures like cease-and-desist letters. Before these attempts, the pictures of her house was an obscure entry posted in a large database, one of more than twelve thousand entries showing pictures of almost the entire California coastline. The photo with her house had been downloaded a mere six times, at least twice by Streisand's attorneys.[4] Search engines had not indexed this picture as connected in any way to Streisand and instead had listed it merely as "image 3850." All that changed once her attempts to remove it by legal action drew attention to the picture. (Now you know about it, too.) The journalist Mike Masnick dubbed this the "Streisand Effect," and it plays out again and again in different settings, just as it did in Egypt's censorship of the internet during Tahrir protests.[5]

Later governments would not repeat Mubarak's digitally naïve, counterproductive moves. They were more suited for an era in which the public sphere was dominated solely by print and broadcast mass media that could be centrally cut off once and for all, as the military government in Turkey had been able to do in 1980. But a new era has brought new methods to the fore—methods that, ironically, include using a version of the Streisand effect as a way to suppress crucial information.

To be effective, censorship in the digital era requires a reframing of the goals of censorship not as a total denial of access, which is difficult to achieve, but as a denial of attention, focus, and credibility. In the networked public sphere, the goal of the powerful often is not to convince people of the truth of a particular narrative or to block a particular piece of information from getting out (that is increasingly difficult), but to produce resignation, cynicism, and a sense of disempowerment among the people. This can be done in many ways, including inundating audiences with information, producing distractions to dilute their attention and focus, delegitimizing media that provide accurate information (whether credible mass media or online media), deliberately sowing confusion, fear, and doubt by aggressively questioning credibility (with or without evidence, since what matters is creating doubt, not proving a point), creating or claiming hoaxes, or generating harassment campaigns designed to make it harder for credible conduits of information to operate, especially on social media which tends to be harder for a government to control like mass media.

The aim of twenty-first-century powers is to break the causal chain linking information dissemination to the generation of individual will and agency, individual will and agency to protests, and protests to social movement action. Rather than attempt to break the first link, information dissemination, censorship through information glut focuses on the second link, weakening the agency that might be generated by information.

The initial response of many governments to the internet was to dismiss it as a virtual and frivolous realm and to take few actions to effectively control it. For example, before 2011, there was relatively little draconian censorship online in Turkey. Court orders blocked many websites, but the blocks were halfhearted and were implemented in crude and easily circumventable ways. The prime minister at the time, who would later become a strong proponent of internet restrictions, joked that he himself circumvented the court-ordered internet bans easily, and he encouraged citizens to do the same. By the time the government started treating the internet as a genuine threat to its rule, in the aftermath of the Gezi protests, the internet was firmly entrenched in the country and was also used heavily by the government and businesses to provide a variety of services. It was no longer possible just to unplug it without great damage to the economy.

Censorship is often thought of as blocking information from getting out, but that is an outdated conception in an era where there are as many cell-phone subscriptions on the planet as there are people. Although many countries still block websites, and a few, like China and Iran, even attempt to build a virtual wall around their national internet, blocking alone is not very effective in most circumstances.

Easily installed virtual private networks (VPNs) can circumvent internet censorship by disguising a user's original "IP address"—the user's exact location on the network—and putting all of a user's communications through an encrypted channel. This makes both surveillance and censorship more difficult. Governments can take the additional step of trying to block VPNs, but this also makes internet commerce and business difficult. Another option is the use of Tor, a specialized browser that hides both user origin and the content of communication. Tor is often slow, but it allows for both anonymity and circumvention of censorship and surveillance. Governments can try to block Tor, too, but this adds to the complexity of the system of censorship.

Censorship is often thought of as simply blocking *individuals* from accessing information, but information is experienced and disseminated *collectively* and *socially*. Information travels in social networks; hence circumvention of censorship is also a collective, networked undertaking. Many users are networked in friendship and social groups, especially on easy, widely used chat applications that are encrypted end-to-end, such as WhatsApp. End-to-end encryption means that even Facebook (WhatsApp's owner) cannot read the content of the communication. News travels far and wide in such groups, and this type of communication does not require that every person practice active circumvention. All that is needed is one person to circumvent censorship in accessing the information and then share the information on a network.

Indeed, in countries like Iran, applications like Telegram (another messaging app that allows channels and chatting) often function like broadcast systems, and many people simply absorb and learn about news that is distributed by a few people. Hence circumvention statistics—the percentage of a country that uses Tor or VPNs—do not give a true sense of the scale of circumvention. Frequently, all that is required is that the information reach, someplace and somehow, even a few people who can serve as credible intermediaries, and, importantly, that others have the will to acquire that information as well.

Despite the possible ways to circumvent censorship, the information environment in many countries remains challenging for an ordinary person interested in finding and understanding credible and factual news reports. The forces of censorship have learned how to exploit new weaknesses. In the past, there was too little information, and there were too few means to broadcast it to the masses, which meant that it could be censored via blocking. In the networked public sphere, there is too much information, and people lack effective means to quickly and efficiently verify it, which means that information can be effectively suppressed by creating an ever-bigger glut of mashed-up truth and falsehood to foment confusion and distraction.

Without traditional trusted institutional gatekeepers, it is quite difficult for an ordinary person to know what is true and what is a hoax, or who is reliable and who is untrustworthy. People also cannot easily prioritize important news and distinguish it from trivialities because this requires keeping up with and judging a daily onslaught of massive amounts of information. Dispersion and weakening of gatekeeping and the lowering of trust in all information intermediaries, including journalists, academics, and experts in an environment of growing polarization, makes it easy for governments and other groups wanting to oppose a social movement to deliberately sow mistrust and confusion, create information glut and distraction, and harass and abuse dissidents or political opponents. As people search for a heuristic to vet information, trusted individuals often emerge as gatekeepers on social media, but without the support of recognized institutions they can be even more vulnerable targets than institutional media.

The protesters in Tahrir Square in 2011 had power because they were able to capture the world's attention, and the Egyptian government responded by increasing the level of the conflict, which further increased attention. Just as attention is underappreciated as a resource for social movements, distraction and ignorance are underappreciated as methods of repression through denial of attention.

The networked public sphere can empower movements to craft their own narrative and disseminate it in a decentralized manner, bypassing resistance from traditional media and censorship by governments. In response, many governments have learned that ignoring and waiting out a protest may be the best path in some cases, rather than blocking it or creating tension with protesters through tear gas or other violent methods of repression (which, paradoxically, sometimes rejuvenates their spirits).

Nowadays protesters have the means to vie for attention on their own terms, even bypassing the mass media, so it is much harder for a government to both repress a movement and deny it attention because repression is a potent tool for getting attention, and protesters can use social media to get the word out even if the mass media can be forced to censor the story. On the other hand, ignoring a protest and not severely repressing it can also allow it to grow and become an unstoppable avalanche. It is difficult for a government to strike the right balance. These new realities require methods of control and censorship with a level of tactical agility suited to the twenty-first-century networked public sphere. Different governments practice different variations on this theme, depending on the diffusion of the internet in their countries, the state of dissent, and the level of grievances.

Perhaps no other country practices the tactical agility required for effective censorship in the digital era as well as China. Although it is often mistakenly portrayed as a clumsy censor, it is in fact a careful and deliberate one, brandishing a potent mix of selective censorship and distraction. In the international rogues' gallery of nations that censor, China is often singled out for its "Great Firewall"—a comprehensive system that blocks a range of information deemed politically undesirable from reaching mainland China's internet. However, many people overlook China's very active domestic internet, complete with chat applications (like Weibo), social networking platforms (like RenRen), and a system of domestic software companies producing a wide variety of applications and sites. On the Chinese internet, hundreds of millions of people connect to one another, many of them using applications that post their comments as soon as they type them in, thus producing billions of messages per day. At this scale of communication, mere blocking of information from the outside is not enough to control dissent or the diffusion of political messages.

When it was announced in September 2014 that candidates for the scheduled 2017 elections in Hong Kong—which has its own government and laws, although the Chinese government is the ultimate authority—would be subject to prior screening by the mainland Chinese Communist Party, outraged students on the island acted. They first organized a boycott of classes. On September 26, 2014, they followed this with an occupation of the Admiralty neighborhood, a key shopping and financial district, crowded and important for Hong Kong's economic activity. Centrally located, this area was also a frequent destination for visitors from mainland China. The movement called itself "Occupy Central" at first, clearly harking back to the Occupy protests around the world. This was the first major confrontation the Chinese government faced in the age of widespread internet use. Its actions afterward showed that it had been carefully watching prior protests and learning from them.

As in many other protests, the use of tear gas by the police in Hong Kong was a catalyst for outrage and mobilization, especially by young people. After students used umbrellas to protect themselves from the tear gas and pepper spray, some journalists dubbed the protests the "umbrella movement."[6] The students adopted the name, and soon scenes of hundreds of colorful umbrellas confronting the police became a visual metaphor for the movement as a whole.

Images of police brutality have coalescing power for protests. In the Gezi Park protests, it was the image of a woman in a red dress being brutally pepper-sprayed up close that had helped spread the initial outrage. In Occupy protests, the severe pepper-spraying in New York of four young women already "kettled in," surrounded by police barriers, caused a spike in media coverage of the protests and provoked outrage. At the University of California at Davis, a small sit-in became national news when a police officer walked over to a line of students sitting down in protest and methodically pepper-sprayed them while the students screamed in pain. Other protesters chanted "The whole world is watching" and "Shame on you," and the words felt true. The images from the scene spread far and wide.

Hong Kong's umbrella movement appeared to be on this track, too, as pictures of teargassed young protesters spread around the world, generating broad media coverage. Other aspects of this occupation, too, were familiar. The area overflowed with youthful energy. Students poured into the Admiralty's wide streets, setting up tents, libraries, and messaging trees where they wrote about their wishes on sticky notes. Art was everywhere. The street was regularly cleaned and even over-cleaned, just as at other protests.

But after the first burst of energy of the protest, events took a different, slower turn than in many other protests. This seemed to be a deliberate strategy on the part of the government. On October 3, 2014, some "locals" who the students said were associated with "triad gangs" (a type of organized crime gang) attempted to beat up the students, who had shut down the high-traffic shopping district and thus caused financial losses. There were some arrests. Then there was a relatively quiet period again. About two weeks later, on October 15, there were further scuffles between police and protesters, but they did not get out of hand. A week later, on October 21, a student delegation met with government officials, but the meeting was unfruitful. The protest settled back into a calmer rhythm again, with little police activity confronting the students. About a month later, on November 10, when courts issued injunctions to clear the protest areas, the protest had already lost much of its initial energy. When the area was cleared on November 25 and 26, there was little resistance.

Over this three-month period, while the Chinese government adopted a watch-from-a-distance strategy after the initial confrontation, the occupation lost its energy and, to an extent, its support. There were few incidents like the initial pepper-spraying and teargassing of students that could re-energize the movement and reignite unity among the protesters who had become involved in bitter internal debates. Although the government undertook significant censorship to keep news of the protests from spreading within mainland China, it never cut off the internet in Hong Kong, as many feared, and it also did not disperse the occupation by massive force. Both of those acts would likely have galvanized international attention, as well as concerns in Hong Kong. Occupy Central had suffered from the strengths and weaknesses of other digitally fueled movements. It was able to scale up quickly and control its own narrative. However, it was unable to effectively respond to the government's countermeasures and advance the momentum of the movement. Meanwhile, the Chinese government managed, through tactical patience and deliberate shunning of attention, to diffuse the protest's energy.

The Chinese government's strategy for managing the internet is also centered on a deep understanding of the importance of attention and capacity to movements, rather than merely blocking information. It might seem impossible to understand how and why the secretive Chinese government censors what it does, but in a remarkable series of articles, a team of researchers from Harvard University managed to do just that.[7] The researchers downloaded millions of social media posts from more than a thousand social media services all over China (recall that China has a strong domestic software industry and a wide variety of platforms). For each post, they "examined its content, placed it on a timeline according to topic area, and revisited the Web site from which it came repeatedly thereafter to determine whether it was censored." Thus they were able to determine which postings had survived, and which had been taken down by the censorship apparatus. The results provided a window into what the Chinese government considers worthy of censorship, and what it leaves up.

The researchers indeed uncovered a vast and speedy apparatus of censorship that could coordinate and take down a large number of posts quickly—most within twenty-four hours. Contrary to most people's assumptions, however, Chinese government censors were not suppressing criticism of the state or the Communist Party. Internet posts that contained "scathing criticisms" of the government and Chinese leaders were not more likely to be censored than other content. In fact, the censors allowed harshly critical posts. But the research team found that they swiftly censored posts that had any potential to encourage collective action.

The censors were especially likely to act if posts tending toward action were concentrated within a single geographical area. If the people making the posts were near each other, there would be more likelihood that they could come together and do something. For example, posts on local web pages supporting an environmentalist who ironically was also supported by the central government were severely censored, "likely because of his record of organizing collective action." The censorship apparatus seemed to value passivity in the population above all—remarkably, even when it appeared that people wanted to organize in favor of the government. The government's concern could be stated in this way: "Once people learn to mobilize, even if they do so to support us, who knows what they will try next?"

It is arguable that allowing critical content to remain online can actually benefit authoritarian rule by providing a feedback mechanism to foster rebalancing, albeit a toothless one as it suits an authoritarian regime. By allowing complaints about the government to surface and coalesce online (while drastically censoring calls to action and stories with the potential to rouse the populace to action), it may well be that the Chinese government is solving a critical problem for authoritarian regimes: their lack of feedback about their weaknesses and blind spots. This is especially a problem for a country the size of China, with a vast and sprawling territory composed of a huge and diverse array of provinces, differing ethnicities and cultures.

Democracies, as imperfect as they may be, tend to be more stable not only because they have more legitimacy than authoritarian regimes, but also because they can engage in self-correction more easily, since voter dissatisfaction with a government leads directly to a change in its leaders. A rigid power structure that does not hold regular elections or have a free press has numerous blind spots and little means to discover when it has gone seriously astray from a stable course. This limited view at the top partly explains authoritarian regimes' vulnerability to sudden rebellions—often ignited by information cascades—that seem to come from nowhere. In truth, repression had hidden the underlying instability. Once people start rebelling, the government unravels in a cascade of uncontrollable events.

In China, a ritual called "memorial to the throne," involving people from outer provinces petitioning the emperor, goes back more than a thousand years. These memorials took the form of letters, often by locals from distant areas who would travel to the seat of the sprawling empire to express their grievances about corrupt local officials.[8] These memorials were also a means for the emperor to stop local corruption from becoming a threat to his power. During the Ming dynasty, Emperor Zhu Di (known as the Yongle emperor) once learned that some of these petitions had not made their way to him because officials considered them minor. He was not pleased and angrily thundered, "Stability depends on superior and inferior communicating; there is none when they do not. From ancient times, many a state has fallen because a ruler did not know the affairs of the people."[9] In the twenty-first century, thanks to social media, the Chinese government may well have discovered how to maintain that communication between "superior and inferior" without threatening its own monopoly hold on power.[10]

Allowing criticism to flourish online certainly comes with risks. What if all the dissent does coalesce into a threat that has the power to ignite collective action? In a second remarkable article, the same team of Harvard researchers elucidated the mechanism by which China's authoritarian rulers blunted the impact of the spread of disapproval online.[11] For topics that they deemed important enough to create a threat, their remedy was straightforward: distraction.

It has long been rumored that China has a so-called "50 Cent Party" of online commentators, so named because they allegedly are paid fifty cents per post they put up online supporting the government. In truth, we do not know how much they are paid, and until recently, we did not know exactly how this vast enterprise—possibly employing hundreds of thousands of people—worked. Do members of the 50 Cent Party enter into arguments online? Do they attack critics? Do they harass them? Do they challenge them to arguments?

The team of Harvard researchers analyzed a cache of leaked documents about this apparatus and also looked at big data footprints of this "50 Cent Party," along with conducting an ingenious survey aimed at a rough identification of this group. It turns out that the 50 Cent Party does exist, but not necessarily to respond to criticism or attack critics. Instead, the members are directed to post at high volume during critical junctures, such as anniversaries and sensitive events, but not about the topics that are sensitive and critical. These critics are also instructed not to argue with government opponents.

Instead, members of this virtual party—most of whom turned out to be government employees, according to the researchers—post on unrelated topics in order to create alternative focal points of attention at a time when activists might be trying to get attention to their own topics. They do this all at once and at high volume to create the appearance of something important that one should pay attention to, and thus to drown critical posts in a sea of other topics. This strategy is similar to yelling "Look behind you" to distract an opponent in a fight, except that in this case the distraction is directed at the audience to get them to look away from the fight.

This elaborate scheme makes sense if one conceptualizes attention rather than information as the key commodity that a social movement needs. Without attention, information means very little. The insight that attention, not information, is the prize in the struggle for power is not new. Almost two thousand years ago, the Roman satirical poet Juvenal wrote about how people's demands for representation could be diluted by "panem et circenses" (bread and circuses), that is, by providing distracting entertainment while also making sure that they were fed.[12] In the twenty-first century, the same dynamics hold, but this time, the circus is online.

Very few countries have the kind of vast censorship apparatus that can carefully censor much of the information coming from outside the country and respond in real time by taking down potentially effective posts. China and Iran's response of essentially splitting the internet from most of the rest of the planet is relatively rare and is difficult for most countries to implement effectively, not only because it requires extensive resources and personnel to operate now, but also because the Great Firewall was built from the ground up in a project that began decades ago. If you were not already thinking like China and Iran in the 1990s, it is quite expensive and difficult to switch to that model now. Further, the Chinese model of control requires a homegrown software industry to provide the services for domestic users instead of Facebook or Twitter, which are blocked. This in turn requires a population that is large enough to make it work. Iran started its censorship efforts early, but it does not have a domestic software industry like that of China. As a result, it is estimated that tens of millions of Iranians are able to use circumvention techniques and have accounts on non-Iranian social media.[13] The Russian government may well try to build a system like this in the future, but the cost and the scale of the investment make late-starter success less likely and quite expensive. Thus Russia and other governments with authoritarian tendencies cannot easily duplicate China's methods exactly.[14] Instead, many such countries use information glut and targeted harassment as their modes of censorship.

It has been widely reported that Russia's government employs a huge number of people in what is often called an "army of trolls."[15] The "trolls"—a term inspired by mythical creatures but now adapted to the online era— are commentators, often pseudonymous, who try to raise people's hackles by making deliberately provocative comments. Trolling comments are not meant to convince or even to generate a back-and-forth argument, but just to upset people. Many people assume that such trolls are bored teenagers, just passing time by being silly or offensive under the protection of anonymity. However, Russia's "troll army" is anything but a bunch of bored teenagers and the consequences are anything but a joke.

Because the troll army is not official, it is difficult to pin down, although there have been many newspaper reports that include interviews with current and former employees. To understand how it works, it is best to consider an example. When Sweden was discussing whether to join NATO—a move Russia strongly opposes—it suddenly found its online forums flooded with "distorted and outright false information" and with claims that were "alarming" and shocking. Messages were posted wondering if it was true that "if Sweden, a non-NATO member, signed the deal, the alliance would stockpile secret nuclear weapons on Swedish soil," or whether "NATO could attack Russia from Sweden without government approval." Questions were raised whether "NATO soldiers, immune from prosecution, could rape Swedish women without fear of criminal charges."[16]

This went on and on, one outrageous claim after another, often disguised as questions.[17] These claims were all false, but these disturbing questions spilled over into traditional news media. The Swedish defense minister, touring the country in an attempt to discuss Sweden, NATO, and Russia, found himself being grilled about these fake stories. People were scared that these stories might be true, confused about what to believe, and unsure about how to deal with this flood of negative stories.

Censorship by disinformation focuses on attention as the key resource to be destroyed and credibility and legitimacy as the key components necessary for a public sphere that can support dissident views—or indeed, any coherent views. Rand Corporation researchers refer to this phenomenon as the "firehose of falsehood" propaganda model.[18] The primary goal is simple: "to confuse and overwhelm" the audience.[19] As in many such cases, it is impossible to pin down responsibility for the campaign, but "numerous analysts and experts in American and European intelligence point to Russia as the prime suspect, noting that preventing NATO expansion is a centerpiece of the foreign policy of President Vladimir V. Putin, who invaded Georgia in 2008 largely to forestall that possibility."[20]

Often, these campaigns do not feature sophisticated comments. The language can be full of grammatical mistakes and may not always make sense.

But there are enormous numbers of posts and claims—far too many for a person to wade through. The goal is to drown out the voices of informed commentators, dissidents, and social movement activists in an online cacophony, and to make it practically impossible to use social media to hold a sane political conversation based on facts and a shared broadly empirical framework among the populace. As a Finnish researcher, Saara Jantunen, who published a book on this topic and then was savaged by these fake commentators, explained:[21] "They fill the information space with so much abuse and conspiracy talk that even sane people start to lose their minds."[22]

In the past, gatekeepers were fewer but they had broader reach. They were trusted, or at least expected, to undertake the necessary sorting of facts from deliberate misinformation. They were not always correct and could even be manipulated to spread misinformation. For example, in the lead-up to the Iraq War of 2003, many major newspapers in the United States were manipulated into publishing what turned out to be false claims that Iraqi strongman Saddam Hussein had stored weapons of mass destruction. Their errors and submissiveness to power was disastrous because it led to a war, with many negative consequences still causing turmoil in the region. However, these gatekeepers had normative standards to judge factual error, and many newspapers published investigations later about how they got the reporting in the run-up to the war so wrong. Their failures were recognized as failures, or at least as departures from standards they were supposed to uphold. However, these failures have contributed to declining trust in traditional media, making the public sphere even more vulnerable to disinformation campaigns. Our new era is marked by the multitude of people and institutions with the capacity to broadcast, each with different normative standards—and some with no concerns about accuracy even as a standard that is not always upheld—with a polarized public with little trust in any intermediary, and drawn to information that confirms preexisting biases. The result is a frayed, incoherent, and polarized public sphere that can be hostile to dissent because the incoherence displaces politics. Unlike mass media failures, it is often not even clear who to hold responsible, or how to improve the situations.

Nation-states and other powerful actors have often carried out clandestine campaigns of misinformation, since long before the rise of digital media. The United States has often been accused of deliberately spreading misinformation against regimes it wanted to overthrow or destabilize in many countries. Politicians have been known to resort to starting rumors about their opponents. None of this is without precedent.

However, what is more striking in the twenty-first century is that the disinformation campaigns are not necessarily carried out to persuade people or to make them believe any particular set of alleged facts. Instead, the goal is often simply to overwhelm people with so many pieces of bad and disturbing information that they become confused and give up trying to figure out what the truth might be—or even the possibility of finding out what is true. Often, such campaigns also include a proliferation of conspiracy theories. Social media's business model financed by ads paid out based on number of pageviews makes it not just possible but even financially lucrative to spread misinformation, propaganda, or distorted partisan content that can go viral in algorithmically entrenched echo chambers. The final effect is often not credulity that leans toward any one set of alleged facts, but a sense within people that the truth is simply unknowable, and an attitude of resignation that leads to withdrawal from politics and to a paralysis of action. This may well serve the powerful since those who want to bring about change need to convince people, whereas those who want to stay in power may need only to paralyze them into inaction.

If you cannot destroy the message because access to techniques to circumvent censorship means that people have too many sources of messages to block them effectively, and because the Streisand effect means that targeting a single message may paradoxically draw even more attention to its contents, why not shoot the messenger? In the networked public sphere, this often means shooting or demonizing the whole medium.

In Russia, for example, a 2012 law labeled all nongovernmental organizations that received any funding from a foundation outside the country "foreign agents," which, in the Russian context, carried connotations of espionage.[73] It was an attempt to demonize the nongovernmental sector as a whole, a tactic that has been repeated in many regions, from the Middle East to Southeast Asia. The Russian law, however, not only attempted to charge all NGOs with foreign interventionism but also imposed unrealistic, draconian measures on all social media platforms. They were required to move all user data, not just Russian users' data but the data of anyone whose writing might be read in Russia, to servers within Russia.[24] This rule is not necessarily meant to be fully implemented, but it serves as a threat that can help portray non-Russian social networks as lawbreakers that do not respect Russian laws.

During the Gezi Park protests of 2013, the Prime Minister (later President) of Turkey had called Twitter a "menace" to society. Now, in March of 2014, he declared, "We'll eradicate Twitter. I don't care what the international community says. Everyone will witness the power of the Turkish Republic."[25] He threatened other platforms, too, and said: "We are determined on the issue, regardless of what the world may say. We won't allow the people to be devoured by YouTube, Facebook or others. Whatever steps need to be taken we will take them without wavering."[26]

Much of the media reporting on this topic was incredulous that the government would attempt such a drastic ban, blocking all of Twitter, and many commenters noted that Turkey's active Twitter community had quickly moved to circumvent the ban. There were more tweets than ever coming out of Turkey, and now, in a striking demonstration of the Streisand effect, there was even more international attention on Turkey because of the ban. Was the censorship backfiring? Only if you believe that this was a move aimed at blocking the medium—social media platforms and Twitter in particular—rather than demonizing it.

Most of the commentary from government officials and government supporters focused on demonizing Twitter, the whole medium, as a source of information. Prime Minister Erdoğan's talking points in rallies and in speeches were less about political uses of Twitter and more about cases (often true) of Twitter causing mayhem in the lives of ordinary Turkish people.

In one example that Prime Minister Erdoğan repeated often during rallies, he referred to a housewife in Turkey who had been impersonated on Twitter as a porn star. She was quite distraught, unable to stop this account from impersonating her and contacting her family. She consulted a lawyer who sued Twitter in the Turkish courts—a jurisdictional challenge since Twitter, at the time, did not answer court requests from Turkey. The case was certainly distressing, and it was a consequence of the business model of social media, where a user base of hundreds of millions of people is handled with minimal staffing. Politicians routinely spoke about and highlighted cases of malicious impersonation, defamation, hate speech, and insults (which have less stringent regulation in U.S. law but are taken more seriously in Turkey, both culturally and legally) that happened online.

"What if Twitter is used to sell organs of little children?" I saw a pro-government account tweet. They were on Twitter to argue that Twitter wasn't safe. Twitter was called a CIA plot, a tool of imperialist intervention, a method to destroy the family and spread propaganda, and worse. It did not help that the United States, like other large powers, had attempted interventions of this nature, even trying to create a fake social media platform in Cuba with the goal of trying to overthrow the Cuban regime.[27]

Fearing that its whole platform would be censored in Turkey, Twitter responded to the Turkish government's court-ordered censorship requests, but in a very specific way. A censored tweet would be withheld only from users within the country. That said, Twitter enabled a setting that allowed people to easily change their claimed country; thus a Turkish Twitter user could simple indicate she was in the United States to once again be able to see the "withheld" tweet. Thus circumvention didn't even require a VPN, only flipping a setting within the application. Judged by effectiveness, neither the total ban nor the single tweet blocking worked as a wall of censorship; almost anyone with a minimal desire to circumvent could walk right over them.

The Turkish government, however, was not being naïve the way Mubarak's government had been. It had to be aware that circumvention was so easy that it made the censorship mostly moot, and that many methods of circumventing censorship were frequently shared among social media users in Turkey. It did not matter—the goal probably had been less to keep all of Turkey off Twitter than to keep about half the country, those who supported the government, off Twitter by portraying it as a "menace" that threatened national priorities and family values. The AKP activist base—especially those who wanted to be on Twitter to argue with dissidents or to push their own point of view—and the top AKP leadership—including ministers, mayors and many others—remained quite active on Twitter. However, those people were already highly committed to the party, unlike ordinary party supporters, whose sole relationship might be going to the voting booth occasionally.

The method seemed to focus on scaring novice users or government supporters off the platform and discouraging them from circumventing the block.[28] It was more a campaign of persuasion and questioning of credibility than one of creating a Turkish equivalent of China's "Great Firewall."

A poll conducted in Turkey later that year reflected the polarization in choice of medium: only about half the people received their news about protests and dissent from social media (49 percent).[29] The rest of the people received their information from government-controlled mass media. In Russia, too, a poll found that only 17 percent of the respondents received their information about Russia's involvement in Ukraine from the internet, and over half of the population believed the Russian mass media to be unbiased.[30] For a regime in power in a polarized country, these results suggest that potential challenges can mostly be contained by control of the mass media, and by demonizing alternative sources of information online.

If Turkey's or Russia's policies—which are not identical—are judged in the light of old-style censorship, they would seem to have failed because circumvention was not made difficult or impossible. Information still flows to people who are motivated to seek it. However, seen through the lens of demonization of the medium, keeping it use as a credible source of information from spreading, and wrapping it up in culture wars and polarization within the country, both countries' policies have greatly succeeded.

Information flows can also be hampered by the lack of intermediaries who can verify information and distinguish credible information from not credible—the role traditional journalism is supposed to serve, however imperfect in practice. In the summer of 2015, the situation in southeast Turkey took a dramatic turn for the worse. The conflict between Kurdish insurgents and the Turkish government reignited. During the following year, the government routinely declared round-the-clock curfews in a variety of places, from small neighborhoods in big cities to entire towns with tens of thousands of residents. Many civilians were trapped amid the fighting, and claims and counterclaims about misconduct were rampant.

Unlike in the past—say, the 1990s—information kept flowing out of the area, but not through journalists. They were banned from traveling to the region, and the few who were already there were constrained by the curfew. Turkey's mass media, most of the time, simply channeled government claims as news. Their reporting did not inspire trust. Independent journalists could not report on the ground. The internet continued to function, however, though slowly at times, and cell-phone networks mostly stayed up. Like many people, I turned to social media and citizen journalism to try to better understand these difficult new developments.

It turned out to be futile.

The news seemed awful. People posted pictures of women and children who had been shot, houses that had been destroyed, and streets that were littered with ammunition. Every picture that went viral, though, was immediately met with the claim that it was either a hoax, a Photoshopped picture, or that it came from another war or another location, such as Gaza, Chechnya, or Egypt. The locations were always claimed to be someplace else—anywhere but Turkey.

In one particularly heartbreaking case, a photograph circulated on Turkey's social media. The photograph appeared to show something wrapped in plastic, placed in a refrigerator. It was reported that the family said that a young girl had been killed in the cross fire, but the family, unable to bury her because of the curfew, had stored instead her body in a large refrigerator, the kind ordinarily used to store items for sale in a store. Immediately, though, there were counterclaims: the fridge was not the type found in the region; the picture was from another war; the area did not have electricity so the fridge wasn't useful; the girl was killed by the insurgents; the girl did not exist; the whole thing was a hoax; the family was non-existent; the picture was Photoshopped, and more. I could no longer confidently judge the truth of what I was seeing. This aggressive challenge to the credibility of posts followed almost every picture or video that made it out of the region. Words like "fake," "Photoshop," and "hoax" trailed every image, every story, every claim.

Sometimes the pictures *were* from Gaza. Some *were* hoaxes. I came across people on social media who said they were government supporters and said that they were deliberately planting hoaxes to prove that dissidents were too gullible or were committed to spreading misinformation. Some facts were misreported by people who defined themselves dissidents, too. Some of the misreporting was ordinary gullibility; people chose to believe stories and pictures that portrayed the side they were closer to as the victims, and denied victimhood to their political opponents. Activists made errors, jumped to conclusions and retweeted dubious claims without checking. Misinformation spread. It seemed clear to me that civilians were getting hurt in the cross fire, but it was impossible to establish even the scale of the deaths or injuries. People, trapped in their homes, were not reliable witnesses either.

I talked to other journalists, including the team at 140journos, a citizen journalism verification and dissemination platform profiled in chapter 2, whose members had developed some of the most advanced methods I had seen for verification of citizen media in Turkey. They were also stumped.[31] There was rarely enough information to do the kind of thorough checking they can do when citizen journalists are reporting from the ground. The round-the-clock curfew had made most of their ordinary methods useless. Unable to verify, they, too, resorted to the "here are some claims, and here are some counterclaims" style of reporting, which did not offer clarity. The only options were to believe whatever you might have believed initially or to give up trying to make any sense of it all. The result was that the mood of Turkish social media wavered between a sense of outrage among people who likely had held that view anyway before the latest tragic turn of events, and, more commonly, a sense of resignation. I watched online as people I knew who were used to commenting on news retreated from the discussion, often discouraged by the constant challenging of all statements and assertions of fact. As this book went to press, the 140journos group took a "breather" from their citizen journalism reporting. "We can't do what we set out to do if we are reduced to reporting claims like this with no clarity or verification," one of the founders told me. They weren't giving up, but they needed to find a new way to add value to the networked public sphere.

I heard similar stories from activists around the world: that citizen media were becoming less useful, not because there were fewer reports, but because there was an enormous increase in challenges to their credibility, ranging from reasonable questions to outrageous and clearly false accusations.[32] These took place using the same channels, and even the same methods, that a social movement might have used to challenge false claims by authorities—claims that would have been believed by many. Now, these methods of challenging authority and expertise were being mobilized to bury claims by dissidents and activists, who were often portrayed as "elites," and to make any insistence on facts and truth as a form of "elitism." Often the crucial aspect was not necessarily whether the challenges were sound, but rather their volume and consistency. Amidst the noise, it wasn't possible to pick out the signal.

In the early days of the internet, when I interviewed activists, I was often asked how to circumvent censorship or even to hide identity. Nowadays, the questions I get are different: "How can I verify that my pictures were real? That I took them? How can I verify their time and place?" In a remarkable turn of events, asserting not only the authenticity of identity (I posted this picture) but also the veracity of its metadata (information about the content rather than the content itself: this picture was taken on this date and in this place) has become a key challenge for activists and social movements because sowing doubt has become an increasingly potent strategy of both governments and counter-movements. Ironically, very few technology activists focus on this question: instead, much effort and resources goes to circumvention tools aimed at getting around blocks, rather than tools that increase the reliability of information that does get out.

In September 2015, a boat full of refugees capsized on its way to Greece from the coast of Turkey. One of the victims was a three-year-old boy, Aylan Kurdi, whose lifeless body was photographed on a Turkish beach. His five-year-old brother, Galib, too, had died along with their mother, Rehana. The tragedy was all too common—hundreds of refugees were drowning each month.

Because I had so many contacts in the region, I had, unfortunately, seen many other pictures of dead children, washed up on various shores. Aylan Kurdi's picture was different, perhaps because in it he looked almost as though he might have been sleeping—a picture of innocence wearing a red shirt, a blue pair of shorts, and shoes with Velcro fasteners. I noticed that unlike most pictures documenting the tragedy of the refugee outflow from Syria, this one seemed to have been taken by a professional, or at least with professional equipment. The image was high resolution and clear. I saw the photograph before it hit the Western media because I had

so many people from Turkey on my social media networks, including journalists, and it was spreading among them. I made brief inquiries and
quickly determined where and when the photograph had been taken.

I pondered for a while whether to help publicize this picture through my
own social media feeds, like Twitter. I knew that it was striking and might
make an impact. But it was also a very difficult picture to look at, especially
if one was unprepared and were to see it without warning. I had hundreds
of thousands of followers on Twitter, and, more important, many journalists. I had had some success before with publicizing little-known events
that were tied to much larger news stories.

I do not share on Twitter every tragic photograph I come across—doing
so would be too overwhelming. I always felt badly about ignoring any of
them, but I inevitably had to. On some days, I could not bear logging on to
Facebook, where my friends from the Middle East would post picture after
picture of the war's horrors. Like many others, I wavered between feelings
of outrage and a sense of helplessness. Earlier, I had written especially
about the refugee outflow from Turkey because I had followed the issue
and had noted the food-subsidy cuts in Jordan (to refugees who were already not doing well) and the loss of hope among refugees in Turkey who
had neither legal rights to work nor a path to citizenship. As I agonized, the
topic was trending on Turkish Twitter, #kıyıyavuraninsanlık, or "humanity washes up ashore," as people who felt heartbroken shared the image. I
decided to post Aylan's picture on my public Twitter feed.

"He was five. Another flimsy boat sunk. 12 dead. Three kids. Cost of not
providing safe passage to people fleeing war." I got his age wrong because
I confused it with that of his deceased brother. I heard from many people,
including parents, how hard it was to see it. Some people got upset with
me for posting such a graphic image. I understood. Many told me how sad
it made them. The picture, indeed, was on its way to worldwide attention,
would be featured on the front page of newspapers around the world, and
would even lead newscasts (to be clear, my posting the picture turned out
to be irrelevant to how far it spread). It would especially shake Canada, where
the family had been headed to live with relatives already there, because the
family had tried to immigrate legally but had failed. The public outcry
helped create a temporary softening of the anti-refugee sentiment that was

rising worldwide, and Canada especially stepped up its campaign to accept many more refugees.

Soon after, though, I encountered claims that the picture was a hoax, that the boys had never died, that they were not refugees, that the picture was staged, or that it had been faked using Photoshop image-editing software. And I was not hearing this only from a random, marginal fringe of people. On Facebook, I noticed that my friends were arguing with their Facebook friends who were telling them that the image was a hoax. I was struck by the proximity of these arguments coming from ordinary people with whom I had friends and acquaintances in common. On the far right, the conspiracy-oriented but popular site Breitbart—whose manager would go on to manage Donald Trump's presidential campaign—ran a story explaining how the picture was staged.[33] The Breitbart writers at least agreed that the boys had drowned, but the site's commenters did not believe even that much. Many claims of fabrication focused on a second picture taken that day of Aylan's brother, who washed up on a different part of the beach. The hoax theories sometimes claimed that Aylan's body was moved from that rocky part to a more "photogenic" location, not understanding that there were two little children who drowned that day, and the second picture was not of Aylan but of his older brother. Some claimed that the pictures were all Photoshopped since the two photographs—of Aylan and his brother—had inconsistencies. Again, it was simply because there were two separate victims.

Reluctantly, and with the help of some journalists in Turkey, I dug into the story to find the photographer and interviews with the soldiers who had been called to the scene after beachgoers discovered the bodies, as well as the other photographs from the scene. It was very sad to have to look at many more pictures of this family's tragedy. We managed to put together a series that showed the different pictures, including ones with other angles than that of the one that had been central to the hoax claims. However, after more discussion, we decided that this was likely futile for the moment—the hoax theories were not going to end if I put forth more pictures. And the widespread reach of the photographs disseminated by legitimate news outlets seemed to make the cries of "Hoax!," "Photoshop!," and "Staged!" less relevant. It was, however, a sad lesson in today's reality:

even the most heartbreaking tragedy is immediately accused of being false, a hoax, a staged event. Had this picture been taken by an ordinary citizen, without the trail of evidence that a professional photographer generated, many more people might never have accepted it as real—or, at least, would have just been left in doubt.

This tactic of sowing doubt as a means of forestalling opposition certainly predates the internet. Sowing doubt occurs through natural polarization in the populace (when each side challenges the other), grassroots efforts (organized campaigns), astroturfing (when corporations or governments pay people to create the appearance of grassroots efforts), direct nation-state intervention, or direct corporate campaigns.

For example, for years, the fossil-fuel industry in the United States actively campaigned to cast doubt on the growing scientific consensus that human-made emissions from burning fossil fuels—coal, oil, and natural gas—were slowly but surely changing the climate. They funded NGOs that acted as fronts for their industry, and they commissioned reports that were used by the press to support an "on-the-one-hand, on-the-other-hand" type of "balanced" reporting that presented the matter to the general public as an issue for doubt and debate long after scientific consensus had actually been reached.[34] The result was that decades passed without meaningful action that might have hurt the profits of the fossil-fuel industry but might have stopped the disastrous climate change that seems inevitable now. And it was not the only industry to do this. A 1969 memo by a tobacco industry executive was titled "Doubt Is Our Product," and it was a successful product. A small, loosely connected network of scientists who had ties to the tobacco industry managed to cast doubt on the idea that tobacco is addictive, and to deny the link between smoking and cancer long after it had been scientifically established.[35]

Confusion and doubt do not have the same effects on those in power as on the movements that challenge power; there is a fundamental asymmetry. Social movements, by their nature, attempt change and call for action, but doubt leads to inaction that perpetuates the status quo. The paralysis and disempowerment of doubt leads to the loss of credibility, spread of confusion, inaction and withdrawal from the issue by ordinary people, depriving movements of energy. If everything is in doubt, while the world is run by secret cabals that successfully manipulate everything behind the scenes, why bother?

Another method that is often cited as one of the key tools by which governments attempt to counter activists is surveillance. Government surveillance is a major concern for a variety of reasons. A prospective whistleblower, for example, might never find the courage to act if she is certain of being exposed, and journalists might be prevented from investigating government wrongdoing. It is certainly true that the internet has greatly increased tracking powers of governments. Hacking software that can break into phones and laptops is available for purchase, and there have been many known incidents of governments using these capabilities against activists and dissidents. Many technology-based efforts to support dissidents around the world have focused on anti-surveillance and anonymization technology.

During the Gezi Park protests, many people would check their phones often, and those with smartphones used them to tweet and post status updates on Facebook. Text messages were also commonly used to share news and updates. Each time the park was teargassed, I noticed that people would take their phones out almost as soon as they could breathe, sometimes while still coughing. In Turkey, though, all cell phones are registered to persons using their unique citizenship number, and the telecommunication infrastructure is mostly owned by, or accessible to, the government. Unless those people had gone to extraordinary measures before coming to the protest—unlikely since the protest had grown so quickly and unexpectedly, and many protesters I interviewed were not experienced activists—the Turkish government knew each and every one, including me.

I asked many of them whether they were worried. "Well, there are so many of us," one shrugged. "What will they do to a million people?" Indeed, it seemed like an instance of the saying about owing money to a bank: if you are out of money and you owe $10,000 to a bank, it's your problem; if you owe $10 billion, then it's the bank's problem. The mass surveillance certainly caused concern, but in the face of a mass movement that was already gathering momentum and becoming quite large, it seemed less dangerous.

Activists are often targeted for surveillance. Movements grow by expanding their networks, and when it comes to surveillance, networks are as weak as their weakest point. All activists trying to expand their networks know that they cannot avoid contact with people they do not know. In fact, that is often exactly what they are trying to do: carry their message beyond their existing network. Just as governments have been known to send informants to open meetings, they also create social media profiles for the sole purpose of joining activist forums online. For activists in movements trying to grow, surveillance is a fact of life that cannot be avoided with higher levels of technological security, since the weakness is inherent and structural: talking to people you do not know well, even if everything is encrypted to hide it from those outside the conversation, opens doors to surveillance. Eventually, a recipient in a growing network will turn out to be either an informant or a well-wisher who's careless with information that was supposed to be nonpublic. Many activists respond to this by embracing publicity, which often fits their political aims anyway. They are trying to attract attention, not hide from it.

I interviewed one activist about a year after the Gezi protests. He had become quite well known and had been openly challenging the government about a scandal that had been dogging it. After we met, raising our voices to be heard in a crowded café in a trendy part of Istanbul, I noticed that an undercover police officer was following us. This is not an uncommon occurrence in Turkey; most activists know how to recognize them, and some even get to know them by sight as they do have somewhat durable "places of work"—somewhere they hangout regularly, often a café or area popular with activists. "Does this happen to you often?" I asked. He shrugged.

We moved to another café, bringing our involuntary follower with us. I turned around and gestured to the man to join us instead of obviously straining to hear us from the next table. It was more annoying than anything else—I was interviewing this activist to publicly write about it. As we walked, our phones—whose location is very easy for a government to track—were moving together, and thus the government could easily know that we were moving together anyway. I asked this activist what he thought of this surveillance.

"I don't care," he said. "I don't care if they torture me; I don't care if they kill me." I was startled. He continued, "I got arrested before, and there was a Twitter campaign to free me. It worked, too. I don't care what they do to me," he said, "I won't change my behavior because of surveillance or threats."

"So, you change nothing about how you behave?" I asked, wondering more about his digital tools, and whether he used technical methods that make surveillance more difficult. He waved his phone, repeating how his phone and Twitter protected him—through publicity, which he valued over freedom from surveillance. His argument was that digital technologies feel empowering to him because their power to publicize is more important to him than their power to surveill.

Then he paused.

"Well," he said, "I do change my behavior for one thing," he said, his shoulders visibly slumping. "I can't have a girlfriend. Or even try to date. It would make my mother sad; she wants me to get married soon, but . . . ."

The story that unfolded was both personal and political. This activist, like others I would talk with, was not worried about surveillance of his political activities. He took it for granted and was mostly resigned to the consequences, and excited about the upsides of social media and digital connectivity. However, he was most afraid of hurting and disappointing his loved ones—especially his mother, who had lost another child to political violence in Turkey—through leaking of personal information that wasn't illegal, or even bad, but just sensitive. Indeed, he knew of prominent activists who had been snared through personal matters that hurt or disappointed their loved ones—an extramarital affair, an embarrassing photograph, or a family feud.

He could defy the threats he faced personally, but the idea of hurting his already-bereaved mother was a red line for him. He knew that his more traditional family wanted him to get married as soon as possible and would see dating as antithetical to what they wanted their surviving son to do, that is, get married to a woman they already had in mind. Surveillance and digital surveillance had restricted his life, but not in the way that many western anti-surveillance activists might envision. It wasn't censorship and it wasn't tracking his political communication.

This tactic of ensnaring activists via surveillance of personal lives is not new, but it has certainly acquired a new life thanks to digital tools. This tactic is so common in central Asian and ex-Soviet countries that it has a name, "kompromat," from "compromising" pictures.[36] In Azerbaijan, for example, as the communications scholar Katy Pearce documents, many female dissidents have been targeted by secret recordings of their bedrooms and living rooms, and investigative journalists have been defamed by fabricated sex tapes that feature actors who resemble them. Digital tools provide activists with important means to spread their public message, but we increasingly conduct our private lives through digital technology as well. E-mails, texts, and private social media conversations leave digital traces that can be hacked, exposed, and used to threaten or blackmail people. Targeted surveillance of personal information may turn out to be a significant threat to social movement activists, beyond surveillance of their political activities, most of which take place in a public or quasi-public manner anyway.

As this book went to press, a striking and drastic story broke out in the United States, creating questions about a potential new instance of these methods being used as a means of political sabotage. The *New York Times* reported that according to the United States intelligence agencies, as well as analyses of digital forensics by independent companies, a foreign government had hacked and strategically dumped internal campaign information and private e-mails from the Democratic political party, targeting races from the presidency to local congressional districts.[37] This wasn't the same as using personal information to target an activist, but the logic was the same: private, internal strategic communication (from one side) was hacked and made public, and asymmetrically offered to both mass media and opposing politicians.

Governments can also mobilize social media to defend themselves from illegitimate attempts to overthrow them. As pictures of tanks in Istanbul continued to fill the television screen in the airport, I turned to my phone again—just like everyone around me in the Antalya terminal. People in Ankara, the capital of Turkey, were reporting sonic booms from low-flying jets and machine-gun fire from helicopters. There was panic online, on television screens, and around me in the airport. There was talk of many dead. Around 11 p.m., a few hours after it all began, the prime minister finally called in to a television station and confirmed what was already apparent: the military, or at least a portion of it, was attempting to take over the country. It was a coup.

"Folks, yes, by all indications this is an ongoing coup attempt in Turkey," I tweeted out. It would be retweeted 747 times, my short sentence reaching hundreds of thousands of people. As I watched my tweets travel, I wondered how the coup would play out this time, when taking over all the mass-media outlets would be insufficient—let alone a single television station, as in the 1980 coup. The coup forces would have to cut the internet completely if they were to succeed in keeping people in the dark. That was not happening, at least not yet.

The prime minister was alive, but the fact had little impact on the airport crowd I was in, or on the online conversations I was following. He was seen as a weak political figure because he had recently been appointed at the behest of the powerful president, Recep Tayyip Erdoğan. Most power in the country revolved around the president, who had been elected in 2014, had served as prime minister for twelve years before that, and had previously been the mayor of Istanbul, the country's biggest city. He had become both a popular and a polarizing figure in the country, and his fate was the most crucial piece of the puzzle of what was going on and where it would end up. The president himself was yet nowhere to be seen.

My phone kept buzzing with social media notifications, texts, and messages from chat applications like WhatsApp messages. I considered leaving the airport as soon as possible, without retrieving my checked-in luggage, but decided against it. As uneasy as I was about being at the airport, an obvious target in a coup, I was not completely sure that it was safe to go anywhere else either. But I also knew that a coup might mean weeks of curfew or, even worse, fighting. I thought that it would be better to have my belongings with me if I was going to end up stuck in one place for a long time. I had already made friends at the airport; a woman had invited me to her home about an hour away. People were exchanging phone numbers and adding each other on WhatsApp.

Soon, airline personnel conceded that things were extraordinary and that nobody was flying anywhere. Workers went to retrieve our luggage. Shortly after midnight, as I was figuring out when I should leave and where I would stay, an aide to the president was trying to use Periscope, a live-video app in Twitter, to let the nation know that Erdoğan was alive. He had apparently left his Marmaris hotel minutes before coup-controlled paratroop commandos had arrived to find him, and now he wanted to call the people into the streets to resist the coup, to take to the major squares around the country, and to occupy important buildings, especially airports.

However, in a twist of history, the president's aide was not logged on to Twitter on his phone from his usual account. Instead, he accidentally broadcast from a personal account with only a few followers rather than the one where he was known as the president's aide. Almost no one saw the broadcast via Periscope. Consequently, most of the country still did not know whether the president was even alive.

A few minutes after the failed attempt at a Twitter broadcast that almost nobody saw, the coup forces took over TRT, the state television, and forced an anchor to read a manifesto declaring that a military council had taken over. It looked as though it was really happening.

For the next fifteen minutes or so, the messages I saw online, as well as the way the anchors on television had started speaking, turned grimmer and grimmer. What people had been pondering and fearing as a possibility—a successful coup—was looking more and more likely. Maybe this was a replay of 1980, the military coup that had set the country on a new path. That event still shaped the political landscape thirty-six years later, with many deleterious effects. The constitution that had been passed under the military dictatorship was still in effect to a large extent, molding Turkey's electoral and judicial systems. Were we about to live through another such time?

About half an hour after midnight, an anchor on CNN Turkey fiddled with her phone. CNN Turkey was a news channel that had largely but not completely succumbed to Turkey's restrictive regime, under which media owners were forced to adopt a pro-government cheerleading stance, either voluntarily as a means to acquire preferential treatment for other corporations in their sprawling holdings, or through coercion via punitive fines and threats. Her hair was pulled up in a ponytail; her face was bereft of makeup. She was wearing a simple white blouse, and her earpiece wasn't even disguised, spiraling back out of her right ear.

"Just a moment," she said, and then, "I apologize for doing it this way," and turned the phone around, holding a small handheld microphone right next to the phone's speakers.[38] "Is Mr. President ready?" she asked into her phone. She repeated herself, waiting for a response, which would determine the fate of the country. The nation heard the voice of the aide who had earlier tried to broadcast via Twitter. "Here's the president," the anchor said, her face tense, and just like that, the president's face appeared on the phone via FaceTime, an easy-to-use live video app that comes with every iPhone.

The president's face looked tiny on the bottom third of the phone screen, under what appeared to be fluorescent lights, in front of white curtains, almost lost in the large frame of the television. It was not at all how people were used to seeing him. The light made him look pale, and the shadows made his face look pallid. But it was unmistakably him.

The president addressed the nation, his voice echoing from the phone. He said that rogue elements in the military were involved in an illegitimate attempt to take over the government. The culprits would be tried in courts and punished. He called on people to take to city squares, major buildings, and airports and to resist the attempted coup.

And just like that, the whole situation was transformed.

The news traveled like wildfire on social media, as well as on other television channels. The resistance had already been bubbling up: the hashtag "#darbeyehayır" (no to the coup) had started trending as soon as it had become obvious that this was a coup. However, confirmation that the president was alive was a major turning point because it made clear that the coup had not yet succeeded, and that whatever happened, there would likely be resistance. In a later survey, about 83 percent of the country said they had watched the president address the nation on television via an iPhone. Yet another survey showed that a majority of the respondents took to the streets after hearing the call from the president on television.[39]

I could see the results of the president's speech immediately. By then, I had decided to drive back to my hotel, an hour away from the airport, and along the way, I saw throngs of people in the streets or in their cars, flags in one hand, phones in the other. People's faces glowed in the light of the phones; many were taking selfies, which would be used to call others to come out to the streets. "Look, here we are." My own WhatsApp and Twitter were also buzzing with the news: the president was alive, and people were taking to the streets as the fighting continued.

Social media was important, but it was not the only place that the information and resistance to the coup spread. Around 1:30 a.m., the government also activated the loudspeaker network of the mosques, all of which had equipment to use for the call to prayer, usually broadcast five times a day at scheduled times. Instead of calling to prayer, though, the mosque loudspeakers broadcast the "sela," a special prayer usually used after funerals and for Friday prayers.[40] It was a call to action; letting people around the country know that something unusual was happening, and imploring them to resist. The mosque loudspeakers could not confirm to people that the president was alive, but social media took care of that as people informed one another. The television stations that were still operating (more would later be occupied by the coup forces) rebroadcast the FaceTime interview with the president.

The coup leaders seemed to have some airpower on their side, but they commanded very limited land forces. Consequently, they went from TV station to TV station, attempting to take them over one by one. However, since television no longer had a monopoly on the transmission of information, the strategy backfired. As soon as they showed up at a TV station, calls went out on social media for people to go to that location and take it back, and people did just that. The nation watched on television as soldiers appeared during live newscasts to shut down the television station. We watched the awkward shot of the empty anchor chair, the camera frozen, and sounds of gunfire or shouting from a distance, somewhere in the building but out of sight, echoing in our living rooms and phone screens. Hashtags bubbled up on Twitter, calling people to action, and we watched as people took television stations back from the soldiers, the same anchor now explaining that she had been forced to read their manifesto with guns pointed at her.

On the small, vertical screen of a live-streaming phone, we watched as jets repeatedly bombed the Parliament building. Deputies from both the governing party and opposition parties huddled together, phones in their hands, as anchors from the still-functioning television stations held their phones, showing the live streams to the TV cameras.

Beside these live streams, Twitter floated pastel-color hearts, as it does with many live streams, as if someone were streaming from a street concert rather than from a parliament resisting attack by jets. In one stream from the phone of a female deputy from the ruling party, a speaker from the opposition party making an impassioned speech against the coup was interrupted by a blast that shook the Parliament, and the phone spiraled down as she took shelter. In another live stream, the Speaker of the Parliament debated whether members should move the session to the basement to be safe from the bombs. A minister went to the lectern, surrounded by other deputies, all of them holding and checking their phones, and said, "If we close the Parliament and go downstairs, people will think the Parliament is afraid. They will leave the squares. What we must do tonight is to die here." The deputies applauded. And they stayed.

What if the deputies, the ministers, and the president had not had phones that could live-stream? A phone call alone might have been possible; but it would have been far less convincing. The only person whose voice is nationally recognizable is the president's, and because he has played such a major role in the country's politics for many years, there are plenty of comedians and actors who can convincingly imitate his voice and his speaking style. Given that Photoshop-doctored pictures and other fake news are not uncommon occurrences on Turkish mass media, people would likely not have entirely trusted a voice-only connection.[41]

Later, journalists who had been involved in the attempts to connect the president to television stations that night told me not only that they had made sure that it was a live stream rather than a phone call, which they could have made earlier, but also that it had been purposefully broadcast from a television station that was known not to be completely subservient to the government. Under fire, the powerful regime had discovered the importance of an independent press that could keep its credibility.

The next day, it looked as though the coup attempt was being defeated, but we would learn later that hundreds had died resisting it. Most mass-media stations were back under the control of their original owners. Even so, government officials and sources continued to use social media heavily to get their message out. But that was not all.

Sending tweets and WhatsApp messages all night, I was running out the data allowance on my Turkish cell phone. I need not have worried. Turkey's telecommunication companies, all of which had close ties to the government, had increased my data plan, along with that of every other subscriber, free of charge. For a nation of netizens used to telecommunication companies throttling or blocking social media, this was a signal that the power of the internet did not belong to any one group.

Epilogue: The Uncertain Climb

THE UNIVERSITY OF TEXAS AT AUSTIN, where I completed my graduate work, has one of the fewer than fifty surviving copies of the Gutenberg Bible, one of the first major printed books in the Western world. It is truly beautiful, with intricate gilded drawings framing each page. The printing press was the center of a world-historical transformation involving forces of production, communication, and media, in some ways like the one we have been living through. Gutenberg's moveable type heralded the Industrial Revolution and the gains in productive power possible with interchangeable parts and mechanical reproduction. However, the book's gorgeous hand-drawn decorations—the paintings with gold leaf called illuminations and the beautiful colored letters called rubrication—were actually an effort to stay anchored in the past—an effort that would prove futile.

If you were Gutenberg or a cardinal of the Catholic Church around the 1450s, you might have boasted about how this invention was going to greatly empower the Catholic Church. At the time, the Catholic Church was in the business of issuing indulgences—notes promising, for a price, a reduction of time to be spent in Purgatory for sins they or their loved ones had committed.

Movable type and the printing press were a way for the Catholic Church to almost literally print money, with the mass production of standardized indulgences. No more would there be unfilled demand because of the shortage of clerical labor required to produce painstakingly handwritten indulgences.[1] Gutenberg's first datable printed document was one of these indulgences, not a copy of his now famous Bible; other printers serving various prominent Catholic officials enthusiastic about this new tool, also started printing these get-out-of-purgatory tickets. By 1500, hundreds of thousands of indulgences had been printed, and church scribes could merely fill in a sinner-cum-customer's "name, date, and place."[2] Pope Leo X issued a substantial number of (printed, of course) indulgences in the 1510s in order to finance the building of Saint Peter's Basilica in the Vatican.

It's no surprise that the first mass market created by the print revolution was in indulgences. Individual copies of the Bible were not only very expensive, but also of use only to the literate, sometimes only to those literate in Latin. Early printers exacerbated this problem by printing Bibles in a manner that did not take advantage of the new affordances of the printing press. The Gutenberg Bible was made to look like previous handwritten and decorated bibles, hiding the novel technology used to produce it. Soon, though, other people would improve capabilities and affordances of movable-type printing, creating cheaper, mass-produced texts that were no longer adorned to look like they were one of a kind. And instead of serving the Catholic Church, these rebels would use the printing press to mass publish pamphlets challenging the church's control over religious affairs and ultimately ushering in the Protestant Reformation.

Perhaps the most famous such pamphlet is Martin Luther's "95 Theses," a fiery denunciation, in part, of the practice of selling indulgences—and a sign that the printing press would be a major weapon in the battle against the deluge of indulgences, a phenomenon also bolstered by the printing press.[3] Luther's pamphlet looked plain, even crude, but it was reprinted quickly and circulated widely. And so, in 1517, Luther went viral.[4] The insurgents also began to mass-produce the Bible, previously very expensive and available almost exclusively in Latin, in the vernacular. The Catholic-Protestant "war of pamphlets" launched by the 95 Theses was, initially, at least, won handily by the Protestants, in part because of the advantage given by Luther's widely published 1522 New Testament translation in German.[5] The dissemination of these ideas set the stage for centuries of religious war and for the creation of new nations, new ideas, and the emergence of modernity.[6]

* * *

What does the era of the printing press teach us in our current period of transition? Barely a decade into a global upheaval in technology, communication, and connectivity, the new state of affairs already appears deceptively familiar. The internet now connects almost every corner of the globe; powerful computers are found in almost every pocket; and algorithms influence decisions in almost every sphere of life. Whenever there is a protest somewhere, people readily look for the associated Twitter hashtag and expect a video livestream, probably from a small phone in one person's hands, but with the power to reach millions.

Yet we have barely begun to understand what this all may mean. The transformation has been very rapid. There are many parts of the world where there was no electricity just a decade ago, and now where even children have cellphones—and there still may not be electricity, at least not regularly.[7]

One key lesson from the past is that our familiarity with a new and rapidly spreading technologies is often superficial, and the full ramifications of these technologies are far from worked out. Another lesson is that what appears to empower one group can also empower its adversaries, and introduce novel twists to many dynamics.

Historian Melvin Kranzberg's famous dictum holds true: "Technology is neither good nor bad; nor is it neutral."[8] Neither are technology's effects static; everything evolves as people invent, innovate, and appropriate technologies for their purposes. This dynamism does not mean that technology provides a level playing field, where each side is equally empowered and equally able to appropriate technologies for its purposes. Not only social forces determine the transformation—features and characteristics of technologies are relevant and these affordances are sometimes beyond the control of these technologies' designers. Any analysis must necessarily embrace this complexity and try to avoid the false dichotomies: optimists versus pessimists; utopians versus dystopians; humans versus technology. I am not arguing for some sort of "technological centrism," but simply for understanding the complex and at times contradictory relationship between different effects of digital technologies.

The story of the printing press should serve as a warning about the dialectical nature of technological-historical transformations; the very technology that enabled the mass printing of indulgences to enrich the Catholic Church led to their opportunistic profusion, feeding the outrage that led to new rebellions against the Church. These rebellions used this same technology for their own purposes but even more effectively, touching off centuries of struggle.

Before 2011, Middle East activists often told me about their efforts to use digital tools to document human rights abuses. They were thrilled to have access to this emergent networked public sphere with few censors. The activists would obtain documents leaked (sometimes from disgruntled state employees) that showed corruption and bribery, and would put them online. Sometimes, police would film themselves beating up or torturing detainees, and the activists would find and use this documentation to expose brutality. In Tunisia, activists used online tools to track how the dictator's wife was using the presidential plane to go shopping in Paris and other trendy cities—the activists put her travels on a Google map which was shared widely.[9]

The lack of gatekeepers felt empowering, and it was.

Just a few years later, in 2016, investigations revealed that various forms of misinformation and fraudulent news had gone viral on Facebook leading up to the US presidential election. Some of these were "fake news" sites—hastily published webpages that were pretending to be legitimate news sites, hoping that people would share them. These sites had a high degree of versimilitude to actual news sites, sometimes including fake tabs for "weather" or "traffic." For example, millions saw false stories, shared hundreds of thousands of times, claiming that the Pope had endorsed Donald Trump (when, in fact, they disagreed vociferously about refugee policies, and the Pope does not endorse presidential candidates) or that Wikileaks documents showed that Trump's opponent, Hillary Clinton, had sold weapons to ISIS.[10]

These sites' operators could use Facebook's advanced targeting capabilities to find willing audiences, hoping some of those readers would share the story with their own network. If a story hit a nerve, it could be seen by millions of people, some of whom would click on the link, making money for the creators of the site through ads displayed on the site. Both the expense and the profit was low: each click might return a fraction of a penny, but the cost per viewer was lower still. To spend $50 targeting on Facebook and make a return of $100 in Google or Facebook ad money was perfectly fine if you were, say, a Macedonian teenager pumping out a dozen stories per day, collecting on those that hit paydirt.

Analyses after the elections showed that some of these "fake news" sites were outperforming many of the actual news stories that had also gone viral.[11] Another study showed that middle school students felt hopelessly lost trying to distinguish fraudulent sites from real news. A survey taken shortly after the 2016 election showed that almost a third of Americans remembered seeing such stories, and that upwards of 80–90 percent of the people who remembered those stories could not tell that they were fake. This group included supporters of Hillary Clinton, even though an overwhelming majority of the fake stories seemed to be in favor of Donald Trump, who would go on to win the electoral college by the small margin of about a hundred thousand votes in three states.[12]

Such disinformation campaigns exploiting the affordances of search and social media platforms' architecture, algorithms, and ad-financed business models that make it lucrative to spew false propaganda can have consequences beyond one presidential election: viral misinformation is also part of ongoing ethnic cleansing campaigns in Myanmar.[13]

After the election, with outrage over such misinformation becoming a public relations nightmare for Facebook, Mark Zuckerberg tentatively announced some early steps to curb this traffic. Meanwhile, NBC News interviewed some of the teenagers in a small town in Macedonia where fake news had become the new gold rush—with hundreds of people spending their days pumping out false stories, waiting for any one of them to go viral.

One Macedonian teenager, whose stories, including "JUST IN: Obama Illegally Transferred DOJ Money to Clinton Campaign!" and "BREAKING: Obama Confirms Refusal to Leave White House, He Will Stay in Power!", had gone viral before the election, shrugged over the consequences. "I didn't force anyone to give me money," he said. "People sell cigarettes, they sell alcohol. That's not illegal, why is my business illegal?"[14] These teenagers had caused a happy crisis for the local nightclubs, which lacked the capacity to accommodate all their new party-goers, ordering ice buckets filled with large bottles of vodka.

I checked back with activists in the Middle East who confirmed that such fake news—often aimed at discrediting dissidents—had gone viral in their own countries, too. One Tunisian activists told me that he thought it was a major reason a secular party had lost one election. Another blogger wrote about the spread of fake news in Egypt, and lamented: "The social media is always highlighted for its role in the Arab spring, especially in the Egyptian revolution. Well, I think it is time to let the world know that the social media is also destroying the Arab Spring."[15]

Fake news and other forms of misinformation could proliferate for some of the same reasons that these same activists could earlier easily share their own content documenting corruption and exposing wrong-doing. The hands-off approach of most of the platforms regarding the distribution of such content meant that there was nobody watching what spread; traditional gatekeepers, now dependent on these platforms to spread their own stories, were critically weakened. The internet made it easy for anyone to quickly set up a webpage, and Facebook's user interface made it hard to tell the legitimate news outlets such as the *New York Times* or Fox News apart from fake ones such as the "Denver Guardian"—whose story about a fictional FBI agent killed in a suspected murder-suicide implied that Clinton had murdered someone for leaking her e-mails. The affordances of digital connectivity; globalization of information flows; business models, policies, and algorithms of the few dominant platforms; ease of setting up sites; and enterprising young people had combined in yet another perfect storm.

The moral of this story isn't that "fake news" definitely swung the US election in 2016, or somehow the past was an ideal place of only facts and reasoned dialogue in the public sphere. In fact, various forms of misinformation and propaganda have always been part of the public sphere, and the success of "fake news" rested on many antecedent dynamics. Mass media had already been losing credibility both due to its own missteps and failures, but also due to a sustained attack against its normative function as gatekeeper for facts. There had also been decades of challenge to authorities and information intermediaries from the left and the right—these attacks often stemmed from somewhat different reasons, but the net effect was weakening of trust in all gatekeepers. Partisan sources of news, which spread misinformation by framing a small kernel of a fact into a misleading story, or flat-out falsehoods, were also a stable of the media ecology by the time the 2016 election rolled around. The polarization in the population was also deeply set. "Fake news" virality rising on affordances of digital technology and Silicon Valley business models added to these existing trends. Everything has many causes in a close election, a single factor can swing the result, but only if you assume all other factors are fixed. Further, even when you confine yourself to one factor, causation is not always straightforward; clearly, the demand for this type of information existed, and for some of the readers the fake stories operated more as an excuse or retrospective justification for their actions than as a cause. The lack of trust in elites and gatekeepers is a story with deep roots and a long history.[16]

I am also not arguing that we should return to some idealized past. Jürgen Habermas's concept of the early-modern public sphere, discussed earlier in the book, as a place of rational, fact-based discussion, where issues of power, identity, flaws in cognition, and deception, among others, are less relevant, is a selective idealization. As the sociologist Craig Calhoun points out, "Habermas tends to judge the eighteenth century by Locke and Kant, the nineteenth century by Marx and Mill, and the twentieth century by the typical suburban television viewer."[17] Neither should we judge the networked public sphere merely by comparing an in-depth investigative story in the *New York Times* or ProPublica with a viral fake story in the "Denver Guardian."

Like the printing press and the industrial revolution, this historical transformation in digital connectivity and computing is a complex, dialectical processes with no clear teleology, no predetermined outcome or preset group of winners and losers. The same undermining of gatekeepers that has permitted social movements to bring the facts to the public despite active repression by authoritarian regimes or casual indifference also enable the effective suppression of the facts through the proliferation of fake news. Perhaps the best approach is not to seek unified overarching answers, but to identify and delineate mechanisms and dynamics introduced by these new technologies and how they entangle with political, social, and cultural forces, with the aid of empirically grounded conceptual tools like those I and others have attempted to provide.[18]

　　As I conclude, I will review some of the conceptual tools that this book has developed and dynamics that it has examined, especially in the context of some of challenges that social movements face going forward—but always keeping in mind that this story is far from over.

The emergence of the digitally networked public sphere has not necessarily introduced new fundamental social mechanisms—humans still behave like humans. Digital technologies have, however, drastically altered the conditions under which these mechanisms operate on social movements.[19]

　　Take, for example, homophily—the tendency people have to connect and interact with others they perceive as fundamentally similar to themselves—and pluralistic ignorance—the tendency potential dissidents have to feel isolated and marginal because of a lack of awareness that many others share their viewpoint. These are crucial mechanisms for community formation in general—homophily for the ties that bind, pluralistic ignorance for policing the boundaries. Social media enables the emergence of long-distance homophily based on viewpoint, including political viewpoints, and thus the formation of a new kind of political community. Digital technologies also change the many ways we interact with our social ties, a common source of movement recruitment.[20] Political scientist Bruce Bimber discusses this as "accelerated pluralism" in the context of interest groups, but these dynamics also foster movement formation, and create a strong mechanism for triggering information cascades (what happens when pluralistic ignorance collapses) as well.[21] Such possibilities, have, of course, always existed.[22] Charles Kurzman's groundbreaking book about the Iranian Revolution of 1979, shows how this operated in the context of the revolution, with radio, pamphlets, street protests, and funerals making revolutionary social change a visible and thinkable option—almost all at once.[23] Nowadays, though, such processes, through which people find and signal to one another to reveal previously private opinions, form communities, and create polarization with other communities are all also done online through digital connectivity. A process that was difficult before has now become common; one result is that this sort of process need not have the results, like revolution, that it had in the past.

This book develops a *capacities* and *signals* approach to social movements which allows shifting the analysis from outcomes and indicators like protest size and number of rallies to underlying capacities and capabilities, and to better comprehend the dialectic and co-evolving landscape of threat, leverage, and challenge between social movements and the powerful. Looking at protest and other acts of social movements as *signals* of underlying capabilities help us examine how digital technologies can simultaneously empower movements and increase their capabilities but also complicate social dynamics, introduce new ones, and even fuel fragilities.

While I specifically focus mostly on three capacities—narrative, electoral or institutional, and disruptive—these are not an exhaustive list of movement capabilities, and the method can be expanded. This approach also allows multiple dynamics to be considered in relationship to one another, and us to analyze the complex impact of digital technologies. Capabilities are like muscles that need to developed; digital technologies allow "shortcuts" which can be useful for getting to a goal, but bypass the muscle development that might be crucial for the next step. It is difficult, if not impossible, to develop one set of muscles without also developing others that work in support and coordination; digital technologies can sever or alter this link, allowing for the social movement equivalent of a bodybuilder with massive pectorals but no biceps or deltoids to speak of.

Applying this framework to antiauthoritarian movements on the left, I have looked at how these effects interact with the culture and sensibilities of those movements.[24] For example, the desire to organize on the fly through "adhocracy"—tasks being taken care of without formal structures, often with few people using digital tools and on the basis of whomever shows up—originates in part from participatory nature and the "leaderless" sensibility of these movements, which is not a mere accident of the affordances of digital technologies. This method has also become a common way for movements to raise and mobilize for resources.[25] Adhocracy allows for the organization, for example, of big protests or major online campaigns with minimal effort and advance-work, but this empowerment can come along with a seemingly paradoxical weakness. I find that many such movements lose out on *network internalities* or the gains in resilience and collective decision-making and acting capacity that emerge from the long-term work of negotiation and interaction required to maintain the networks as functioning and durable social and political structures. In the past, this was more organic to the process of tak- ing care of tasks and preparation for acts of protest, from rallies to marches to producing dissident media—there was no other way to do it quickly or on-the-fly. Taking care of such tasks through digital adhocratic methods leads to many significant consequences, ranging from inverted movement trajectories (protest first, organize later unlike the past where a large protest was the culmination of long-term work) to complex frailties including *tactical freeze*, where movements cannot quickly respond to changing conditions and have an inability to negotiate and delegate when necessary—since they have no strong means of collectively making decisions and adapting to new cir- cumstances. On the other hand, this means that movements cannot be eas- ily "decapitated" by killing, coopting, or corrupting a few leaders, and the participatory structure is the very reason many people join protests in the first place.

Collective action has always required a balance between empowering the individual voice and expressing the will of the group. Digital technology can often amplify this tension. Sometimes, great unity and collective iden- tity can emerge as people coalesce around hashtags that sing the song of the excluded and the marginalized. But networked movements have few means of dealing with the inevitable internal conflicts of politics, as well as the natural jockeying for status and attention. Who speaks for the movement as a whole when members can speak through their individual social media accounts, but there is no mechanism for closure or decision making?

Digital technologies also highlight the importance of *attention* as a key resource, no longer to be conflated with mass media, and no longer under the sole control of traditional elites.[26] In the networked public sphere, cen- sorship, too, needs to be understood in new configuration, as a denial of attention through multi-pronged strategies, not just blocking something from being published in a newspaper or discussed on television. Adding to the complexity, many of the key platforms on which social movements operate—Facebook, Twitter, and YouTube, are in the business of monetiz- ing attention, and not necessarily in ways that are conducive to health or success of social movements or the public sphere. The shift from dissemination of scarce information as the challenge social movements face to those of credibility, trust, and information glut has been jarring for many movements. That said, new intermediaries are already emerging to respond to these challenges: citizen journalist collectives, employing new modes of verification and gatekeeping designed for social media.[27]

The other side of the dialectical coin is present as well. Leaderless and horizontal movements, with all their strengths and challenges, long predate the internet. Jo Freeman's feminist treatise from the 1970s, "The Tyranny of Structurelessness," examines how an informal and seemingly horizontal style of organization can lead to the tyranny of a few who jockey informally to exercise power without accountability. That analysis applied to "closed-door" or "private network" meetings between people who appoint themselves as a movement elite, but a greatly exacerbated version of that problem continues in the open in networked movements; indeed, the business models, policies, algorithms, and ideologies of the governing commercial platforms that activists use promote it. As Nobel Prize–winning economist Herbert Simon wrote in 1971, in an information-rich world, the real scarcity is in attention, and the key question is how "to allocate that attention efficiently among the overabundance of information sources that might consume it."[28] Social media platforms are designed for inefficient allocation of attention; they aim to increase the amount of time spent on their site, often to the detriment of efficient consumption of important information.

Therefore, these sites often reward quarrelsome or even extreme behavior within movements—attention getters, stunts, and spectacles. Corporate platforms can also entrench echo chambers because hearing only those views one agrees with makes people feel more comfortable and thus more likely to spend more time on the site. But these platforms also encourage polarization because people whose views are strengthened in these echo chambers then find people from the other side to argue with online. All of this creates a spectacle more people want to watch, and corporate platforms can use this opportunity to bombard users with more ads and gather more behavior data to help profile users for the benefit of advertisers. Worse, much of this activity is public and permanent by default, causing movements to re-litigate old fights again and again.[29] This makes for movements brimming with activity, but much of it is chaotic and even self-defeating. Thus, Freeman's secret movement elite can morph into a micro-celebrity movement elite, based on the manufactured structureless-ness of the social media attention economy.

Social media sites also mix people's personal lives with their political trajectories. In the 1960s, the feminist movement correctly identified that the personal is political: individual experiences are embedded within structures of power. Now it appears also that everything political is personal, since movement politics is experienced in environments that combine multiple contexts from the personal to the political, all homogenized because multiple audiences who might otherwise be separated by time and space are all on the same Facebook page.[30] Many personal aspects of one's life and interactions expressed on social media—tastes in music, travel, offhand statements about current cultural events—have become part of political expression, and the multiple social roles that each person plays—a natural part of human society—have become harder to maintain. All of this feeds political conflict, which is now deeply personal as well.

Hate, harassment, and counter-movements also thrive online.[31] Activists find themselves battling their opponents' harassment and counter-movements, and although the authorities may not as easily censor their speech formally, the need to battle armies of abusive and threatening trolls can lead to self-silencing and self-censorship.[32] What started as a space of free expression and free assembly has increasingly become a danger to social movement activists who find themselves targeted, their private information leaked as a means to intimidate them, and their voices drowned out or distorted by ad-friendly algorithms. At the same time, movements based on ethnosupremacy or extremism also spring to life online as those on the fringe find one another and set their own narrative, recruit followers, and push the boundaries of acceptable discourse.

Activists must go where people are, and network effects mean that once a platform gathers a larger user base, it effectively shuts out competition. Commercial online spaces that provide a few tools for organizational strength and decision making but make it easy for a few people to dominate conversations have become the hegemonic activist tools. A few such platforms are so dominant and consequential that the tyranny of structurelessness has merged with the tyranny of the platforms.

* * *

Repression has always been one of the most important challenges movements face.[33] Digital technologies have altered movement resilience to repression by developing some capabilities social movements seek, while weakening them in other. However, digital technologies have also added new dimensions to what the powerful can attempt to repress or demobilize movements. Governments, too, have developed increasingly sophisticated strategies against threats that networked movements in the new public sphere poses to their hold on power, even though they can no longer effectively censor in the old ways; as an oft-quoted aphorism by internet pioneer John Gilmore goes, "The Net interprets censorship as damage and routes around it."[34] There is even a name for the phenomenon of attracting more attention by attempting to hide something, just as Barbra Streisand inadvertently publicized the location of her home by battling to remove images of her mansion from the California Coastal Records Project.

There is also increasingly a sort of "reverse Streisand effect"—a deliberate information glut can hide the truth by denying attention or credibility to events or facts inconvenient to those in power. As a result of this, instead of an aware public, there is often a lot of distraction, confusion, and partisan polarization about which claims are true. One of the networked public sphere's strengths for social movements is that it allows them to bypass and weaken gatekeepers, but as discussed in the case of fake news, its vulnerability to censorship by information glut and distraction stems from the same mechanism: the lack of broad agreement about who is an expert or what constitutes expertise, combined with the lack of the usual indicators of expertise provided by gatekeeping institutions, makes it easier for those in power to induce political paralysis through confusion and doubt. The effects are not symmetric. Challengers need attention and authority to persuade people to mobilize, while those in power merely need to keep them from acting. Muddying the waters is often good enough for the powerful.

One of the earliest means of protest on the on the internet by dissidents had been the "DDOS," or the denial-of-service attack in which thousands of people, bots, or scripts would repeatedly ping a website, overwhelming its capacity to respond, thus taking it down. For example, the website of a corporation that had just undertaken an unpopular action may go down as people around the world coordinate to drown it in requests. Nowadays, however, governments and the powerful, along with other authoritarians, have adopted parts of this playbook: by kicking up massive clouds of claims, accusations, misinformation, and controversies, they can overwhelm the capacity of the public and traditional media to respond to any one of them; thus causing a type of paralysis. It's as if the networked public sphere, and indeed traditional institutions of democracy, can be DDOSed via releasing large numbers of flares, each attracting and consuming attention, thus making focus and sustained conversation impossible.

Censorship via blocking is not an end but a means to prevent political action; if hiding information is not feasible, confusion may work just fine. Indeed, confusion and misinformation, whether deliberate or a by-product of information glut, have emerged as significant political problems for social movements.

This coevolution of power and protest is far from over, and social movements are far from static.[35] Many social movements, too, are testing new arenas, developing new tools, and building new capacities. They are flexing new muscles. It is wrong to label movements that struggle as failures, just as it is wrong to conclude that a large protest, measured by the number of people on the street, is a sure sign of success. The past offers limited guidance because similar looking moments in 2017 and 1965 or in China and the United States do not necessarily correspond to the same moment in the movement's trajectory or signal the same capacity to influence governments or enact change.

Digital tools have altered the narrative, disruptive, and electoral and institutional capacities of movements and the ways in which they can signal those capacities, resulting in strengths, weaknesses, and complexities. After an initial shock, the powerful have learned to read the digital signals of these capacities more accurately, and they have figured out ways of responding, sometimes even by mobilizing similar capacities and methods. In response, many movements are now looking to shore up both their own capabilities and those of their tools, digital and non-digital.

Some movements, including the left-leaning, horizontalist, and antiauthoritarian ones most examined in this book, have turned to engaging the electoral-institutional sphere, which they had long avoided, and using digital tools, including new ones created by movement actors, to leverage their influence in that sphere as well. In the United States, Black Lives Matter—a movement named after a hashtag—has managed not just to draw attention to a long-neglected issue, racial injustice in law enforcement and sentencing, but also to affect the electoral landscape. After decades when tough-on-crime platforms were a no-brainer for aspiring district attorneys, with literally no downside, suddenly prosecutors and district attorneys known for being weak on curbing police abuses or on pushing for accountability in the criminal justice system have been voted out of office.[36]

The Occupy movement in the United States may have largely withered away, but its themes remain relevant and resonant. Some of its activists found a political opening in the unlikely presidential campaign of Bernie Sanders, a quirky septuagenarian senator from Vermont who calls himself a "democratic socialist" and who mounted a surprisingly strong challenge to the institutionally backed and initially much better resourced candidacy of Hillary Clinton. Sanders followed in the footsteps of Howard Dean's and Barack Obama's presidential runs,[37] which had used digital tools to create a movement rather than a strictly hierarchical campaign.[38] Although Sanders lost the nomination to Clinton, the strength of the challenge from such a seemingly unlikely quarter surprised many political observers. Clinton then lost the general election to another surprise candidate, Donald Trump, a reality-television celebrity and businessman whose unconventional candidacy benefited from some of the technologies discussed in this book.

Elsewhere in the world, from Greece to Spain to Iceland, new political parties born of protest movements have either formed governments or have come close. In Spain, a party called Podemos was formed from the Indignados movement—the wave of protests and occupations that especially shook southern European countries in 2011. Podemos quickly catapulted to being the second-biggest party in Spain while still continuing many of its participatory practices, such as grassroots assemblies. In Greece, Syriza, a political party born of the protests centering on Syntagma Square in central Athens, came to power and found itself wrestling with deep structural issues within Greece and the European Union. None of these parties have been free of tensions and challenges, of course. Such insurgent political parties find themselves battling a deluge of inherited problems: entrenched bureaucracies, global power structures, their own inexperience in government, the tensions between their horizontal roots and the complexities of decision making and representation, and grassroots activists who remain wary of political power. Still, in the 2016 elections, a platform consisting of Podemos and a few other small parties won the second most votes and the third most parliamentary seats in Spain, a striking result for a political party barely two years old. Such new experiments, fusing both existing strengths and impulses of these movements but attempting to incorporate different tools and strategic visions, are discussed around the world in conversations between activists who consider next steps.

Digital tools continue to evolve, too. Many movements seek decision-making structures that align with their participatory impulses. In New Zealand, technically inclined veterans of its Occupy movement launched a platform called Loomio, a tool designed for horizontalist movements that want to keep the participatory structures of the assembly model to facilitate decision making. I met with one of its cofounders Benjamin Knight in New York. He was only in his twenties, but he was already a veteran of the Occupy movement and frustrated by its lack of tactical and strategic decision-making capacities. Teaming up with other people, he created Loomio, an online platform that blends practical considerations with a movement ethos. A wide range of actors, from activists planning movements to the government in New Zealand organizing a census, use the tool.

In 2014, Knight told me that already about 60 percent of the traffic to Loomio was coming from Spain, where Podemos won crucial offices, including the mayoralty of Madrid, won by a female attorney in her seventies who had started her career defending people detained by Franco's dictatorship and then, after Franco's fall, fighting corruptions in the courts.

In the summer of 2015, I met with a young Spanish activist in Madrid, in a café next to the famous Plaza del Sol, where the indignados movement had begun. It was just a few days after the Podemos-backed candidate for mayor, Manuela Carmena, took office—a striking moment: a brand new political party forged in the heat of a protest occupation winning mayoralty of the capital of the country, unseating the party that had held that office for twenty-four years. Involved in the *indignados* protests from the beginning, this activist was elated by all that had happened. She was also trying to balance optimism and caution. It was a beautiful summer day, and there was no longer an occupation in the square itself. But the rebellious impulse had diffused into the city, and not just to its top office.

Madrid was enveloped by vibrant grassroots activity, often coalescing in councils and assemblies of all kinds: art councils, health councils, and social work councils. But now the local government, too, joined the grassroots efforts. The city decided to stop evictions of families living in subsidized social housing. Similarly, the newly elected Madrid city council now worked in parallel with bottom-up efforts to restructure debts to large banks, announcing that "social sustainability" would come before debt repayments for the city. Citizen assemblies continued to meet, and the new mayor took the subway to work. Movement and governance had blended in new ways whose outcome was uncertain.

We sat outside at the café sidewalk tables and sipped our drinks, shielded from the brilliant sun by a colorful awning. I asked this activist whether she had a sense of where things would go. She tried to ponder some scenarios, but too many unprecedented things had already happened. Prediction was difficult. "I don't know," she said. "We will keep walking, and keep asking questions," she continued, talking mostly in English but occasionally switching to Spanish. I was startled. It was a phrase , as you know from the preface, I had heard almost two decades earlier in the mountains of Chiapas from the indigenous peasants of the Zapatista rebellion: "Preguntando caminamos" or "Asking, we walk"—we make our path, questioning it as we go along.

I first thought that she had consciously evoked the phrase, but then I realized that she might have been too young to have known any details about the Zapatistas. I was about to bring it up, but then I changed my mind. It was important to learn from the past, no doubt. But maybe it was better to keep walking forward and to keep asking questions.

NOTES

Introduction

1. Rasha Abdullah, *Egypt's Media in the Midst of the Revolution* (Washington, D.C.: Carnegie Endowment for International Peace, 2014).

2. An Xiao Mina, "Hashtag Memes: Breaking the Single Story through Humour," Al Jazeera, March 2013, http://www.aljazeera.com/indepth/opinion/2013/03/2013326132026281740.html.

3. Ian Hutchby, "Technologies, Texts and Affordances," *Sociology* 35, no. 2 (2001): 441–56; and Sandra K. Evans, Katy E. Pearce, Jessica Vitak, and Jeffrey W. Treem, "Explicating Affordances: A Conceptual Framework for Understanding Affordances in Communication Research," *Journal of Computer-Mediated Communication*, December 2016.

4. Yochai Benkler, *The Wealth of Networks: How Social Production Transforms Markets and Freedom* (New Haven, Conn.: Yale University Press, 2006).

5. Thomas Schelling, *The Strategy of Conflict* (Cambridge, Mass.: Harvard University Press, 1960), 69; Medhi Shadmehr and Dan Bernhardt, "Collective Action with Uncertain Payoffs: Coordination, Public Signals, and Punishment Dilemmas," *American Political Science Review* 105, no. 4 (2011): 829–51.

6. David A. Snow, E. Burke Rochford, Steven K. Worden, and Robert D. Benford, "Frame Alignment Processes, Micromobilization, and Movement Participation," *American Sociological Review* 51, no. 4 (1986): 464–81, doi:10.2307/2095581; David A. Snow and Robert D. Benford, "Ideology, Frame Resonance, and Participant Mobilization," *International Social Movement Research* 1, no. 1 (1988): 197–217; Robert D. Benford and David A. Snow, "Framing Processes and Social Movements: An Overview and Assessment," *Annual Review of Sociology* 26, no. 1 (2000): 611–39, doi:10.1146/annurev.soc.26.1.611.

7. Mancur Olson, *The Logic of Collective Action: Public Goods and the Theory of Groups* (Cambridge, Mass.: Harvard University Press, 1965); Pamela Oliver, Gerald

Marwell, and Ruy Teixeira, "A Theory of the Critical Mass. I. Interdependence, Group Heterogeneity, and the Production of Collective Action," *American Journal of Sociology* 91, no. 3 (1985): 522–56.

8. Jennifer Earle, "Political Repression: Iron Fists, Velvet Gloves, and Diffuse Control," *Annual Review of Sociology* 37 (2011): 261–84.

9. An Xiao Mina, "#Hashtagging the Streets," The Civic Beat, December 5, 2014, https://medium.com/the-civic-beat/hashtagging-the-streets-7fb8ca777076#.ru8632wdl.

10. Malcolm Gladwell, "Small Change," *New Yorker,* October 4, 2010, http://www.newyorker.com/magazine/2010/10/04/small-change-malcolm-gladwell.

11. Keith N. Hampton, Inyoung Shin, and Weixu Lu, "Social Media and Political Discussion: When Online Presence Silences Offline Conversation," *Information, Communication and Society* 0, no. 0 (2016): 1–18.

Chapter 1. A Networked Public

1. Benedict Anderson, *Imagined Communities: Reflections on the Origin and Spread of Nationalism* (London: Verso, 1991).

2. Meltem Ahiska, "Occidentalism: The Historical Fantasy of the Modern," *South Atlantic Quarterly* 102, nos. 2–3 (2003): 351–79.

3. Anderson, *Imagined Communities.*

4. Anthony Giddens, *The Consequences of Modernity* (Stanford, Calif.: Stanford University Press, 1990).

5. Jürgen Habermas, *The Structural Transformation of the Public Sphere: An Inquiry into a Category of Bourgeois Society* (Cambridge, Mass.: MIT Press, 1989).

6. Gerard A. Hauser, "Vernacular Dialogue and the Rhetoricality of Public Opinion," *Communication Monographs* 65, no. 2 (1998): 83–107, doi:10.1080/0363775 9809376439.86.

7. Nancy Fraser, *Rethinking the Public Sphere: A Contribution to the Critique of Actually Existing Democracy* (Milwaukee: University of Wisconsin–Milwaukee, Center for Twentieth-Century Studies, 1990).

8. Habermas, *Structural Transformation of the Public Sphere.*

9. Manuel Castells, *The Rise of the Network Society* (Chichester: Wiley-Blackwell, 2011).

10. Jim Dwyer, "When Official Truth Collides with Cheap Digital Technology," *New York Times,* July 30, 2008, http://www.nytimes.com/2008/07/30/nyregion/30about.html.

11. Walter J. Ong, *Orality and Literacy: The Technologizing of the Word* (London: Methuen, 1982).

12. Michael Rapport, *Year of Revolution* (New York: Basic Books, 2008).

13. Fraser, *Rethinking the Public Sphere.*

14. Miller McPherson, Lynn Smith-Lovin, and James M. Cook, "Birds of a Feather: Homophily in Social Networks," *Annual Review of Sociology* 27 (2001): 415–44.

15. Anthony Giddens, *Modernity and Self-Identity: Self and Society in the Late Modern Age* (Stanford, Calif.: Stanford University Press, 1991); Ulrich Beck and Mark

Ritter, *Risk Society: Towards a New Modernity* (London: Sage Publications, 1992); Harrison Rainie and Barry Wellman, *Networked: The New Social Operating System* (Cambridge, Mass.: MIT Press, 2012).

16. Theda Skocpol and Vanessa Williamson, *The Tea Party and the Remaking of Republican Conservatism* (Oxford: Oxford University Press, 2012); Andreas Madestam, Daniel Shoag, Stan Veuger, and David Yanagizawa-Drott, "Do Political Protests Matter? Evidence from the Tea Party Movement," *Quarterly Journal of Economics* 128, no. 4 (2013): 1633–85, doi:10.1093/qje/qjt021.

17. Madestam et al., "Do Political Protests Matter?"

18. Marc Lynch, *Voices of the New Arab Public: Iraq, Al-Jazeera, and Middle East Politics Today* (New York: Columbia University Press, 2010).

19. Amnesty International, "Tunisia: Journalist Faces Imprisonment for Covering Gafsa Unrest," February 2010, https://www.amnesty.org/en/documents/mde30 /006/2010/en/.

20. Eric Gobe, "The Gafsa Mining Basin between Riots and a Social Movement: Meaning and Significance of a Protest Movement in Ben Ali's Tunisia" (working paper, 2010), https://halshs.archives-ouvertes.fr/halshs-00557826.

21. Jamai Al-Gasimi, "Ben Ali Rescues Facebook from Censorship," *Middle East Online,* September 3, 2008, http://www.middle-east-online.com/english/?id =27687.

22. Evgeny Morozov, *The Net Delusion: The Dark Side of Internet Freedom* (New York: PublicAffairs, 2011); Evgeny Morozov, "From Slacktivism to Activism," *Foreign Policy,* September 5, 2009, http://foreignpolicy.com/2009/09/05/from -slacktivism-to-activism/. My criticism of *The Net Delusion* here is about the concept of slacktivism. There was much else about the book to recommend, though I found it too internet-centric in its analysis of politics in the digital age. My full review can be found at Zeynep Tufekci, "Delusions Aside, the Net's Potential Is Real," *Atlantic,* January 12, 2011, http://www.theatlantic .com/technology/archive/2011/01/delusions-aside-the-nets-potential-is-real /69370/.

23. Doug McAdam and Ronnelle Paulsen, "Specifying the Relationship between Social Ties and Activism," *American Journal of Sociology* 99, no. 3 (1993): 640–67, doi:10.1086/230319.

24. Henry Farrell, "The Tech Intellectuals," *Democracy Journal* 30 (2013), http:// democracyjournal.org/magazine/30/the-tech-intellectuals/.

25. Tim Wu, "Book Review: 'To Save Everything, Click Here' by Evgeny Morozov," *Washington Post,* April 12, 2013, https://www.washingtonpost.com/opinions/book -review-to-save-everything-click-here-by-evgeny-morozov/2013/04/12/0e82400a -9ac9-11e2-9a79-cb5280c81c63_story.html?utm_term=.doab73ff3c64.

26. For in-depth explorations of "reality" in the digital age and online spaces, see pioneering work by Annette N. Markham, *Life Online: Researching Real Experience in Virtual Space,* 1st ed. (Walnut Creek, Calif.: AltaMira Press, 1998); Annette Markham and Nancy K. Baym, eds., *Internet Inquiry: Conversations about Method,* 1st ed. (Los Angeles: Sage, 2008); N. K. Baym, "The Emergence of

Community in Computer-Mediated Interaction," in *Cybersociety: Computer-Mediated Communication and Community*, ed. S. G. Jones (Thousand Oaks, Calif.: Sage, 1995), 138–63. For the term "digital dualism" see Nathan Jurgenson, "When Atoms Meet Bits: Social Media, the Mobile Web and Augmented Revolution," *Future Internet* 4, no. 1 (2012): 83–91, doi:10.3390/fi4010083.

27. Racha Mourtada and Fadi Salem, "Facebook Usage: Factors and Analysis" (Arab Social Media Report, Dubai School of Government, 2011), http://unpan1.un.org/intradoc/groups/public/documents/dsg/unpan044212.pdf.

28. Marc Lynch, *The Arab Uprising: The Unfinished Revolutions of the New Middle East* (New York: Public Affairs, 2012).

29. Rasha A. Abdulla, "The Revolution Will Be Tweeted," The Cairo Review of Global Affairs, Special Report on the Internet, 2011, p. 3, http://www.aucegypt.edu/GAPP/CairoReview/Pages/articleDetails.aspx?aid=89.

30. Ethan Zuckerman, "Cute Cats to the Rescue? Participatory Media and Political Expression," 2013, http://ethanzuckerman.com/papers/cutecats2013.pdf.

31. Mike Isaac, "Facebook Said to Create Censorship Tool to Get Back into China," *New York Times*, November 22, 2016, http://www.nytimes.com/2016/11/22/technology/facebook-censorship-tool-china.html.

32. Mark S. Granovetter, "The Strength of Weak Ties," *American Journal of Sociology* 78, no. 6 (1973): 1360–80.

33. Eytan Bakshy, Solomon Messing, and Lada A. Adamic, "Exposure to Ideologically Diverse News and Opinion on Facebook," *Science* 348, no. 6239 (2015): 1130, http://science.sciencemag.org/content/348/6239/1130.

34. Michael Suk-Young Chwe, *Rational Ritual: Culture, Coordination, and Common Knowledge* (Princeton, N.J.: Princeton University Press, 2003).

35. Wael Ghonim, *Revolution 2.0: The Power of the People Is Greater Than the People in Power: A Memoir* (Boston: Houghton Mifflin, 2012); Jose Antonio Vargas, "How an Egyptian Revolution Began on Facebook," *New York Times*, February 17, 2012, http://www.nytimes.com/2012/02/19/books/review/how-an-egyptian-revolution-began-on-facebook.html; personal interviews with Wael Ghonim on multiple occasions by the author in 2015 and 2016.

36. Zeynep Tufekci and Christopher Wilson, "Social Media and the Decision to Participate in Political Protest: Observations from Tahrir Square," *Journal of Communication* 62, no. 2 (2012): 363–79, http://doi.org/10.1111/j.1460-2466.2012.01629.x.

37. Henry W. Fischer III, *Response to Disaster: Fact versus Fiction and Its Perpetuation*, 3rd ed. (Lanham, Md.: UPA, 2008).

38. Artist Ai WeiWei's disporportionate repression in China for just tweeting is one example of this.

39. Timur Kuran, "Sparks and Prairie Fires: A Theory of Unanticipated Political Revolution," *Public Choice* 61, no. 1 (1989): 41–74.

40. Clay Shirky, "The Political Power of Social Media," *Foreign Affairs*, December 20, 2010, https://www.foreignaffairs.com/articles/2010-12-20/political-power-social-media.

Chapter 2. Censorship and Attention

1. I concluded that it was not the Zapatistas themselves but the solidarity networks in more developed countries, especially in North America, that were using the newly emergent digital tools to organize in support of the Zapatistas. The North American network consisted of many groups that had organized to stop NAFTA and had failed, and the Zapatistas had launched their own uprising the very day NAFTA had gone into effect. A group that had just lost had thus found a cause and sprung into action. The Zapatistas were significant because they were a movement in the internet era, not because they themselves were heavy (or even light!) internet users.

2. As I will explore in chapter 9, censorship is now increasingly performed by spreading disinformation, flooding with too much information so some stories are deprived of attention, and creating distrust and confusion in a manner that diffuses attention.

3. Todd Gitlin, *The Whole World Is Watching: Mass Media in the Making and Unmaking of the New Left* (Berkeley: University of California Press, 1980).

4. Gitlin, *Whole World Is Watching*.

5. Susan Corke, Andrew Finkel, David J. Kramer, Carla Anne Robbins, and Nate Schenkkan, "Democracy in Crisis: Corruption, Media, and Power in Turkey," *Freedom House Special Report* (2014), http://www.freedomhouse.org/sites/default/files/Turkey%20Report%20-%202-3-14.pdf.

6. Sebnem Arsu and Sabrina Tavernise, "Turkish Media Group Is Fined $2.5 Billion," *New York Times*, September 9, 2009, http://www.nytimes.com/2009/09/10/world/europe/10istanbul.html.

7. Marc Champion, "Turkish Premier Defends Media Tax Battle," *Wall Street Journal*, October 5, 2009, http://www.wsj.com/articles/SB125469621389762827; "Dogan Yayin: Unit Tax Fine Slashed to 129 Mln Lira," Reuters, June 1, 2011, http://www.reuters.com/article/doganyayin-amnesty-idUSIST00774020110601.

8. The implication here is not that traditional journalism did not fail but that it had an ethos of facts, and when it failed, it was recognized as a failure.

9. Francis Pisani, "Can Turkey's Contribution to the Web Be Reproduced Elsewhere?," *The Next Web*, February 18, 2012, http://thenextweb.com/me/2012/02/18/can-turkeys-contribution-to-the-web-be-reproduced-elsewhere/; interview with Sedat Kapanoğlu by the author.

10. Numbers on Ekşi Sözlük were provided by the site's founder.

11. Here, "spontaneous" means arising quickly, without anyone planning it or knowing that it was about to happen.

12. Reuters photo, "'Woman in Red' Sprayed with Teargas Becomes Symbol of Turkey Protests," *Guardian*, June 5, 2013, https://www.theguardian.com/world/2013/jun/05/woman-in-red-turkey-protests; see "Looking Back at 30 Years of Reuters Pictures," Reuters, February 19, 2015, http://insideagency.reuters.com/2015/02/looking-back-30-years-reuters-pictures/; and http://insideagency.reuters.com/wp-content/uploads/2015/02/RTR4PF9B1.jpg.

Chapter 3. Leading the Leaderless

1. E. J. Lowe, "For Want of a Nail," *Analysis* 40, no. 1 (1980): 50–52.

2. The term "adhocracy" comes from a very different context: management strategy. The term originated with the management scholars Warren G. Bennis and Philip E. Slater (*The Temporary Society* [New York: Harper and Row, 1964]) and was adopted by futurists Alvin and Heidi Toffler (Alvin Toffler, *Future Shock* [New York: Bantam Books, 1970]). It was touted as a management strategy in the 1980s. (For example, see Robert H. Waterman, *Adhocracy: The Power to Change* [New York: W. W. Norton, 1993].) For a history of the term, see Timothy E. Dolan, "Revisiting Adhocracy: From Rhetorical Revisionism to Smart Mobs," *Journal of Futures Studies* 15, no. 2 (2010): 33–50, http://www.jfs.tku.edu.tw/15-2/A03.pdf. Although the strategy has not been widely adopted in the business world, it has become a very common method for taking care of tasks in protests, with the help of digital technologies to coordinate them. For an early invocation of the term in reference to networked social movements, see Jesse Hirsh of the "TAO collective"—a Canadian-based collective that provided free technical support, e-mail, and web hosting especially to dissidents and movements—who referred to their efforts as "geek adhocracy." Recounted in Naomi Klein, "The Vision Thing," *Nation*, June 22, 2000, https://www.thenation.com/article/vision-thing/.

3. See especially W. Lance Bennett and Alexandra Segerberg, "The Logic of Connective Action," *Information, Communication and Society* 15, no. 5 (2012): 739–68.

4. "Egypt: The Legacy of Mohammed Mahmoud Street," BBC News, November 19, 2012, http://www.bbc.com/news/world-middle-east-20395260; also conceptually reintroduced in the context of social movements and digital technology by scholars of the early internet, including in the book *Smart Mobs* by Howard Rheingold.

5. Abulkasim al-Jaberi, "Out of Sight, but Not out of Mind: Mohamed Mahmoud Remembered," *Egypt Independent,* November 19, 2012, http://www.egyptindependent.com/news/out-sight-not-out-mind-mohamed-mahmoud-remembered.

6. Reem Abdellatif, "Back in Tahrir, Business Booms," *Daily News Egypt,* November 25, 2011, http://www.dailynewsegypt.com/2011/11/25/back-in-tahrir-business-booms/.

7. Alice Hackman, "Bringing the World to Tahrir," *Common Ground News Service,* December 20, 2011, http://www.commongroundnews.org/article.php?id=30821&lan=en&sp=0.

8. "On the 'Digital Frontline,' Social Media Reporters and Editors Exposed to Vicarious Trauma," *Columbia Journalism Review,* 2016, http://www.cjr.org/first_person/social_media_reporters_and_vicarious_trauma.php; "Viewing Violence on Social Media Linked to PTSD Symptoms," *Psychiatry Advisor,* May 7, 2015, http://www.psychiatryadvisor.com/ptsd-trauma-and-stressor-related/violent-news-social-media-ptsd-symptoms/article/413366/.

9. "Needed Urgently in Zenhom Mourge: Coffins and Money زي نهم م شرحة اح د ياجات ف, لوس و ضروري ت واب يت," @TahrirSupplies (microblog), November 21, 2011,

https://twitter.com/TahrirSupplies/status/138623935653744640; "Zenhom Mourge out of Coffins. This Is a Sad Day. Moment of Silence for All the Dead," @Tahrir-Supplies (microblog), November 21, 2011, https://twitter.com/TahrirSupplies/status /138624142659420160.

10. al-Jaberi, "Out of Sight, but Not out of Mind."

11. Ibid.

12. Farah El-Akkad, "The Square Effect," *Al-Ahram Weekly,* June 6, 2013, http://weekly.ahram.org.eg/News/1118/30/The-square-effect.aspx.

13. Howard Rheingold, *Smart Mobs: The Next Social Revolution* (Cambridge, Mass.: Perseus, 2003).

14. I explore signaling of capacity to power in greater depth in chapter 8.

15. This movement has been richly documented by too many scholars to summarize in a few citations. However, for a book that highlights the capacity building of long-term organizing, see Kenneth T. Andrews, *Freedom Is a Constant Struggle: The Mississippi Civil Rights Movement and Its Legacy* (Chicago: University of Chicago Press, 2004). For importance of tactical innovation and shifts, see Doug McAdam, "Tactical Innovation and the Pace of Insurgency," *American Sociological Review* 48 (1983): 735–75, doi:10.2307/2095322.

16. Jo Ann Gibson Robinson, *The Montgomery Bus Boycott and the Women Who Started It: The Memoir of Jo Ann Gibson Robinson* (Knoxville: University of Tennessee Press, 1987).

17. Ibid.

18. "The March Should Be Stopped," *New York Herald Tribune,* June 25, 1963; cited in Jervis Anderson, *Bayard Rustin: Troubles I've Seen, a Biography* (New York: HarperCollins, 1997), 250.

19. Jerald Podair, *Bayard Rustin: American Dreamer* (Lanham, Md.: Rowman and Littlefield, 2008).

20. "NPR: Behind the Scenes of the March on Washington," 2016, accessed October 17, 2016, http://www.npr.org/news/specials/march40th/part1.html; Gary Younge, "Bayard Rustin: The Gay Black Pacifist at the Heart of the March on Washington," *Guardian,* August 23, 2013, World News section, https://www.theguardian.com/world/2013/aug/23/bayard-rustin-march-on -washington.

21. Garth E. Pauley, "John Lewis, 'Speech at the March on Washington' (28 August 1963)," 2010, http://voices-of-democracy.org/wp-content/uploads/2014/07 /pauley-lewis-ii.pdf.

22. Konda Gezi Raporu, June 5, 2014, http://www.vanityfair.com/news/2016/12/the -year-the-trolls-won-by-monica-lewinsky.

23. Gianpaolo Baiocchi, "Emergent Public Spheres: Talking Politics in Participatory Governance," *American Sociological Review* 68 (2003): 52–74.

24. For an in-depth description of how some civic organizations help generate activists over time, see Hahrie Han, *How Organizations Develop Activists: Civic Associations and Leadership in the 21st Century* (Oxford: Oxford University Press, 2014).

25. Jo Freeman, "The Tyranny of Structurelessness," *Berkeley Journal of Sociology* 17 (1972–73): 151–64.

26. Zeynep Tufekci, "'Not This One': Social Movements, the Attention Economy, and Microcelebrity Networked Activism," *American Behavioral Scientist*, March 2013, doi:10.1177/0002764213479369.

27. Zeynep Tufekci and David Talbot, "A Leading Voice of the Egyptian Revolution Says Social Media Failed to Sustain the Movement and Talks about What Comes Next," *MIT Technology Review*, April 16, 2016, https://www.technologyreview.com/s/601241/remaking-social-media-for-the-next-revolution/.

28. Mahmoud Salem, "You Can't Stop the Signal," *World Policy Journal* 31, no. 3 (2014): 34–40. Also see Marc Lynch, "Twitter Devolutions: How Social Media Is Hurting the Arab Spring," *Foreign Policy* 7 (2013).

29. McAdam, "Tactical Innovation and the Pace of Insurgency."

Chapter 4. Movement Cultures

1. Paolo Gerbaudo, *Tweets and the Streets: Social Media and Contemporary Activism* (London: Pluto Press, 2012), and "The Indignant Citizen: Anti-Austerity Movements in Southern Europe and the Anti-Oligarchic Reclaiming of Citizenship," *Social Movement Studies* 16, no. 1 (2017): 36–50.

2. John Chalcraft, "Horizontalism in the Egyptian Revolutionary Process," *Middle East Report*, no. 262 (2012): 6–11; Paul Mason, *Why It's Still Kicking off Everywhere: The New Global Revolutions* (London: Verso, 2013); Marina Sitrin, "Horizontalism: From Argentina to Wall Street," *NACLA Report on the Americas* 44, no. 6 (2016): 8–11.

3. Steven M. Buechler, "New Social Movement Theories," *The Sociological Quarterly* 36, no. 3 (1995): 441–64; and Jeffrey M. Ayres, Beth Schaefer Caniglia, Sean Chabot, Marco G. Giugni, Michael Hanagan, Tammy L. Lewis, Gregory M. Maney et al., *Globalization and Resistance: Transnational Dimensions of Social Movements* (Lanham, Md.: Rowman and Littlefield, 2002).

4. This question about free riding and how collective action occurs in the first place, since people can stay at home and hope that others do the work, was posed formally by the economist Mancur Olson in 1965 and has generated much interest since. Mancur Olson, *The Logic of Collective Action: Public Goods and the Theory of Groups* (Cambridge, Mass.: Harvard University Press, 1965).

5. See William H. Sewell, "Historical Events as Transformations of Structures: Inventing Revolution at the Bastille," *Theory and Society: Renewal and Critique in Social Theory* 25, no. 6 (1996): 841–81.

6. William Wordsworth, "The Complete Poetical Works," Bartleby.com, 1999.

7. Émile Durkheim, *The Elementary Forms of the Religious Life* (New York: Free Press, 1965); Joseph R. Gusfield and Jerzy Michalowicz, "Secular Symbolism: Studies of Ritual, Ceremony and the Symbolic Order in Modern Life," *Annual Review of Sociology* 10 (1984): 417–35.

8. Doug McAdam, Sidney Tarrow, and Charles Tilly, *Dynamics of Contention* (Cambridge: Cambridge University Press, 2001).

9. "The New Social Movements: A Theoretical Approach," *Social Science Information* 19 (1980): 199–226; Jürgen Habermas, "New Social Movements," *Telos,* no. 49 (1981): 33–37; Claus Offe, "New Social Movements: Challenging the Boundaries of Institutional Politics," *Social Movements* 52, no. 4 (1985): 817–68.

10. Aynur Yolcu, "Gezi Parkı'nın hızla büyüyen kütüphanesi," *Hürriyet,* June 5, 2013, http://www.hurriyet.com.tr/gezi-parkinin-hizla-buyuyen-kutuphanesi -23435469.

11. Michael Kelley, "Court Orders NYPD to Pay $360,000 for Raid That Destroyed Occupy Wall Street Library," *Raw Story/Business Insider,* April 10, 2013, http:// www.rawstory.com/2013/04/court-orders-nypd-to-pay-360000-for-raid-that -destroyed-occupy-wall-street-library/.

12. Karl Marx, *Capital: A Critique of Political Economy,* trans. Ben Fowkes, vol. 1 (London: Penguin, 1976).

13. Chris Buckley and Keith Bradsher, "Hong Kong Protesters Lose a Last Bastion, but Vow to Go On," *New York Times,* December 11, 2014, http://www.nytimes .com/2014/12/12/world/asia/hong-kong-protests.html.

14. Francesca Polletta, *Freedom Is an Endless Meeting: Democracy in American Social Movements* (Chicago: University of Chicago Press, 2002).

15. Archon Fung, Erik Olin Wright, and Rebecca Abers, *Deepening Democracy: Institutional Innovations in Empowered Participatory Governance* (London: Verso, 2003).

16. Students for a Democratic Society, *The Port Huron Statement* (New York: Students for a Democratic Society, 1964).

17. Christopher Hayes, *Twilight of the Elites: America after Meritocracy* (New York: Crown Publishers, 2012).

18. Jo Freeman, "The Tyranny of Structurelessness," *Berkeley Journal of Sociology* 17 (1972–73): 151–64.

19. Doug McAdam, "The Biographical Consequences of Activism," *American Sociological Review* 54, no. 5 (1989): 744–60.

20. Molly Crabapple, *Drawing Blood* (New York: HarperCollins, 2015).

21. Francesca Polletta and James M. Jasper, "Collective Identity and Social Movements," *Annual Review of Sociology* (2001): 283–305.

22. Robert D. Putnam, *Bowling Alone: The Collapse and Revival of American Community* (New York: Simon and Schuster, 2000).

23. Harrison Rainie and Barry Wellman, *Networked: The New Social Operating System* (Cambridge, Mass.: MIT Press, 2012).

24. Rebecca Solnit, *A Paradise Built in Hell: The Extraordinary Communities That Arise in Disasters* (New York: Viking, 2009).

25. Susannah Rosenblatt and James Rainey, "Katrina Takes a Toll on Truth, News Accuracy," *Los Angeles Times,* September 27, 2005; Brian Thevenot and Gordon Russell, "Rape. Murder. Gunfights," *New Orleans Times-Picayune,* August 3, 2015.

26. Patrick Kingsley, "Egyptian Police 'Killed Almost 900 Protesters in 2011 in Cairo,'" *Guardian*, March 14, 2013.

27. Subcommandante Marcos from comunicado del 28 de mayo de 1994 of the Zapatistas: "El Viejo Antonio: 'En la montaña nace la fuerza, pero no se ve hasta que llega abajo,'" http://palabra.ezln.org.mx/comunicados/1994/1994_05_28.htm.

28. Sherry Turkle, *Alone Together: Why We Expect More from Technology and Less from Each Other* (New York: Basic Books, 2011).

29. Durkheim, *Elementary Forms of the Religious Life;* Randall Collins, *Interaction Ritual Chains* (Princeton, N.J.: Princeton University Press, 2004); Erving Goffman, *The Presentation of Self in Everyday Life* (Garden City, N.Y.: Anchor Books, 1959).

Chapter 5. Technology and People

1. Clay Shirky, *Here Comes Everybody: The Power of Organizing without Organizations* (New York: Penguin Press, 2008).

2. Yochai Benkler, *The Wealth of Networks: How Social Production Transforms Markets and Freedom* (New Haven, Conn.: Yale University Press, 2006).

3. Anthony Giddens, *The Consequences of Modernity* (Stanford, Calif.: Stanford University Press, 1990); and Michael Rapport, *Year of Revolution* (New York: Basic Books, 2008).

4. George Orwell, "Reflections on Gandhi," *The Orwell Prize*, January 1949, http://www.theorwellprize.co.uk/the-orwell-prize/orwell/essays-and-other-works/reflections-on-gandhi/.

5. Elizabeth L. Eisenstein, *The Printing Press as an Agent of Change* (New York: Cambridge University Press, 1980).

6. Sandra K. Evans, Katy E. Pearce, Jessica Vitak, and Jeffrey W. Treem, "Explicating Affordances: A Conceptual Framework for Understanding Affordances in Communication Research," *Journal of Computer-Mediated Communication*, December 2016; and James J. Gibson, "Theory of Affordances," in *The Ecological Approach to Visual Perception: Classic Edition* (New York: Psychology Press, 2014).

7. Raymond Williams, "The Technology and the Society," in *Television: Technology and Cultural Form*, 2nd ed. (London: Taylor and Francis, 2005).

8. Ralph Schroeder, *Rethinking Science, Technology, and Social Change* (Stanford, Calif.: Stanford University Press, 2007).

9. Caitlin Dewey, "Is the Internet Giving Us All ADHD?," *Washington Post*, March 25, 2015.

10. Lawrence D. Frank, Martin A. Andresen, and Thomas L. Schmid, "Obesity Relationships with Community Design, Physical Activity, and Time Spent in Cars," *American Journal of Preventive Medicine* 27, no. 2 (2004): 87–96; Graham Moon et al., "Fat Nation: Deciphering the Distinctive Geographies of Obesity in England," in "Eleventh International Medical Geography Symposium," special issue, *Social Science and Medicine* 65, no. 1 (2007): 20–31.

11. Sanae Inagami et al., "Body Mass Index, Neighborhood Fast Food and Restaurant Concentration, and Car Ownership," *Journal of Urban Health* 86, no. 5 (2009): 683–95.

12. For an overview, see Andrea Falcon, "Aristotle on Causality," in *The Stanford Encyclopedia of Philosophy*, ed. Edward N. Zalta, Spring 2015, http://plato .stanford.edu/archives/spr2015/entries/aristotle-causality/.

13. Marc Lynch, *Voices of the New Arab Public: Iraq, Al-Jazeera, and Middle East Politics Today* (New York: Columbia University Press, 2006).

14. Theories of causality are a deep academic subfield with millennia of writing. For a brief overview, see Henry E. Brady, "Causation and Explanation in Social Science," in *The Oxford Handbook of Political Methodology*, ed. Janet M. Box-Steffensmeier, Henry E. Brady, and David Collier (Oxford: Oxford University Press, 2011), 217–49, for social science; and Judea Pearl, *Causality: Models, Reasoning, and Inference* (Cambridge: Cambridge University Press, 2000), for modeling and inference.

15. George Orwell, "George Orwell: You and the Atomic Bomb," 1945, http://orwell .ru/library/articles/ABomb/english/e_abomb.

16. Melvin Kranzberg, "Technology and History: 'Kranzberg's Laws,'" *Technology and Culture* 27, no. 3 (1986): 544–60. (Quote is on page 545.)

17. Tarleton Gillespie, Pablo J. Boczkowski, and Kirsten A. Foot, eds., *Media Technologies: Essays on Communication, Materiality, and Society*, 1st ed. (Cambridge, Mass.: MIT Press, 2014); Paul M. Leonardi, Bonnie A. Nardi, and Jannis Kallinikos, *Materiality and Organizing: Social Interaction in a Technological World*, 1st ed. (Oxford: Oxford University Press, 2013).

18. Peter L. Berger and Thomas Luckmann, *The Social Construction of Reality: A Treatise in the Sociology of Knowledge* (Garden City, N.Y.: Doubleday, 1966); Ian Hacking, *The Social Construction of What?* (Cambridge, Mass.: Harvard University Press, 2000).

19. Michael Omi and Howard Winant, *Racial Formation in the United States: From the 1960s to the 1990s* (New York: Routledge, 1994).

20. Christine B. Hickman, "The Devil and the One Drop Rule: Racial Categories, African Americans, and the U.S. Census," *Michigan Law Review* 95, no. 5 (1997): 1161–265.

21. David R. Roediger, *Working toward Whiteness: How America's Immigrants Became White; The Strange Journey from Ellis Island to the Suburbs* (New York: Basic Books, 2005).

22. Émile Durkheim, Steven Lukes, and W. D. Halls, *The Rules of Sociological Method* (New York: Free Press, 1982).

23. Hans K. Klein and Daniel Lee Kleinman, "The Social Construction of Technology: Structural Considerations," *Science, Technology and Human Values* 27, no. 1 (2002): 28–52.

24. Massimo Ragnedda and Glenn W. Muschert, *The Digital Divide: The Internet and Social Inequality in International Perspective* (New York: Routledge, 2013); Eszter Hargittai, "The Digital Divide and What to Do about It," in *New Economy Handbook*, ed. Derek C. Jones (San Diego: Academic Press, 2003), 821–39.

25. John Perry Barlow, "A Cyberspace Independence Declaration," 1996, https://w2
.eff.org/Censorship/Internet_censorship_bills/barlow_0296.declaration.

26. In fact, "exclusion" in a digital world implies a whole host of differences from
living in a predigital one where nobody was included. It is one thing not to have
a telephone number in a world where nobody has one; it is a different thing to
be a person without a phone in a world in which it is expected that one will have
a phone to perform most basic functions: apply for a job, connect with people, or
have a political life.

Chapter 6. Platforms and Algorithms

1. He did not ask me to keep his identity secret, but I am not using his name on
principle, to avoid any clumsy attempts by repressive regimes to entangle his
views with mine.

2. Marc Lynch, *Voices of the New Arab Public: Iraq, Al-Jazeera, and Middle East Politics Today* (New York: Columbia University Press, 2010).

3. Hossein Derakhshan, "The Web We Have to Save—Matter," *Matter*, July 14, 2015,
https://medium.com/matter/the-web-we-have-to-save-2eb1fe15a426; Hossein Derakhshan, "Iran's Blogfather: Facebook, Instagram and Twitter Are Killing the
Web," *Guardian*, December 29, 2015, https://www.theguardian.com/technology
/2015/dec/29/irans-blogfather-facebook-instagram-and-twitter-are-killing-the
-web.

4. Zeynep Tufekci and Christopher Wilson, "Social Media and the Decision to Participate in Political Protest: Observations from Tahrir Square," *Journal of Communication* 62, no. 2 (2012): 363–79, http://doi.org/10.1111/j.1460-2466.2012.01629.x.

5. Platforms are not easy to define. In this book, I use the term "platforms" to
mean companies providing mass access online in centralized locations with
sets of corporate-defined rules for interconnectivity and visibility, such as Facebook, Twitter, and Google (especially its search function and YouTube). Apple,
Microsoft, and, in commerce, Amazon also can be included under this umbrella, but in different ways. For lengthy discussions, see José van Dijck, *The
Culture of Connectivity: A Critical History of Social Media* (Oxford: Oxford University Press, 2013); Tarleton Gillespie, "The Politics of 'Platforms,'" *New Media
and Society* 12, no. 3 (2010): 347–64; and Kate Crawford and Catharine Lumby,
"Networks of Governance: Users, Platforms, and the Challenges of Networked
Media Regulation," *International Journal of Technology Policy and Law* 1, no. 3
(2013): 270–82.

6. Yochai Benkler, *The Wealth of Networks: How Social Production Transforms
Markets and Freedom* (New Haven, Conn.: Yale University Press, 2006); Steven
Johnson, "Can Anything Take Down the Facebook Juggernaut?," *WIRED*,
May 16, 2012, https://www.wired.com/2012/05/mf_facebook/.

7. Sheera Frenkel, "This Is What Happens When Millions of People Suddenly
Get the Internet," BuzzFeed, November 20, 2016, https://www.buzzfeed.com

/sheerafrenkel/fake-news-spreads-trump-around-the-world; Hereward Holland, "Facebook in Myanmar: Amplifying Hate Speech?" Al Jazeera, June 2016, http://www.aljazeera.com/indepth/features/2014/06/facebook-myanmar-rohingya-amplifying-hate-speech-2014612112834290144.html.

8. Rebecca MacKinnon, *Consent of the Networked: The World-wide Struggle for Internet Freedom* (New York: Basic Books, 2012).

9. Astra Taylor, *The People's Platform: Taking Back Power and Culture in the Digital Age* (New York: Metropolitan Books, 2014).

10. Don Clark and Robert McMillan, "Facebook, Amazon and Other Tech Giants Tighten Grip on Internet Economy," *Wall Street Journal*, November 5, 2015, http://www.wsj.com/articles/giants-tighten-grip-on-internet-economy-1446771732.

11. "Network externalities" is a different term for the same concept.

12. Good places to start learning about the economic theory of network effects are Michael L. Katz and Carl Shapiro, "Network Externalities, Competition, and Compatibility," *American Economic Review* 75, no. 3 (1985): 424–40; and Joseph von R. Farrell and Garth Saloner, *Standardization, Compatibility and Innovation* (Cambridge, Mass.: Deptartment of Economics, Massachusetts Institute of Technology, 1984). For more discussion in the context of the Internet, see Jonathan Zittrain, *The Future of the Internet and How to Stop It* (New Haven, Conn.: Yale University Press, 2008); and MacKinnon, *Consent of the Networked*.

13. Zeynep Tufekci, "As the Pirates Become CEOs: The Closing of the Open Internet," *Daedalus* 145, no. 1 (2016): 65–78; Ethan Zuckerman, "The Internet's Original Sin," *Atlantic*, August 14, 2014, http://www.theatlantic.com/technology/archive/2014/08/advertising-is-the-internets-original-sin/376041/.

14. Zuckerman, "Internet's Original Sin"; Zeynep Tufekci, "Mark Zuckerberg, Let Me Pay for Facebook," *New York Times*, June 4, 2015.

15. Leo Mirani, "Millions of Facebook Users Have No Idea They're Using the Internet," *Quartz*, February 9, 2015, http://qz.com/333313/millions-of-facebook-users-have-no-idea-theyre-using-the internet/.

16. John D. H. Downing, *Radical Media: Rebellious Communication and Social Movements* (Thousand Oaks, Calif: Sage Publications, 2000).

17. Jürgen Habermas, *The Structural Transformation of the Public Sphere: An Inquiry into a Category of Bourgeois Society* (Cambridge, Mass.: MIT Press, 1989).

18. Aleksandra Gjorgievska, "Google and Facebook Lead Digital Ad Industry to Revenue Record," Bloomberg.com, April 21, 2016, http://www.bloomberg.com/news/articles/2016-04-22/google-and-facebook-lead-digital-ad-industry-to-revenue-record.

19. The literature is vast. Two of the most influential articles on social movements and media are William A. Gamson and Gadi Wolfsfeld, "Movements and Media as Interacting Systems," *Annals of the American Academy of Political and Social Science* 528 (1993): 114–25; and Robert D. Benford and David A. Snow, "Framing Processes and Social Movements: An Overview and Assessment," *Annual Review*

of Sociology 26 (2000): 611–39. For an overview, see Rens Vliegenthart and Stefaan Walgrave, "The Interdependency of Mass Media and Social Movements," in *The Sage Handbook of Political Communication* (London: Sage, 2012), 387–98. For an inquiry into alternative media used by social movements, including discussions before the Internet, see John Downing, *Radical Media: Rebellious Communication and Social Movements* (London: Sage, 2001).

20. David Kirkpatrick, *The Facebook Effect: The Inside Story of the Company That Is Connecting the World* (New York: Simon and Schuster, 2010). Mark Zuckerberg has since evolved in these views, but this early invocation shows the power of ideologies of founders on platform affordances and policies.

21. Stephen J. Whitfield, *A Death in the Delta: The Story of Emmett Till* (New York: Free Press, 1988).

22. On Facebook, a page administrator basically controls the contents of the page and acts as the final authority for posting and monitoring—these include keeping or deleting comments, posting updates or photos, conducting polls, changing privacy settings, creating or modifying events. The role is much more than that of an editor; it is more like being the publisher and journalist of a social space where users can also post.

23. Danny O'Brien, "Facebook Gets Caught up in Egypt's Media Crackdown—Committee to Protect Journalists," *Committee to Protect Journalists*, December 1, 2010, https://cpj.org/blog/2010/12/facebook-gets-caught-up-in-egypts-media-crackdown-1.php.

24. This was covered widely in blogs and the tech press. For a sampling, see Violet Blue, "Facebook Nymwars: Disproportionately Outing LGBT Performers, Users Furious," *ZDNet*, September 12, 2014, http://www.zdnet.com/article/facebook-nymwars-disproportionately-outing-lgbt-performers-users-furious/; and Bay City News Service, "San Francisco Supervisor Calls for Facebook, Drag Queens to Meet over Profile Name Crackdown," *Mercury News*, September 15, 2014, http://www.mercurynews.com/2014/09/15/san-francisco-supervisor-calls-for-facebook-drag-queens-to-meet-over-profile-name-crackdown/. The incidents can also be found under the hashtag #nymwars because users took to Twitter, which allows pseudonyms, to take issue with Facebook.

25. For example, during the 2016 Olympics, many users—some with tens of thousands of followers—were suspended from the service for posting video clips or Graphics Interchange Format (GIF) files from the Olympics. Tim Chester, "Twitter User's Account Shut Down after Posting Olympic Videos," *Mashable*, August 9, 2016, http://mashable.com/2016/08/09/twitter-account-olympics/. Meanwhile, throughout most of 2016, Twitter would do fairly little to take down prominent racist or misogynist accounts that were using the platform to organize harassment of minorities. For example, in that same year, I reported a Twitter account that did nothing but tweet pictures of dead children to relatively high-profile accounts, including mine. The response I got from Twitter dryly said, "We reviewed your report carefully and found that there was no violation

of Twitter's Rules regarding abusive behavior." On most platforms, a copyright claim is the demand for censorship or takedown that gets enforced most quickly while sustained and organized efforts to drive women, minorities, and dissidents of the twenty-first-century public squares are allowed to flourish.

26. Bilge Yesil, "Press Censorship in Turkey: Networks of State Power, Commercial Pressures, and Self-Censorship," *Communication, Culture and Critique* 7, no. 2 (2014): 154–73. doi:10.1111/cccr.12049; Susan Corke, Andrew Finkel, David J. Kramer, Carla Anne Robbins, and Nate Schenkkan, "Democracy in Crisis: Corruption, Media, and Power in Turkey," *Freedom House Special Report* (2014), http://www.freedomhouse.org/sites/default/files/Turkey%20Report%20 -%202 -3-14.pdf.

27. Adrian Chen, "Inside Facebook's Outsourced Anti-porn and Gore Brigade, Where 'Camel Toes' Are More Offensive than 'Crushed Heads,'" *Gawker,* February 16, 2012, http://gawker.com/5885714/inside-facebooks-outsourced-anti-porn -and-gore-brigade-where-camel-toes-are-more-offensive-than-crushed-heads.

28. Adrian Chen, "The Laborers Who Keep Dick Pics and Beheadings out of Your Facebook Feed," *WIRED,* October 23, 2014, https://www.wired.com/2014/10 /content-moderation/; Catherine Buni and Soraya Chemaly, "The Secret Rules of the Internet," *Verge,* April 13, 2016, http://www.theverge.com/2016/4/13/11387934 /internet-moderator-history-youtube-facebook-reddit-censorship-free-speech.

29. Bill Moyers, "Transcript, September 12, 2008," *Bill Moyers Journal,* http://www .pbs.org/moyers/journal/09122008/transcript_anti.html.

30. "Shi Tao-Imprisoned for Peaceful Expression," *Amnesty International USA,* http://www.amnestyusa.org/our-work/cases/china-shi-tao.

31. Joseph Menn, "Exclusive: Yahoo Secretly Scanned Customer Emails for U.S. Intelligence-Sources," Reuters, October 5, 2016, http://www.reuters.com/article /us-yahoo-nsa-exclusive-idUSKCN1241YT.

32. Christian, Sandvig, Kevin Hamilton, Karrie Karahalios, and Cedric Langbort, "Automation, Algorithms, and Politics; When the Algorithm Itself Is a Racist: Diagnosing Ethical Harm in the Basic Components of Software," *International Journal of Communication* 10 (2016): 19.

33. Zeynep Tufekci, "The Medium and the Movement: Digital Tools, Social Movement Politics, and the End of the Free Rider Problem," *Policy and Internet* 6, no. 2 (2014): 202–8, http://doi.org/10.1002/1944-2866.POI362.

34. M. Eslami et al., "'I Always Assumed That I Wasn't Really That Close to [Her]': Reasoning about Invisible Algorithms in News Feeds," *Conference on Human Factors in Computing Systems—Proceedings* (April 2015): 153–62.

35. R. M. Bond et al., "A 61-Million-Person Experiment in Social Influence and Political Mobilization," *Nature* 489, no. 7415 (2012): 295–98.

36. Bond et al., "61-Million-Person Experiment"; Jonathan Zittrain, "Facebook Could Decide an Election—without Anyone Ever Finding Out," *New Republic,* June 1, 2014, https://newrepublic.com/article/117878/information-fiduciary -solution-facebook-digital-gerrymandering.

37. Lorenzo Coviello et al., "Detecting Emotional Contagion in Massive Social Networks," *PLoS ONE* 9, no. 3 (2014): e90315, http://doi.org/10.1371/journal.pone.0090315.

38. In 2016, Facebook added a set of "reactions," perhaps in response to criticism about the limiting nature of having only the "Like" button available to express emotions. The new reactions chosen included "love," "sad," "angry," "wow," and "haha." "Like," however, still remains the default reaction, and the others are accessible only after clicking to a new menu.

39. Robert Epstein and Ronald E. Robertson, "The Search Engine Manipulation Effect (SEME) and Its Possible Impact on the Outcomes of Elections," *Proceedings of the National Academy of Sciences* 112, no. 33 (2015): E4512–E4521, http://doi.org/10.1073/pnas.1419828112.

40. Zeynep Tufekci, "Algorithmic Harms beyond Facebook and Google: Emergent Challenges of Computational Agency," *Journal on Telecommunication and High Tech Law* 13 (2015); Zeynep Tufekci and Deen Freelon, "Introduction to the Special Issue on New Media and Social Unrest," *American Behavioral Scientist* 57, no. 7 (2013): 843–47.

41. Topsy, "Trending Topics on Twitter on August 13, 2014," accessed March 29, 2015, http://topsy.com/s?q=august%2013%2C%202014.

42. Trevor Timm (@trevortimm), "#Ferguson livestream has almost 40K viewers right now. For comparison, that's almost 10% of CNN's average viewership," August 13, 2014, https://twitter.com/trevortimm/status/499742916315582464.

43. Tufekci, "Algorithmic Harms beyond Facebook and Google."

44. For a prescient exploration of this danger, see Eli Pariser, *The Filter Bubble: How the New Personalized Web Is Changing What We Read and How We Think* (New York: Penguin Books, 2012). For a deep dive into how homophily and cosmopolitanism do and don't operate online, see Ethan Zuckerman, *Digital Cosmopolitans: Why We Think the Internet Connects Us, Why It Doesn't, and How to Rewire It* (New York: W. W. Norton, 2014).

45. Eytan Bakshy, Solomon Messing, and Lada A. Adamic, "Exposure to Ideologically Diverse News and Opinion on Facebook," *Science* 348, no. 6239 (2015): 1130, http://science.sciencemag.org/content/348/6239/1130; Zeynep Tufekci, "Facebook Said Its Algorithms Do Help Form Echo Chambers, and the Tech Press Missed It," *New Perspectives Quarterly* 32, no. 3 (2015): 9–12.

46. Nicholas Carlson, "Upworthy Traffic Gets Crushed," *Business Insider,* February 10, 2014. http://www.businessinsider.com/facebook-changed-how-the-news-feed-works—and-huge-website-upworthy-suddenly-shrank-in-half-2014-2.

47. Sam Thielman, "Facebook News Selection Is in Hands of Editors Not Algorithms, Documents Show," *Guardian,* May 12, 2016.

Chapter 7. Names and Connections

1. Athima Chansanchai, "Reddit Aggregates Porn, 'Jailbait' and Racist Commentary," TODAY.com, March 28, 2011, http://www.today.com/money/reddit-aggregates

-porn-jailbait-racist-commentary-124179; Adrian Chen, "Unmasking Reddit's Violentacrez, the Biggest Troll on the Web," *Gawker,* October 12, 2012, http://gawker.com/5950981/unmasking-reddits-violentacrez-the-biggest-troll-on-the-web.

2. Adrian Chen, "Unmasking Reddit's Violentacrez, the Biggest Troll on the Web," *Gawker,* October 12, 2012, http://gawker.com/5950981/unmasking-reddits-violentacrez-the-biggest-troll-on-the-web.

3. Howard S. Becker, *Outsiders* (New York: Simon and Schuster, 2008).

4. Zick Rubin, "Disclosing Oneself to a Stranger: Reciprocity and Its Limits," *Journal of Experimental Social Psychology* 11, no. 3 (1975): 233–60.

5. Tricia Wang, "Talking to Strangers: Chinese Youth and Social Media" (Ph.D. diss., University of California, San Diego, 2013).

6. danah boyd, *It's Complicated: The Social Lives of Networked Teens* (New Haven, Conn.: Yale University Press, 2014).

7. This topic is covered in depth in chapter 9.

8. Brendan O'Connor, "YouBeMom: The Anarchic Troll Hub That's Basically 4chan for Mothers," *Daily Dot,* August 8, 2014, http://www.dailydot.com/unclick/youbemom-4chan-for-moms/.

9. The site is not truly anonymous because the site administrators can trace each participant (unless the person uses privacy-preserving options like TOR or VPNs), but they are anonymous to one another and cannot trace posting history.

10. Emily Nussbaum, "Mothers Anonymous," *New York Magazine,* July 24, 2006, http://nymag.com/news/features/17668/.

11. Sherry Turkle, *Life on the Screen: Identity in the Age of the Internet* (New York: Simon and Schuster, 1995).

12. John Perry Barlow, "A Cyberspace Independence Declaration," 1996, https://w2.eff.org/Censorship/Internet_censorship_bills/barlow_0296.declaration.

13. Jessie Daniels, *Cyber Racism: White Supremacy Online and the New Attack on Civil Rights* (Lanham, Md.: Rowman and Littlefield, 2009); Lisa, Nakamura, *Cybertypes: Race, Ethnicity, and Identity on the Internet* (New York: Routledge, 2002).

14. R. Stuart Geiger, "The Lives of Bots," in *Critical Point of View: A Wikipedia Reader,* ed. Geert Lovink and Nathaniel Tkacz (Amsterdam: Institute of Network Cultures, 2011), http://www.escholarship.org/uc/item/7bb888c6.

15. Jamie Condliffe, "Google and Facebook May Be Using Algorithms to Fight Terrorism," *MIT Technology Review,* June 27, 2016, https://www.technologyreview.com/s/601778/facebook-and-google-may-be-fighting-terrorist-videos-with-algorithms/.

16. "H.R.2281—105th Congress (1997–1998): Digital Millennium Copyright Act," October 28, 1998, https://www.congress.gov/bill/105th-congress/house-bill/2281.

17. Esther Addley, "Syrian Lesbian Blogger Is Revealed Conclusively to Be a Married Man," *Guardian,* June 13, 2011, https://www.theguardian.com/world/2011/jun/13/syrian-lesbian-blogger-tom-macmaster.

18. Melissa Bell and Elizabeth Flock, "'A Gay Girl in Damascus' Comes Clean," *Washington Post,* June 12, 2011, https://www.washingtonpost.com/lifestyle/style/a-gay-girl-in-damascus-comes-clean/2011/06/12/AGkyHoRH_story.html?utm_term=.05cd0f74cc2d.

Chapter 8. Signaling Power and Signaling to Power

1. The archive of their page can be found at https://web.archive.org/web/2004 0904214302/www.guinnessworldrecords.com/content_pages/record.asp ?recordid=54365.
2. Michael Tackett, "U.S. Protests Savvier, but Slim on Clout," *Chicago Tribune*, February 26, 2003, http://www.chicagotribune.com/chi-0302260383feb26-story.html.
3. Edwin Amenta, Neal Caren, Elizabeth Chiarello, and Yang Su, "The Political Consequences of Social Movements," *Annual Review of Sociology* 36 (2010): 287–307.
4. There have been major protests with more substantial participation, like the ones in Bahrain in 2011–12 that may have involved more than half the population. However, they were in a small country with fewer than six hundred thousand citizens.
5. Jennifer Earle, "Political Repression: Iron Fists, Velvet Gloves, and Diffuse Control," *Annual Review of Sociology* 37 (2011): 261–84.
6. See Charles Tilly, *Social Movements, 1768–2004* (New York: Routledge, 2004). Charles Tilly, an eminent scholar of social movements, talks about how movements strive to display "WUNC": worthiness, unity, numbers, and commitment. I chose to develop a capabilities approach because I think the question remains open: what is it about numbers, commitment, or unity that has power and the potential for impact? Do all movements with these indicators on their side have impact? As I argue in the rest of this chapter, such indicators indeed feed into capacities—electoral, narrative, and disruptive—but are not sufficient by themselves. A movement—especially one that is scaled up with the help of digital tools—can be large in number and quite committed, yet falter because of lack of organizational infrastructure and collective decision-making capacity, which makes it hard for it to wield its "WUNC" in ways that threaten those in power.
7. "Capacity" and "capability" are arguably somewhat interchangeable terms, but I use "capacity" because it fits the social movement context better, since I am talking about collective capacity rather than capabilities of individuals.
8. In human development, Sen wanted to move away from narrow economic measures of output, such as GDP, and instead focus on people's potential for agency. He called this "beings and doings" that empowered and satisfied people, such as having good health or literacy. In this approach, rather than asking how much money a person has, we focus on what she is able to do with her life, including capacities that may lead to earning money. Rather than counting how many fish a person has caught this year, we look at the things that make one able to catch fish. See Amartya K. Sen, "Capability and Well-Being," in *The Quality of Life,* ed. Martha Nussbaum and Amartya K. Sen (Oxford: Clarendon Press, 1993), 30–53, and *Development as Freedom* (New York: Knopf, 1999); and Martha Nussbaum, "Capabilities as Fundamental Entitlements: Sen and Social Justice," *Feminist Economics* 9, nos. 2–3 (2003): 33–59. For overviews, see http://www.iep.utm.edu/sen-cap/ and http://plato.stanford.edu/entries/capability-approach/.
9. On strategic capacity building, see also Marshall Ganz, *Why David Sometimes Wins: Leadership, Organization, and Strategy in the California Farm Worker Movement* (Oxford: Oxford University Press, 2009).

10. For an overview, see Robert D. Benford and David A. Snow, "Framing Processes and Social Movements: An Overview and Assessment," *Annual Review of Sociology* 26 (2000): 611–39.

11. For a starting point on this vast academic literature, see Claus Offe, "New Social Movements: Challenging the Boundaries of Institutional Politics," *Social Movements* 52, no. 4 (1985): 817–68.

12. Many studies show the influence of donors and wealthy people on policy at the expense of ordinary voters. For an example, see Benjamin I. Page, Larry M. Bartels, and Jason Seawright, "Democracy and the Policy Preferences of Wealthy Americans," *Perspectives on Politics* 11, no. 1 (2013): 51–73.

13. For an overview of signaling theory, including its use in studying online social media, see Judith Donath, "Signals in Social Supernets," *Journal of Computer-Mediated Communication* 13, no. 1 (2007): 231–51. For an overview of signaling theory as applied to other social sciences, see Brian L. Connelly et al., "Signaling Theory: A Review and Assessment," *Journal of Management* 37, no. 1 (2011): 39–67; Rebecca Bliege Bird et al., "Signaling Theory, Strategic Interaction, and Symbolic Capital 1," *Current Anthropology* 46, no. 2 (2005): 221–48; and Lee Cronk, "The Application of Animal Signaling Theory to Human Phenomena: Some Thoughts and Clarifications," *Social Science Information* 44, no. 4 (2005): 603–20.

14. For probably the earliest application of signaling theory to social science questions, see Michael Spence, "Job Market Signaling," *Quarterly Journal of Economics* 87 (1973): 355–74.

15. For more on the concept of "cheap talk," see Joseph Farrell and Matthew Rabin, "Cheap Talk," *Journal of Economic Perspectives* 10, no. 3 (1996): 103–18.

16. This site by Carl T. Bergstrom, a biology professor, has a good overview of honest signaling theory, also with references to the (vast) primary literature on this topic: http://octavia.zoology.washington.edu/handicap/honest_biology_01.html. For a brief overview of signaling, including costly signaling, as it may appear to social settings, see Connelly et al., "Signaling Theory." There are also theories of "partially honest signaling" since "talk" and signals can vary between being absolutely cheap and being absolutely honest. See Kevin J. S. Zollman, Carl T. Bergstrom, and Simon M. Huttegger, "Between Cheap and Costly Signals: The Evolution of Partially Honest Communication," *Proceedings of the Royal Society B: Biological Sciences* 280, no. 1750 (2012).

17. Judith Donath, "Signaling Identity," 2007, http://smg.media.mit.edu/papers/Donath/SignalsTruthDesign/SignalingAbstracts.1.pdf.

18. Thorstein Veblen, *The Theory of the Leisure Class* (New York: Penguin Books, 1994).

19. Alice E. Marwick, *Status Update: Celebrity, Publicity, and Branding in the Social Media Age* (New Haven, Conn.: Yale University Press, 2013); Judith Donath, *The Social Machine: Designs for Living Online* (Cambridge, Mass.: MIT Press, 2014); and Judith Donath, "Signals in Social Supernets," *Journal of Computer-Mediated Communication* 13 (2007): 231–51.

20. Todd Gitlin, *The Whole World Is Watching: Mass Media in the Making and Unmaking of the New Left* (Berkeley: University of California Press, 1980).

21. See Francesca Polletta and James M. Jasper, "Collective Identity and Social Movements," *Annual Review of Sociology* 27 (2001): 283–305; and Benjamin Heim Shepard and Ronald Hayduk, *From ACT UP to the WTO: Urban Protest and Community Building in the Era of Globalization* (London: Verso, 2002), on ACT UP and similar movements, especially on the question of collective identity.

22. William A. Gamson and Gadi Wolfsfeld, "Movements and Media as Interacting Systems," *Annals of the American Academy of Political and Social Science* 528 (1993): 114–25. The quote is from page 122.

23. Frances Fox Piven and Richard Cloward, *Regulating the Poor: The Functions of Public Welfare* (New York: Knopf Doubleday Publishing Group, 2012).

24. Reliable statistics are hard to find since the federal government does not keep track of such killings despite the obvious importance of the issue. A few newspapers have since started keeping track, and the federal government may finally start doing so, but only as a response to the movement.

25. A later Department of Justice report failed to completely resolve the issue or the contradictory eyewitness testimonies. However, at the time, there was widespread belief that he indeed had his hands up at the time of the shooting, although he may also have scuffled with the police officer inside the police car before running away.

26. U.S. Department of Justice, Civil Rights Division, *Investigation of the Ferguson Police Department*, 2015, https://www.justice.gov/sites/default/files/opa/press-releases/attachments/2015/03/04/ferguson_police_department_report.pdf.

27. Daniel Cox, Juhem Navarro-Rivera, and Robert P. Jones, *Economic Insecurity, Rising Inequality, and Doubts about the Future* (PRRI, 2014), http://www.prri.org/research/survey-economic-insecurity-rising-inequality-and-doubts-about-the-future-findings-from-the-2014-american-values-survey/.

28. Catherine E. Shoichet, "Racism Is a 'Big Problem' to More Americans, Poll Finds," CNN, November 25, 2015, http://www.cnn.com/2015/11/24/us/racism-problem-cnn-kff-poll/index.html.

29. Clay Shirky, *Here Comes Everybody: The Power of Organizing without Organizations* (New York: Penguin, 2008).

30. Lizzie Widdicombe, "Preoccupied," *New Yorker,* October 24, 2011.

31. Jules Boykoff, "Framing Dissent: Mass-Media Coverage of the Global Justice Movement," *New Political Science* 28, no. 2 (2006): 201–28, doi:10.1080/07393140600679967.

32. Sarah Gaby and Neal Caren, "Occupy Online: How Cute Old Men and Malcolm X Recruited 400,000 US Users to OWS on Facebook," *Social Movement Studies* 11, nos. 3–4 (2012): 367–74, doi:10.1080/14742837.2012.708858.

33. Nicholas Kristof, "The Bankers and the Revolutionaries," *New York Times,* October 1, 2011, http://www.nytimes.com/2011/10/02/opinion/sunday/kristof-the-bankers-and-the-revolutionaries.html.

34. See, for example, Katrina vanden Heuvel, "The Occupy Effect," *Nation,* January 26, 2012; and C. Robert Gibson, "Four Years Later: Occupy Succeeded Despite Its Flaws," PopularResistance.Org., September 19, 2015, https://popularresistance.org/four-years-later-occupy-succeeded-despite-its-flaws.

35. Erik Sherman, "America Is the Richest, and Most Unequal, Nation," *Fortune*, September 30, 2015; Jill Hamburg Coplan, "12 Signs America Is on the Decline," *Fortune*, July 20, 2015.

36. Ganz, *Why David Sometimes Wins*.

37. Annie Lowrey, "Protesting Student Debt with Astra Taylor," *New York Magazine*, May 17, 2015, http://nymag.com/daily/intelligencer/2015/05/astra-taylor -encounter.html.

38. Sidney Tarrow, "Why Occupy Wall Street Is Not the Tea Party of the Left," *Foreign Affairs*, October 10, 2011. https://www.foreignaffairs.com/articles/north -america/2011-10-10/why-occupy-wall-street-not-tea-party-left.

39. Richard Hofstadter, "The Paranoid Style in American Politics," *Harper's Magazine* 229, no. 1374 (1964): 77–86.

40. Zachary Courser, "The Tea 'Party' as a Conservative Social Movement," *Society* 49, no. 1 (2012): 43–53; Theda Skocpol and Vanessa Williamson, *The Tea Party and the Remaking of Republican Conservatism* (Oxford: Oxford University Press, 2012); and Andreas Madestam, Daniel Shoag, Stan Veuger, and David Yanagizawa-Drott, "Do Political Protests Matter? Evidence from the Tea Party Movement," *The Quarterly Journal of Economics* 128, no. 4 (2013): 1633–85, doi:10.1093/qje/qjt021.

41. Jules Boykoff and Eulalie Laschever, "The Tea Party Movement, Framing, and the US Media," *Social Movement Studies* 10, no. 4 (2011): 341–66; Skocpol and Williamson, *Tea Party*; Tarun Banerjee, "Media, Movements, and Mobilization: Tea Party Protests in the United States, 2009–2010," *Research in Social Movements, Conflicts and Change* 36 (2013): 39–75.

42. Christopher M. Mascaro, Alison N. Novak, and Sean P. Goggins, "Emergent Networks of Topical Discourse: A Comparative Framing and Social Network Analysis of the Coffee Party and Tea Party Patriots Groups on Facebook," in *Web 2.0 Technologies and Democratic Governance*, ed. Christopher G. Reddick and Stephen K. Aikins (New York: Springer, 2012), 153–68.

43. Skocpol and Williamson, *Tea Party*, 199.

44. Yochai Benkler, Hal Roberts, Robert Faris, Alicia Solow-Niederman, and Bruce Etling, "Social Mobilization and the Networked Public Sphere: Mapping the SOPA-PIPA Debate," *Political Communication* 32, no. 4 (2015): 594–624.

45. Marco G. Giugni, "Was It Worth the Effort? The Outcomes and Consequences of Social Movements," *Annual Review of Sociology* 24 (1998): 371–93; John Higley and Michael G. Burton, "The Elite Variable in Democratic Transitions and Breakdowns," *American Sociological Review* 54, no. 1 (1989): 17–32, doi:10.2307/2095659.

Chapter 9. Governments Strike Back

1. Turkey has had a string of coups. Some have been full-blown military takeovers, while others have been military threats that ousted governments. The latter are sometimes called "soft" or "postmodern" coups. Just as the Inuit are said to have many words for snow, people in Turkey distinguish types of coups with a range of terminology for each type.

2. I am indebted to Rahul Mahajan for the phrase.

3. Bianca Bosker, "Egypt's Only Internet Provider Still in Service," *Huffington Post,* January 31, 2011, http://www.huffingtonpost.com/2011/01/31/egypt-internet -noor-group_n_816214.html.

4. *Streisand v. Adelman et al.* Decision, Superior Court, State of California, Case SC 077 257, December 3, 2003, http://www.californiacoastline.org/streisand /slapp-ruling-tentative.pdf.

5. Mike Masnick, "Photo of Streisand Home Becomes an Internet Hit," *Techdirt,* June 24, 2003, https://www.techdirt.com/articles/20030624/1231228.shtml.

6. "Hong Kong Protests: Timeline of the Occupation," BBC News, China, December 11, 2014, http://www.bbc.com/news/world-asia-china-30390820.

7. Gary King, Jennifer Pan, and Margaret E. Roberts, "How Censorship in China Allows Government Criticism but Silences Collective Expression," *American Political Science Review* 107, no. 2 (2013): 326–43, doi:10.1017/S0003055413000014; and Gary King, Jennifer Pan, and Margaret E. Roberts, "Reverse-Engineering Censorship in China: Randomized Experimentation and Participant Observation," *Science* 345, no. 6199 (2014).

8. Timothy Brook, *The Confusions of Pleasure: Commerce and Culture in Ming China* (Berkeley: University of California Press, 1998); Kevin J. O'Brien and Lianjiang Li, *Rightful Resistance in Rural China* (Cambridge: Cambridge University Press, 2006).

9. Brook, *Confusions of Pleasure*; O'Brien and Li, *Rightful Resistance in Rural China.*

10. King, Pan, and Roberts, "Reverse-Engineering Censorship in China," and "How Censorship in China Allows Government Criticism."

11. Gary King, Jennifer Pan, and Margaret E. Roberts, "How the Chinese Government Fabricates Social Media Posts for Strategic Distraction, Not Engaged Argument" (working paper), August 26, 2016, http://gking.harvard.edu/50c.

12. Juvenal, *Satire* 10.77–81.

13. Helia Ighani, "Facebook in Iran: The Supreme Leader," *The Iran Primer, United States Institute of Peace,* April 16, 2013, http://iranprimer.usip.org/blog/2013/apr /16/facebook-iran-supreme-leader.

14. Leonid Ragozin and Michael Riley, "Russia Just Ratified a Rigorous New Cyberspace Law," Bloomberg.com, August 26, 2016, http://www.bloomberg.com/news /articles/2016-08-26/putin-is-building-a-great-russian-firewall.

15. Adrian Chen, "The Agency," *New York Times,* June 2, 2015, https://www.nytimes .com/2015/06/07/magazine/the-agency.html; Daisy Sindelar, "The Kremlin's Troll Army," *Atlantic,* August 12, 2014, http://www.theatlantic.com/international /archive/2014/08/the-kremlins-troll-army/375932/.

16. Neil Macfarquhar, "A Powerful Russian Weapon: The Spread of False Stories," *New York Times,* August 28, 2016, http://www.nytimes.com/2016/08/29/world /europe/russia-sweden-disinformation.html.

17. Jon Henley, "Russia Waging Information War against Sweden, Study Finds," *Guardian,* January 11, 2017, https://www.theguardian.com/world/2017/jan/11 /russia-waging-information-war-in-sweden-study-finds; Martin Kragh and

Sebastian Åsberg, "Russia's Strategy for Influence through Public Diplomacy and Active Measures: The Swedish Case," *Journal of Strategic Studies* (2017): 1–44.

18. Christopher Paul and Miriam Matthews, "The Russian 'Firehose of Falsehood' Propaganda Model: Why It Might Work and Options to Counter It," Rand Corporation, 2016, http://www.rand.org/content/dam/rand/pubs/perspectives/PE100/PE198/RAND_PE198.pdf.

19. Giorgio Bertolin, "Conceptualizing Russian Information Operations: Info-War and Infiltration in the Context of Hybrid Warfare," *IO Sphere* (Summer 2015): 10.

20. Neil Macfarquhar, "A Powerful Russian Weapon: The Spread of False Stories," *New York Times*, August 28, 2016, http://www.nytimes.com/2016/08/29/world/europe/russia-sweden-disinformation.html.

21. Saara Jantunen, *Infosota: Iskut kohdistuvat kansalaisten tajuntaan* (Helsingissä Kustannusosakeyhtiö Otava, Finland, 2015).

22. Andrew Higgins, "Effort to Expose Russia's 'Troll Army' Draws Vicious Retaliation," *New York Times,* May 30, 2016, http://www.nytimes.com/2016/05/31/world/europe/russia-finland-nato-trolls.html.

23. Fred Weir, "Russian NGOs Say New Law Makes Them Look like Spies (+Video)," *Christian Science Monitor,* November 26, 2012, http://www.csmonitor.com/World/2012/1126/Russian-NGOs-say-new-law-makes-them-look-like-spies-video.

24. Anton Nossik, "Russia's First Blogger Reacts to Putin's Internet Crackdown," *New Republic,* May 15, 2014, https://newrepublic.com/article/117771/putins-internet-crackdown-russias-first-blogger-reacts.

25. Terence McCoy, "Turkey Bans Twitter—and Twitter Explodes," *Washington Post,* March 21, 2014, https://www.washingtonpost.com/news/morning-mix/wp/2014/03/21/turkey-bans-twitter-and-twitter-explodes/.

26. "Turkey's Erdogan, Fighting Corruption Scandal, Threatens to Ban Facebook, YouTube," *US News and World Report,* March 7, 2014, http://www.usnews.com/news/world/articles/2014/03/07/turkish-pm-threatens-to-ban-facebook-youtube.

27. Zeynep Tufekci, "Bay of Tweets," Politico, April 4, 2014, http://www.politico.com/magazine/story/2014/04/cuba-twitter-bay-of-tweets-105382.html.

28. This block was later lifted but would come back occasionally as throttling—slowing access to social media rather than blocking.

29. "Turks Divided on Erdogan and the Country's Direction," *Pew Research Center's Global Attitudes Project,* July 30, 2014, http://www.pewglobal.org/2014/07/30/turks-divided-on-erdogan-and-the-countrys-direction/.

30. "Interfax: TV Main Source of Info for Most Russians on Ukraine Events; over Half Believe It Is Unbiased," *Johnson's Russia List,* September 2, 2014, http://russialist.org/interfax-tv-main-source-of-info-for-most-russians-on-ukraine-events-over-half-believe-it-is-unbiased-poll/.

31. Nieman Reports, "5 Questions for Engin Onder," January 19, 2017, http://niemanreports.org/articles/5-questions-for-engin-onder/.

32. Ethan Zuckerman, "Who Benefits from Doubt? Online Manipulation and the Russian—and US—Internet," *My Heart's in Accra,* July 23, 2015, http://www

.ethanzuckerman.com/blog/2015/07/23/who-benefits-from-doubt-online -manipulation-and-the-russian-and-us-internet/.

33. James Delingpole, "The 5 Awkward Questions They Won't Answer about the Drowned Boy, Syria and Our 'Moral Duty,'" Breitbart.com, September 8, 2015, http://www.breitbart.com/london/2015/09/08/the-5-awkward-questions-they -wont-answer-about-the-drowned-boy-syria-and-our-moral-duty/.

34. George Monbiot. *How to Stop the Planet from Burning* (London: Penguin, 2006).

35. Naomi Oreskes and Erik M. Conway, *Merchants of Doubt* (New York: Bloomsbury Press, 2010).

36. Katy E. Pearce, "Democratizing Kompromat: The Affordances of Social Media for State-Sponsored Harassment," *Information, Communication and Society* 18, no. 10 (2015): 1158–74.

37. Eric Lipton, and Scott Shane, "Democratic House Candidates Were Also Targets of Russian Hacking," *New York Times*, December 13, 2016, http://www .nytimes.com/2016/12/13/us/politics/house-democrats-hacking-dccc.html; Eric Sanger, David E. Lipton, and Scott Shane, "The Perfect Weapon: How Russian Cyberpower Invaded the U.S.," *New York Times*, December 13, 2016, http://www .nytimes.com/2016/12/13/us/politics/russia-hack-election-dnc.html.

38. "Erdogan on Skype, Announcement (Turkey Military Coup) 16.07.2016," YouTube, July 15, 2016, https://www.youtube.com/watch?v=w3uN34oXHyc.

39. Konda survey, "Demokrasi Nöbeti Araştırması: Meydanların Profili," July 26, 2016, http://konda.com.tr/demokrasinobeti/.

40. H. Akin Unver and Hassan Alassaad, "How Turks Mobilized against the Coup," *Foreign Affairs*, September 14, 2016, https://www.foreignaffairs.com/articles /2016-09-14/how-turks-mobilized-against-coup.

41. The recent announcement of new software by Adobe that can recreate anyone's voice if sufficient sampling exists makes this even more salient. In the near future, it may not be possible to verify audio-only recordings of any politician.

Epilogue

1. Elizabeth L. Eisenstein, *The Printing Press as an Agent of Change* (Cambridge: Cambridge University Press, 1980); Peter Stallybrass, " 'Little Jobs': Broadsides and the Printing Revolution," in *Agent of Change: Print Culture Studies after Elizabeth L. Eisenstein,* ed. Sabrina Alcorn Baron, Eric N. Lindquist, and Eleanor F. Shevlin (Amherst: University of Massachusetts Press, 2007), 315–41.

2. Peter Stallybrass, "Printing and the Manuscript Revolution," in *Explorations in Communication and History,* ed. Barbie Zelizer (New York: Routledge, 2008), 111–18.

3. Here, of course, I am saying not that indulgences were a product of printing, simply that the mass market in them, and thus the proliferation that so offended Luther, was.

4. "How Luther Went Viral," *Economist,* December 17, 2011, http://www.economist .com/node/21541719.

5. Mark U. Edwards Jr., *Printing, Propaganda, and Martin Luther* (Minneapolis, Minn.: Fortress Press, 2004).

6. Anthony Giddens, *The Consequences of Modernity* (Stanford, Calif.: Stanford University Press, 1990).

7. Annie Gowen, "Men's Attitudes about Women Were Changing in One Indian Village. Then a Dowry Dispute Turned Deadly," *Washington Post,* December 9, 2016, http://www.washingtonpost.com/sf/world/2016/12/09/mens-attitudes -about-women-were-changing-in-this-indian-village-then-a-dowry-dispute -turned-deadly/.

8. Melvin Kranzberg, "Technology and History: 'Kranzberg's Laws,'" *Technology and Culture* 27, no. 3 (1986): 544–60, doi:10.2307/3105385.

9. Anthony Olcott, *Open Source Intelligence in a Networked World* (London: A&C Black, 2012).

10. Craig Silverman, "This Analysis Shows How Fake Election News Stories Outperformed Real News on Facebook," BuzzFeed, November 16, 2016, https:// www.buzzfeed.com/craigsilverman/viral-fake-election-news-outperformed -real-news-on-facebook; Craig Silverman and Alexander Lawrence, "How Teens in the Balkans Are Duping Trump Supporters with Fake News," BuzzFeed, November 3, 2016, https://www.buzzfeed.com/craigsilverman /how-macedonia-became-a-global-hub-for-pro-trump-misinfo; and Zeynep Tufekci, "Mark Zuckerberg Is in Denial," *New York Times,* November 15, 2016, http://www.nytimes.com/2016/11/15/opinion/mark-zuckerberg-is-in-denial .html.

11. Silverman, "This Analysis."

12. Sue Shellenbarger, "Most Students Don't Know When News Is Fake, Stanford Study Finds," *Wall Street Journal,* November 22, 2016, http://www.wsj.com /articles/most-students-dont-know-when-news-is-fake-stanford-study-finds -1479752576; Craig Silverman and Jeremy Singer-Vine, "Most Americans Who See Fake News Believe It, New Survey Says," BuzzFeed, December 6, 2016, https://www.buzzfeed.com/craigsilverman/fake-news-survey.

13. Sheera Frenkel, "How Facebook Spreads Fake News and Anti-Muslim Views in Myanmar," BuzzFeed, November 20, 2016, https://www.buzzfeed.com/sheer afrenkel/fake-news-spreads-trump-around-the-world.

14. Alexander Smith and Vladimir Banic, "How Macedonian Teens Earn—and Spend—Thousands from Fake News," NBC News, December 9, 2016, http:// www.nbcnews.com/news/world/fake-news-how-partying-macedonian-teen -earns-thousands-publishing-lies-n692451.

15. Zeinobia, "Egyptian Chronicles: Egypt's Internet Trolls: The Union 'Ep.1,'" *Egyptian Chronicles,* December 6, 2016, http://egyptianchronicles.blogspot.com /2016/12/egypts-internet-trolls-union-ep1.html.

16. Chris Hayes, *Twilight of the Elites: America after Meritocracy* (New York: Crown/ Archetype, 2012); Nicco Mele, *The End of Big: How the Internet Makes David the New Goliath* (London: Macmillan, 2013); and Moises Naim, *The End of Power:*

From Boardrooms to Battlefields and Churches to States, Why Being in Charge Isn't What It Used to Be (New York: Basic Books, 2014).

17. Craig J. Calhoun, "Introduction: Habermas and the Public Sphere," in *Habermas and the Public Sphere* (Cambridge, Mass.: MIT Press, 1992), 33.

18. Charles Tilly, "Mechanisms in Political Processes," *Annual Review of Political Science* 4, no. 1 (2001): 21–41, doi:10.1146/annurev.polisci.4.1.21.

19. For other explorations of uses of digital technology and its intersection with movement organization, see Bennett W. Lance and Alexandra Segerberg, *The Logic of Connective Action: Digital Media and the Personalization of Contentious Politics* (Cambridge: Cambridge University Press, 2013); and Jennifer Earl and Katrina Kimport, *Digitally Enabled Social Change: Activism in the Internet Age* (Cambridge, Mass.: MIT Press, 2011).

20. Doug McAdam and Ronnelle Paulsen, "Specifying the Relationship between Social Ties and Activism," *American Journal of Sociology* 99, no. 3 (1993): 640–67.

21. Bruce Bimber, "The Internet and Political Transformation: Populism, Community, and Accelerated Pluralism," *Polity* 31, no. 1 (1998): 133–60, doi:10.2307/3235370.

22. Karl-Dieter Opp and Christiane Gern, "Dissident Groups, Personal Networks, and Spontaneous Cooperation: The East German Revolution of 1989," *American Sociological Review* (1993): 659–80.

23. Charles Kurzman, *The Unthinkable Revolution in Iran* (Cambridge, Mass.: Harvard University Press, 2009).

24. Movements are always intertwined with culture, emotions. and passion. For an introduction to this important realm, see Jeff Goodwin, James M. Jasper, and Francesca Polletta, *Passionate Politics: Emotions and Social Movements* (Chicago: University of Chicago Press, 2009); Jürgen Habermas, "New Social Movements," *Telos* 49 (1981): 33–37; and Thomas R. Rochon, *Culture Moves: Ideas, Activism, and Changing Values* (Princeton, N.J.: Princeton University Press, 2000).

25. John D. McCarthy and Mayer N. Zald, "Resource Mobilization and Social Movements: A Partial Theory," *American Journal of Sociology* (1977): 1212–41.

26. Rens Vliegenthart, Stefaan Walgrave et al., "The Interdependency of Mass Media and Social Movements," *Sage Handbook of Political Communication* (2012): 387–98.

27. Zeynep Tufekci, "'Not This One' Social Movements, the Attention Economy, and Microcelebrity Networked Activism," *American Behavioral Scientist* 57, no. 7 (2013): 848–70, doi:10.1177/0002764213479369; and Jen Schradie, "Qualitative Political Communication: Labor Unions, Social Media, and Political Ideology: Using the Internet to Reach the Powerful or Mobilize the Powerless?" *International Journal of Communication* 9 (2015): 21.

28. H. A. Simon, "Designing Organizations for an Information-Rich World," in *Computers, Communication, and the Public Interest,* ed. Martin Greenberger (Baltimore, Md.: Johns Hopkins University Press, 1971), 40–41.

29. I lived through this once, after the local North Carolina GOP headquarters were firebombed by unknown assailants in the middle of a tense election season in the fall of 2016. The tensions had already been high locally, and there were indications of potential for violent reprisals. On Twitter, I suggested that the Clinton presidential campaign donate use of office space to the GOP to smother the rapidly spreading rumors among fringe groups that the firebombing was done by Democrats in order to win the election through violent means. I had conceived of the idea as a gesture—not intended to convince the core members of fringe groups who might undertake violence, but to make it harder for them to rationalize their actions to their own networks—something both research and my own experience from Turkey showed was important in heading off these spirals of violence early on.

    An African American colleague of mine had a daughter who went to school blocks from the firebombed GOP headquarters, and she was in agreement in the need for a gesture—she feared for her daughter's safety, as did others. Meanwhile, inspired by my tweets about donating office space or showing up in person to help clean up the place, a friend of mine in Boston set up a "GoFundMe" campaign—raising money that was earmarked only for repairs to that firebombed building, and not otherwise available for electoral activities. Along with many others, I retweeted the campaign, which quickly raised $13,000. Many people cited Michelle Obama's then recent speech when she had said "when they go low, we go high." I had not actually conceived of the initial gesture in that manner. As someone who works locally in assisting refugees in North Carolina, I was not naïve about the politics in my state. I didn't even donate to the GoFundMe campaign—it closed very quickly—but I thought any gesture was fine as long as money was properly earmarked; only the building, no electoral activities. Along with this, I publicized calls for people to donate to the North Carolina NAACP or groups working to help queer youth in the state. In fact, I would later learn that the money never went to the GOP as the earmarking had not yet been legally solved; and may yet end up in a charitable cause like a food pantry.

    Nonetheless, the campaign sparked a backlash. People were concerned that the money would be used for electoral work and toward discriminatory policies. This was a reasonable concern and fairly easy to clear up since the funds were strictly earmarked. However, for months, the organizers of the campaign and I got accused of supporting North Carolina GOP's policies against transpeople and minorities—a set of policies that in reality I stood in steadfast opposition to. My colleague who feared for her childrens' safety even jumped on Twitter to try to explain to my (many out-of-state) attackers that the threat of violent reprisals was real, and a gesture was both necessary and seemed effective in the local context. She couldn't get through either.

    What was striking about the experience was how it was lived and relived online: how many people just wanted to quote old tweets of mine out of context, but not to try to disagree or even fight with me on the topic, but as a performative display at their supporters own audiences. My tweets would pop up here and there out of context. They would be "quote-tweet"ed—a Twitter affordance that allows taking a quote in a thread out of context, and displayed to one's supporters, rather than a "reply"—a means to engage me. Sometimes, it would be a screenshot of my tweets so that I would not even know of the accusations being hurled. Such screenshots were often preceded with wild charges that could have been cleared up quickly had I actually been asked—but the point of screenshots was to do this without notifying the person, and thus without giving anyone the ability to respond.

This dynamic was frustrating, but also sadly familiar: I had watched movements tear themselves apart internally in Egypt, Turkey, and elsewhere through such online reliving and re-litigating disputes or accusations. A brawl, a screenshot, or a put-down was an easy way to go viral, as people watched as if driving by a wreck. In some countries, this type of vicious and seemingly perpetual infighting had helped paralyze the movements even as authoritarian parties or even the military came to power, indiscriminately repressing all the groups that had been busy fighting among themselves. Movement infighting is not a new phenomenon; however, the persistence of screenshots and old tweets makes it harder to move on since as long as brawls garner retweets and reshares, they are relived.

For a discussion of such destructive dynamics in the context of Egypt and elsewhere, see Mahmoud Salem, "You Can't Stop the Signal," *World Policy Journal* 31, no. 3 (2014): 34–40; and Marc Lynch, "Twitter Devolutions," *Foreign Policy*, February 7, 2013, https://foreignpolicy.com/2013/02/07/twitter-devolutions/.

30. M. Wesch, "Context Collapse," *Digital Ethnography*, July 31, 2008, http://mediatedcultures.net/projects/youtube/context-collapse.

31. Tahi L. Mottl, "The Analysis of Countermovements," *Social Problems* 27, no. 5 (1980): 620–35.

32. K. Hampton, L. Rainie, W. Lu, M. Dwyer, I. Shin, and K. Purcell, "Social Media and the 'Spiral of Silence,'" Pew Research Center, August 26, 2014, http://www.pewinternet.org/files/2014/08/PI_Social-networks-and-debate_082614.pdf; and Amanda Lenhart, Michele Ybarra, and Myeshia Price-Feeney, "Online Harassment, Digital Abuse, and Cyberstalking in America," *Data and Society and CIPHR Report*, November 21, 2016, https://www.datasociety.net/pubs/oh/Online_Harassment_2016.pdf.

33. Jennifer Earl, "Tanks, Tear Gas, and Taxes: Toward a Theory of Movement Repression," *Sociological Theory* 21, no. 1 (2003): 44–68, doi:10.1111/1467-9558.00175.

34. Philip Elmer-Dewitt, "First Nation in Cyberspace," *Time*, December 6, 1993, http://www.chemie.fu-berlin.de/outerspace/internet-article.html.

35. Sidney G. Tarrow and J. Tollefson, *Power in Movement: Social Movements, Collective Action and Politics* (Cambridge: Cambridge University Press, 1994).

36. "Voters Tell Prosecutors, Black Lives Matter," *New York Times,* March 18, 2016, http://www.nytimes.com/2016/03/18/opinion/voters-tell-prosecutors-black-lives-matter.html.
37. The Obama 2008 and 2012 campaigns were run quite differently in terms of digital tool use and other dimensions as well. See Micah L. Sifry, *The Big Disconnect: Why The Internet Hasn't Transformed Politics (Yet)* (New York: OR Books, 2014).
38. Daniel Kreiss, *Taking Our Country Back: The Crafting of Networked Politics from Howard Dean to Barack Obama* (New York: Oxford University Press, 2012); and Becky Bond and Zack Exley, *Rules for Revolutionaries: How Big Organizing Can Change Everything* (White River Junction, Vt.: Chelsea Green Publishing, 2016).

ACKNOWLEDGMENTS

TO SAY THAT EVERY BOOK IS A collective effort is an understatement. The following is necessarily an incomplete list of all those I must thank.

Supportive academic settings at every step of the way made this book possible. At the University of North Carolina, I benefited from the support of my incredible dean, Gary Marchionini, as well as the encouragement, collaboration, and warm environment provided by my many amazing colleagues at Chapel Hill at the School of Information, where I'm based, as well as in so many other departments. The Berkman Klein Center for Internet and Society at Harvard has been a second home for me through the years; it houses a remarkable and marvelous community that I've counted on for intellectual sustenance. I workshopped much of the work that went into this book in many talks; one at the Center for Civic Media at MIT is memorable for the deeply insightful and productive feedback I received. My colleagues at UNC in the sociology department, where I also hold an appointment, provided thoughtful and crucial input as I developed my conceptual toolkit. I started thinking about this book the year I was at the wonderful Center for Information Technology Policy at Princeton University—and just as my time there was ending, the Gezi Park protests erupted, carrying me to my home country, and to more tear gas and fieldwork. I started my academic career at the University of Maryland, Baltimore County, and will always remain grateful to the faculty, leadership, and students at one of the best universities in the country. It's hard to imagine an environment that is both as supportive and intellectually rich as academia. To every academic friend, colleague, and student who gave me feedback, mentorship, and support over the years, you are so numerous that I can express my gratitude only collectively: thank you.

Eileen Clancy was an invaluable collaborator on the many iterations of this book; her keen intellect, work ethic, and integrity came to the rescue too many times to count. We met as I sought assistance with research, but she provided much more. She took every question I posed and came back with answers that were better than my questions.

Didem Turkoglu was vital in helping this book navigate the treacherous path it took between general and academic readerships, and provided essential assistance in shaping the bridges to more academic literature without losing readability.

Mark Gubrud read many drafts of this book and helped me clarify and cut to the chase without losing substance. Without his editing, this book would have been bogged down more than it is.

My editor at Yale, Joseph Calamia, was instrumental in bringing this book to life, from convincing me to write it two years ago to providing helpful feedback, editing every draft, and accommodating changes to our deadline and the scope of this book. Writing a book about current events, illustrated by stories of real people, provided many challenges. Some of the delays resulted from having to scrap some early material because I was concerned that the activists I was writing about were in countries that were descending into turmoil and civil war; some were jailed. Then there was the time I found myself witnessing an attempted coup in Turkey—weeks before I was to turn in my final draft! Yale University Press has been incredible in its support and understanding over the years, even arranging an accelerated publishing schedule so that I could include lessons from the coup attempt in the book. I don't know the identities of the three peer reviewers who commented on my book for the press, but every review was so helpful and constructive. I'm awed and filled with gratitude for the people who know they will remain anonymous but still put so much effort into being so perceptively critical yet graciously helpful. Their every suggestion and criticism made the book better.

Faruk Eczacibasi has been an inspiration, muse, and intellectual partner over the years. We met just as social movements began sweeping the Middle East. He introduced himself as the chairman of the Turkey Informatics Foundation, and it was supposed to be a short, polite meeting to discuss the state of the information technology sector in Turkey. Once we started, we kept talking and talking and talking, and other people finally had to barge in to pry us from his office many, many hours later—each of us had blown through every other appointment and obligation for the day. We haven't stopped talking. His unconventional and vibrant mind has had an impact on much of this book. It's not too often that one gets to acquire a family late in life, and it is hard for me to overstate the value of his friendship, his intellectual company, and the warm welcome that he and his wife, Füsun, have provided to me over the years.

Rahul Mahajan has the sharpest mind and the most powerful intellect one could ever have in a critic and a collaborator. Any part of this book that remains incoherent or poorly thought out is because I did not give him the draft in time. He did not just fix my writing but made it better, deeper, richer, and smarter. As he read drafts, his intellectual challenges were always razor-sharp, his points incisive, and his observations penetrating. He helped my writing become better in the sense that Orwell identified so many years ago: "The slovenliness of our language makes it easier for us to have foolish thoughts." It's hard to thank him for any specific thing, since he's responsible for making the book better at every turn and doing his best to prevent me from making it worse.

Finally, my biggest and deepest gratitude goes to the thousands of protesters and activists I've met over the decades as they struggled to do their part to make the world a better place; some I have formally interviewed for this book. I am grateful to the many people who opened up their hearts, thoughts, and lives to me—among whom I marched, walked, and faced tear gas and worse. I cannot thank all of them individually, not just because they are too numerous, but also because so many of them put their lives and their livelihoods on the line to bring about a better world and would be at more risk if named. If not for people like them throughout our history, none of the good things we have would be possible. Their sacrifices allow people after them to live better lives. But, as I have tried to explain throughout this book, while they sacrifice much, they also gain the world through the beloved community they find in rebellion. I'm most grateful to have been welcomed into that community.

INDEX

ACT UP AIDS awareness movement, 204–5

adhocracy: culture emphasizing, 83; organizational structure of, 53, 54, 58, 269–70, 284n2

advertising: ad-financing model for platforms, 128, 136–37, 138, 140, 241; capacity signaling affected by, 194, 195; social media use in, 59–60; social movement themes in, 8

algorithms/algorithmic control: capacity signaling and, 207; definition of, 121; name and identities in relation to, 180, 185; platform function based on, 133, 134, 137–38, 145, 154–63, 263, 265, 272; social-technological interactions based on, 121, 127, 129–30

Al Jazeera: forum organized by, 175; public sphere influence of, 13, 15–16, 19

ALS ice-bucket challenge, 156, 158–59, 162

altruism, mutual, 88, 104–5

"Amina" (false identity), 183–85

anonymity: anonymous harassment and threats, 176–83, 238–39, 272;

anonymous social interaction, 172–76. *See also* pseudonymity

antiauthoritarian movements: "Black bloc" in, 213; capacity signaling via, 198, 209–16, 221–22, 274–75; culture of, 83–112; early adoption of technology in, 13; Occupy movement as, 38, 81, 83, 86, 87, 91, 93, 95–100, 209–16, 217, 221–22, 275, 276; organizational structure of, 81, 215, 217, 269–70, 276; Seattle WTO protests in, 86, 213

antiwar movement: capacity signaling by, 189, 190, 204, 205, 221; cause and effect dynamics in, 123; culture of protest in, 100–101

Arab Bloggers Conference, 23, 115–16

Arab uprisings/Arab Spring, 7, 18, 19, 41, 58, 118, 122, 123–24, 175–76, 190, 266. *See also specific protests*

Aristotle, causation theory of, 120–23

Armenia, Yerevan protests in, 93

assemblies, culture of protest and use of, 95–100

attention, 28–48; accuracy and verification of, 38–40, 41, 42–43, 240,

attention (*cont.*)
   244–51, 270–71; attention economy, 79, 272; cell phones impacting, 29, 30, 36, 39, 47; censorship as denial of, 30, 31, 32, 33–37, 41, 47–48, 228–29, 231–32, 234–35, 237–38, 274, 283n2 (*see also* censorship); curating citizen media for, 39, 41–43; dismissal of power of networked journalism for, 40, 44, 45; disruptive capacity to garner, 197–99; gatekeepers shaping and influencing, 38–40, 134, 271; mass media role in, 30–31, 35, 124, 204–5, 208, 210–15; meme and humor culture creating, 45; narrative or persuasive capacity to garner, 192, 193–95, 202, 204–6, 208–9, 210–14, 222; negative attention, 31, 198–99, 270; networked protests garnering, 31–32, 37–38, 42–43, 45–48, 210–16; networked public sphere evolution impacting, 29, 31, 32–38; 140journos creating, 37, 38, 40–43, 47; organizational coordination and communication need for, 56, 79; overview of, 270–72; platforms and algorithms creating, 31–32, 36, 37, 38, 40–43, 47–48, 270–71; publicity attracting, 252–53
automobiles, social-technological interaction analogies with, 120–21, 125
Azerbaijan, "kompromat" in, 254

Bahrain, networked protests in, 13, 296n3
Barlow, John Perry, "Cyberspace Independence Declaration," 130, 131
Ben Ali, Zine El Abidine, 14–16, 20
"Black bloc," 213
Black Lives Matter movement: anonymous harassment and threats to, 177–78; capacity signaling via, 197, 205–9, 275, 298nn23–24; platforms and algorithms affecting, 154–56

bots: DDOS via, 273; Magic Recs bots, 129; threats and harassment via, 177, 180
Bouazzizi, Mohammad, 14
Breitbart, 249
bridge ties, 21–22, 24
Brown, Michael, 154, 206–7, 208, 298n24
Brutsch, Michael, 168–69

Canada, refugee acceptance in, 248–49
capacity signaling, 189–222; agency and, 296n7; antiwar movement's, 189, 190, 204, 205, 221; attention needed for, 192, 193–95, 197–99, 202, 204–6, 208–16, 222; Black Lives Matter movement's, 197, 205–9, 275, 298nn23–24; censorship affecting, 194, 220–21; cheap talk and, 200–201; civil rights movement's, 193, 197; concepts underlying, 191–93, 199–203, 221–22; costly signals in, 200–201, 203; deceptive signals in, 199–200, 202; digital technologies affecting, 202–21; direct or violent conflict not foundation of, 190; disruptive capacity in, 192, 197–99, 202, 204–5, 213, 222; elite unity or disunity affecting, 220; financial considerations in, 194, 195, 196, 197; government countermeasures affecting, 190, 191, 194, 199, 212, 220–21; growth rate of capacity and, 209–16; Indignados protests's, 210, 275, 276; institutional or electoral capacity in, 192–93, 195–97, 205, 208–9, 214–16, 217–18, 219–20, 274–77; mass media affecting, 194, 198, 204–5, 206, 207–8, 210–15; narrative or persuasive capacity in, 192, 193–95, 202, 204–6, 208–9, 210–14, 222; number of protesters *vs.* bystanders considered with, 190–91, 296n3; Occupy movement's, 209–16,

221–22, 275; organizational structure for capacity building and, 61, 64–66, 69–70, 71, 75–77, 192, 220; overview of, 269, 274–75; signaling theory on, 199–203; Tahrir Square protests's, 197, 202–3, 210; Tea Party movement's, 216–18; WUNC approach vs., 296n5

cause and effect dynamics: efficient cause in, 121–23; final or root cause in, 122–23; formal cause in, 121, 122; material cause in, 120, 122–23; multiple layers in, 123; necessary cause in, 123–24; in social-technological interactions, 119–24; sufficient cause in, 123–24

cell phones: attention garnered via, 29, 30, 36, 39, 47; cause and effect dynamics applied to, 121; data allowances on, 260; early adoption of, 13; government countermeasure knowledge via, 255–60; government countermeasures targeting, 226–27; introduction of, 30; mobile revolution and internet access via, 29; organization and communication via, 50–51; social-technological interactions via, 118, 121, 125, 130; surveillance of postings via, 251

censorship, 28–48; attention denial via, 30, 31, 32, 33–37, 41, 47–48, 228–29, 231–32, 234–35, 237–38, 274, 283n2; backfire of, 226–28; capacity signaling hampered by, 194, 220–21; circumvention of, 221, 229–30, 238, 242, 243; credibility denials vs., 244–51; demonizing medium vs., 242, 243–44; government countermeasure knowledge restricted via, 225; information inundation and disinformation vs., 39–40, 228–29, 230–31, 236–41, 245–46, 265, 273–74, 283n2; mass media's, 13, 19, 26, 29, 31, 32, 33–37, 47–48, 148–49, 160, 194,

225, 245, 256, 258; overview of, 270–71; platforms and algorithms affecting, 20, 134, 137, 141–42, 149–54; in public sphere, 13, 14–15, 18, 19, 27, 32, 33–37; social-technological interactions opposing, 129; Streisand Effect of, 228, 241, 273; tactical and strategic use of, 231–36; virtual private networks circumventing, 221, 229–30

cheap talk, 200–201. See also capacity signaling

child pornographers and pedophiles, online community of, 164–69

China: anonymous social interaction in, 173–74; capacity signaling in, 203; censorship and repression in, 20, 27, 142, 153, 229, 232–36, 238; "50 Cent Party" in, 237; government countermeasures in, 20, 27, 142, 153, 179, 229, 232–38; "Great Firewall" in, 232, 238; Hong Kong democracy protests in, 87, 93, 99, 232–36; information inundation and disinformation in, 236–38; "memorial to the throne" in, 236

cities: identity anonymity in, 171; public sphere dynamics in, 5–6, 11; street protest participation in, 47

civil rights movement: bus boycott in, 61, 62–66, 140, 193, 197; capacity signaling by, 193, 197; Civil Rights Act of 1964 following, 70; culture of protest in, 94; government countermeasures to, 64–65, 66; "I Have a Dream" speech in, 62, 66, 67, 69–70; internal strife in, 65, 69; leaflet distribution in, 63–64; March on Washington in, 62, 66–70; mass media coverage of, 65, 66, 68, 134; Occupy movement and, 96–99; organizational structure of, 61–70, 81–82; tactical innovation of, 81–82; Till murder influencing, 140

cleanliness of protests, 92–93

clothing and housing supplies: culture reflected in, 87–88, 92; organizational coordination of, 50, 51

CNN, 167, 168–69

CNN International, 48

CNN Turkey, 37, 48, 256–57

collective effervescence, 89–90

collective identities, 83–85, 111

Colvin, Claudette, 62, 63

commodity fetishism, 91–92

community: of child pornographers and pedophiles online, 164–69; communities of belonging in protest culture, 88–90, 94, 102–5, 111; community policing of platforms, 143–45, 146, 153, 165, 181; homophily as search for, 9, 172, 268; "imagined communities," unification of, 4–5; internal norms and customs of, 164–65, 166, 167–69; LGBT community, 105–7, 108, 142, 144, 145, 183–85; networked public sphere formation of, 10–11, 12; scale of, identity interaction with, 172, 179

"compromising" pictures, 254

credibility: accuracy and verification of attention for, 38–40, 41, 42–43, 240, 244–51, 270–71; denials of, as government countermeasure, 244–51; false news without, 39–40, 41, 43, 183–85, 239–40, 264–68; hoaxes lacking, 183–85, 244–51

Creepshots subreddit, 165, 168

crowdfunding, 53, 60

culture of protest, 83–112; ad hoc organization support in, 83; antiauthoritarian protest culture, 83–112; assemblies and human microphones in, 95–100; cleanliness conveying sacredness in, 92–93; collective identities and, 83–85, 111; communities of belonging in, 88–90, 94, 102–5, 111; decision making challenges in, 95–100; de facto leadership in, 102;

demographic skew in, 100; digital technologies supporting, 84, 86, 94, 102, 110–11, 112; free-rider phenomenon vs., 87, 89, 286n4; generational differences in, 85; of Gezi Park protests, 84, 85, 90–91, 92–94, 99, 102–10, 111–12; of Hong Kong democracy protests, 87, 93, 99; horizontalism focus in, 83, 94; of Indignados protests, 87, 93, 99; institutional distrust in, 83, 90, 106; libraries supported in, 87–88, 91; longevity and durability of networks formed in, 85–86, 102–3; mutual altruism in, 88, 104–5; of Occupy movement, 83, 86, 87, 91, 93, 95–100; participation emphasis in, 83, 94–95, 100–102; pluralism and diversity in, 105–10; reasons for protest participation, 87, 88–94, 99, 112; reverse commodity fetishism in, 91–92; self-expression in, 88–90, 111; summary of goals in, 101–2; of Tahrir Square protests, 83, 84, 85–86, 93, 99, 102, 105; of Zapatista protests, 85, 94, 109–10

"cute cat theory" of activism, 20

"Cyberspace Independence Declaration" (Barlow), 130, 131

DDOS (denial of service attacks), 273–74

Dean, Howard, 275

debt collective movement, 215

decision making mechanisms: culture of protest challenges of, 95–100; organizational structure underlying, 73–77, 81, 215, 269–70

de facto leadership, 79, 98–100, 102, 271

denial of service attacks, 273–74

"digital dualism," 17, 130

digital technologies: cell phones using (see cell phones); government countermeasures to use of (*see* government countermeasures); networked protests using (*see* networked protests); networked public sphere using (*see* networked public sphere); platforms and algorithms of (*see* platforms and algorithms; *specific platforms*); social-technological interactions, 115–31

"Digital Troublemakers" panel, 43–45

disinformation and information inundation, 39–40, 228–29, 230–31, 236–41, 245–46, 265, 273–74, 283n2. *See also* false news; hoaxes

disruptive capacity, 192, 197–99, 202, 204–5, 213, 222

doubt, credibility denials or hoax claims creating, 244–51

doxing, 178

Durkheim, Émile, 89–90, 127

eBay, network effects of, 135–36

education, national public sphere evolution impacting, 3–4

Egypt: capacity signaling in, 190–91, 197, 202–3, 210; censorship and repression in, 13, 18, 141–42, 226–28, 231; culture of protest in, 83, 84, 85–86, 93, 99, 102, 105; dismissal of networked power in, 18, 133–34; election boycotts in, 80; Facebook usage in, 18, 20, 22–24, 27, 132, 133–34, 227; false news in, 266; Mubarak's resignation in, 8, 23, 77, 190; networked protests in, 8–10, 16, 22–24, 27, 53–60, 77–78, 79–80, 83, 84, 85–86, 93, 99, 102, 105, 133–34, 197, 202–3, 210, 226–28, 231; Said murder protests in, 22–23, 139–42; soccer fans as protesters in, 107; social-technological interactions in, 118; Tahrir Square protests in, 8–10, 23–24, 77–78, 79–80, 83, 84, 85–86, 93, 99, 102, 105, 133–34, 197, 202–3, 210, 226–28, 231; Tahrir Supplies in,

38, 53–60; Twitter usage in, 53, 54–60, 118, 139, 227

Ekşi Sözlük, 44, 47

electoral or institutional capacity, 192–93, 195–97, 205, 208–9, 214–16, 217–18, 219–20, 274–77

elite unity or disunity, 220

end-to-end encryption, 230

Europe: antiausterity protests in, 99; capacity signaling in, 196, 210; People's Spring in, 7; platforms and algorithms in, 134, 147; public sphere evolution in, 5. *See also specific countries*

Facebook: acquisitions of smaller platforms by, 137; ad-financing model for, 128, 136–37, 138, 140; algorithms and algorithmic control of, 133, 154–63, 207, 265; Arabic version of, 13–14, 20; attention garnered via, 47, 270; backchannel communication via, 138; bias in, 160–62; bridge ties between weak ties via, 21–22, 24; capacity signaling via, 202, 211, 214, 218; censorship by, 20, 141–42, 149–54; coffee shop or gathering place function of, 138; communication architecture of, 55–56; community policing of, 143–45, 146, 153; content governance and restrictions on, 146–54, 292n22; credibility denials of posting via, 249; "cute cat theory" of activism via, 20; demonizing, 242; employees of, 143, 151–52; experiments on power of, 157–58; false news via, 264–67; founding of, 30; gatekeeping by, 162; government censorship of, 227, 238; "Like" button, 125, 128, 133, 149, 158–59, 160, 161–62; mass media criticism of, 147; networked public sphere via, 13–15, 18, 19–24, 27, 133–34, 162; network effects of, 20–21, 135–36, 137; number

Facebook (*cont.*)
of users, 135; organizational coordination and communication via, 51; platform expansion, 132, 133–34, 135–38; reaction buttons, 161–62, 294n37 (*see also* "Like" button *subentry*); "real-name" policy of, 139–46, 171, 182–83; report and takedown policing model for, 143–45, 146, 153; reputation development on, 171; social-technological interactions via, 118, 128; surveillance of postings via, 251; technodeterminism due to, 119; "We Are All Khaled Said" page on, 22–23, 139, 140–41
FaceTime app, 257
false news, 39–40, 41, 43, 183–85, 239–40, 264–68. *See also* hoaxes
Ferguson protests: capacity signaling via, 206–8; culture of protest of, 93; platforms and algorithms affecting, 154–56, 158–60, 161–62
"50 Cent Party," 237
"firehose of falsehood" propaganda model, 239
food preparation and supplies: culture reflected in, 84, 87–88, 92; organizational coordination of, 50, 52, 68
4Chan, 170, 171
France: French Revolution in, 88, 94; public sphere evolution in, 3–4, 6, 11
freedom of speech, 167, 176, 178, 179, 219
Freeman, Jo, "The Tyranny of Structurelessness," 102, 271–72
free-rider phenomenon, 87, 89, 286n4
fundraising and donations: crowdfunding for, 53, 60; organizational structure supporting, 50, 53, 58, 60

Gafsa protests, 14
gatekeepers, media, 39–40, 134–35, 138, 162, 231, 240, 266–67, 271
gender: anonymous harassment and threats related to, 178, 179–80; cyberspace free of, 130, 179–80;

women's movement on issues of, 193–94. *See also* LGBT community
Gezi Park protests: attention and censorship of, 32, 37, 45–48, 160; culture of protest in, 84, 85, 90–91, 92–94, 99, 102–10, 111–12; library services in, 50, 52, 90–91; organizational structure of, 49, 50–53, 70–75, 81, 99; plurality and diversity of protesters in, 105–10; "spirit of Gezi," 74, 81, 84, 103, 105, 112; surveillance of protesters, 251
Ghonim, Wael, 22–23, 78, 79, 140–41
Global Voices, 15, 22–23
Google: ad-financing model for, 136–37, 138; anti-SOPA/PIPA stance of, 219, 220; gatekeeping by, 162; network effects of, 135–36, 137; organizational coordination using Google docs, 57; search engine platforms and algorithms, 135–37, 138, 154, 159, 161; YouTube ownership by, 146
government countermeasures, 223–60; attention denial as, 30, 31, 32, 33–37, 41, 47–48, 228–29, 231–32, 234–35, 237–38, 274; backfire of censorship as, 226–28; blindspots in, 235–36; capacity signaling in face of, 190, 191, 194, 199, 212, 220–21; censorship as (*see* censorship); coups as, 31, 75, 148, 223–25, 254–60, 299n1; credibility denials or hoax claims as, 244–51; culture of protest in face of, 104–6; demonizing medium as, 241–44; digital technologies used in, generally, 225–26; dismissal of networked power and failure of, 16–19, 40, 44, 45, 133–34, 229; information inundation and disinformation as, 39–40, 228–29, 230–31, 236–41, 245–46, 265, 273–74, 283n2; isolation and alienation empowering, 25–26; "kettling" as, 212; negotiation as, 71, 72–74, 77, 78; in networked public sphere, 6–7, 8, 13, 14–15, 18, 19, 25–26,

27, 32, 33–37; organizational coordination and communication in response
to, 50, 51, 53–54, 58–59, 60, 64–65,
66, 71, 72–74, 77–78; platform
content restrictions of violence of,
147–48; pseudonyms used in, 179,
182, 183; publicity countering, 252–53;
report and takedown policing as, 153;
social media mobilization for
government self-defense as, 254–60;
surveillance as, 251–54; tactical and
strategic use of, 231–36; taxation as,
33; throttling as, 301n28
Greece: capacity signaling in, 196;
Indignados protests in, 210; political
party formation in, 81, 196, 275–76;
soccer fans as protesters in, 107

harassment, online anonymous,
176–83, 238–39, 272
hate speech, banning, 180–81
historical comparisons, 261–64, 268.
See also civil rights movement
hoaxes, 183–85, 244–51. *See also* false
news
homophily, 9, 172, 268
Hong Kong democracy protests: culture
of protest in, 87, 93, 99; government
countermeasures to, 232–36; "Occupy
Central" title of, 232–33, 234;
"umbrella movement" name of, 233
horizontalism: culture of protest focus
on, 83, 94; organizational structure
based on, 50, 51–53, 76–77, 81, 82,
271, 276
human microphones, culture of protest
and use of, 95–100
humor as political criticism, 45, 111–12
Hurricane Katrina, mutual altruism
following, 104
Hurricane Sandy, Occupy participant
involvement after, 215

"I Have a Dream" speech (King), 62,
66, 67, 69–70

India, capacity signaling in, 197
Indignados protests: capacity signaling
via, 210, 275, 276; culture of protest
in, 87, 93, 99
information inundation and disinformation, 39–40, 228–29, 230–31,
236–41, 245–46, 265, 273–74, 283n2.
See also false news; hoaxes
Instagram, 36, 47, 137, 150
institutional or electoral capacity,
192–93, 195–97, 205, 208–9, 214–16,
217–18, 219–20, 274–77
intellectual property rights: content
restrictions based on, 146, 152,
293n25; SOPA/PIPA on, 219–20
internet Relay Chat (IRC), 13, 129, 176
iPhone, 30, 36, 121, 257. *See also* cell
phones
Iran: capacity signaling in, 191;
censorship circumvention in, 230,
238; Facebook usage in, 133; government countermeasures and censorship in, 179, 229, 238; Iranian
revolution, 191, 268; tactical freeze of
protests in, 81
ISIS, platform content restrictions on,
147–48, 152
Italy, Indignados protests in, 210

Jailbait subreddit, 165–69, 178

karma reputation system, 165, 166,
169, 171
Kenya, mobile revolution and internet
access in, 29
"kettling," 212
King, Martin Luther, Jr., 62, 64,
66–67, 69–70, 94
"kompromat," 254
Kurds and Kurdish conflict, 32–37, 106,
109, 148–52, 244–46

leadership: assembly facilitators
managing, 95–100; de facto leadership, 79, 98–100, 102, 271;

leadership (*cont.*)
  leaderlessness in organizational
  structure, 72, 77, 78–79, 81, 82, 99,
  215, 217, 269–70; leadership-
  participation balance, 82; tactical
  freezes due to lack of, 71, 75, 77–82,
  215, 270
LGBT community: "Amina" hoax
  falsely identifying with, 183–85; Gezi
  Park protest role of, 105–7, 108;
  "real-name" policy issues for, 142,
  144, 145
libraries: culture of protest supporting,
  87–88, 90–91; organizational
  coordination of, 50, 52
logistics coordination, 49–51, 53–66, 220
Loomio, 276
Luther, Martin, "95 Theses," 262

Macedonia, false news generated in,
  265–66
Magic Recs, 129
March on Washington, 62, 66–70
Marcos (Zapatista protest leader),
  109–10
mass media: attention awarded by,
  30–31, 35, 124, 204–5, 208, 210–15;
  capacity signaling affected by, 194,
  198, 204–5, 206, 207–8, 210–15;
  censorship of, 13, 19, 26, 29, 31, 32,
  33–37, 47–48, 148–49, 160, 194, 225,
  245, 256, 258; civil rights movement
  coverage by, 65, 66, 68, 134; demonizing alternatives to, 244; dismissal of
  networked power by, 17; gatekeepers
  in, 39–40, 134, 240; journalists
  banned from, 36–37; media watchdog
  organizations monitoring, 33;
  organizational coordination not
  covered by, 60–61; platforms and algorithms *vs.*, 134–35, 138–39, 147,
  148–49, 150–51, 159–60; public sphere
  evolution role of, 4–5, 6; technology
  focus in social-technological interaction coverage by, 118–19

medical care, organizational coordination of, 50, 52, 53–60, 68
memes, political criticism via, 45, 111–12
Mexico: mobile revolution and internet
  access in, 29; Zapatista protests and
  culture in, 28, 85, 94, 109–10, 277,
  283n1
mic checks, culture of protest and use
  of, 95–100
Microsoft, censorship by, 153
Middle East and North Africa: Arab
  uprisings/Arab Spring in, 7, 18, 19, 41,
  58, 118, 122, 123–24, 175–76, 190, 266;
  censorship in, 13, 14–15, 18, 19;
  Facebook usage in, 13–15, 18, 19–24,
  27, 31; false news in, 266; networked
  public sphere in, 12–27; platforms and
  algorithms in, 134, 147; Twitter usage
  in, 31–32. *See also specific countries*
mobile phones. *See* cell phones
movements. *See* social movements
Mubarak, Hosni, resignation of, 8, 23,
  77, 190
mutual altruism, 88, 104–5
Myanmar: ethnic cleansing campaigns
  in, 265; platforms and algorithms in,
  134
MySpace, 136

names and identities, 164–85; ad-
  financing model benefits from, 140;
  anonymous harassment and threats
  without, 176–83, 238–39, 272;
  anonymous social interaction
  without, 172–76; child pornographers
  and pedophiles obscuring, 164–69;
  collective identities and culture,
  83–85, 111; credibility and, 183–85;
  doxing or disclosure of, 178; free
  speech arguments related to, 167, 176,
  178, 179; hoaxes using false, 183–85;
  internal norms of communities
  without, 164–65, 166, 167–69;
  pseudonym use for, 12, 22, 139–42,
  144, 153, 164–85; "real-name" policies,

139–46, 153, 171, 182–83; reputation development and, 164–65, 166, 167, 168–69, 170–72, 175; scale of community interaction with, 172, 179; "special masks" identifying, 171; "stranger on a train" effect with, 172; "vulgar" name restrictions, 145–46

national language, evolution of, 4

Nawaat, 15, 41

negotiations, organizational structure hampering, 71, 72–74, 77, 78

networked protests: attention garnered by (*see* attention); capacity signaling of (*see* capacity signaling); censorship of (*see* censorship); culture of protest in, 83–112, 286n4; government countermeasures to (*see* government countermeasures); historical comparisons to, 261–64, 268 (*see also* civil rights movement); names and identities in (*see* names and identities); networked public sphere affecting (*see* networked public sphere); organizational structure of (*see* organizational structure); overview of, 268–77; platforms for (*see* platforms); social-technological interactions in, 115–31; street protests *vs.* (*see* street protests)

networked public sphere, 3–27; architecture of connectivity in, 18; attention garnered in, 29, 31, 32–38; bridge ties between weak ties in, 21–22, 24; censorship in, 13, 14–15, 18, 19, 27, 32, 33–37; community formation in, 10–11, 12; "cute cat theory" of activism in, 20; definition and description of, 5, 6; dismissal and misunderstanding of power of, 16–19, 44, 45, 133–34, 229; early adopters of technology in, 13, 16, 18–19, 22–23; emergence of, 29; empowerment of, 26–27; Facebook influence on, 13–15, 18, 19–24, 27, 133–34, 162; gatekeepers in, 39–40,

162; government countermeasures in, 6–7, 8, 13, 14–15, 18, 19, 25–26, 27, 32, 33–37; historical public sphere evolution preceding, 3–8, 31, 32–38; homophily search via, 9, 268; interests *vs.* demographics as unifier of, 8–11, 103; isolation and alienation *vs.*, 24–26; networked protests intervention in, 8–10, 12, 14–16, 19, 22–24; network effects in, 20–21; overview of, 268; platforms and algorithms connecting, 20–21, 133–34, 162; pluralistic ignorance weakened in, 26–27, 268; "slacktivism" of, 16–17; unification of "imagined communities" in, 4–5

network effects or externalities: definition of, 75; in networked public sphere, 20–21; network internalities *vs.*, 75; of platforms and algorithms, 20–21, 135–36, 137, 272

network internalities, 75–76, 82, 269–70

"95 Theses" (Luther), 262

nongovernmental organizations (NGOs): capacity signaling via formation of, 205; credibility denials by corporate-funded, 250; Gezi Park protests involving, 51–52, 72; media attention for, 31

Obama, Barack, 275

"Occupy Central" movement, 232–33, 234. *See also* Hong Kong democracy protests

Occupy movement: assemblies in, 95–100; capacity signaling via, 209–16, 221–22, 275; civil rights movement and, 96–99; culture of protest in, 83, 86, 87, 91, 93, 95–100; hand signals in, 96, 97; human microphones in, 95–100; library services in, 87, 91; organizational structure of, 81, 215, 217, 276; Sanders's campaign participation by

Occupy movement (*cont.*)
members of, 216, 275; speed of
expansion of, 38, 209, 215
140journos, 37, 38, 40–43, 47, 246
organizational culture. *See* culture of
protest
organizational structure, 49–82;
adhocracy or ad hoc organization in,
53, 54, 58, 269–70, 284n2; capacity
building in, 61, 64–66, 69–70, 71,
75–77, 192, 220; of civil rights
movement, 61–70, 81–82; clothing and
housing supplies in, 50, 51; communication in, 50–51, 67–68; decision making mechanisms in, 73–77, 81, 215,
269–70; de facto leadership in, 79, 271;
food preparation and supplies in, 50,
52, 68; fundraising and donations in,
50, 53, 58, 60; of Gezi Park protests,
49, 50–53, 70–75, 81, 99; government
countermeasures necessitating, 50, 51,
53–54, 58–59, 60, 64–65, 66, 71,
72–74, 77–78; horizontal *vs.* hierarchical, 50, 51–53, 76–77, 81, 82, 271, 276;
internal strife in, 65, 69, 79, 82;
leaderlessness in, 72, 77, 78–79, 81, 82,
99, 215, 217, 269–70; leaflet distribution in, 51, 63–64; library services in,
50, 52; logistics coordination in, 49–51,
53–66, 220; medical care in, 50, 52,
53–60, 68; negotiation difficulties due
to, 71, 72–74, 77, 78; network internalities in, 75–76, 82, 269–70; overview
of, 269–70; political party formation
from, 81; tactical freezes *vs.* tactical
shift capacity in, 71, 75, 77–82, 215, 270;
of Tahrir Supplies, 53–60; transportation logistics in, 49, 57, 61, 64, 68
Orwell, George, 116–17

Parks, Rosa, 62, 63, 67
participation: culture of protest
emphasis on, 83, 94–95, 100–102;
leadership-participation balance, 82;
reasons for protest participation, 87,
88–94, 99, 112
people-technology interactions. *See*
social-technological interactions
Periscope, 256
platforms, 132–63; acquisitions among,
137; ad-financing model for, 128,
136–37, 138, 140, 241; algorithms/
algorithmic control of, 121, 127,
129–30, 133, 134, 137–38, 145, 154–63,
180, 185, 207, 263, 265, 272; attention
garnered via, 31–32, 36, 37, 38, 40–43,
47–48, 270–71; backchannel
communication via, 57, 138; bias in,
160–62; blogging impacted by,
132–33, 134; capacity signaling via,
202, 203, 207–8, 211, 214, 218;
censorship by, 20, 134, 137, 141–42,
149–54; coffee shop or gathering
place function of, 138; community
policing of, 143–45, 146, 153, 165, 181;
content governance and restrictions
on, 146–54, 180–82, 272, 292n22,
292–93n25; cost of market entry
impacting, 136; definition of, 290n5;
denial of service attacks against,
273–74; experiments on power of,
157–58; gatekeeping via, 134–35, 138,
162; intellectual property right considerations for, 146, 152, 219–20, 293n25;
mass media *vs.*, 134–35, 138–39, 147,
148–49, 150–51, 159–60; networked
protests influenced by, 133–34;
network effects of, 20–21, 135–36, 137,
272; pseudonym allowances via, 12,
22, 139–42, 144, 153, 164–85; "real-
name" policies of, 139–46, 153, 171,
182–83; report and takedown policing
model for, 143–45, 146, 153, 165, 181;
social-technological interactions
using, 116, 118, 121, 128–29, 129–30.
See also specific platforms
pluralism and diversity, culture of
protest supporting, 105–10

pluralistic ignorance, 26–27, 111, 217, 268
Port Huron Statement, 100–101
printing press, 261–62, 263–64
protest culture. *See* culture of protest
protests. *See* networked protests; street
    protests
pseudonymity, 12, 22, 139–42, 144, 153,
    164–85. *See also* anonymity
"public goods," 87
public sphere. *See* networked public
    sphere

Qatar: Al Jazeera forum in, 175; Al
    Jazeera headquarters in, 19; culture
    of protest in, 85

race: anonymous harassment and threats
    related to, 177–78, 179–80; Black Lives
    Matter movement on issues of, 154–56,
    177–78, 197, 205–9, 275, 298nn23–24;
    cyberspace free of, 130, 179–80; social
    construction of, 126–27
real-name politics, 139–46, 153, 171,
    182–83. *See also* names and identities
Reddit: "Ask Me Anything" sessions on,
    165; child pornographers and
    pedophiles using, 164–69; Creep-
    shots subreddit on, 165, 168; internal
    norms of communities on, 164–65,
    166, 167–69; Jailbait subreddit on,
    165–69, 178; karma reputation
    system on, 165, 166, 169, 171;
    pseudonym use on, 164–69, 170, 171;
    Reddit Gold symbol, 165; report and
    takedown policing model for, 165
refugee deaths, credibility denials of,
    247–49
RenRen, 232
reputation: anonymous social interac-
    tion without accrual of, 175; journal-
    ism accuracy and, 43; online
    development of, 164–65, 166, 167,
    168–69, 170–72, 175; Reddit's karma
    representing, 165, 166, 169, 171

Russia: communication restrictions in,
    117; government countermeasures
    and censorship in, 179, 238–39, 244;
    platforms and algorithms in, 134;
    "troll army" in, 238–39
Rustin, Bayard, 66–68

Said, Khaled and Said murder protests,
    22–23, 139–42
Sanders, Bernie, campaign of, 81, 216,
    275
Seattle WTO protests, 86, 213
self-expression, culture of protest
    supporting, 88–90, 111
Sen, Amartya, 191, 296n7
September 11th terrorist attacks, 104, 213
Sidi Bouzid protests, 14–15
signals. *See* capacity signaling
"slacktivism," 16–17
"smart mobs," 60
smartphones. *See* cell phones
Snapchat, 118, 172
soccer fans: censorship during media
    broadcast to, 225; as Gezi Park
    protesters, 107–8
social media, networked protests using.
    See networked protests; *specific
    platforms*
social movements: antiauthoritarian
    movements as, 13, 38, 81, 83–112, 198,
    209–16, 217, 221–22, 269–70, 274–75,
    276; antiwar movement as, 100–101,
    123, 189, 190, 204, 205, 221; Black
    Lives Matter movement as, 154–56,
    177–78, 197, 205–9, 275, 298nn23–24;
    civil rights movement as, 61–70,
    81–82, 94, 96–99, 134, 140, 193, 197;
    networked protests of (*see* networked
    protests); Occupy movement as, 38, 81,
    83, 86, 87, 91, 93, 95–100, 209–16,
    217, 221–22, 275, 276; street protests
    of (*see* street protests); Tea Party
    movement as, 11–12, 216–18; women's
    movement as, 193–94

social-technological interactions, 115–31; affordances in, 118, 124–26, 128–29; anticensorship objectives in, 129; at Arab Bloggers Conference, 115–16; architecture of connectivity in, 129–31; cause and effect dynamics in, 119–24; consequences of, 123, 124–26, 130; context influencing, 116–17, 118; ecological effects of, 117–18; innovation in, 129; mass media technology focus with, 118–19; social construction of technology, 126–29; technodeterminism and, 119; technology as tool in, 119, 124–25

Spain: capacity signaling in, 196, 210, 275–77; Indignados protests in, 87, 93, 99, 210, 275, 276; political party formation in, 81, 196, 275–77

spammers, reporting activists as, 144

"special masks," 171

Stop Online Piracy Act and Protect Intellectual Property Act (SOPA/PIPA), 219–20

"stranger on a train" effect, 172

street protests: capacity signaling of, 203; civil rights movement protests as, 61–70, 81–82, 94, 96–99; Gafsa protests as, 14; Gezi Park protests as (see Gezi Park protests); Occupy protests as (see Occupy movement); Sidi Bouzid protests as, 14–15; social-technological interactions via, 131; Tahrir Square protests as (see Tahrir Square protests); Tahrir Supplies supporting, 38, 53–60; Tea Party protests as, 11–12, 216–18; weather impacting, 11–12

Streisand Effect, 228, 241, 273

surveillance, 251–54

"swatting," 180

Sweden, NATO membership disinformation about, 239

Syria: "Amina" hoax in, 183–85; networked journalism in, 42

tactical freezes, 71, 75, 77–82, 215, 270

Tahrir Square protests: backfire of censorship during, 226–28; capacity signaling via, 197, 202–3, 210; culture of protest in, 83, 84, 85–86, 93, 99, 102, 105; governmental countermeasures during, 226–28, 231; networked public sphere affecting, 8–10, 23–24; organizational structure of, 77–78, 79–80, 83; platforms and algorithms influencing participation in, 133–34; "Republic of Tahrir," 84, 112

Tahrir Supplies: organizational coordination and communication of, 53–60; speed of expansion of, 38, 53

taxation: as government countermeasure, 33; Tea Party protests on, 11–12, 216–17

Tea Party movement, 11–12, 216–18

technodeterminism, 119

technologies. See digital technologies

Telegram, 230

terrorism: content restrictions and censorship for ties to, 147–48, 150, 152, 180; mass media portrayal of conflict as, 32, 34; September 11th terrorist attacks, 104, 213

threats, online anonymous, 176–83, 238–39, 272

throttling, 301n28

Till, Emmett, 140

Tor, 230

traditional protests. See street protests

transportation technologies: organizational logistics using, 49, 57, 61, 64, 68; public sphere impacts of, 7–8; social-technological interactions affected by, 123

"troll army," 238–39, 272

Trump, Donald, 157–58, 218, 249, 264, 265, 275

Tumblr, 137, 219, 220

Tunisia: Arab Bloggers Conference in, 23, 115–16; censorship and repression in, 13, 14–15, 41; culture of protest in, 84–85; Facebook usage in, 14–15, 20; false news in, 266; Gafsa protests in, 14; networked protests in, 14–16, 19, 41; Sidi Bouzid protests in, 14–15; soccer fans as protesters in, 107

Turkey: anonymous harassment of literary figure in, 176–77, 182; censorship in, 19, 31, 32, 33–37, 47, 148–52, 160, 220–21, 225, 229, 242, 243–44, 245; coups and attempted coups in, 31, 75, 148, 223–25, 254–60, 299n1; credibility denials in, 244–49; culture of protest in, 84, 85, 90–91, 92–94, 99, 102–10, 111–12; "Digital Troublemakers" panel in, 43–45; Ekşi Sözlük platform in, 44, 47; Facebook usage in, 31, 47, 51; Gezi Park protests in, 32, 37, 45–48, 49, 50–53, 70–75, 81, 84, 85, 90–91, 92–94, 99, 102–10, 111–12, 160, 251; Kurds and Kurdish conflict in, 32–37, 106, 109, 148–52, 244–46; LGBT community in, 105–7, 108; meme and humor culture in, 45, 111–12; networked protests in, 31–32, 36–38, 42–43, 45–48, 49, 50–53, 70–75, 81, 84, 85, 90–91, 92–94, 99, 102–10, 111–12, 160, 251; 140journos in, 37, 38, 40–43, 47, 246; platforms and algorithms in, 134; public sphere evolution in, 3–4, 6, 31, 32–38, 43–45; refugee outflows from, 247–49; soccer fans in, 107–8, 225; surveillance in, 251–54; Twitter usage in, 31–32, 36, 37, 38, 47–48, 51, 52, 70–71, 111, 144, 224, 242–44, 255

Twitter: ad-financing model for, 136; anonymous harassment and threats via, 177–79, 182; attention garnered via, 31–32, 36, 37, 38, 40–43, 47–48, 270; backchannel communication via, 57; capacity signaling via, 203, 207–8, 211, 275; chronological vs. algorithmic control of, 154, 155–56, 159–60, 162; communication architecture of, 55–58; content governance and restrictions on, 146–47, 182, 292–93n25; credibility denials of posting via, 247–49; culture of protest expressed via, 85, 90, 111; demonizing, 242–44; "egghead" threats via, 177, 182; founding of, 30; freedom of speech ideologies of, 176, 178; government censorship of, 227, 238, 242, 243; government countermeasure knowledge via, 224, 255–56, 257–58, 260; hashtags in, 9, 52, 54, 90, 111, 116, 118, 129; jailing or limiting number of tweets via, 57–58; "mentions" feature of, 55–56, 177, 182; networked public sphere via, 9–10, 11, 133, 134; 140journos on, 38, 40–43; organizational coordination and communication via, 51, 52, 53, 54–60, 70–71; platform expansion, 133, 134, 137; pseudonym use on, 170, 171, 172, 176–77, 182; report and takedown policing model for, 144; reputation development on, 171; social-technological interactions via, 116, 118, 128–29; technodeterminism due to, 119; Twitter bot Magic Recs, 129

"The Tyranny of Structurelessness" (Freeman), 102, 271–72

Umbrella movement, 233. See also Hong Kong democracy protests

United States: ACT UP AIDS awareness movement in, 204–5; anonymous social interaction in, 174–75; antiwar movement in, 100–101, 123, 189, 190, 204, 205, 221; Black Lives Matter movement in, 154–56, 177–78, 197, 205–9, 275, 298nn23–24; capacity

United States (*cont.*)
   signaling in, 189, 190, 193–94, 196,
   197, 204–18, 221–22, 274–75; civil
   rights movement in, 61–70, 81–82,
   94, 96–99, 134, 140, 193, 197;
   Confederate flag debate in, 197–98;
   credibility denials in, 250; culture of
   protest in, 83, 86, 87, 91, 93–94,
   95–100; Ferguson protests in, 93,
   154–56, 158–60, 161–62, 206–8;
   government countermeasures in,
   240–41, 243, 250; Hurricane Katrina
   in, 104; Hurricane Sandy in, 215;
   information inundation and disinformation in, 240–41; Occupy movement
   in, 38, 81, 83, 86, 87, 91, 93, 95–100,
   209–16, 217, 221–22, 275, 276;
   platforms and algorithms in, 134, 143,
   144, 152–53, 181–82; political sabotage
   and false news in, 254, 264–65, 266;
   report and takedown platform liability
   in, 143, 144, 181; Sanders's campaign
   in, 81, 216, 275; Seattle WTO protests
   in, 86, 213; September 11th terrorist
   attacks in, 104, 213; social construction
   of race in, 126–27; State Department
   terrorist organization list in, 150; Tea
   Party movement in, 11–12, 216–18;
   Wisconsin anti-union bill protests in,
   93, 210; women's movement in,
   193–94
Upworthy, 161
urban areas. *See* cities

virtual private networks (VPNs), 221,
   229–30
"vulgar" name restrictions, 145–46

"We Are All Khaled Said" Facebook
   page, 22–23, 139, 140–41
Weibo, 203, 232
WhatsApp: attention garnered via, 47;
   end-to-end encryption of, 230;
   Facebook acquisition of, 137;
   government countermeasure
   knowledge via, 224, 255, 257–58,
   260; organizational coordination and
   communication via, 52; platform
   expansion of, 137; "real-name"
   policies of, 171; reputation development on, 171
Wikipedia, 219
Wisconsin anti-union bill protests, 93,
   210
women's movement, capacity signaling
   by, 193–94
writing, as technology: printing press
   and, 261–62, 263–64; public sphere
   impacts of, 7
WUNC (worthiness, unity, numbers,
   and commitment), 296n5

Yahoo, 136, 137, 153
Yerevan protests, 93
YouBeMom, 170, 171, 174–75
YouTube: attention garnered via,
   270; content governance and
   restrictions on, 146, 147–48; demonizing, 242; platform expansion,
   134; speed of news aggregation
   via, 29

Zapatista protests and culture, 28, 85,
   94, 109–10, 277, 283n1
Zuckerberg, Mark, 140, 142